W9-ABI-242

Negotiating Control

Negotiating Control reports on a major empirical investigation of news sources. It is the first major study to take up the question of the power of news sources, and its variation across and within different institutions, from the perspective of the sources themselves.

The authors undertake a series of ethnographic studies on news sources involved in law and criminal justice, especially those representing law enforcement agencies (police and courts), and those engaged in policy formation and law-making (the legislature). There is also a comparison with private-sector sources, including those who represent private corporations and various citizens' interest groups, and a study of letters to the editor of a major newspaper.

The research reported in this study addresses two central concerns. One is the effect that news has on organizations – how the desire to either attract or avoid news coverage influences routines, affects careers, and promotes organizational change and stability. The other relates to remedies available to sources in the face of unreasonable coverage.

The data acquired are rich and fascinating. They underscore the power of the news media in controlling the public conversation, and in influencing ideology. They have a powerful influence over a wide variety of organizations who need to control the level and nature of public awareness of their activities. And the news media offer few if any effective remedies to those who feel that they have received inadequate or unfair coverage.

In a society where knowledge is a principle of social hierarchy at least as important as property, the power of the news process is enormous. Sources and journalists can be seen as joining together to articulate the contours of 'the knowledge society,' reproducing the power/knowledge structures of bureaucratic life and, thereby, the authoritative apparatus of society.

RICHARD V. ERICSON is Professor at the Centre of Criminology, University of Toronto, and the author of *Reproducing Order*. He is co-author, with Patricia M. Baranek, of *The Ordering of Justice* and, with Baranek and Janet B.L. Chan, of *Visualizing Deviance*.

PATRICIA M. BARANEK is Assistant to the Vice-President, Business Affairs at the University of Toronto and former Research Associate at the Centre for Criminology.

JANET B.L. CHAN is a Lecturer in Sociology at the University of Sydney.

Negotiating Control:
A Study of
News Sources

RICHARD V. ERICSON

PATRICIA M. BARANEK

JANET B.L. CHAN

UNIVERSITY OF TORONTO PRESS

Toronto Buffalo London

© University of Toronto Press 1989
Toronto Buffalo London
Printed in Canada

ISBN 0-8020-2659-1 (cloth)
ISBN 0-8020-6691-7 (paper)

Printed on acid-free paper

Canadian Cataloguing in Publication Data

Ericson, Richard V., 1948–
  Negotiating control: a study of news sources

  Bibliography: p.
  Includes index.
  ISBN 0-8020-2659-1 (bound) ISBN 0-8020-6691-7 (pbk.)

  1. Reporters and reporting. 2. Attribution of news. 3.
  Journalistic ethics. I. Baranek, Patricia M., 1946–   . II.
  Chan, Janet B. L. (Janet Bick Lai), 1948–   . III. Title.

  PN4781.E75 1989   070.4'31   C88-094046-8

Contents

Acknowledgments

In conducting the research for this book we have benefited from the goodwill
and direct assistance of many people in several institutions. In the process
our respect for these people and their institutions has been enhanced greatly.

In particular we are grateful to the subjects of our research. It is dis-
comforting to open one's institution to scrutiny by academics, and risky to
support them without knowing what they will focus upon. Yet, committed
to the value of scholarly enquiry, the subjects of our research were willing
to be open and to take risks. Reporters on newsbeats and editors in newsrooms allowed us to observe their relations with news sources and what they
made of them. News sources in various institutions – courts, police forces,
legislatures, public bureaucracies, private corporations, and citizens' interest
groups – in turn accounted for their relations with journalists and what they
made of them. Only through the generosity of these people were we able to
pursue our academic interest in what they know and how such knowledge
both enables and limits their activities.

Several institutions have been generous in their financial support. The
Social Sciences and Humanities Research Council of Canada funded our work
through two research project grants (nos. 410-83-0748 and 410-84-0004) and
through a leave fellowship (no. 451-84-3311) granted to Richard Ericson.
Another important source of funding was the Ministry of the Solicitor General
of Canada, through both its fund for independent research and its contribution
program to the Centre of Criminology, University of Toronto. This book has
been published with the help of a grant from the Social Science Federation
of Canada, using funds provided by the Social Sciences and Humanities
Research Council of Canada.

The University of Toronto and the University of Cambridge provided academic support. At Toronto our work has been enhanced in untraceable ways

by the rich intellectual environment at the Centre of Criminology. We are the beneficiaries of the foundation laid by the first director of the Centre of Criminology, Professor J.Ll.J. Edwards, of the sustained encouragement and help of the current director, Professor A.N. Doob, and of the support of the acting director during 1986–7, Professor J.M. Beattie. We have benefited a great deal from the resources of the centre's library, and from the resourcefulness of librarians Catherine Matthews, Jane Gladstone, and Pearl Hsing. At Cambridge, Richard Ericson benefited from the scholarly environment that he enjoyed as an Overseas Fellow of Churchill College, and as a Visiting Fellow of the Institute of Criminology, during the 1984–5 academic year.

Several people have contributed at various stages of the research process. Sophia Voumvakis offered a great deal of insight as a research assistant. Donald Edwards was helpful in providing advice and assistance on statistical analyses. Kristine Ericson provided accurate transcriptions of tape-recorded interviews. Marie Pearce and Mary Jackson were admirably efficient and patient in the word-processing of successive drafts.

Seven scholars have enhanced the intellectual quality of this book by providing detailed comments on an earlier draft. These include three anonymous reviewers for the publisher, as well as Professor David Altheide of Arizona State University, Professor John Eldridge of the University of Glasgow, Professor Paul Rock of the London School of Economics and Political Science, and Professor Robin Wagner-Pacifici of Swarthmore College.

Finally, it is a pleasure to acknowledge our association with the publisher. Virgil Duff and John Skelton have been enthusiastic and helpful in seeing this manuscript through to publication. In the production of the manuscript, our burden was eased considerably by the copy-editing skills of Beverley Beetham Endersby and by the index preparation of Dianna Ericson.

In the chapters that follow we continue to record our appreciation of those who participated in the research and of their respective institutions. We hope that in reading this record they will learn more about how people in institutions think, and arrive at the conclusion that their co-operation and support were worthwhile.

RVE
PMB
JBLC

Negotiating Control

1

Negotiating the News

The Significance of News Sources

Sociological research on news work has been based primarily in news organizations and grounded in the perspective of journalists (e.g., Altheide, 1976; Chibnall, 1977; Schlesinger, 1978; Tuchman, 1978; Fishman, 1980; Ericson et al, 1987). Existing research addresses journalists' relations with sources but studies them in terms of the social and cultural arrangements of the news organization more than of the source organization. The research reported in this book begins with the perspective of sources, focusing on their organizational demands and expectations in making news.

In *Visualizing Deviance* (Ericson et al, 1987), we documented that although there is an enormous array of knowledge sources potentially available – official documents, academic texts, survey and trend statistics, and direct observation – journalists tend to limit themselves to the 'performatives' of news releases and interview quotations from sources. Moreover, the reliance on selected people as knowledge resources is itself limited mainly to key spokespersons for particular bureaucratic organizations. While individuals without an organizational affiliation are cited – especially in designated places such as letters-to-the-editor columns, or for specific purposes such as to inspire 'fear and loathing' over a tragic event in a news story – they are a small minority statistically (Ericson et al, forthcoming). Typically, the journalist seeks a source in the know to say it is so, and has a routine, predictable supply of such sources in established organizations.

Visualizing Deviance explained how and why journalists have this orientation in terms of their news organization's structure and culture. In this book we not only refine this analysis, but go beyond it by documenting the processes of negotiation and struggle between sources and journalists as experienced by sources themselves. Given that most news sources are located in bureaucratic organizations, our primary focus is on the ways in which various source bureaucracies organize to communicate through the news media. We examine their internal organizational arrangements for producing news discourse, and for limiting the terms of that discourse. We are thus concerned with the strategies and tactics sources use to control how their organizations and activities are visualized in the news. This approach entails consideration of how journalists are able to negotiate alternative visualizations and the degree to which they or their sources maintain relative autonomy in the process. While news sources can do various things to routinize and influence the process of news communication, they remain vulnerable to journalists' demands for news of deviance, and to the journalistic thrust for policing and reforming organizational life. Thus, we consider not only how sources organize to influence news flow, but also how they respond when the flow of their organization is disrupted by news of deviance and demands for more control over their organization.

This book incorporates rich data on sources' relations with journalists in various institutional settings. Prior to analysis of those data, however, it is necessary to establish the framework within which we seek an understanding of news sources. Hence, the remainder of this chapter is an exercise in conceptualizing the relation between source and news organizations. The appropriateness and power of this conceptualization is made evident as the subsequent substantive chapters unfold.

In concert with that of *Visualizing Deviance*, the central concern of this book is the dialectic between knowledge and power. We demonstrate that control over knowledge – in this case, over good and bad news as it is worked out through source-journalist transactions – is contextual, equivocal, transitory, and unresolved. In order to demonstrate this premise, we provide ethnographic detail on the cultural and organizational ecology of knowledge-work, and on the institutional umbrella within which various groups negotiate their way through the news. This detail casts light upon the micropolitics of accounting practices, on the reflexive quality of agency and constraint in social control of knowledge, and on the institutional, cultural, professional, and personal interests that are played out in the eternal dance of secrecy and revelation characterizing knowledge/power relations.

Several major themes are entwined in our analysis of the knowledge/power dialectic. We focus on the recurrent problems and tensions faced by all organizations in defining the margins of secrecy, confidence, censorship, and publicity. This focus entails consideration of the relative autonomy of sources and reporters, and the related problems of trust, reciprocity, collaboration, co-optation, and assimilation as they negotiate their work and the news. A central question here is the degree of convergence, socially and in discourse, between sources and journalists. To what extent do sources adapt media logic, formats, and power (Altheide and Snow, 1979; Altheide and Johnson, 1980; Altheide, 1985) to achieve particular purposes? To what extent do sources and journalists begin with different discursive strategies for composing an event and news about it, but end up, through negotiation, with a convergence and consensus? Addressing these questions raises another theme, namely the nature of authority (legitimate power) as it pertains to the enabling and disabling forces affecting news sources and journalists. How do spokespersons for bureaucracies perceive their authority in their own organization and as it articulates with the public domain? Are they able to constitute their preferred version and vision of authority in the particular instance of news coverage? What are the obstacles to doing so in terms of the powers and preferences of the news media?

In summary, this research explores a central terrain for the reproduction of the knowledge society. Our analysis of the negotiated production of public knowledge about courts, police, lawmakers, and private-sector organizations allows us to expand collective understanding of newsmaking, media discourse, legal discourse, professional sense, common sense, and the reflexivity between knowledge and power. The research materials presented in subsequent chapters allow us to activate a broadly based enquiry into the commodification of knowledge (the knowledge trade, in both meanings of the term), the micropolitics of professions concerned with lawmaking and enforcement, the relationship between specialized knowledge and 'the common sense,' the relevance of knowledge control for legal control, the meaning of cultural contests *over* meaning, and the recursive relation between conflict and order in the knowledge society.

We recognize limitations on our own knowledge and how it was produced. This enquiry is restricted to one level of analysis, and limited to explorations along particular paths. This study focuses on culture more than on structure, on microanalysis and agency more than on macroanalysis and institutional architecture, on the state as a shadowy Leviathan more than as a vector of political economy.

AUTHORITATIVE SOURCES AND NEWS

News is a representation of authority. In the contemporary knowledge society news represents *who* are the authorized knowers and *what* are their authoritative versions of reality. As such, it is every person's daily barometer of 'the knowledge-structure of society' (Böhme, 1984; Böhme and Stehr, 1986). It offers a perpetual articulation of how society is socially stratified in terms of possession and use of knowledge. It indicates who is in possession of knowledge as 'cultural capital,' and thereby articulates who are members of the 'new class' who derive their labour and property membership from the production, distribution, and administration of knowledge (Berger, 1977; Konrád and Szelényi, 1979; Gouldner, 1979). At the same time that it informs about who are the authorized knowers, it suggests, by relegation to a minor role and by omission, who is excluded from having a say in important matters.

News also constitutes an authoritative vision of social order through what sources are cited as saying. Sources are used to cite the facts of the matter without further investigation (Tuchman, 1978; Ericson et al, 1987), and to give credibility to what the reporter visualizes. Most news is bad news, visualizing deviance and advancing preferred control solutions (Cohen and Young, 1981; Glasgow University Media Group [GUMG], 1976, 1980, 1982; Ericson et al, 1987, forthcoming). Sources are asked to explain the behaviour that has been designated as deviant within prevailing cultural criteria of rational acceptability. The preferred causal imagery – for example, underscoring that deviance is motivated by the rational calculus of pleasure against the pain of punishment if caught, or is a result of individual pathology – carries implicit recommendations for control (e.g., more control in the form of stiffer punishment or more intense treatment). Sources are also used to offer tertiary understanding, addressing the question 'What is it like to be involved?' For example, news conveys cathetic scenarios of police and other agents of order coming to the rescue of citizens in distress, including their accounts of how they managed to get the job done this time. These images of everyone's 'salvation army' are a matter of the heart as well as the head. This type of understanding can bolster an affinity with particular ideologies, for example, a belief in the authoritative-control apparatus of the state (cf O'Neill, 1981; Schneider, 1977). Sources are also mobilized to convey their evaluations and recommendations for the control of the deviance. Here, too, only some sources have warrant to address social control needs, and among these some are more warranted than others. The relevant state policing authorities are routinely called upon to give their official imprint to particular control solutions.

It is hard to imagine a mainstream newscast or newspaper that cites only the man on the street, the cop on the beat, the hospital porter, the House of Commons back-bencher, the university student, and the clerk of the court. It is thus easy to see why they must cite the executive in his office, the chief of police, the hospital administrator, the cabinet minister, the professor, and the chief justice. These are the people who are recognized socially to be in a position to know. They have been authorized to give an account that serves the public expectation that their organization is accountable.

These are also the people who sustain the image that the particular media outlet is an authoritative news voice. Without them the news outlet would disappear from the ranks of the respectable mass media, and be relegated to the level of the disreputable 'fringe' media. The news outlet would take on the character of being deviant, rather than being the most pervasive and authoritative vehicle in society for designating deviance and promoting social control. In other words, through the process of displaying the place of authorized knowers in the knowledge structure of society, and conveying the type of knowledge that gives them that place, news organizations underscore their own authority. News organizations thereby join with key source organizations in representing the authoritative apparatus of society. News becomes a vehicle for communication among those towards the top end of the knowledge structure of society, while those towards the bottom end are left to spectate.

THE CONVERGENCE OF SOURCE AND NEWS ORGANIZATIONS

Source organizations and news organizations converge on different levels, and are best viewed as part of each other.

Convergence is evident at the institutional level. The media élite is not separate from the élites who control many of the government and corporate bureaucracies that are reported on (Porter, 1965; Clement, 1975, 1977; Royal Commission on Newspapers [RCN], 1981; regarding the United States, see Dreir, 1982). They interlock with these organizations in ownership, management participation, and social participation, sustaining an élite culture that circumscribes the ability of the news media to be analytically detached from the élite persons and organizations they report on. It is extremely difficult to document precisely how the values of élite culture filter down and influence decisions in the particular newsroom. Values do not operate in a deterministic manner, but shape perceptions and the recognition of how things ought to be done. Moreover, human organizations are obdurate, with any system of values being subject to translation, and at least partial transformation, into the values and social practices of the particular organization. Hence, it is not possible to sustain empirically an instrumentalist view of the media élite and their governmental and corporate allies pulling the strings by which newsworkers dance. Nevertheless, it is evident that there are many strings attached to being a journalist in a news organization whose interests are ultimately bound at the élite level to those source organizations being reported on. There are also many strings attached to being a source spokesperson who must represent simultaneously the authority of his office and the authoritative apparatus of the élite culture.

At a much more concrete and empirically specifiable level, it is possible to document what sources representing what component of the authoritative apparatus of society are given the favour of access to the news. By *access* we mean the news space, time, and context to reasonably represent the authority of their office. Such access is distinguished from *coverage*, which may entail some news space and time but not the context for favourable representations.

For example, Gitlin (1980) shows how the Students for a Democratic Society movement in the United States strategically acquired ample coverage but, because it was not access, were eventually splintered and delegitimated through this coverage.

Sources have access in a number of ways. Most routinely, they are cited as an authority in stories pertaining to their sphere of organizational life. More directly, they write news releases that are cited in whole or in part, contributing substantially to the final news item. Similarly, they compose letters to the editor that allow their original texts to be published in whole or in part, making an authoritative contribution to ongoing themes in the news. Most directly, sources are asked to write stories, features, or columns on an ongoing basis. They become employees of a news organization as well as of a source organization, extinguishing any doubt about convergence.

Sources and journalists also converge to the extent that journalists rely upon sources to function as 'reporters.' It is reasonable to argue that the real reporters are source spokespersons, who do all the essential 'signwork' (Manning, 1986) within their organization in order to produce an acceptable news account. The reporter for the news organization then functions as an 'editor,' determining what aspects of this material will be used along with accounts tailored for the purpose of news discourse by other sources. '[S]ources are continually deciding whether certain information should be revealed, which details should be highlighted or discarded, when the story should be offered to the press. Every such decision, which makes some data visible to the press and relegates other data to invisibility, is an act of news management' (Roscho, 1975: 84–5). It is not that the journalist could not, in many cases, obtain the information more independently, contacting other sources in the organization or acquiring original documents. Rather, it eases the practice of newswork to have colleagues in source organizations who are only too willing to do the basic signwork. The ease of news flow typically takes precedence, even though the probable consequence of this process is to transmit the source organization's 'bureaucratic propaganda,' defined as '[a]ny report produced by an organization for evaluation and other practical purposes that is targeted for individuals, committees, or publics who are unaware of its promotive character and the editing processes that shaped the report' (Altheide and Johnson, 1980: 5).

This convergence is most evident on newsbeats, the 'routine round of institutions and persons to be contacted at scheduled intervals for knowledge of events' (Tuchman, 1978: 144). On most beats the source symbolizes incorporation of news reporting into the organization by having office facilities for journalists. On beats, journalists are not only physically part of the source organization, but over time become part of it socially and culturally. They become socialized into the occupational culture of sources on the beat to the point where the relation between their understanding and values coheres with that of their sources. This level of socialization means that the signwork done by sources does not conflict with what the journalist finds agreeable. 'Even though the reporter takes the social setting of the beat as the object of reporting, reporters are part of that object. They participate in the activities that they report ... reporters and their beats are *reflexively* related' (Fishman, 1980: 30). Again, one possible effect is that the news organization becomes a useful appendage to the self-reporting apparatus of the source organization. Through ongoing reciprocity among journalists and sources on the beat, sources are able to refine their account ability in the terms of news discourse, which in turn allows them to achieve organizational accountability to the publics that concern them.

The reciprocity on newsbeats includes knowledge being passed from journalists to sources. The journalist can offer a source knowledge about upcoming plans or events of other organizations that are relevant strategically to the source. He can provide the source with facts about things he is working on, as well as his speculative interpretations of events, processes, or states of affairs. He can inform the source about other people in the source organization, or elsewhere, whose activities might have a bearing on those of the source. Perhaps most significantly, the journalist can provide guidance to the source regarding how to formulate news accounts in a manner that will ensure access.

Just as sources contribute regularly as authors of features and columns, and sometimes move full time to the newsroom, so journalists find a career path from the newsroom to public-relations work for source bureaucracies. Many public-relations units of governmental and corporate bureaucracies are staffed by journalists who acquired their news sense on the floor of newsrooms. Reporting is a vocation for the young (RCN, 1981), and it is often the case that the newsroom is staffed with reporters less experienced in the craft than those in the public-relations unit of the source bureaucracy. Within the source bureaucracy public-relations personnel work primarily as reporters for their own organization, mediating between the senior members of their organization and the news media to ensure that the right information is released and access assured. The fact that public-relations personnel have considerable recipe knowledge of the craft and an established network of associates within newsrooms again signals convergence.

THE RELATIVE AUTONOMY OF SOURCES: REGIONS AND CLOSURES

Most researchers have concluded that these institutional and organizational ties leave journalists in a state of dependency with respect to sources (e.g., Chibnall, 1977; Hall et al, 1978; Fishman, 1980; see Lane, 1923, and Fraser,

1956, for historical examples). Confronted with a bureaucratically constructed universe, the journalist can only reproduce bureaucratic constructs for public consumption. Simply by working within the constraints of his job the journalist functions as a conduit pipe for the flow of prefigured signs from his sources. As Sir John A. Macdonald once remarked, 'When you see what a journalist will write unbribed, why then, there's no need to bribe them, is there?' (cited by Black, 1982: 215).

Just as sources face the problem of obtaining access to the news rather than mere coverage, so journalists have the problem of obtaining access to a source organization rather than the opportunity for mere coverage. There is a great difference between being in a position to give coverage to a source organization's event, process, or state of affairs, and having access that allows for the story the journalist needs for his news organization's purposes. Sources effect varying degrees of restriction on access to the back regions of their organization, and even their front regions are controlled in time, space, and social arrangements. Concomitantly, the knowledge available in the front regions is subject to degrees of closure.

Every human being and organization requires a workable level of privacy, defined as 'those places, spaces, and matters upon or into which others may not normally intrude without the consent of the person or organization to whom they are designated as belonging' (Reiss, 1987: 20; see also Bok, 1982: 10–11). Indeed, privacy is a necessary condition for the possibility of an organization's arising in the first instance (Rock, forthcoming), and for its continuation.

> [N]o organization seems possible – whether that of the personality, a family
> or friendship, or more formal organizations, including the state – without
> its private matters or secrets. For the capacity to act is predicated in part
> on preserving a unique form of organization that sets it apart from others.
> Moreover, any competitive advantage one may have stems in part from being
> able to 'keep others guessing.' There appears to be an implied threat even
> in sharing that information with others; its disclosure makes one vulnerable.
> At the core, then, of one's private matters or space is a fear that one is
> vulnerable to others. Hence, one seeks to protect that space against intrusion.
> (Reiss, 1987: 27–8)

Our subsequent analyses are centrally concerned with how sources work to protect their organization against intrusion by journalists, while concomitantly achieving favourable publicity, which is seen as an important means of maintaining control over the organizational environment. This work is extremely complex and difficult because of the porosity of bureaucratic organizations, the volume of knowledge available, the elusive nature of knowledge,

Figure 1
Regions and closures

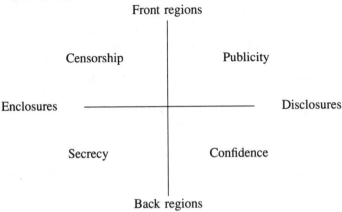

and the fact that knowledge can be taken without ever leaving its place. In order to capture the complexity of this work we have devised the model presented as figure 1. This model is inspired by the pioneering work of Goffman (especially Goffman, 1959), and the subsequent refinements of Giddens (1984: 122–6). However, Goffman and Giddens were primarily concerned with the individual's preservation and presentation of self by relying upon spatial preserves of privacy alternating with public places for the staging of appearances. In addition to this social-psychological framework, we are interested in the sociological level of how organizations protect and present their activities by policing spatial regions and knowledge.

Figure 1 represents the possibilities for journalists' physical access to regions and sign access to knowledge in source organizations. The parameters sketched here are filled with empirical detail in chapters 3 to 6, where we undertake a comparative analysis of regions and closures within the courts, police, legislature, and private-sector organizations without newsbeat arrangements.

The back regions are spaces where organizational work transpires and decisions are taken but which are open only to the purview of those who are officially authorized to be there. Excluded are not only those who do not have an official role in the organization, but also those whose official role is limited to some regions and not others. For example, in the courts key decisions are taken in the Crown attorney's office as the police, Crown attorney, and defence lawyer make plea-bargaining deals to settle criminal cases without trial. The accused and victim are routinely excluded from this setting where the 'real trial' occurs, as are other members of the public, including the reporter (Ericson and Baranek, 1982). Judges' chambers are even more exclusive, as even other court officials are excluded except as the judge might summons them to discuss a case.

The front regions consist of those areas where the public business of the organization is transacted. In normal circumstances not only those with an official role, but also those who wish to do business with the organization, are allowed access to front regions. In many public bureaucracies members of the public can attend these spaces merely as spectators, without any official business. For example, in courts and legislatures designated public-gallery sections are normally open to any member of the public, including journalists.

Enclosure refers to efforts to circumscribe or extinguish the signs that are given off in various regions. An effort to keep signs or knowledge from others is an attempt at secrecy. An obvious way to maintain secrecy is to exclude from back regions those persons whom one wants to keep knowledge away from. For example, in the courts we studied, the reporters were excluded from plea-bargaining sessions in the Crown attorney's office. Enclosure is not restricted to back regions. '[T]he differentiation between front and back regions by no means coincides with a division between the enclosure (covering up, hiding) of aspects of the self and their disclosure (revelation, divulgence). These two axes of regionalization operate in a complicated nexus of possible relations between meanings, norms and power' (Giddens, 1984: 126). For example, there are provisions in law that allow a judge to censor even that which transpires in the public forum of the courtroom. Censorship is a restriction on publicizing more broadly that which is made public in one narrower context. Thus, there are occasional publicity bans on what transpires in the courtroom.

Disclosure entails efforts to communicate signs in various regions. An effort to communicate to the unauthorized that which is normally communicated only to the authorized, and the expectation that it is not to be made known to others, is a confidence. Confidence, the revelation of private matters with mutual trust, normally pertains to work activities that transpire in the back regions. For example, a Crown attorney might tell a reporter that an accused decided to plead guilty as a result of a plea bargain involving the withdrawal of some charges and a favourable sentence recommendation, but expect the reporter not to include that in his filed story. Disclosure in the front regions is the normal condition of publicity. What is said in the courtroom, in interviews in the corridors of the courthouse, or through 'proper channels' over the telephone has been prefigured and preformulated for public consumption. Here the source organization works hard to give off signs that make it appear to be doing what interested publics think it should be doing.

There is considerable variation in access to source regions and knowledge, depending on the type of source organization involved, and the type of knowledge being sought within a given source organization. For example, prisons are relatively closed institutions for the purposes of news. It is rare to find a regular 'prison beat' reporter, the exceptions being communities where prisons are dominant (as with the *Whig–Standard* in Kingston, Ontario) or where there are special ties between the prison administration and a particular local news outlet (as occurred in Chicago over a twenty-five–year period – see Jacobs, 1977). Prisons are run in terms more of administrative discretion than of external review and public accountability, and this veil of administrative decency has effectively kept out the news media. This observation is borne out by content studies that indicate that stories emanating from prisons, or about prisons, are rare statistically compared to court coverage and especially police coverage (Graber, 1980; Garofalo, 1981; Ericson et al, forthcoming).

Courts are relatively less closed. Reporters are given an office and develop ongoing relations with reporters from other news organizations, and with sources, in a distinctive beat culture. However, they are restricted to particular public physical spaces (e.g., the courtroom, but not the Crown attorney's office during plea-bargaining sessions), and to particular organizational documents. This restriction emanates from a combination of formal source control (including the law), work expediency, and norms of propriety that evolve among journalists and their sources (Epstein, 1975; Fishman, 1980; Dreschel, 1983). Key actors in the court are reluctant to divulge knowledge because they are legally restricted from doing so, or have been socialized into being reticent about talking to the news media about their cases. This case especially applies to judges, who will not 'second-guess' their decisions to a reporter and are even reluctant to talk about issues on a regular basis for fear of tainting the image of their office as independent. The reporter is left to convey what the court organization has pre-established as public information, knowable through its presentation in public-display settings such as the courtroom.

The police have become relatively more open. Unlike the courts, they often have full-time public-relations specialists and news-media officers who are proactive in disseminating knowledge and arranging for 'media events.' While this aspect of openness may be taken as a sign that efforts are being made to exert more control over the news media, it is also a sign that the police recognize the need to be more open and accommodative to perpetual demands for news-media coverage (Hickling-Johnston, 1982). In the face of being used at the forefront of public debates about the relation between the individual and the state, and as a sign of governmental accountability, the police recognize the importance of allowing reasonable access to the news media and the account ability allowed by its discourse (Brogden, 1982; Jefferson and Grimshaw, 1984; Reiner, 1985). An additional consideration is that the membership of a police bureaucracy is very large, and varied in functions and subunit loyalties. In contrast to the small-city situation studied by Fishman (1980), the large urban police organization is open to multiple communication channels because of its size (often several thousand members), and internal divisions, which make control through guidelines and official contexts (news releases, the press room) only partial (Chibnall, 1977).

Political beats appear relatively most open. In this sphere public accountability must be shown routinely, and the news media are seen as the most significant vehicles for displaying it. Political beats are characterized by myriad full-time media-relations personnel and consultants whose job is to represent political interests through gaining news access. Politicians and senior civil servants recognize the importance of the news media not only to the authority of their office, but also to their ability to stay in office (Sigal, 1973; Cockrell et al, 1985; Golding et al, 1986). Access means maximizing their sources and objects, magnifying their coherence and hegemony; mere coverage can have the effect of the news media's minimizing their sources and objects, magnifying their incoherence and fragmentation. In the interest of maximizing their access while relegating the opposition to mere coverage, political interests expend enormous resources through a variety of proactive media strategies, and allow considerable access to some back-region settings.

It is wrong to say 'reporters expose themselves *only* to settings in which formally organized transactions of official business occur' (Fishman, 1980; emphasis added). Reporters' *primary* exposure may be in such front-region settings, but these are not the exclusive settings of their work (Ericson et al, 1987). Moreover, it is not just a matter of what reporters expose themselves to, but of what sources allow them to be exposed to. Even back-region access may not yield reportable material because relevant information is still enclosed (secrecy) or disclosed with the understanding it will not be published (confidence). Front-region access may not yield reportable material because what is presented there is enclosed (legally or otherwise restricted) or is a highly structured, mediated, and partial account. The nature and degree of exposure is always at issue, varying in time and place within a source organization, and by the type of source organization. We document this subsequently through our comparative analyses of the court, police, legislature, and non-state organizations.

THE RELATIVE AUTONOMY OF REPORTERS:
RECONTEXTUALIZING ORGANIZED LIFE

In *Visualizing Deviance* we documented that journalists do have some relative autonomy from their sources in spite of the many signs of their dependency. News and source organizations are entwined, but they are not one. It is an illusion to think there can be a near total or effective control of knowledge, just as it is an illusion to think that efforts at secrecy and control are neutral and carry no risks of their own (Bok, 1982: 285). Journalists are adept at devising alternative means of penetrating organizational life, and at policing what they visualize as unsavoury interests that seem to carry risks for their conception of the public good.

The relative autonomy of journalists is indicated by a number of considerations. As noted earlier, the journalist on the newsbeat becomes part of the organization she reports on. She is literally given an 'office' (Weber, 1946) by the source organization, and in that sense has a defined role to play as much as any other member of the source organization. In that role she is privy to knowledge relevant to the role, just as other members are privy to knowledge pertinent to their roles. For example, in a police organization the police constable has some knowledge exclusive to her role. The chief of police is not aware of a lot of this knowledge, just as the constable is not aware of much knowledge available to the chief. Similarly the police reporter develops knowledge exclusive to her role, as part of the division of labour within the police organization. While the reporter may be several steps removed from the symbolically constructed reality she reports on – and is frequently forced to rely upon the organizationally mediated texts of line police personnel and public-relations officers (Wheeler, 1986) – senior administrators, including the chief of police, are in the same position of being at the nth level of knowledge production regarding work on individual occurrences or internal practices and politics.

It is too simplistic to say that the reporter is only an 'observer' of what goes on in the source organization. The other members of the source organization are themselves 'observers' of virtually all of their organizational activity, since they deal with already socially constructed knowledge rather than participate directly in the activity being constructed. Again taking the example of the police organization (Ericson, 1981, 1982), the typical scenario involves the patrol officer talking to a complainant about an event that occurred previously. Often the victim did not participate in the event directly (e.g., was absent when her house was broken into); and the patrol officer, also not directly involved, is not able to make direct observations. The patrol officer writes an occurrence report that is read and possibly amended by a patrol sergeant, is read again and possibly amended by a staff sergeant, and is then possibly sent on to a detective sergeant who again reads it and possibly makes amendments. If detectives are assigned to work on it they may seek further accounts from the complainant, try to generate witnesses, and, one hopes, also obtain a suspect who can come the closest to giving a first-hand account. Any accounts generated are scrutinized further, and possibly amended, at the detective-sergeant and detective-inspector levels. At all levels, the actors in this process serve as 'reporters' of socially constructed knowledge and 'editors' of the documentary realities they have been presented with. Like the journalist, they are rarely dealing with observed activity in nature, but rather with others' symbolically constructed versions of reality.

The journalist, within the role he negotiates and establishes as part of the source organization, becomes another component in this knowledge-reproduction process. Like those in other roles within the source organization, he has considerable control over what he decides to attend to, how much attention it deserves, how it should be reconstructed, and so on. He is a *participant* in the process of giving meaning to the texts of the source organization, and of having those texts enter back into the source organization to affect social relations and practices there. He is *interdependent* with his fellows in the source organization regarding both knowledge production and its various uses inside and outside the organization.

This view is in contradistinction to the dominant one in the research literature, as represented for example by Roscho (1975: 63), who states that 'the mass-media reporter is prototypically an observer, describing the issues others frame, the problems they raise, the solutions they offer, the actions they take, the conflicts in which they engage. Thus, the nature of news as a form of knowledge makes the reporter dependent upon news sources for most of the knowledge he will transpose into media content.' As a producer of a news text about activities involving the source organization, the journalist has control over aspects of how it is framed and how the other texts that are used to construct it are contextualized. Thus, the source is very likely to have her own understandings and meanings escape her as they become translated and objectified in the news text (cf Giddens, 1979: 73–4). The common complaints of persons who know something more directly about the matter being reported on in the news are that it is distorted, taken out of context, biased, and inaccurate. These complaints are inevitable since the news text is not formulated in terms of the source's context and attendant criteria of rational acceptability, but reformulated to meet the terms and contexts of news discourse.

Sources wishing to communicate in the news media must share values with journalists, including core values of the dominant culture. 'Those actors who want their actions and beliefs signified as legitimate by the news media must contrive to associate themselves with the positive legitimating values' (Chibnall, 1977: 21–3). Journalists develop special affinities with sources, with whom they share the same sense of news values (Nimmo, 1964). Sources are generally constrained by the need to conform with the working ideology of journalists. There is an 'elective affinity' – what Weber (1946: 280) referred to as *Wahlverwandschaft* – between the ideas and interests of journalists and their sources. In the process sources learn to bring their accounts into conformity with the form and content established by journalists *vis-à-vis* their view of what constitutes legitimate, reportable material (Altheide and Snow, 1979; Altheide and Johnson, 1980; Altheide, 1985). Every journalist learns through a 'vocabulary of precedents' (Ericson et al, 1987) what constitutes a reportable account, and he in turn develops a vocabulary of precedents with his sources so that they give him an account that is reportable.

Of course reporters and their sources can manipulate news values to justify their particular constructions of knowledge. For example, it is well established that the news requirement for objectivity, fairness, and balance – 'the strategic ritual of objectivity' (Tuchman, 1978) – means that sources are safe in giving accounts that will only be challenged by the *representations* of an opposing source, rather than by independent *evidence* generated by the journalist. 'Quite inadvertently, the fairness standards encourage rhetoric and even demagoguery, at least to the degree that spokesmen in a controversy are aware that their arguments are not likely to be questioned' (Epstein, 1974: 265).

Journalists have partially adjusted to this dilemma by dropping the pretense of objectivity in some instances, practising a 'new journalism' that has political purpose and practical effect as it aims to police organizational life. Moreover, there has developed an emphasis on 'vox pop' journalism, going to the people in addition to those in positions of authority. This emphasis is partly intended as a corrective to the bias inherent in seeking validation only in the accounts of official spokespersons elevated in the hierarchy of credibility. While reliance upon the accounts of authorized knowers, within the point / counterpoint format, remains predominant, there has been some recognition of the bias this entails. Smith (1980: 170, 173–4) comments on the objectivity strategic ritual and its implications for reproducing the knowledge structure of society:

> Arguably the industry has emerged in the 1980's with a newly adjusted
> version of the doctrine, liberalized to accommodate some of the most skillful
> proponents of the subjectivism of the sixties but substantially the same set of
> occupational ideals ... [Prior to this adjustment the] bias to which reporting
> unwittingly gave itself stemmed from the procedures that tied journalism
> to its sources, forcing it to use methods of validation that left information
> culled from socially underprivileged sources structurally invalid. Journalism
> helplessly underpinned a social system that was content with and depended
> upon a kind of objective truth that that very social system constrained, even
> crippled.

Journalism continues to contribute to structured inequality in the knowledge society. It does so inevitably because knowledge as 'cultural capital' and a source of power is unevenly distributed. As Böhme (1984) observes, 'the old antagonism resulting from the different participation in the material resources of society is now ... rivalled by another antagonism resulting from the different participation in the intellectual resources of society.' The news media contribute to structured inequality in relation to the spokespersons they do or do not allow to make imprints on versions of reality. As a form of cultural capital itself, the news media are a competitive resource differentially available to different sources.

There are also many signs of how the cultural capital of news communication is effectively controlled by news outlets. The fact that the source has few formal controls over copy, such as a right to see filed copy before it is published or broadcast, is an indication that sources lose control of their accounts. The fact that there are few effective remedies for unreasonable news coverage again signals the power of news outlets over and against those who seek to use them for cultural capital gains (see chapter 6). The fact that organizations expend considerable fiscal resources in paid advertisements to present or to correct the record on matters of public importance to them is another clear sign that journalists do not always represent the source's bureaucratic propaganda in the terms the source would prefer.

It is best to assume that there is relative autonomy between reporters and sources, varying by types of source organizations and news organizations. As we document in subsequent chapters the large, urban news-media culture is multifaceted. Reporters have multiple and varied sources of knowledge, and sources have multiple media outlets to convey their preferred versions of what appears to be the case. That is not to say that the market is 'free.' Rather, it is regulated and controlled in complex ways. It entails positive and negative freedoms for both journalists and sources, and for citizens who are left to spectate and speculate. Moreover, as Altheide has instructed through his series of studies, sources, journalists, and other citizens are collectively constrained by the dominant modes of media formats and logic (Altheide 1976, 1985; Altheide and Snow, 1979).

CONSTRUCTING ORGANIZATIONAL ORDER

Sign Struggles

Journalists and sources construct order and effect change both in their everyday transactions and in the news texts produced out of their transactions. In their exchanges with each other an order emerges regarding what knowledge is available under particular conditions, in designated places, and at certain times. In their news texts they display the order of authoritative actors and organizations within the knowledge structure of society. These two aspects of constructing organizational order are entwined, and play back upon each other in perpetual dialectic. In playing back upon each other they provide for both organizational and social change, leaving their mark on an array of public and private arenas for action.

In the knowledge society there is continual struggle over what is proper procedure for organizations to follow in pursuing their interests, *vis-à-vis* the interests of others and the public interest (Habermas, 1975). The specification of the norm and the anomaly, the deviant and the conforming, along with attendant control remedies, is an essential feature of this process and entails a struggle over signs. Signs have multiple meanings or a multi-accentual character (Williams, 1976). Opposing interests compete for preferred meanings that will further their interests. 'Signs don't command "general acceptance" in privileged isolation from the contending forces which exist within any society. People struggle over what they should signify, and over what choice of orientation for a given sign counts' (Hartley, 1982: 23).

A key terrain for this struggle is news discourse. The news media are the most immediate and widely circulated vehicles for turning multi-accentuality into more unified values for signs. Sources compete for access to the news media in order to traffic in their preferred values for signs. In particular, they seek to defend their organization against others' imputations of deviance, and thrust to control them, while advancing their own claims about the deviance of other organizations and how they should be controlled. In these terms news access means to be given preference for one's particular meanings that articulate with one's particular interests. Through journalists, sources seek to construct an organizational order that is partial: partial to their own interests, and offering only a partial version of social order.

This partial organizational order requires sources to develop a common stock of rationales (reasons and rationalizations) (cf Brandt, 1969; Bok, 1982), a task made easier when there are key words in the culture that sources can recite with legitimation effect (Rodgers, 1987). 'Democracy' (Williams, 1976a), 'community' (Cohen, 1985), 'national security' (Bok, 1982), and similar 'hurrah words' make readily apparent that the organization is doing good and thus create a sense of self-evident legitimacy. The news is filled with redundant preferred meanings of preferred sources (GUMG, 1976, 1980, 1982). To the extent such preferred meanings can be produced by a small stock of political language, the task of preferred sources is made quite simple. However, this language and the myths it signifies are always equivocal to a degree, and they remain a product of active generation by sources and journalists. The fact that source organizations do not see the matter as unequivocal is clearly revealed in the considerable personnel and fiscal resources they invest in public-relations work. Legitimation work has become a most legitimate expense for organizations in the knowledge society (Blyskal and Blyskal, 1985).

Privacy and Publicity

As introduced earlier, the core component of an organization is its private culture. Private culture is necessary to get the work of the organization done, and has many features that must be mystifying or kept out of the public culture altogether (Gusfield, 1981). News carries the potential for making the source organization vulnerable to further probes that might puncture the private culture. The greater the public knowledge the greater the vulnerability of the organization, and the greater the need for more accounts to achieve accountability. The most obvious means of enclosing this amplifying spiral is secrecy. One key aspect of structured inequality in the knowledge society is the differential ability of organizations to maintain privacy through secrecy. This differential ability includes being able to protect against unwanted attention by journalists regarding private spheres of organizational life. 'The power to keep an occurrence out of the news is power over the news' (Tuchman, 1977: 53). No news can be good news.

Selection and Deception

Since total secrecy is neither desirable nor possible, the common approach is to patrol the facts through selection and deception. Selection is an offensive strategy, trying to bring to news attention only particular events and particular formulations of those events. By keeping reporters preoccupied with things they are bound to be interested in, and by easing their workload in the process, sources can offset the likelihood of incursions into private spheres.

Deception is a defensive strategy. Akin to lying, it is the intention to mislead (cf Warnock, 1971). It thus differs from fiction, which requires suspension of disbelief on the part of a person willing to be taken in by it (Ericson et al, 1987: chap. 8). Deception may seem required in a situation because it will prevent a harm. Preventing a harm becomes more valued than telling the truth. For example, a *New England Journal of Medicine* article advises medical professionals:

> Above all, remember that it is meaningless to speak of telling the truth,
> the whole truth, and nothing but the truth to a patient. It is meaningless
> because it is impossible – a sheer impossibility ... Since telling the truth is
> impossible, there can be no sharp distinction between what is true and what
> is false.

... Far older than the precept, 'the truth, the whole truth, and nothing
but the truth,' is another that originates within our profession, that has always
been the guide of the best physicians, and, if I may venture a prophecy, will
always remain so: So far as possible, do no harm. You can do harm by the
process that is quaintly called telling the truth. You can do harm by lying
... But try to do as little harm as possible. (Henderson, 1935; cited by Bok,
1979: 12–13)

Entwined with this aim of deception is deception for the purpose of
some benefit to the source organization and/or their conception of the public
good. Among the more candid persons demonstrating this aspect is Sir Robert
Mark, former commissioner of the Metropolitan Police of London. According
to Chibnall (1979: 147):

[I]n his celebrated Dimbleby Lecture on BBC television in 1973, Sir Robert
Mark (1973) virtually denied the association between pornography and
police corruption although he was well aware of its existence. He admitted
sometime later that his aim had been the restoration of morale within the CID
[Criminal Investigation Division], which was also a factor in his attack on
unscrupulous elements within the legal profession.

   'I was like a surgeon who had to cut out a major cancer without killing
the patient, in other words I had got to do great execution amongst the CID
while at the same time maintaining their morale and to some extent maintaining public belief in them. Well this isn't a simple operation, you know,
you've got to ... mask your real intentions behind your words occasionally.
I would have thought that this was a classic example of walking that very
dangerous tightrope but producing the results we wanted to produce.' (BBC
interview, 12 July 1977)

Sir Robert also provides an illustration of another purpose of deception:
giving the appearance of veracity. All efforts at communication require a degree of trust between senders and receivers. Without trust in communication,
language and action are only 'stabs in the dark' (Bok, 1979: 19). Ironically,
sometimes it is necessary to deceive in order to sustain the belief that one
is still trustworthy. The appearance of veracity becomes more important than
veracity itself. Hence, Sir Robert argues that on occasion 'police/public relations are not governed by the truth necessarily. They are governed by the
appearance of truth' (*The Listener*, 25 August 1966, quoted by Chibnall,
1977: 173).

Deception can also be justified by reference to principles of justice and
fairness, which are related to considerations of burdens and benefits. Does
deception allow the source to give people 'their due treatment, reward, pun-

ishment, or share' (Bok, 1979: 86)? For example, social scientists sometimes construct their research reports to protect the confidentiality of subjects. Any scientific distortion that ensues is justified as a professional obligation with respect to the subjects' right to confidentiality.

Deception also arises in the more subtle contexts of interpersonal relations. Especially when people face situations in which they feel forced to say something – as when the student persists in questioning the professor or the journalist probes the source – there is a desire to fill any void, even if it is with deceptive statements. On a rather different level than intentional strategies and tactics of deception is the compulsion a person might feel to deceive in order to fill the air. As Jean-Jacques Rousseau says in *Reveries of a Solitary* (1927: 92), 'Never have I lied in my own interest; but often I have lied through shame in order to draw myself from embarrassment in indifferent matters, or matters which did not interest any but myself, when, having to sustain discussion, the slowness of my ideas and the dryness of my conversation forced me to have recourse to fictions in order to say something.'

All efforts at patrolling the facts, by either offensive selection or defensive deception, can be construed in terms of protecting interests. Sometimes it is the interests of the source organization, or some subunit within; sometimes it is conceived and formulated as being interests beyond the source organization, for example, the public interest; in truth, it is often some combination of the source's interest and the public interest.

Time and Space

Source strategies and tactics are also framed in terms of time and space considerations (Giddens, 1984). Often it is not a matter of whether or not to release knowledge, but the occasion on which to release it. Organizations require time and private spaces to foster and contemplate policy options, to avoid harm to others who may be affected by different options, to avoid giving unfair gains to others who may capitalize on information disclosed in advance, and to maintain the strategic value of surprise that comes with controlling the time and place of revelation. Conflict between organizations is not only over whose signs will be given a preferred reading in the news media, but also over when and where these signs will be communicated publicly.

Too much control over regions and knowledge suffocates freedom. Organizations with substantial control of regions and closure can perpetuate their authority in part through the representations they make rather than from being direct representatives of the people. For the people, the trouble with representations is that it is difficult to know what to encourage or challenge because of the limitations on what one is permitted to see. However, too much access and disclosure is no more a source of freedom than is too little. 'With no control over secrecy and openness, human beings could not remain either sane or free' (Bok, 1982: 24).

Policing Organizational Life

The news media function as a social-control agency, policing organizational life to the point of significantly shaping it. If having a social-control effect is on the newsroom agenda, then it is not simply a matter of accepting the bureaucratically constructed barrier erected by the source. Journalists are no different from social-science ethnographers in exploiting the fact that 'the secrets of one group are revealed most readily by members of another group' (Van Maanen, 1979: 545 n 8). If they are stonewalled by one organizational representative they can go to another, with the possibilities being multiple within large bureaucracies. If the members of one organization remain unforthcoming, they may pursue representatives of another organization who may themselves have reason to control the original organization in question. In turn reporters can confront members of the original organization with what they have learned from the whistle-blowers, ultimately puncturing at least part of the private culture and making it part of the culture of public problems.

Along with their sources, journalists must reflect upon the values that articulate with their decisions about secrecy and attendant construal of the facts. For example, they must decide what they know but should not report (confidence); whether to report something as fact without attribution to a source who deserves to be kept secret; and how to write an account that shapes the direction of things to come for members of both the source organization and the news outlet.

When it comes to the crunch of using deceptive methods to obtain snippets from a private culture, journalists face the same dilemmas as sources. For example, the Canadian Broadcasting Corporation's guide, *Journalistic Policy*, asks journalists to weigh up the harm done by deceptive methods *vis-à-vis* benefits to the public interest. Having stated that 'Deception must not be used to gain information' (p. 26), this guidebook then goes on to detail techniques of deception and when they might be permissible. Thus, the journalist is advised to identify himself as a journalist, and then is told it might be advisable not to do so in some circumstances (p. 26). Hidden microphones and cameras are said to be forbidden, then recommended if there is an important social purpose behind using them, for example, revealing antisocial behaviour, such as someone selling drugs to children (p. 27). Elsewhere it is stated that using technological devices for surveillance is permissible when it 'does not infringe the law and when such use could be regarded as in the public interest. The information to be gained must serve an important purpose, must be indispensable to that purpose and must be unobtainable by more open means. On these occasions approval of the divisional Vice-President or by his or her authorized delegate is required for their use' (p. 49). This manual reads no differently than those available to other investigative trades, such as the police (Inbau and Reid, 1967). In a similar way to these other manuals, it indicates that it is legitimate to use deviant practices for the suppression of the deviant activity of others. In other words, deviance is sometimes necessary to keep the lid on the deviance being perpetrated and perpetuated by others.

By penetrating organizational life and blowing the whistle on procedural deviance the news media can serve as guardians against the excesses of secrecy. Yet, journalistic effort to lift the veil of administrative decency that covers so much of organizational life is sporadic. Its sporadic nature means that in news discourse it is difficult to distinguish legitimate secrecy, and legitimate efforts to invade it, from its excesses.

Moreover, journalistic enterprise carried out in the name of exposing organizational secrets can have the effect of contributing further to secrecy. Journalists look for sensational acts of organizational deviance, exposed on an individual-case basis, rather than for an understanding of organizational process and structure that might explain what they uncover. Hence, their revelations often leave a bad taste akin to that of rotten apples. The organizationally structured nature of the deviance, and the legitimacy of its place in the private culture of the organization, is not addressed. Journalists thereby invest in the source's 'secrecy corporation' (Brodeur, 1983: 510) and are only paid dividends sporadically in the form of salacious, but not seditious, exposés. As Brodeur observes regarding journalistic efforts to 'cover' the illicit affairs of the RCMP Security Service that led to the McDonald royal commission:

> The attitude of investigative journalism toward the exposure of deviant po-
> litical policing is somewhat akin to the behavior of the tabloids toward sex
> scandals. The scandal sheets try to hide their pornographic character by pre-
> tending to denounce what they prey upon, thus partaking in what they affect
> to repudiate. Similarly, investigative journalism presents as sensational feats
> of intelligence the numerous cases of police delinquency which it succeeds in
> unearthing, thereby suggesting that these wrongdoings are occurring behind
> a leaden veil of secrecy which only the 'free press' can lift. The growing
> banality of these so-called 'revelations' bears witness to the fact that political
> policing has become a reservoir for fishing out deviance, in order to increase
> plummeting circulation rates. (ibid)

There are, of course, many stocked ponds from which journalists can cull their deviance and control stories and send them to the canning factories managed by their editors. And, as one pond dries up, the others can be relied upon until it is restocked and ready once again to contribute.

News Significance

It is a paradox that news texts are treated with scepticism (RCN, 1981a), and yet are taken so seriously. As we document subsequently, sources complain bitterly about being misrepresented, but feel compelled to make another representation next time they are asked. One explanation for this behaviour is the recognition by sources that news is crucial to the constitution of authority in the knowledge structure of society, even if its veracity and contributions to understanding are in doubt. Resources must be devoted to newswork if one wants to be recognized as an authorized knower, if one's organization wants to both promote and protect its image as accountable, if legitimation work is required to respond to and sustain the myths of one's institutional environment. Both public bureaucracies and private corporations recognize this fact, as signified by the corps of public-relations staff they employ for these purposes.

Marginal organizations that challenge the dominant culture and its articulation in legitimate organizations are also compelled to address the news media, even if they recognize that the media are destroying them. Being up against the authorities as an 'outsider' (oppositional) reform group entails confronting the news media also, since they literally represent the authorities (McMahon and Ericson, 1987). As Gitlin (1980: 242–4) observes, social-movement groups in political opposition foster media attention for rational purposes, such as the recruitment of members, the challenging of authority, the neutralizing of third forces, protection, agenda-setting, the visualizing of cultural alternatives, the redressing of grievances, the enhancing of individual egos, and the obtaining of a wider audience. 'Toward these ends it is difficult to see how an opposition movement can avoid addressing the mass media at some point in its career' (ibid). Yet, in the very process of needing to challenge the authorities through the news media that represent them, the reform group becomes absorbed into, or alternatively, expelled from, the existing knowledge structure of society. '[T]his sort of access can also be delusory, to the extent that media-made reputation is confused with substantive social power over public decisions' (ibid).

Research Questions

Our deliberations to this point can be summarized and formulated as a series of research questions. The sociology of newswork has emphasized that sources hold the upper hand in the news process. Sources are portrayed as effectively policing the boundaries of their organizations, so that they remain 'primary definers.' Journalists are thus left to reproduce sources' 'bureaucratic propaganda,' as 'secondary definers.' We start with the assumption that these findings may be an artefact of the researchers' methods, and not a full picture of the complexities involved in negotiating the news. Research that visualizes reporter/source relations in this way is largely grounded in observations of journalists at work, or it is at the greater distance of speculative readings of news content without any effort to observe or consult with sources or journalists. We begin with the possibility that a very different picture might emerge if knowledge is also grounded in the perspectives of sources. Therefore, we have raised research questions and designed empirical enquiries grounded in the perspectives of sources.

Current research also suggests that the news-negotiation process is much the same regardless of the type of news organization involved ('popular' or 'quality'), the medium (radio, television, newspaper), and the type of source organization involved. All journalists are severely constrained by the social and cultural organization of their work, including especially the bureaucratic edifice constructed by their sources. We begin with the assumption that the news-negotiation process is not uniform. We assume that there is variation across types of news organization and the medium they work with. We also assume variation across types of source organization, in terms of what they hope to accomplish in the news process, and the strategies and tactics they use to achieve it. In particular, we focus on the fact that different sources have very different requirements of enclosure and disclosure of knowledge. These differences are likely to be particularly evident in the distinctive news cultures that arise on different newsbeats. Each newsbeat has its own culture related to the news requirements of the source organization; the requirements of the news outlets operating there; the social relations that emerge among source individuals and reporters; and the social relations that emerge among reporters from different news outlets. We assume that the news process is 'multicultural,' that is, the news product varies according to the framework of regions and closures on each beat, and how different news organizations adapt their own needs to that framework in each instance.

This 'multiculturalism' is reflected in the research studies that follow on court, police, legislature, and private-sector news sources. The focus on organizations concerned with deviance, law, and social control is especially propitious, because it accentuates the core features of the news-negotiation process. As Leigh (1982: 74) observes: 'Knowledge is, of course, power. So to discuss the way information is shared out in society is to talk about the politics of information gathering. The relationship between journalists, private citizens and government organisations in the criminal justice system

– police, courts, and prisons – is a particularly interesting one, because three ideas about information collide – sometimes nastily – in this arena. These are the concepts of publicity, privacy, and secrecy.'

Sources are as able as journalists to use the news to *enact* their environment (Weick, 1979). Just as we have enquired into how journalists do so (Ericson et al, 1987), so we examine the strategies, tactics, and perceived success of sources in this regard. How do sources use news to set a public agenda? to recruit financial, membership and ideological support? to prevent a harm? to neutralize opposing interests? to rectify a harm? Consideration must be given to what the source sees as the interests at stake in a public issue or event she participates in through news communication. Is publicity part of the organization's mandate? How will publicity affect the source organization in a positive or negative direction? Will publicity allow the organization to sustain a sense of veracity, appear accountable, and therefore underpin its authoritative position in the knowledge structure of society?

These more abstract questions can be studied concretely at the interpersonal level of participation in the news process. Does the source feel 'compelled' to talk in the context of situational dynamics of being questioned by reporters? Conversely, do his concerns in a particular context lead him to seal off access to the advantage or disadvantage of his own career and that of his organization? Is publicity an intrinsic reward for those whose work is otherwise mundane? Does being in the media spotlight – even if it entails only a snapshot or ten-second clip – reward the spokesperson because it reinforces his sense of elevated status in the knowledge structure of society?

We conceive source organizations as having a dual mandate in their dealings with news organizations. On the one hand, they seek access to news outlets rather than mere coverage; on the other hand, they seek to deny access to their private culture. They want the public face of their organization to be covered in the news, and their private face to remain under cover. The ability to do this is far from routine or fixed. Rather, it is always equivocal and tentative, with the attendant sense that understandings could fall apart. The obvious threat for the source is the news thrust to police organizational life by exposing deviance and pushing for particular control remedies. A more subtle threat is the 'self-enclosure' that arises among sources and journalists who deal with one another regularly. Through 'group think,' sources and journalists can unwittingly neglect to ask certain questions of one another, to consult relevant documents, or to otherwise communicate aspects of mutual interest.

The essence of the regular source's relation to journalists is negotiating the terms of news accounts of social-control efforts by or against the source. Sources wish to use news discourse to further their arguments for control over other organizations in their environment, and to defend against the efforts of other organizations to use news communications to justify infringements on their autonomy. Obviously negotiation with journalists is itself an exercise in social control: control over organizations in the environment requires control over the news.

Negotiations for control of the news take place on three terrains: the physical, the social, and the cultural. Each of these terrains must be investigated empirically to understand the news communications that are forthcoming from each beat.

The physical terrain is the actual physical arrangements available for journalists to do their work on the beat. Are office facilities provided for journalists? Does the source have public-relations specialists, with their own offices? Are journalists restricted to these spaces, or are other means of entry and engagement possible in both front and back regions? How effective is the telephone, and other less direct means of penetrating organizational space, for obtaining information? Entwined with these questions of space is the matter of time. When are sources available? When is it permissible not only to obtain information, but to publish it? Disclosure is usually not an either/or matter, but a matter of when and where news communication is appropriate from the source's point of view.

On the terrain of social relations the analyst must map the network among journalists and sources, what holds the web of relations together and what is significant about it. Communication networks are strung together on the basis of trust and reciprocity among members. They also depend in part on the physical arrangements, which literally provide a concrete form to how the social relations are established and sustained. In the news business there is also considerable flow of personnel, who move from working for news outlets as journalists to working for source organizations as public-relations officers, and vice versa. This flow creates a continuity in social relations between sources and journalists, and a consistency through a sharing of craft knowledge.

The matter of craft knowledge brings us to the cultural terrain. Here questions abound concerning how webs of social relations are spun into webs of cultural significance that can be communicated as news. Do sources and journalists share similar news values and/or similar values in the dominant culture? If so, does this sharing come about through on 'elective affinity' (Weber, 1946) and/or through the routine demands of their respective occupational environments? If not, how do they manage news communication? Do they experience an 'uneasy relation'? What problems does this uneasy relation create for the parties involved?

In summary, the task is to capture how the physical, social, and cultural terrains merge on the landscape of each beat and affect the news product. How does the source engage these terrains to develop both offensive and defensive tactics and strategies for managing the news? How does the source process a large, variable, and equivocal volume of knowledge, and yet act upon it swiftly in the production of news accounts? What are the effects of source efforts at routinization? Do they allow the source to limit the terms of news to the point where his preferred version of his organization becomes visualized in the news? Once such access is gained, how is it sustained without lapsing into mere coverage? When it becomes mere coverage, or worse still negative coverage, what remedies are available to correct the record and eventually return to routine access? Can this be done through a reworking of more routine procedures, or are formal mechanisms of protest and remedy required?

Answering these questions allows us to address grander questions. What is the relative autonomy of different types of sources in the news process? In turn, what does the differential autonomy of sources tell us about the contribution of news to their place in the knowledge structure of society, and to processes of control and change in that society?

Research Approaches

NEWSBEAT ETHNOGRAPHIES

Ethnographic research is most appropriate for ascertaining the distinctive news culture that arises on each beat, and the spatial and social practices that are in accord with that culture (Ericson et al, 1987: chap. 3). Only through direct observation can the analyst accurately map the web of social relations, and the nature of cultural values, as they are struggled with in actual decision-making. While interviews removed from the situation can reveal structures of thinking and suggest what to look for, 'We cannot depend on being told, we have to observe the actual situation' (Holy and Stuchlik, 1983: 12). While organizational documents reveal the criteria of rational acceptability by which the organization accounts for its work, they are otherwise limited for research purposes because they do not address directly research questions but rather administrative questions. Only ethnographic observation provides a means of documenting independently what people do, as opposed to what they say they do in interviews or organizational documents. Indeed, observation allows an assessment of how subjects' words in the abstract – whether in organizational documents or research interviews – are related to their deeds. This assessment includes the opportunity to analyse how they construct their written and verbal accounts for organizational purposes, how their words are also deeds.

With these considerations in mind, all three authors participated in extensive field-work during 1982 and 1983. We undertook long-term observation, interviewing, and scrutiny of sources' and reporters' documents in court, police, and legislature (Ontario provincial parliament) beats. These beats were

TABLE 1.1
Court, police, and legislature beats: comparisons on regions and closures

Characteristics of regions and closures	Beat		
	Court	Police	Legislature
Media-relations facilities	Minimal	Considerable	Extensive
Proactivity	Minimal	Considerable	Extensive
Back-region access	Minimal	Minimal	Considerable
Vulnerability to back-region disclosure	Minimal	Considerable	Extensive
Front-region enclosure	Extensive	Considerable	Considerable

chosen because they are primary locations for news of lawmaking and law enforcement. The police beat is the location for the reporting of events of deviance, and of the routine procedures – sometimes also visualized as deviant – used by the police as *the* primary agency of social control. The court beat is the location for reporting the process by which the captured deviant is formally dealt with, emphasizing both procedural values (rights, justice, fairness, equality) and outcomes. The legislature beat is the location for governmental reaction to deviant events, processes, or a state of affairs in the form of legislation or policy reform. Safety in the streets, zoning for halfway houses for deviants, police efficiency, the growth of citizens' groups for crime prevention and justice, ministerial reaction to major events, mismanagement or corrupt practice by civil servants or politicians: these and many more matters of deviance and control are defined as inherently political by newsworkers. As argued in recent criminological writing (Foucault, 1977; Rothman, 1980; Ericson, 1985, 1987; Rock, 1986), the political-reform process is as much a part of crime control as the police, courts, and prisons.

These beats were also chosen because they offer considerable variation in how they are organized to deal with the news media. As such, they provide a basis for comparing how different physical, social, and cultural arrangements on a beat are related to the news product. As presented schematically in table 1.1, the court beat is most closed, the police beat more open, and the legislature beat most open. Documentation of these differences is presented in chapters 2 to 4.

In conducting the ethnographies on each beat, we attached ourselves to particular reporters who occupied desks within the beat newsroom. Reporters were observed in the beat newsroom and as they made their rounds. Several key aspects were the focus of data collection. We looked for differences in the reporters' occupational culture, compared to general-assignment reporting, brought about by working daily with journalists from different news organizations and by the greater autonomy from their own news organizations than is available to the general-assignment reporter. We focused upon the ways in which beat journalists systematized their searches for information, including their exchanges with one another, related to the issue of 'pack journalism.' We examined the criteria used by journalists to discover and decide upon newsworthiness, being relatively more autonomous from assignment-editor control of these judgments compared to general-assignment reporters. We examined interpersonal ties with sources as these related to criteria of what is reportable and how it is to be reported – for example, how do these ties influence what is to be treated as 'fact' without attribution? What is the relation between credibility of sources and the decision to report? The data from these newsbeat ethnographies were indexed for qualitative analysis.

SOURCE INTERVIEWS

Additional data were generated by interviewing a range of sources. We chose a theoretical sample of sources involved in stories we observed on the police, court, and legislature beats, as well as other sources who were cited regularly in news of deviance and control. Interviews allowed us to probe further regarding the strategies and tactics used by sources in news communication, and how these might be explicable in terms of the social and cultural criteria of their particular organizations. Interview data obtained from sources who were regular participants on the court, police, and legislature beats were related to stories we observed 'in the making' while conducting the newsbeat ethnographies. It is well established that as an interview technique, discussion of specific matters an interviewee was involved in is preferable to asking questions about concepts and processes in the abstract (Holy and Stuchlik, 1983). The fact that we also observed aspects of these specific matters is an additional means for us to understand the source-interview data.

We generated a theoretical sample of ninety-three sources representing different institutional spheres. A detailed breakdown of the sample is given in table 1.2. These persons were chosen a / on the basis of being involved in stories we had observed during our observational field-work on the beats or with general assignment reporters in newsrooms (cf Ericson et al, 1987), and b / in terms of representing a range of organizational types, organizational roles, and hierarchical positions within organizations. The criminal-justice and other government categories correspond to the beat organizations we observed in field-work. The non-government category was added to incorporate private organizations or individuals who were involved in stories we observed in which they were either subject to imputations of deviance or made such imputations against other organizations or individuals. Their newsmaking activities are analysed in chapter 5.

An open-focused interview schedule was designed to address three major topics related to our research questions. First, we focused upon source

TABLE 1.2
Sources interviewed

Source type	N	%
Criminal Justice		
Police commissioner	1	1.1
Police executive	2	2.2
Police superintendents	4	4.3
Police inspectors	4	4.3
Police constables	3	3.2
Crown attorneys	3	3.2
Trial court co-ordinators	2	2.2
Coroner	1	1.1
Judges	5	5.4
Subtotal	25	27.0
Other Government		
Federal civil servants	6	6.4
Provincial cabinet ministers	3	3.2
Provincial members of parliament	5	5.4
Provincial party assistants	3	3.2
Provincial civil servants	12	12.9
Municipal mayors	3	3.2
Municipal aldermen/councillors	4	4.3
Municipal civil servants	2	2.2
Subtotal	38	40.8
Non-Government		
Citizen interest groups	11	11.8
Corporations	5	5.4
Occupational associations	5	5.4
Lawyers	6	6.4
Individual	3	3.2
Subtotal	30	32.2
Total	93	100.0

perspectives regarding how the news media organize and the news criteria they utilize. Included were questions on the role of the news media, adequacy of coverage, and the nature and locus of problems sources experience with the news media. Sources were asked to assess the nature of news judgment: the criteria of newsworthiness, the criteria for selecting sources, the locus of news interpretation, the nature and locus of bias, and conceptions of objectivity, fairness, neutrality, and balance. They were also asked for their views on news-organization and media differences regarding these criteria.

Second, we probed for strategies and tactics used by sources to obtain reasonable coverage. Sources were questioned regarding their criteria for limiting news-media access, and the specific forms of knowledge control they engaged in. They were asked to discuss the degree and nature of proactive contact with news organizations, and the advantages and disadvantages of being proactive. The question of accessibility to the news media was addressed, and how it varies for individual reporters, different news organizations, and different media. Probes were made regarding sources' advance preparation for scheduled interviews, and interpersonal styles and approaches in interviews. On a more general level sources were asked to enunciate and explain their preferences for particular news formats, news organizations, and news media. They were also asked to give details on their use of specialist staff to deal with the media, the training of their personnel to handle the media, and what internal controls they had to influence the decision about who within their organization acted as a spokesperson. Sources were requested to articulate how news coverage affected their organization positively and negatively, and what they had learned over time was the best way to 'manage' the news media.

Third, we questioned sources about possible remedies for unreasonable coverage and their accounts of actual efforts at remedy. In the context of considering specific problems encountered with the news media, the remedies of calling the journalist concerned, contacting supervising editors, writing letters to the editor, seeking corrections and retractions, complaining to the Ontario Press Council, complaining to the Canadian Radio-television and Telecommunications Commission, and taking legal action were addressed. Also considered were sources' reasons for continuing to co-operate with the news media in face of unreasonable coverage. Data from these questions provide the basis for our analysis of remedies presented in chapter 6.

The interviews were tape-recorded with consent of the interviewee, and the tapes were transcribed for ease of access. The transcribed interview material was scrutinized to develop a coding manual for quantitative classification and analyses, and for the preparation of a qualitative index.

LETTERS TO THE EDITOR

The research approaches outlined above were designed to explore ways in which journalists and sources are part of each other's organizations, and how news texts are negotiated products of their physical, cultural, and social contexts. These research approaches also provide a vehicle for understanding how news texts play back on members of the source organizations involved in making them, and how they affect their social relations, including their further efforts at news communication.

An important consideration is how these further efforts at news communication in turn have an influence upon, and must be dealt with by, the particular news outlet involved. In order to understand the communication cycle back into the news organization, we decided to study the letters-to-the-editor process in one major newspaper. Many letters come from sources who are in the news regularly. Our thesis is that, as such, letters are treated by the news organization as simply another type of input by sources, only in this case the source provides the actual 'filed copy' in the form of a letter. Letters are treated in the same way as all other filed copy in news organizations: the same criteria of newsworthiness, the same news values, and the same parameters regarding play and layout are considered by the editor.

To explore this thesis, the letters editor of a major newspaper was observed for eight days, including two preliminary days, followed by six days during which we tape-recorded the editor's verbalizations of his decisions: why he accepted or rejected a letter; and if accepted, its priority, expected use in play and layout, and reasons for the particular substantive copy-editing of the letter. Over this six-day period 366 letters were dealt with, 124 or 33.9 per cent of which were accepted. These letters were copied for our research files; the copies of the accepted ones include the copy-editing markings. The tape-recordings of the editor's verbalized judgments of these letters were transcribed for ready access. Letter content and the editor's verbalizations were coded for quantitative analysis in tabular form, and also provide a rich source of qualitative data.

The analysis begins with a description of the letter editor's place and function in the newsroom. This analysis is followed by that of his decision to accept or reject letters in terms of characteristics of letter writers (organizational affiliation, status, whether they cite other sources); contexts and issues addressed in letters (government or private sector, institutional fields, issues); and levels of understanding and assessment in letters (primary/factual, secondary/explanation, tertiary/empathy, implications, evaluations, recommendations). The analysis includes both cross-tabulation and discriminant techniques, as well as qualitative data in illustration. We then describe and analyse the editor's own reasons for his decisions to accept or reject letters. Finally, we examine the editor's decisions regarding editing and play of accepted letters. This examination is accomplished through consideration of the editor's own accounts and our scrutiny of the edited copies of the accepted letters and published content. The results of these analyses are presented in chapter 6. In conjunction with our other research approaches, these analyses provide a comprehensive picture of the terms and conditions in which the news is negotiated, and how it flows perpetually in and out of source organizations and news organizations.

Keeping in mind the frames we have developed for its production, we now set this picture in motion. In chapters 2 to 5 we undertake a comparative study of how different source organizations and institutions organize to achieve an acceptable level of privacy and publicity. In chapter 2 we analyse the courts as an example of a source organization that is relatively closed to access by journalists except on very specific and controlled terms. In chapter 3 consideration is given to the police beat as an example of a somewhat more open source organization, yet with a sophisticated system for patrolling interpretations of its activities. In chapter 4 the legislature is examined as the most open newsbeat, where oppositional forces, including news organizations, develop and trade knowledge in an active and relatively pluralistic market of symbolic politics. In chapter 5 we compare and contrast the strategies and tactics of various private-sector sources (business corporations, citizen-interest groups, individuals), most of whom do not have a newsbeat system as part of their organizations. In chapter 6 we explore the crucial, yet neglected, research question of how sources of all types seek remedy in the face of unreasonable news coverage. These data are especially instructive about the nature and potency of media power/knowledge as experienced by sources. We further our analysis of remedies by focusing on letters to the editor as the most significant forum for remedy. This empirical investigation serves as an excellent vehicle for summarizing the materials on source/journalist relations presented previously, and underscores the relative autonomy of the news media. In chapter 7 we summarize the instruction offered by our empirical investigations and we draw conclusions about how sources and journalists negotiate symbolic order to constitute the knowledge society.

2

The Courts

News Culture and Ideas

The news is not simply a product of social arrangements and a unitary culture in the newsroom, as depicted in much of the research literature. It is produced in the context of a network of microcultures that arise on different newsbeats. It is necessary to analyse these microcultures, and how they differ from each other and from newsroom cultures, in order to understand news texts.

In this section we analyse the spatial, temporal, social, and cultural aspects of the court beat. We consider what journalists take to be newsworthy about the courts, and whether or not sources share this view. The process of discovery of newsworthy items is examined in detail, including how story ideas originate. In the next section we consider how sources control knowledge about cases and actors through spatial and temporal arrangements, tacit agreements, exclusion, legal ideology, and the law itself. We examine knowledge networks among reporters, as they use one another to find out about newsworthy cases, to discover and construe the facts, and generally to make their work more manageable. In the final section consideration is given to sources' views of the influence of news texts on their work. We examine how news plays back into the court environment and orders relations there.

There is relatively little research on newsmaking in the courts. Sustained analyses are provided by Drechsel (1983) and Stanga (1971), and some attention to the courts is offered by Epstein (1975), Chibnall (1977), and Fishman (1980). In contrast, the police beat and legislature beat have been researched in greater depth. This research emphasis parallels the news, which gives relatively little attention to the courts compared to what it gives the police and legislative branches of government. In nineteenth-century England (Tunstall,

1971: 92), the United States (Drechsel, 1983: 48–9), and Canada (Craven, 1983), the emphasis in crime reporting was on court cases, with verbatim transcripts or long accounts published in newspapers. In the late twentieth century the courts are given minimal attention in broadcast journalism. Print journalists report on only a tiny fraction of cases, almost never attend the entire hearing of the cases they do cover, and reduce a complex matter into a few column-inches. In terms of both the number of journalists assigned and the quantity of stories, news outlets pay more attention to police efforts at crime control, and to politicians' and civil servants' policy talk about the control of crime and other forms of deviance.

In spite of the historical shift away from courts as a major forum for news, most news outlets still give some coverage to court cases. Courts remain attractive for a number of reasons. Matters arising in the courts are easy to construe as newsworthy. Court stories articulate with the major functions of news, simultaneously providing for entertainment, signs of social order and change, and fourth-estate opportunities. One newspaper we studied had a full-time court reporter but no full-time reporter on the police beat. As a senior editor explained, 'If you have a police beat, what you're expecting is a whole bunch of stories every day on local crime ... and I don't know what that does to the sum total of knowledge of your particular society.' In contrast, 'In the courts ... you're there because the rules of the game are being either changed or confirmed. And it's important for people to know what's happening to the rules of the game and it's a decision-making body.'

Courts also allow journalists to meet their claim that they are standing in on behalf of the public to see that governmental processes are just and that government officials are accountable. Except for a notorious case or a case in which they are directly involved, citizens do not attend court. The 'public' aspect of court hearings is defaulted to journalists, and their selection of what cases and what details the public should know. This defaulting was clearly evident in our court observations, as the public gallery of a courtroom often contained more reporters than other citizens. On one occasion seven of the nine persons in a courtroom, other than court officials, were reporters.

For editors looking to fill the column-inches provided for by advertising, and especially those spaces on the back pages that are more awkward to fill with other material, court stories are ideal. The regular place and time of court hearings offers a steady and ready supply of stories to use or discard as they can be 'fitted to print.' Hence, at the time of our research the mass-market Toronto *Star* had several reporters and a secretary on the court beat to provide editors with a predictable supply to choose from. The popular *Sun* had two full-time reporters, while the quality *Globe and Mail* had only one.

The Court Newsroom

Journalists on the court beat had a newsroom in the county court house. The Supreme Court of Ontario and the provincial courts were each within two minutes' walk, so that a range of courts could be covered with ease from the beat newsroom. The beat newsroom was occupied on a regular basis only by reporters from the three Toronto daily newspapers, and a free-lance reporter who derived most of his work from one television station and one radio station. Hence, the practice of referring to the newsroom as the 'press room' was not anachronistic. This beat was a print-oriented one. With the exception of one television station whose reporter did not use court-newsroom space, no broadcast-news organization had a journalist exclusively on the court beat. Broadcast journalists typically covered at least two beats, for example, police and courts, or City Hall (which was next door to the county-court building) and courts. For these broadcast journalists the court beat was an add-on to their primary beat, the police or City Hall.

Each beat reporter was his own assignment editor. To that end a date file was kept on upcoming cases he planned to follow or further hearings for cases already being followed. Beat reporters worked on more 'featurish' stories over time, usually when there was a lull in the cases they were covering or when they had already 'bagged' their quota of two or three court-case stories at an early point in the day.

Work was also managed by relying on one another for tips about what cases were worth covering, and about the timing of cases being covered. This process allowed each reporter to ensure he would be in court for key testimony and summations. In order to manage the coverage expected by editors, reporters could rarely afford to sit through an entire case or even a substantial portion of it. They had to rely on their colleagues from other newspapers on the beat to tell them when to 'pop into' a courtroom for some quotable quotes, and to provide them with quotations and other information when they missed being in court at the appropriate time. By pooling *some* of their resources in this way, they could achieve the goal of covering 'all' the 'significant' cases, and 'all' the details of these cases, as judged by their editors. This sharing was crucial to reporters whose newspapers devoted minimal resources to the court beat.

Reporters also managed their work by relying on sources. Sources were useful in the same way as fellow reporters: they provided tips on upcoming cases, quotable quotes, and knowledge about aspects the reporter missed by not being in court. A prominent local lawyer expressed the prevailing view among regular sources that for reporters in routine cases, 'the key is ties that they have with people who know what is coming up.' This finding is in keeping with Drechsel's (1983: 94–5).

Relations with Sources

Compared to their colleagues on the police and legislature beats, court reporters had a more distant relationship to sources, mainly because lawyers, Crown attorneys, and judges have less need to use the news media to serve the purposes of the court system or their personal causes. They are content to restrict reporting to the formal 'majesty, justice and mercy' (Hay, 1975) of the courtroom, and to keep it out of the informal, hectic, tariff-based marketplace of plea-negotiation sessions from which the accused and victims are also excluded (Ericson and Baranek, 1982). The distance between reporters and sources kept their encounters fairly formal and 'business-like.' Reporters we spent time with did not routinely cultivate sources by, for example, extensive informal chats or going to lunch with them.

While court-beat reporters were given a legitimate place *within* the courts through the provision of office space, their work was not facilitated further by full-time news-media officers, as provided on other beats. The trial co-ordinators at different court levels were assigned the task of co-operating with reporters regarding time and location of hearings and questions of access to documents and to judges. In addition they proactively offered tips to the newspaper reporters who were regulars on the beat. However, according to one trial co-ordinator, this 'co-operation' amounted to no more than one-half hour of her time each day and was largely a 'hit-and-miss' affair.

Apart from the cost of maintaining news-media officers, it is clear that the role of such personnel is not consistent with the way the courts are organized and how legal professionals see their relation to the news media. A reporter's place is in the courtroom, supplemented by access to selected documents such as judgments and brief interviews with Crown attorneys to get a clarification of the facts. A full-time news-media–relations person would be in effect a 'reporter' for the courts. Such a person would add another level of interpretation and translation to the process and, as such, would entail 'second-guessing' what went on in court or what was meant by the judge who wrote the judgment. Moreover, there is always the risk that, instead of patrolling the facts, this person might venture into the back regions of the courts on behalf of reporters to reveal the workings there.

That is not to say that court-beat reporters had no regular contacts with sources for the purpose of managing their work. Trial co-ordinators in particular had ongoing good relations with reporters and were a vital resource in news management. Individual lawyers and Crown attorneys also had regular contact with beat reporters, especially with one reporter who had been on the beat for more than a decade. One Crown attorney described this reporter as a fixture: 'I'd see him every day just as much if not more than you see the judges in court, just always there.' He also noted that the formal relations that are supposed to prevail among court officials can be eroded with familiarity, and this is no less true of relations with reporters than it is with police, Crown attorneys, and judges.

> [W]hen you see a reporter every day for several years, you can't help become friendly with him, I mean he's part of the court almost, he's there every day and that's true, that can happen, but that can happen in any sphere of activity. I mean a Crown being with a judge too long, they can get too friendly, or with a defence lawyer ... [I]t goes with the territory I suppose ... [S]ure there are disadvantages to it, but on the whole, you're better to have seasoned people who are there all the time reporting what's going on, than throwing a lot of inexperienced people in. Now, a new broom may sweep clean and ... a fresh view of the thing is sometimes helpful but sometimes it isn't if the person that's covering the story doesn't know what he's doing, particularly with a court case.

Reporters' Knowledge

The Crown attorney cited above raises *the* predominant concern among all news sources in the courts, namely the reporters' knowledge. Similar to what Drechsel (1983: 111) found, court officials we interviewed complained repeatedly about reporters' lack of specialist knowledge of the law. Many felt it is the responsibility of news organizations to ensure that court reporters are educated in law. This finding is particularly significant because judges are generally unwilling to be interviewed about points of law as they pertain to particular cases. The reporter is expected to make educated interpretations based upon what he hears in court or reads in a judgment. If he does not know the law he cannot make educated interpretations.

Even the regular court-beat reporters did not have specialist training in law (the situation is very different elsewhere – see Hess, 1981; Dennis, 1974–5). Moreover, in our observations reporters frequently confronted their ignorance of the law and were forced either to ask Crown attorneys or defence counsel about it or to drop it with attendant consequences for what they reported. Indeed, regulars in the court newsroom did not even seem to have a good knowledge of the law pertaining to what they could report, the law of contempt. On one occasion reporters in the court newsroom discussed a case they were all covering, and disagreed over what was reportable legally at this particular stage. Later one reporter, who was a regular on the beat, talked to his desk editor about the case. The reporter volunteered his opinion that it would be worthwhile for him to learn the law related to reporting because he did not have a good working knowledge of it.

Reporters demonstrated repeatedly that they lacked knowledge of the court and legal system. Neither a court reporter nor his editor knew if there was a federal court in Toronto. A reporter who had been on the beat for over a year did not know the meaning of an 'audit hearing.' A court-beat reporter of considerable experience went to the appeal court and scanned three judgments, eventually commenting to the researcher, 'They're incomprehensible, and that means they're not reportable.' Reporters mainly covered the county-court trials, while also paying some attention to the provincial courts in a nearby building, but the hearings of the Supreme Court of Ontario were attended rarely. On one occasion an experienced court-beat reporter decided to attend a Supreme Court of Ontario case because of its significance in relation to the Canadian Charter of Rights and Freedoms. He repeatedly asked questions of our researcher and others in the Court about the procedures, and did not know the identity of any of the five judges presiding.

Regular reporters on the court beat were critical of less-experienced colleagues, especially those who were not regulars on the beat. These criticisms focused on their colleagues' lack of knowledge of court procedures in terms of when it was appropriate to interview a witness; what questions were appropriate to ask; and what proceedings, such as voir dires, could not be reported on. Violations of reporting propriety, and legal propriety, were pointed out with regularity, a fact borne out by our own direct observations of general-assignment reporters who were parachuted into the courts for a single day or single case. Some literally did not know where to look or to whom to talk. We observed general-assignment television reporters who relied on their cameraman, because he at least had recipe knowledge of the courthouse spatial regions. General-assignment reporters also turned to our researchers for advice and knowledge about court procedures.

Among legal professionals, the locus of the superficial and distorting nature of court reporting was said to be in reporters' lack of both specialist and recipe knowledge. A lawyer stated: 'Where I think they fall down, and fall down very badly, is that because journalists are not properly trained on the one hand and because they usually don't have continuity within a case on the other hand, I think the public often does not get a proper flavour of what goes on in the context of a trial. It's only the rare case where, for example, one journalist from a newspaper is assigned to cover the case throughout ... When that happens you get great coverage, but generally the coverage is atrocious.'

Many sources believed that, with the exception of one newspaper, the court beat served as a relatively low-status training ground for junior, inexperienced reporters lacking specialist or recipe knowledge. A judge summarized the view of many: 'Well I think the news media function is to report accurately the proceedings in court and to do that I feel they have to have much more continuity of reporters than they do. It seems to be a training ground to break in new reporters. It may be different in other cities but I seem to hear the same complaint from other judges that it's not looked upon very highly within the newspaper hierarchy and I don't think that we get adequately trained or adequately prepared people reporting on court activities.'

Sources seemed to expect news discourse to be in the familiar terms of legal discourse. They are bound to be disappointed, since news discourse sets out to 'edit' legal discourse so that it is more manageable and can be communicated within the common sense. Legal discourse involves qualifiers and et cetera clauses; news discourse requires the opposite. News managers do not require reporters who are knowledgeable in law and court procedure, they need someone who can retell the stories of others within the requirements of news discourse. The courts are an ideal setting because the reporter just has to sit in court and let others unfold the story for her. While legal analysis has its place in the courtroom, it is literally out of place in news texts.

The same can be said for journalistic analyses of the administration of justice. Occasional features do appear on 'problems' such as plea bargaining, heavy dockets, inadequate resources, court delays, and the connections among these issues. However, such features are rare and constitute no more than an ideology of special pleading for more resources and bureaucratic efficiency. More evident is the 'eternal recurrence' (Rock, 1973) of criminal-court cases in which the names change but everything else remains innocent. A lawyer observed:

> Reporting on the criminal court is the reporting that I watch mostly. It's utterly stereotyped. It's being done in exactly the same way it was being done seventy-five years ago. It hasn't progressed one moment. It's the crime reporters' technique that you see on the late movies. And the language is the same, the structure of paragraphs is the same ... You rarely go on even to the second level, which was developed in the thirties, which was the human-interest, sob story, where you take the criminal and tell something about the criminal's background. What you don't ever see is an analysis of the social functions involved and the social roles. And it's just like they didn't exist. It's like there's only one role for a criminal and that was to be criminal in the stereotyped sense. Only one role for a judge and that's to be either soft or hard, depending on the two roles available for a judge ... There's no analysis of social structure involved. And very little understanding therefore of the criminal process, which is structural beyond belief.

Reporters' Autonomy

From the reporter's perspective, the court beat represents autonomy, when compared to general assignment. Several court-beat reporters said they had greater autonomy on the court beat, and one said he chose the beat for that reason. Signs of autonomy included the fact that most court stories were generated by the reporter rather than by her desk editor. Some reporters had their own word-processing terminals in the court newsroom, and could therefore submit their filed story without having to return to the main newsroom of their newspaper. Their work was anchored physically and culturally within the court and its newsroom rather than the newsrooms of their respective news outlets.

One newspaper reporter was expected to call her desk editor (assignment editor) twice during the day to inform him about what she was working on. She would sometimes offer her editor options among several possible stories, although choice was negotiated in terms of how the reporter formulated the possibilities to the editor. The reporter would also use these occasions to negotiate for more play. While the editor often made specific recommendations, and ultimately controlled play, any statements he made during these calls did not foreclose the matter. For example, on one occasion the editor told the reporter to 'brief' (three or four column-inches and no byline) a story because there was no room for more. The reporter wanted something more than this, and worked especially hard to develop human-interest aspects through extra interviews outside court and a dramatic lead. She filed a story of thirteen column-inches, and it was published largely intact, complete with her byline.

The control of editors is also evident in their feedback to reporters on stories. The greatest concern to reporters was that a fellow reporter from the court newsroom would cover a story that they had missed, and that their editors would consequently be annoyed. A lesser concern was that a fellow reporter might come up with a better angle, or better quotations, again leading their editors to conclude that they had been 'beaten by the competition.' As documented later, this event was partially covered through exchanges with fellow reporters, a process by which they routinely revealed what they were working on and shared primary facts. It was also covered on occasion by reporters offering one another their most quotable quotes. To the experienced reporter, these quotes were telling in terms of angles and leads.

Reporters worked hard to protect their beat territory from incursions by their colleagues in the same news organization. There were frequent conflicts in this regard. In particular, conflicts arose when a general-assignment reporter or topic-specialist reporter was working on a major continuing story that eventually ended up in a court case. When the matter came before the courts, the court reporter typically wanted to take it over. The reporter who originally worked on it experienced frustration and animosity if he lost the assignment at the court stage, the very point when the most dramatic public revelations and a definitive official conclusion were most likely.

Even when the court-beat reporter knew he had too many newsworthy cases to cover, he sometimes decided not to ask his assignment editor to send a general-assignment reporter to help. This decision was based on the knowledge that what initially appeared as a busy list for the day could easily fall apart, leaving the regular court reporter with little or nothing. We observed several days that appeared promising but fell apart, including some when no stories at all were filed. While court provides a somewhat predictable forum for routine news production, a given case may not go on as planned or proceed as visualized initially.

When she had the case she found most significant, the court reporter did sometimes tip her assignment editor about other possibilities that someone else could cover. Furthermore, when there was a major continuing story, for which the court reporter had already established her property claim, she sometimes asked her editor to send help to interview additional sources and otherwise 'cover all the angles.' The conflicts were over establishing property rights to stories in the first instance. Once it was established that she was in control, the court reporter was often pleased to receive additional resources from her news organization to enhance her coverage.

NEWSWORTHINESS

The court reporter judges newsworthiness with reference to a number of considerations external to the beat and the administration of justice, internal to the beat and the administration of justice, and internal to the news business. We consider these in turn.

External Considerations

The news media are oriented to government, political process, and reform politics. To this end they thirst for signs of wrongdoing, and go after procedural strays (Ericson et al, 1987). Thus, reporters on the court beat are always half watching in terms of another show: how court cases might bear on political issues and public culture. The reporters we observed frequently considered coverage of court cases not because they were of legal significance or involved serious consequences of death and destruction, but rather because they represented potential for exposing politicians and governmental wrongdoing.

In scrutinizing the lists of hearings before court commenced at 10:00 A.M., reporters had a keen eye for cases involving politicians or government departments. One reporter scanned the list of landlord-tenant cases regularly, saying one day he would find a landlord who could be shown to be acting unfairly who was a politician. A court reporter was told by his desk editor to cover what appeared to be a routine theft case, because the accused was believed to be the holder of the mortgage on the house of a prominent politician; this fact was taken to be suggestive of links between the politician and unsavoury characters. There were numerous occasions on which reporters focused on routine litigation against government ministries, with the explicit hope that these cases would be vehicles for a more broadly based attack on the party in power.

It is part of the news-media mandate to police organizational life, and such policing is not restricted to governmental wrongdoing. We observed reporters giving similar selective attention to cases involving professional wrongdoing (e.g., involving lawyers), and questionable business practices (e.g., fraud by a well-known retailer). Reporters for one quality news outlet stressed that corruption, mismanagement, and legal precedent formed their holy trinity of newsworthiness on the court beat. One of these reporters emphasized that regular court coverage with a focus on the procedural deviance of organizations was a vehicle for understanding organizations and institutions in society, and at the same time a means of controlling them.

The bearing of court cases on public issues and problems was also salient. The latest dominant sensibilities about social problems and their solution, and the attendant politics of 'lawandorder,' were always percolating in judgments of newsworthiness. Reporters regularly selected cases to cover that they defined as 'topical.' Prominent examples during our field-work included domestic violence and abortion. As a Crown attorney asserted in interview, it's 'common sense' that 'if there's a bail hearing for Morgentaler [a medical practitioner who ran a free-standing abortion clinic and was a leading pro-choice campaigner] and a bail hearing for some two-bit robber, which do you think would be of interest to the media?' Most pervasive at the level of dominant culture were the notions of rights and equality, given a boost by the passing of the Canadian Charter of Rights and Freedoms. Cases were chosen explicitly on the grounds that the reporter construed them to be a vehicle for furthering rights debates in the public culture. Sources too became aware of this topicality and fed reporters accordingly. Thus, a trial court co-ordinator observed in an interview: 'I give them all of their cases ... just verbally ... [T]hey report on a particular type ... it's the issues that are topical ... human rights ... if it's a civil case they might pick up on a case where it's one of the minority groups who has a problem because that's what everyone right now seems to be interested in ... I can guess which ones they'll pick up on.'

In searching for a focus in their visualizations of deviance, reporters narrow in on cases involving well-known public figures. Court lists are scanned not so much according to the charges listed as to whether the accused is a prominent person about to become a 'fallen idol' (Clarke, 1981); the accused is represented by a lawyer who is prominent and a proven dramatist for the purposes of news discourse; or the victim is a celebrity. In short, persons who have an elevated standing as 'names' in the public culture – a standing that the news media have contributed to significantly in the past – are also likely to receive coverage as their biographies become entangled in court proceedings. Some reporters said their decisions about cases were taken primarily in terms of the 'name' criterion. We observed several instances in which reporters dropped in on court hearings solely because a 'name' was involved, or alternatively ignored serious cases (e.g., involving a murder in a rooming house) because they would entail 'no-name' products.

Court officials recognized the importance of 'names' for coverage. Judges, Crown attorneys, and lawyers we interviewed believed source selection was made in terms of 1 / those who were 'names,' 2 / those 'at the top,' and 3 / those who are talkative. One lawyer we interviewed observed that if 'names' are involved, reporters attend the case even 'when what's going on in there is mundane and uninteresting.' He also noted that 'name' lawyers sometimes serve as sources to the news media regarding legal topics they know nothing about. Another lawyer expressed his opinion that leading lawyers are also leading actors, and their sense of theatre is what endears them to the news media. 'They're all characters. You know, a lot of frustrated actors in the criminal bar. Oh, for real, I mean it's what we're doing is theatre and there are a lot of frustrated actors.'

These comments point to other external criteria of newsworthiness. The unusual in popular terms – that which is intrinsically interesting rather than intrinsically important legally – is a major consideration. An accused who appeared in a priest's robe, although he held no official religious office, was deemed newsworthy. Newsworthiness was also sensed in the case of a woman who was trying to preserve a legal right to stay in her apartment after the tenancy agreement had been terminated on the grounds that her singing and whistling on the balcony in the early hours of the morning were disturbing her neighbours. While court reporters generally emphasized that the entertainment criterion was secondary, it was clear that such 'brighteners' brightened their day.

This emphasis was also revealed by what was not covered. Reporters generally ignored civil cases. On a slow day a reporter approached a Supreme Court trial clerk and asked if there were any interesting cases. She was directed to two courtrooms. One case involved an automobile accident, the other an interpretation of a section of a mortgage act. The reporter quickly dismissed these cases, commenting that the clerk had a strange sense of what is interesting. As a trial court co-ordinator explained to us in interview, reporters routinely cover criminal cases and ignore civil cases because 'it's like an accident, people will stop and they love the gore, they love to see the blood.'

Realizing this to be the case, sources give reporters tips that meet the same criteria. A Crown attorney outlined how he supplied reporters with story ideas he felt would meet their criteria of newsworthiness.

A: [I]n the County Court there'll be ... as many as eighteen trials on a day and on the eighteen trials there may be six robberies. Now there are robberies and there are robberies. You know, a robbery could be a mugging in a bar-room brawl or something like that. Or it could be a bank robbery with a gun, well organized and well planned. Now, all they see is robbery, Joe Smith charged with robbery ... I mean if this is a bank robbery and it's a well-planned bank robbery, guns involved, it seems to me that's one you should be taking interest in. Or this murder case ... It's going to be a fairly lengthy murder case and it's got some particular features to it that I think you'll find are going to be interesting. So, they will know generally what courts they should go to ... what they should be watching for. They're not going to be wasting their time covering a case that's of no interest.

Q: Well now, what's a case of no interest?

A: Well, I don't know. I guess it's, that's, I guess everything's subjective, eh? For the poor victim and for the accused their case is very important but generally speaking I think the cases we were dealing with involved violence and some of them were a little more serious than others.

Q: Well, would you say that cases that you thought would be interesting for the press were the unusual cases ... I mean let's face it, murder is not one of Toronto's big problems.

A: No. That's right, there weren't that many murder cases that were sensational. But there may be a case where you would know the lawyer, for instance, was going to raise the Charter of Rights ... Well, on this case, for instance, Eddie Greenspan [a prominent local lawyer] is the lawyer and I know he's going to do this. Or Dave Humphrey's [a local prominent lawyer] the lawyer in this case and he's served us with notice that he's going to do this. In this case here the Crown is going to ask that the jury be locked up for certain reasons, you may want to keep an eye on that. There are certain unusual features about cases and what's going to go on in them, that I may know that they may not know, so I simply pass it on to them ... I suppose that crimes of violence do tend to attract publicity more than the other cases do and they are of greater interest to the average Crown attorney. Break-and-enter cases really aren't that interesting. Some of them are interesting but on the whole an armed robbery is more exciting. I suppose it's only human nature that you'd tend to concentrate or direct the reporter to that particular case.

This Crown attorney makes evident the 'common sense' criteria of newsworthiness that are deemed 'human nature' not only by him and reporters, but also, he assumes, by the public. He not only summarizes external considerations of newsworthiness we have outlined previously, but also designates many aspects that are internal to the courts and the administration of justice.

Internal Considerations

Court-beat reporters also judge newsworthiness in terms of what they visualize to be deviant about criminal procedure and outcomes. A man pleaded not guilty to a charge of failing to obey a probation order. He was then found unfit to stand trial and incarcerated in a mental-health facility. The defence appealed that decision and won, with the accused again being judged fit to stand trial. The Crown in turn appealed that decision to the Supreme Court of Ontario, the earlier appeal was overturned, and the accused was once again deemed unfit to stand trial and remanded to a mental-health facility until such time as he could be found fit to stand trial. A reporter decided this case was newsworthy in the context of a defence submission at the Supreme Court of Ontario appeal that argued the accused had already been in custody for a longer period than if he had pleaded guilty to the original charge of failing to obey a probation order and received the maximum penalty of six months' imprisonment. When it is evident that 'the process is the punishment' (Feeley, 1979), newsworthiness comes into focus.

Experienced court reporters visualized potential procedural strays simply by 'cruising' the corridors of the courthouse. For example, as a reporter walked along the corridor with a researcher he observed, 'All the left-wing lawyers in Toronto seem to be here today, I'd better check what is going on.' He examined the docket outside the courtroom where the lawyers were mingling and ascertained it was a 'drug case.' The court was in recess, and he noted the case for coverage, depending on whether other possibilities for the day fell apart.

Court reporters proceed with a sense of the order of things, and attend to cases that violate their sensibilities. This perspective characterizes their focus on sentences. Knowing little of the background details of the case, the arguments made, or the reasons for the sentencing decision – because they rarely attend more than brief snippets of the court hearing, and because such detail is not translatable into news discourse anyway – reporters equate an offence category with an imagined sentencing norm, and then construct their story as a complaint that the sentence is inappropriately severe or lenient (cf Doob and Roberts, 1983; Doob, 1984). Reporters use the sentencing process as an important arena in which to articulate and reinforce the moral contours of society, valuing the facts of the sentence according to their visions of social control and order.

The decontextualization of sentencing decisions was a major source of complaint among court officials we interviewed. A defence lawyer offered a case example of a client he had represented:

> The guy went into a bank, walked up to the teller, and said give me your money, she gave him the money and he got away with it. He felt so badly about it that he went and surrendered himself. Now, this guy was a poor, sad, alcoholic, who by the time of sentencing had really done something about his alcohol problem, taken excellent steps. He's returned the money, or he hadn't returned it all but certainly it was in the process of being returned. He'd stabilized his life, he'd got employment, he'd been through Alcoholics Anonymous; he was doing very well. The judge gave him a suspended sentence; he had no previous record, too, a guy in his fifties. The two Toronto papers that covered it, covered it under the heading 'Bank Robber gets Suspended Sentence.' There was no development of why he got a suspended sentence in the story.

Coverage was skewed to 'the big case,' involving serious wrongs and a trial rather than a negotiated plea settlement. This finding is confirmed in studies of news content (Dussuyer, 1979). It may be explicable in part by the fact that reporters were routinely excluded from back-region settings where plea-bargaining arrangements were transacted. Furthermore, a trial entails the possibility of theatrics and quotable 'lines,' essential ingredients of the good story as opposed to the good report. Court reporters 'cruised' for signs of the big trial in the same way as they searched for procedural strays. One cue to the importance of a case was whether it was being held in the largest courtroom in the courthouse. The assumption was that the court administrator would reserve this courtroom for trials of public interest because it could accommodate a larger number in its expanded public gallery. One reporter we studied, when faced with having to 'fish' for stories on a slow day, would check the case in this courtroom as having greater potential than cases located elsewhere.

The news significance of a case decreased if the accused was acquitted at trial. A court unwilling to put the official imprint of offender on the accused, and to put its etch on moral boundaries through sentencing, was in most instances worthy of less attention. After an accused was acquitted, we heard a reporter call his desk editor and preface his comments with the statement, 'This may disappoint you but the accused was acquitted on appeal.' The editor gave him limited space, and the reporter commented later that the newsworthiness of his story had decreased, first because the accused was acquitted, and second because he refused to be interviewed. There was not complete consensus on this aspect. Some reporters from quality news outlets indicated that a conviction itself was not as important as whether the decision was of legal significance. Cases involving the testing of new legal rules or establishing legal precedent, especially as they related to the Canadian Charter of Rights and Freedoms, were especially newsworthy to the court reporter for a quality newspaper. Other reporters for this newspaper argued that conviction was not a paramount concern, but rather whether the court's decision articulated with the corporate values of their newspaper. This finding bears upon criteria of newsworthiness internal to the business concerns of news organizations.

News-Media Considerations

Newsworthiness on the court beat is also visualized in terms of criteria generated within the news business itself. These criteria pertain to internally shaped goals of news, news values, and competitive strategies and tactics of editors and reporters.

The news media have a historic mandate to entertain as well as to inform. Analysts have commented on how these two goals are achievable in the coverage of crime and its control, thus explaining the extensive news coverage in this sphere (Murdock, 1982; Ericson et al, 1987). Court reporters accepted this twin mandate, and gave consideration to covering a case in terms of whether it had entertaining elements. Occasionally cases were selected as 'pure entertainment.' The key to entertainment was to identify leading legal characters, who in turn would draw moral caricatures of the accused, witnesses, and victims, and sometimes of one another. The key to communicating entertainment was the 'quotable quote,' the word or phrase that 'said it all,' that condensed a day's court proceedings into a few column-inches or a ninety-second broadcast item. It was striking how reporters attending court would all seize on the same phrase, either at the time it was uttered or after talking among themselves as to what phrase best captured what was newsworthy. If a suitable phrase was not uttered in the court proceedings, reporters would imagine what should have been said, and then interview a source outside the court in the hope that he or she would see it their way and eventually say it.

Reporters also gave coverage for reasons ultimately traceable to news-media values of fairness and balance. While it was not always adhered to, some news organizations had a policy that if they published the accused's name at the time of reporting the original criminal incident or his arrest, they would also publish the court outcome of his case. Court reporters were directed to cover cases for this purpose.

Court reporters were influenced in other ways by their editors, especially the desk editor. Reporters operated on the assumption that the desk editor's main concern was whether competing outlets had better court coverage because of the cases they chose to cover and how they were reported. This concern translated into a perpetual worry for reporters, and the development of various techniques to manage it. The matter was clear-cut when assignment editors simply directed the court reporter to cover a particular case. Otherwise, as the reporter was contemplating the newsworthiness of a case, he had to take into account whether his editor would be upset if the competition gave it significant play and he did not. Reporters often faced the practical dilemma of whether to cover several stories to match the competition, or to cover only one case more thoroughly in the hope editors would see its significance regardless of what competing outlets did. During the course of our research a new assignment editor was appointed at a newspaper, and the newspaper's court reporter spent considerable time and energy 'testing' her likes and dislikes by filing types of stories that the previous editor did not like but that he presumed this editor might like. It was only over time that he learned to adjust his selection and texts to the context of the new editor's expectations.

Editors' expectations, originating in their mandate to 'cover' the competition, are the key to understanding the sharing in the court newsroom between reporters from different news outlets. The only way some reporters could manage their work and meet editors' expectations was to collectively 'ass cover' with their colleagues in the court newsroom. They exchanged information about what they planned to cover and how they would go about it. They also exchanged on what would not be covered, thus relieving concern that one outlet would have something the other outlet's editor might think it should have too. Editors could not reprimand reporters and otherwise effect control over something they did not even know about.

Reporting Values: The Case of the $1.39 Toothbrush

Our discussion of newsworthiness has dealt with a variety of considerations. In a given case several of these considerations cross the reporter's mind as he decides whether it is of sufficient merit to warrant a filed story, as is revealed in the following vignette.

While in a courtroom for another case, a reporter noticed a lawyer flipping through a file with character testimonials on behalf of his client, including one from a head of state of another country. The reporter also overheard the lawyer mention to the Crown attorney that the matter involved a trivial theft and that a discharge would be an appropriate resolution. With his curiosity aroused, the reporter stayed in the courtroom for the sentencing hearing.

The Crown attorney read in the facts, which amounted to the theft of a

'$1.39 Jordan double-action toothbrush' from a drugstore. The accused had pleaded guilty, and the Crown attorney stated no objection to an absolute discharge. The defence lawyer argued for an absolute discharge. The offender was in Canada on a term appointment. He had a university degree; was a successful businessman in his own country; had been married for thirty years and had four children; and was described as an 'ambassador,' visiting many Canadian provinces and meeting senior officials, including provincial premiers. He was applying for landed-immigrant status in Canada, hoping to establish a business, and immigration authorities were aware of the charge. He had no criminal record. The lawyer presented the judge with several testimonials on behalf of the accused, including some from provincial premiers and at least one from a head of state abroad.

The judge took a ten-minute recess to read the testimonials. The reporter left the courtroom and sat in the lobby area of the courthouse. The reporter described to the researcher the 'moral dilemma' of reporting this case. He said it was newsworthy that someone of such high-status would shoplift a toothbrush, and that he might receive leniency because of testimonials from high status people. The disadvantage of reporting was that it might harm the accused's reputation and cause personal hardship when he had probably suffered enough already. The reporter said his inclination was not to report it, but his desk editor would argue there was no dilemma and it should be reported. He said the editor's position was that everything should be reported. The researcher remarked that that was a rather unusual position, since taken to the extreme it would mean that every case heard in court would have to be reported. The reporter replied that his editor would say the moral thing to do is report it, and would 'have a fit' if he learned that the reporter knew about it but did not report it. The reporter and researcher left the courthouse, but a short distance away the reporter stopped suddenly and wondered aloud whether he was making the correct decision. The researcher suggested he could discover the judge's decision and decide later whether to file a story. The reporter said, 'I like that,' and headed for the courtroom.

The judge opened by remarking that, 'It gives me no pleasure to sentence a man of your stature,' noting that the testimonials were a 'litany' of the accused's contributions to society. The judge then addressed the endemic nature of shoplifting and the fact it was of grave concern to the business community. He remarked, 'Shoplifting is a crime that seems to know no bounds by sex, social class, or age.' The judge noted that even for a first offence he rarely gave an absolute discharge, but rather a conditional discharge and/or community service with probation. He added that he often gave a jail term for a second offence. He said that if the offender was a callow sixteen-year-old it would be different. He said he couldn't argue youth and he couldn't expect community service to be of benefit since the accused had a long history of community service. The judge said the offender had obviously achieved much in life and he should be given 'marks' for that. He then marked his words by giving an absolute discharge.

As he left the courtroom, the reporter remarked to the researcher that it was even more difficult now not to report this case. As he proceeded to the court newsroom, he said that if the offender had been a politician he would have had absolutely no qualms about reporting it. The reporter said that, depending on who was on the desk, the story could be played up to a front-page box. He continued to 'think aloud' about his dilemma. He said he would probably talk with the assistant desk editor, who would be taking over from the other editor in the early afternoon. He said that in contrast to the other editor's '1940s journalism,' the assistant desk editor 'has a good head and is reasonable in discussing things like this.' He decided that his decision to file a story would partly depend on whether he could produce another story during the day: if something 'decent' could be developed on another case, then he would be less inclined to report this one. Apparently pragmatic interest in meeting production expectations could override a moral dilemma. Another case was attended, and no story was filed on this shoplifting case.

Typically, the reporter came across this case by chance. It was initially newsworthy because it represented something out of order, an older man of high status and influence 'reduced' to stealing an everyday item worth $1.39. It was also newsworthy because the court was prepared to give the offender the most lenient disposition possible, with reference to élite testimonials regarding his moral character. In addition to this 'one law for the rich and one law for the poor' angle, the judge's statements added vivid texture to what the reporter decided was worth saying about the case. He was confident that his desk editor would 'love it' and reward him with prominent play. Nevertheless his own sense of fairness, and his own belief that news from court can serve as an instrument of punishment, kept him from filing a story. More than any other means at their disposal, beat reporters stake their claim to autonomy by not reporting everything that they see, even that which they think their supervisors would find significant and reward.

ORIGINS OF STORY IDEAS

News production is lubricated by shared cultural sensibilities developed among all reporters and key sources on the beat. Just as a particular news organization is characterized by its own occupational culture and 'vocabulary of precedents' (Ericson et al, 1987) among its journalists, so the court newsroom had its distinctive shared understandings about how the work is to be done. The reporters representing different news organizations and their key sources developed ideas about how to recognize a case as newsworthy (recognition knowledge), how to proceed to obtain relevant knowledge (procedural knowledge), and what to do with this knowledge to produce an acceptable news account and to be accountable to superiors (accounting knowledge).

Key sources included court clerks and trial co-ordinators. As Drechsel (1983: 88) discovered, these strategically situated persons provided not only tips about what appeared interesting, but guidance as to when, where, and how the reporter should spend her time to maximize the possibility of good story ideas and coverage. A trial co-ordinator saw his job in part as helping reporters to manage their jobs because they could not cover everything. This assistance included providing story ideas and serving as a conduit between reporters and otherwise inaccessible people and paper.

A: Well, they normally come to me pretty well on a daily basis, but always they all come on a Friday to see what's happening in the next week ... I tell them firstly the charges and then synopsize the case for them. Well, you could argue that that is privileged information, but this is where the trust comes in; I wouldn't do that with a reporter I didn't know ... I tell them all the cases and they select ... They're always here and because there is a spirit of co-operation with them, in that they, it's a matter of you scratch my back and I'll scratch yours. I trust them in that I know they won't, certain of them anyway, won't report a story where they haven't got all the facts.

Q: Why is that your concern?

A: Well, on the one hand I could say it's no concern of mine, but on the other hand I feel that my duty is really towards the judges, to the court, and if a reporter doesn't understand the full impact of what [he] may be doing now I think that's irresponsible reporting.

Q: Is part of your job then like a public-relations officer for the court?

A: Well, it is, it's not specified as such but it really is. We just help each other that way ... I field questions in that the judges can't speak for themselves, they are there to, as sort of an umpire; they can't say what they feel, because they're basing their decisions on the facts and on the law. They can't speak up for themselves – if somebody says anything about a judge, he can't write to the paper and clarify anything – so I'm sort of the go-between there. I think that's a big responsibility of mine ... The judges don't really come to me; they trust me enough to know that I'll only give out, I won't give out any privileged information.

The other key source of story ideas for a court reporter is fellow reporters in the court newsroom. As mentioned previously, there were established exchanges between reporters from two newspapers that devoted fewer resources to the court beat than a third newspaper. The expectation about exchanging was reinforced on an occasion when a reporter was about to leave for the day, and a court clerk informed him about a hearing for a notorious accused. The reporter was very upset that his colleague from the other newspaper had not informed him about this hearing. A sign that the exchange relationship was institutionalized beyond personal relationships of regular court reporters was the fact that when a substitute reporter was on the beat because the regular reporter was ill or on holiday, story-idea tips continued to be exchanged between reporters from the two newspapers.

Story-idea tips were not always restricted to exchange between reporters from the two newspapers. To some degree all reporters trafficked freely in their ideas of what was worth covering. As one reporter commented to a researcher, even sitting in the court newsroom allowed him to discover almost every noteworthy case because the other reporters were unable to keep it to themselves: 'Five minutes after they have found a new case they are talking about it in the press room.' On occasion this reporter and his court-newsroom colleagues did keep cases from each other, even going to the extent of using telephones outside the court newsroom to avoid being overheard. On several occasions a reporter we were observing worked hard to keep his colleagues from learning about what case he was covering, only to find them in the same courtroom! Obviously a reporter's nose for news made sense of what was happening in court beyond co-operative exchanges with colleagues.

In comparison to trial co-ordinators, clerks, and court-newsroom reporters, other sources of story ideas were of less significance. Story ideas were on occasion supplied or even ordered by the reporter's desk editor and/or by reporters from her own news organization. Crown attorneys were of some help. One radio reporter said her main source of story ideas was a few Crown attorneys. Crown attorneys were more helpful than defence lawyers. Very few defence lawyers were court regulars, and a given lawyer had only one or a few cases before the courts at a time. In contrast, Crown attorneys were court regulars and could assess the relative newsworthiness of many cases going on simultaneously. Many defence lawyers felt that publicity was an added punishment for their clients, while Crown attorneys sometimes wanted publicity for its stigmatic, general-deterrence, and public-education value. Some defence lawyers interviewed said they did occasionally give story-idea 'tips' to regular court reporters or as a personal favour to a particular reporter. Furthermore, an editor of a publication for lawyers said he fed ideas to reporters on a regular basis, and a few prominent local lawyers occasionally had letters to the editor, articles, and features published in newspapers under their own byline. Entwined within the news-communication process, they were authorized *reporters* as well as sources.

Drechsel (1983: 96, 101) reports that the police provided case tips in the courts he studied, but the police were not a routine source of story ideas in the courts we observed. Even less frequent was any direct contact with judges regarding ideas on what cases to cover. Judges did sometimes communicate through trial co-ordinators and clerks. There were a few occasions on which judges let it be known that what they were about to say in court might be newsworthy. These occasions usually involved a 'blast' at the administration of justice, for example, attacking how two legal-aid lawyers had handled a case, and complaining about delays in bringing a case to trial and expedient conclusion. On such occasions reporters rushed to the courtroom where the pronouncement would be made, indicating both the rarity of such initiatives from the bench and how such a rarity is visualized by reporters as deviant and therefore newsworthy.

Court reporters developed their own devices to fill any gaps in this ideas system. Other newspapers were scanned for story ideas. This practice was more germane to broadcast reporters who were not in the court newsroom full time. As detailed earlier, court dockets were scanned for prominent people to see if newsworthiness could be construed in 'name' terms. The practice of 'cruising' the corridors for signs of significance also helped to fill gaps in ideas as well as time. And, as illustrated in the example of the $1.39 toothbrush case, cases were revealed by chance while the reporter was in court pursuing other matters. These discoveries could only be made in specified public regions, where there was some disclosure of knowledge. We require a better understanding of regions and closures to appreciate more fully the origins of story ideas, and what was eventually reported about the courts.

Regions and Closures

Compared to other areas of government, the courts are not very reliant on news. The knowledge the courts need to take decisions is gathered and formulated by officials in the legal system 'more thoroughly and exhaustively than the press could' (Drechsel, 1983: 21–4) and therefore the substance of news is seen as poor or unreliable knowledge. Also, the knowledge upon which court decisions are taken is specialized. As we have seen already, court reporters contribute to restrictions on their access to knowledge because they do not have specialist legal knowledge. However, even with specialist legal knowledge, reporters would still be limited because a lot of knowledge remains secret and confidential. There are no news-media–relations personnel in court to help reporters access and translate knowledge into news discourse, and some key decision-makers, especially judges, are unwilling to help them access it and translate it except as mediated through the formal legal rationality offered in the courtroom. Since they have very limited requirements for publicity, court officials can easily restrict reporters' access to particular regions of the system, and disclose only particular knowledge as they deem it appropriate in terms of time, place, language, and content. How this restriction is accomplished routinely is revealed in the subsequent analysis of secrecy, confidence, censorship, and publicity in the courts.

BACK-REGION ENCLOSURE: SECRECY

The prevailing view among sources on the court beat was that reporters are only entitled to whatever knowledge is communicated in the courtrooms. Reporters could not patrol the back regions to observe the only 'trial' most accused receive, namely plea-negotiation sessions involving police, the Crown attorney, and the defence lawyer. In our observations reporters did not venture into back regions to observe discovery and plea-negotiation sessions, and rarely even asked about these except as they were raised as an issue in the courtroom. They only ventured into the inner sanctums of Crown attorneys' offices or judges' chambers by invitation, and then only to receive an interview account rather than to directly observe the workings of the court system there. Moreover reporters' requests for interviews and the specific questions they put were frequently ignored or denied. The more seasoned court reporters experienced fewer denials because they had learned not to ask.

All judges we interviewed stressed that the exclusive forum for reporters is the courtroom. Judges refused to be interviewed by reporters about particular cases and the reasons for their decisions as expressed in court or in written judgments. They also severely criticized other court actors, and in particular defence counsel, who talked with reporters while the case was in progress. A judge who commented that 'a newspaper can kill a judge' stated in a research interview that he would not talk to reporters about a case outside the courtroom, and reporters would not ask him to. Another judge was equally adamant:

What goes on in the courtroom, they come and report or do what they like. But I wouldn't discuss a case before or after with a reporter ... There might be an appeal and I might say something that might damage the appellant's case, whether the appellant is the Crown or the accused. You see, we make a report to the Court of Appeal and sum up the cases. I mean, that's where we follow a form and set forth the facts and other things in the report. And that's what the Court of Appeal look at, together with the record of the trial, of course. And what are my feelings about a case are on the public record and are available to the public including the news media ... I can't clarify a judgment. It's written in stone, so to speak. I've said that in open court, those are my reasons, and that's for the Court of Appeal to look at and interpret if they have to. But for me to second-guess myself, I think that's wrong.

One judge we interviewed had, for a period of time, agreed to interviews with reporters about specific judgments he had made. However, he quickly discovered that he was being portrayed as deviant, and he experienced the censure of his colleagues. As 'the judge who would talk,' reporters began to call him about cases he was not involved in himself, and he was even asked to participate in a popular and controversial 'talk show' on television. After a few experiences of what he termed inaccuracy and misquotation, he ceased co-operating.

A senior judge said his court's policy was judicial silence, except regarding issues pertaining to the court and the administration of justice, in which case it is the senior judge who should be the spokesperson. 'We ask them not to talk to the press ... That I do it or [names another senior judge] docs it for the court ... [J]udges are independent cusses you know, and there's the odd one that will sound off. But less and less. We're not out looking for publicity.' Other judges confirmed that there was an unwritten rule not to talk to the news media. One judge said there was no need for official guidelines on the matter because it was simply not the judge's place to talk to the media. Several judges took the view that talking to the news media was tantamount to a political act. In the words of one judge, 'This is what my own guidelines are: I don't think a judge should make any pronouncements on a point of law which has not come before him, you know ... he shouldn't enter the political arena at all.'

The enclosure of judges was revealed in another way in a case we observed. As a judgment on a major case was about to be read in court, reporters asked for the written judgment in advance so that they would have time to digest it. There is a parallel to this at government budget time, when reporters are sequestered and then given an advance copy of the budget so that they can understand its basic elements by the time of official release. In this instance, however, the trial co-ordinator was instructed not to give a copy of the judgment to reporters until the judge had presented it in the courtroom. This event was an indication that even when reporters were willing to give more time to digest and understand a judicial decision, they were unable to do so because of their sources' enclosure on when and where the knowledge would be made available initially.

Judges are agents appointed by and for government. Moreover, with impetus from the Charter of Rights and Freedoms, they are being given an increasing role in the making of political policy (Russell, 1983; McWhinney, 1982). Nevertheless they sustain enclosure on anything that emanates from regions other than the courtroom, thereby reducing the potential for informed comment and criticism in the news media. While they are increasingly getting into print in the legal media, judging by the ever expanding case tomes on the shelves of legal libraries, they remain equally eager not to get into print in the news media. Their perceived need to appear authoritative but not authoritarian (cf Vining, 1986) ensures that this is the case.

Crown attorneys take a similar view to judges, emphasizing that disclosure to reporters, as to other members of the public, should only occur in the courtroom. One Crown attorney defined the court reporter's job as reporting 'accurately and professionally on what they see in the courtroom,' adding 'They have access to anything that's on record in the courtroom.' Plea bargaining sessions, and 'Crown brief' documents pertaining to prosecution, were explicitly ruled out. Another Crown attorney elaborated: 'In a trial there are lots of factual things that the Crown does, you know I don't think the media is entitled to have any access to that. The defence counsel might be able, that's a matter for the defence, but I don't see that the public has any interest in that. All the public's entitled to know is that there's a fair trial going on and it's open to the public and they can see what goes on in the courtroom. But other than that I don't think the media or the public is entitled to anything else.'

Crown attorneys stated that they would not provide verbal accounts of their strategies in handling a forthcoming case or a case in progress. Except in rare instances on the direction of superiors, they did not initiate contacts with reporters. One Crown attorney could recall only one proactive contact, and that was to ask reporters not to publish the fact that there was an investigation into threats against court witnesses because publicity would interfere with the investigation. Occasionally Crown attorneys had the matter of talking to reporters taken over by superiors, even to the level of the office of the attorney general of Ontario. A Crown attorney recalled that, 'On occasion somebody from the attorney general's office would phone and say, "Don't comment on this. He's [the attorney general] going to make an announcement about it this afternoon and we'd prefer you didn't say anything about it."'

Defence lawyers varied in opinions as to whether they wished to encourage publicity. Their decisions depended on the particular case and whether it could be used as a strategy on behalf of their client. However, they did not want coverage of back-region negotiations with police, Crown attorneys, and judges. Moreover, they could usually manage publicity through what they did in the courtroom. Some lawyers took the view that publicity was not a good thing, and asserted that it was not their job to be worried about media presence even in the courtroom. One respondent stated bluntly, 'I haven't got a message for the media. My messages are all directed to the judge.'

The police were more active in pretrial publicity, especially at the point of arrest and attendant investigations (see chapter 3). Occasionally local police departments held a news conference to announce an arrest, and even to display the accused for television visuals and newspaper still photographs. They also displayed evidence seized, such as caches of weapons and drugs.

Some lawyers we interviewed mentioned these publicity displays as an unfair practice, possibly prejudicing a trial. Apart from this, the police shared the view that enclosure of back-region activity was essential. One advantage to the police of out-of-court guilty-plea settlements is that they circumvent the public scrutiny of how their case was put together that comes with a trial (Ericson 1981, 1982). Public scrutiny of plea-negotiation sessions is especially undesirable because these sessions are exploratory, unpredictable, and equivocal, compared to what transpires in trials within the highly structured context of the courtroom (cf Ericson and Baranek, 1982). The police have a need to patrol the facts of a case to the point they are stated in the courtroom. Since they are unlikely to reveal all to everyone in their own organization or to other actors in the criminal process, they are most unlikely to do so to the news media except when it appears appropriate strategically. Thus, when a notorious police informant was scheduled to testify in court, a police officer told a reporter he was not scheduled to testify in the hope of avoiding news coverage of the case.

Subject to effective enclosure through being foreclosed from the back regions, reporters rely on trial co-ordinators and court clerks for accounts of what people are thinking and doing there. For their part, these court officials see their job as minimizing actual access to the back regions, and informing reporters about what procedures *should be* in order to effect 're-sponsible reporting.' Commenting on why he co-operates with reporters as a 'go between,' one person said the alternative of non-cooperation would make reporters 'upset and then it would be irresponsible reporting.' Asked if news coverage was of any help to his office or the court in general, he replied: 'Really, I don't think it can in that if you check into what the court does, I think it would cause more problems if they reported the fact that our judges overextend themselves, which they do, in this court, they really do. It would lead to lawyers getting upset, judges from [other] courts getting upset. I think the least said the better in that kind of situation.'

As the comments from a range of court officials indicate, secrecy is not simply a matter of individual discretion. There is a collective sense among court officials that only what is revealed within the decorum of the courtroom is open to reporters and their publics. To go against this collective expectation would indicate disloyalty and suggest the person should no longer be trusted and accepted within the collective. In an organization where publicity is not of great value, it is easy to understand how the back-region signs remain so tightly enclosed.

Enclosure is also ensured by the law. Court officials frequently referred to the law as justification for not commenting on a case in progress. A lawyer explained, 'I didn't talk with them at all before the decision was made, not because I didn't want to but because the matter was before the courts and as a lawyer I am what you call an officer of the court, you have to be very careful, there's a principle of law that says that you can't discuss a case while it's pending before the courts and of course I had an obligation to adhere to that so I did.'

The law also limits the potential for using the accused, victim, and/or witness as a source while the case is in progress. While journalists sometimes ignored the possibility of contempt-of-court charges by interviewing citizens involved in a case, they did so at their own risk and sometimes with the censure of their court-newsroom colleagues. The belief among journalists we observed was that pretrial 'discovery' was legally possible by obtaining accounts from both plaintiff and defendant in a civil case, or the accused in a criminal case. However such discovery was attempted only rarely, and in major cases, usually where the party or parties had already indicated a willingness to seek publicity. The usual practice was to await the outcome of the case before interviewing the citizens involved. This instance is another in which citizens are subject to 'the ordering of justice' (Ericson and Baranek, 1982), to be seen but not heard from except as provided by the space, time, language, and legal requirements for order in the courtroom.

Court officials believed in the power of the law as a control on publicity. The law of contempt of court was seen as particularly powerful because in most cases its influence was sufficient to effect enclosure without actually being invoked. A prominent defence lawyer comments:

> The press have no interest in a fair trial, the press have an interest in selling
> newspapers and sensationalizing things and if there were not these laws in
> place which constrain what they can say prior to the trial and during and
> after a trial really, I'm sure that the press would join their American friends
> in turning it into a Roman holiday if they could ... I think they're as fair as
> they are required to be by our laws of contempt of court ... I don't conceive
> the media as voluntarily restraining their reporting to ensure a fair trial.
> The law ensures a fair trial, therefore they can tippy-toe up to the line and
> they know that if they go beyond that line they're going to get their wrists
> slapped.

BACK-REGION DISCLOSURE: CONFIDENCE

Reporters obtained knowledge of back-region activities that was understood to be 'off the record,' or usable 'on the record' only under conditions specified by the source. In interviews with regular court reporters, lawyers and Crown attorneys usually did not have to state explicitly what was off the record and what was publishable. There was a tacit understanding that basic facts about a case were on the record, for example, the accused's record (after conviction), demographics, and details of the incident(s) and charge(s). How-ever, when talk was about back-region activity it was understood to be off the record. Several sources we interviewed acknowledged this 'unspoken rule,' adding that talk about back-region activity was a means of helping reporters to understand why particular decisions were taken and outcomes arrived at. It was hoped that such understanding would lead reporters to avoid miscon-struing what transpired in court, and result in a more sympathetic published story.

A judge explained that when he was a lawyer the rule was simple: 'The only quote is what we said in the courtroom,' even though there was consid-erable discussion with reporters outside the courtroom, especially with one reporter who 'had a complete confidant in me … you could speak to him off the record to help him.' A lawyer made a similar point, adding that he sometimes reminded reporters that if they used the back-region knowledge he gave them they could all be implicated in prejudicing a fair trial and possible contempt-of-court charges:

> I might say things to, or give information to, a reporter that is not at that
> time printable by virtue of our contempt-of-court laws, and give it to them on
> the basis that they are professional reporters and that their overview of the
> case should include the knowledge of this, but this, whatever that fact may
> be, is not a printable fact at this stage … I would probably, out of caution,
> remind the reporters that as professional reporters you understand, of course,
> that to print this at this stage would be contempt of court, you must be very
> careful what you print. Particularly since the case is being tried by a jury.
> You don't have to be as careful in a case that's being tried by a judge.

Court officials sometimes expressed their opinions of people involved in a case, and of the process, even though they knew that if they were ever cited saying these things it would be the end of their careers. For example, a Crown attorney at an inquest chatted with a reporter during a recess and remarked that there was really nothing in the inquest, it was 'making a mountain out of a molehill.' He offered negative opinions of members of the bereaved family, and observed that the deceased had many health problems and therefore the death was a 'blessing in disguise.' He noted that the coroner did not like to make his summations on the same day when evidence was submitted, and thus probably would not make his summations until the next day, adding with a laugh that he thought the coroner was paid on a per-diem basis. He said that the only outcome might be a view that the doctors who had treated the deceased were a little careless. This Crown attorney was confident that his careless talk would not be reported, and as it turned out he was correct. Court reporters know that back-region disclosure is a matter of confidence (cf Drechsel, 1983: 90).

This tacit understanding of what is confidential has important implications for what is published about court cases. The social organization of the court and its relation to decisions and procedures (Carlen, 1976; Feeley, 1979; Ericson and Baranek, 1982) remain unknown to the news consumer, who is left with the officially and formally structured account rendered in the courtroom. As Fishman (1980: 71) found in the reporting of a case in which the process of plea bargaining and the accused's social condition were ignored, 'By focusing on bureaucratically appropriate dispositions in their everyday reports, journalists' stories leave invisible the agency procedure and social conditions which give rise to these dispositions. Routine news stories implicitly support the status quo by taking for granted these background factors.' This is not simply a matter of what the reporter does or does not do, a fault with his thinking and initiative. Rather, it is a complex matter of how the reporter participates on the court beat and establishes trust with his sources. In essence, it includes silence about the workings of his sources' private culture, how they actually manage to get their work done. *As a member* of that private culture, the regular court reporter is bound to join with legal officials in reproducing the appearances of formal legal rationality even if he knows that the system works in terms of other criteria.

Confidence includes 'firm trust, assured expectation; telling of private matters with mutual trust' (*The Concise Oxford Dictionary*). Court officials we interviewed emphasized the importance of trust in making disclosures to reporters. Most stated that since trust is only established over time in an ongoing relationship, greatest trust was with the regular court-beat reporters. As quoted previously, a trial co-ordinator said it was her policy to give case-related knowledge only to the regular court-beat reporters. A defence lawyer stated, 'I prefer always to deal with a reporter whom I know because sometimes I have to go ... off the record and I prefer to deal with somebody. who knows the guidelines and whom I feel I can trust.'

In many work settings, back-region disclosure is made possible not only through mutual trust, but also by ongoing reciprocity among the parties concerned. For example, in plea-negotiation sessions the police, Crown attorney, and defence lawyer all have enclosed knowledge that they can disclose gradually to each other, as they work to arrive at a case settlement out of court. The difficulty for the court reporter in the court setting is that he has relatively little that he can offer to the source in exchange for disclosure. He is rarely privy to information about a case that the legal officials involved do not know and could make use of. Even on the rare occasion when he does have such knowledge, the reporter may be reluctant to divulge it because of the implications for his source, or because it might undercut his own uses of it. When this factor is combined with the fact that most court officials do not value publicity to a high degree, the court reporter is effectively without a currency for reciprocity, a situation that underscores the reporter's dependency on his sources. Instead of back-region disclosure being an exchange where the source derives a direct benefit such as reciprocal disclosure or publicity, it is grounded more in a source's individual ego, friendship with a reporter, and/or a genuine desire to further a reporter's understanding of a case.

In comparison to the law-enforcement officials and defence counsel who inhabit the back regions of the courts, the reporter has no legitimate authority or special qualifications to intrude. He is left to rely upon the consent of officials to intrude, but this consent is granted rarely (cf Reiss, 1987: 25). With such clear-cut margins of intrusion, the reporter can at least reduce uncertainty in his working environment, and with it his anxiety over what might be reportable. He is left with official discourse.

However, significant incursions of the back regions do occur. It was the practice of one news organization to use its regular court-beat reporters only for routine reporting of courtroom proceedings or feature pieces sympathetic to court officials. If it was decided that coverage should be given to controversial cases that critically challenged the administration of justice, or to mismanagement or wrongdoing in the administration of justice, reporters other than those on the court beat were brought in to do the dirty work.

The regular court reporters for this organization were critical of regular court reporters from other news organizations whose editors allowed them to do negative or critical pieces themselves. An example was offered to us by a reporter whose editors allowed him to do critical pieces on his own. He filed a story raising questions about the propriety of a judge's dismissing a case after a Crown witness had failed to appear. The accused in the case, charged with a major property offence, was the son of a chief of police. The reporter said he filed the story a week after the judge dismissed the case, having done further back-region work on it after the dismissal. A reporter from the news outlet whose regular beat reporters did not do critical pieces told him that he should not have filed this story. The argument was that it was not proper to report a week after the decision, and that his negative casting of the judge's decision as favouritism shown the son of a chief of police might affect relations with court officials for all court reporters. The reporter who filed the story replied that the other reporter's newspaper had used a general-assignment reporter to do a similar story and that it was published on the same day as his. The other reporter was not aware of this story until it was pointed out to him, and he then began berating his own newspaper for carrying this story, again on the grounds that it might interfere with his relations with sources.

Court officials talked of instances in which they had given back-region disclosure in confidence, only to have it published. A senior judge talked of being burned on one occasion, and his decision thereafter to give written statements to journalists only at the conclusion of a case:

> I thought he was a fiction writer instead of a journalist because he'd been reporting things I did not say. And he took things out of context. Plus the fact that I was under the impression ... it was not something that was going to be reported, it was just kind of a discussion that we were having and then later on we were going to sit down ... I said, 'Fine, as soon as the attorney general releases the document that we had given to him I'll feel free to discuss it with you in detail.' And then all of a sudden, bang, he wrote a lot of stuff that I didn't say and so I thought it was very slanted writing and I would never talk to that guy again, face to face or on the telephone ... [L]ast week ... I just said God, he's probably going to be there so I did what I do not normally do, I wrote out what I was going to say and I had copies here and I gave them to the registrar, and if anybody wants one they can have it. So they couldn't say things that I didn't say because you're always at a disadvantage talking to the press because they have the last word. If you say that you didn't say it or that, there's no point getting into a controversy with them, you can't win ... [This time] I thought well hell, I'll help them out, I'll have these copies ready and they can have them available to them. And each one gets a fair shot at it ... [I]t was just after a couple of other experiences that I wasn't very pleased about and I thought, well, this one I would have under my control anyway. If they can't read it and they can't interpret it that's their fault.

Back-region disclosure was sometimes offered with an understanding that the knowledge might be publishable if certain conditions were met. One pervasive condition concerned timing. Knowledge disclosed before a verdict was often given on the understanding that it would not be published until the verdict was in. In turn, reporters persuaded sources to provide knowledge by saying its use was contingent on a verdict. Indeed, reporters sometimes told a source that their editors would not consider a story without a verdict.

Sources frequently offered knowledge to reporters with the understanding that it could be published, but without their name being used in connection with it. This was done in relation to continuing investigations or court cases in progress where it was inappropriate for a legal official to be seen to be commenting on the case. It was also done when a source had a different view of a matter than a colleague but did not want to be seen to be contradicting the colleague in public.

Another form of controlled disclosure was to allow selected reporters to attend a back-region setting and have their accounts stand for what transpired there. Wire-service reporters were favoured on these occasions because they were seen as more neutral; that is, they serve as a news source dealing mainly with primary facts, rather than secondary or tertiary understanding. For example, during an inquest into a fire death the jurors were taken to the fire site and a wire-service reporter was allowed to accompany them. Other reporters were upset about their own exclusion, as explained by the coroner involved:

> [T]hey always get upset about that ... [T]hey felt that they represented the
> public, and I had to inform [the reporters] the jury represented the public,
> they were just there to observe or report on what they saw. Problems occur
> repeatedly in this type of situation, in say fires ... [Y]ou take the jury to help
> them to understand what the situation was like, look at the scene and try to
> get a better picture of things. This is sometimes dangerous, sometimes very
> confined spaces and certain members of the press feel they have the right
> to be there ... And we attempt on these tours to avoid any questions being
> asked [of] the jury ... We ask them to hold them until they come back to the
> courts so everybody can hear and it's recorded. But they really don't accept
> this, they feel that they question the integrity of officials I guess and this is
> why.

'Go-betweens' were used by sources who believed that back-region disclosure would look inappropriate if they were associated with it. Judges occasionally used clerks and trial co-ordinators in this way. The coroner's office relied upon a news-media–relations officer for the ministry of the attorney general. Corporate interests involved in a major civil case, or an inquest where there was potential for adverse publicity, sometimes used news-media–relations consultants (see chapter 5).

FRONT-REGION ENCLOSURE: CENSORSHIP

The front regions on the court beat include the courtrooms and the corridors and public offices surrounding them. The focal point for reporting is within these front regions, especially the courtrooms. While the courtroom is a public forum, it is subject to enclosure spatially, legally, in language, and by informal agreement.

Spatially, reporters had their place in the order of the court (Carlen, 1976; Ericson and Baranek, 1982: chap. 6). Sometimes this place was a special one in front of the public gallery, and at other times it was simply the public gallery. Regardless, they were not allowed to venture into the well of the court during proceedings, and they were sometimes prevented from doing so for the purpose of interviewing a Crown attorney or defence lawyer before proceedings commenced or after they concluded. Television cameras and other recording devices were banned from the courtroom; thus, the official recording by the court was the only verbatim record available.

Enclosure over knowledge in the courtroom was also effected legally. As related in our discussion of back-region enclosure, the law of contempt-of-court imprinted a sense of order even if it was rarely invoked. This law pertained to what was reported about proceedings in the courtroom, as well as to what transpired elsewhere, and instances arose during our observations in which it became directly salient. A judge threatened a reporter with a contempt of court charge after the reporter construed court testimony to suggest police wrongdoing. The reporter was most upset by the threat, and consulted a lawyer for his news organization and had the lawyer at court at the time he thought the judge might charge him with contempt of court. The judge who threatened the charge on this occasion said in a research interview that he had no intention of following through with an actual charge, indicating he had only made the threat as a means of controlling reporters' accounts of the case as best he could.

I was quite disturbed at what I felt at the time was sensationalism and said so. I had to take that position and instruct the jury strongly or I would have had to declare a mistrial and as it turned out, the trial did proceed and was completed and so far as I know was never appealed ... [T]he import of it was that there was an impropriety on the part of senior officers in the police department for which I had heard no pertinent or relevant or admissable evidence to that effect ... My recollection of the way it came out in the press was that there was a definite named hierarchy that were involved ... The way it came out in the paper was stronger and more definite than I felt any evidence had indicated. And the defence counsel were pressing me to declare a mistrial. I was afraid this was going to turn into the trial of the police department rather than of the accused, perhaps to the prejudice of the Crown and the accused and the police department. My harsh remarks at the press were directed primarily though at preserving the trial ... I indicated I might have to consider [a contempt-of-court charge] but I had never seriously considered it ... [I]f I was able to keep the trial going, that was my main concern and I didn't think that there was a contempt of the court I should seriously get concerned about, unless it had resulted in the loss of the trial, that was the thing I was concerned about. Now you must remember the context that was in. This was what was called the 'Blitz,' and there were judges from all over the province helping out, and great effort had gone into having cases ready to be tried. And the prospect of taking two weeks out of this court's time and the thought of having it, a jury case, blown away by what I felt was sensational press reporting, disturbed me ... I got a letter after the trial, after the sentencing, from someone in the [newspaper] hierarchy that I acknowledged receiving but I did nothing more ... It was a letter of accusation that I had treated their reporter unfairly and, but that's the last I heard of it ... I don't know whether it was coincidental or not, I thought the reporting for the rest of the case was accurate. I thought that they got a transcript of what was said to the jury and they printed it in full with respect to the article, which I thought was a very favourable action on their part and I thought from then on I had no more problem with what was printed.

Court reporters said they consulted lawyers several times a year, and occasionally had their copy 'lawyered' prior to publication. Reporters who were not court regulars seemed to be both ignorant of the law of contempt of court and eager not to be in violation, although they sometimes were. Some reporters working on continuing stories regarding a major case used the technique of looking at the published stories of other news outlets to decide what was reportable legally. In one instance a regular court-beat reporter advised another reporter from his news organization who was working on a major case to use this technique as the easiest route to understanding legal limitations. This event underscores the established fact (Ericson et al, 1987) that, for many journalists, everything one needs to know to produce the news is contained within the news, regardless of the availability and significance of other knowledge.

There were cases in which part or all of a story was dropped for fear that publication would risk contempt-of-court charges. The net effect of the invisible hand of the law is to lead reporters into self-policing, which makes them more conservative than the law itself. As an alternative-newspaper editor said with reference to a court case her newspaper was involved in, '[W]e were constrained in what we could say until the trial was over because of the laws of contempt ... The media are much more strict in observing contempt laws than the courts have ever been in actually enforcing them. The media will drop anything at the slightest whisper of being in contempt of court or "it's before the courts," the favourite excuse of politicians and the media alike.'

Ironically front-region enclosure can force reporters, and sources with an inclination to show and tell, into the back regions for disclosure. What a person says in court may be restricted. Moreover, it is recorded so that there is an official account against which a reporter's account can be assessed. In contrast, an interview account outside the courtroom is more difficult to pin down legally because the reporter might try to protect his source, or the source might say she was misunderstood or misquoted. Both reporters and sources felt that going to sources outside the courtroom was a viable way around front-region enclosure. However, this alternative was not a straightforward one because sources were very reluctant to grant interviews about cases in progress, other than to offer basic primary facts. As one lawyer for a government ministry stated, the law of contempt reaches into the back regions as well. Reporters do not attend most of the proceedings, and expect the lawyers involved to be reporters for them, thus putting the lawyers in jeopardy of contempt. 'I don't want to take a chance on being cited for contempt and this is a trap ... I think that their function is to listen to that evidence and report on it as best they can and if they don't want to do that, I don't think I should supply that deficiency. As I say there are risks to myself and to my client if we undertake that function of reporting on the matter to the press.'

Lawyers in major cases did sometimes agree to talk about a legal action in progress. However, this was very carefully orchestrated through other forms of front-region enclosure, such as a prepared written statement. With an eye to the law, lawyers created specific conditions that would allow them to state facts without straying to matters that might affect the case. For example, a lawyer agreed to a television interview in her office on the condition that she would not be questioned on the merits of the case, and that there would be no editing of the prepared statement of facts she was presenting orally.

Front-region enclosure was also effected through legal powers to ban publication regarding all or parts of the proceedings (Robertson, 1981: chap. 5). In some instances statutory offences exist so that a publication ban relies not upon the discretion of the court but on the election of the applicant (e.g., regarding sexual offences, bail hearings, preliminary enquiries). In other instances publication bans are at the discretion of the court, providing for the exclusion of the public entirely, or allowing reporters to attend but not to publish.

Until recently, except by special leave, reporters could not publish stories on juvenile court cases. Even with the legislative changes under the Canadian Charter of Rights and Freedoms and the Young Offenders Act, which allow reporting of youth court cases, the law provides for exceptions. Section 39 of the Young Offenders Act not only allows a judge to conduct a closed hearing if any evidence is deemed seriously injurious or prejudicial to the accused, witness, or victim, but also if 'it would be in the interest of public morals, the maintenance of order or the proper administration of justice to exclude any or all members of the public from the court room' (cf Beckton, 1983). Court reporters did not include the juvenile courts on their rounds. The law was just in the process of being changed during our field-work period, but to that point it had the effect of ensuring a 'silent system' in terms of news reporting. We observed only one case in whch concerted efforts were made to lift the veil. In this case a juvenile murder suspect was before the court and several news organizations wanted to publish his name and picture.

Reporters commented to us that while their lawyers were formulating their case in terms of 'community interest' in knowing the identity of the suspect, the real interest was the news media's desire to sensationalize for profit.

In adult court, requests for publicity bans arose on several occasions. These were typically high-profile cases in which publicity had been rampant and the Crown attorney or defence lawyer wished to minimize its possible further impact while the trial was in progress. Bans included entire hearings, for example, a preliminary hearing in which reporters were to be seen but not heard from in publication; and, on particular forms of publication, for example, a ban on publishing a sketch or photograph of a police informant. On such occasions the larger and more influential news media quickly mobilized their lawyers to fight restrictions on behalf of all news media. The law allowing publicity bans, when combined with the contempt-of-court restrictions on both front-region and back-region processes, had an inhibiting effect on what was reported. The law was an important, often 'invisible' means by which enclosure was effected on the court beat. As Black (1982: 64–5) observes, 'In terms of the "watching" they allow, the British and Canadian political systems are much more closed than the American is. Legal restrictions in the two Commonwealth countries have the result of focusing the mass media's attention much more closely in the legislature and occasionally on the administration and scarcely at all on the judicial and similar parts of government. The result is a marked imbalance in the political information fed into the public communication system. Some areas of politics, and particularly the legal ones, have been effectively ruled out of bounds for the mass public.'

The law effects enclosure over the courtroom in another respect. The courtroom is *the* setting in which formal legal rationality is displayed and perpetuated (Balbus, 1973; Carlen, 1976; Atkinson and Drew, 1979; Feeley, 1979; McBarnet, 1981; Ericson and Baranek, 1982). While in most cases the 'real trial' consists of settlements reached out of court through remarkably informal procedures, the norms of formal legal rationality and the order it promises are re-enacted ritualistically in court as guilty pleas are entered and sentences passed. Reporters routinely convey this rationality and its promise in their court stories. When trials occur, the legal focus is on the minutiae of procedural form as it relates to the construal of factuality. To the extent court stories are skewed towards the big trial, they highlight this form as if it is typical of case settlement generally. Legal form both resists penetration and provides ideological strength. The news media do not penetrate the legal form through court coverage, but underpin its ideology further by communicating it as common sense. This practice is at once the most subtle and the most pervasive form of front-region enclosure.

Front-region enclosure was also effected by informal agreements between court officials and reporters, without reference to the law. These informal arrangements involved knowledge available in the front regions that a court official either did not want published at all, or did not want published until future events transpired. These requests were typically based on a belief that publicity would have an unjust harmful impact on the citizens involved. A reporter said he agreed to a judge's request not to publish the names of victims of incest. Another reporter said he was asked by a judge not to report anything on a particular day's proceedings, but rather to wait until the next day when evidence would be more favourable to the accused. He said he obliged because to do so was 'good taste' and 'common sense.' A judge who was hearing cases of accused persons charged with offences related to homosexual acts said he was asked by the attorney general to ask reporters not to report the names of the accused.

> [The concern was that] ... lots of people who had been arrested and charged with it [would be deemed] automatically, or suspected to be, a homosexual. Well, a person might have gone there out of curiosity. And I remember when the matters came before me and the attorney general had quite properly stated to me, these people are presumed innocent and it would be good if their names were not published. I had to tell the Crown [attorney] that I had no authority to instruct the press not to publish their names, but I did appeal to their sense of fair play not to publish the names of the persons. After they're convicted, if they wanted to, they could. They did not publish the names.

Court officials discussed direct control over reporters' accounts. Crown attorneys and a trial co-ordinator said 'experienced reporters' consulted them if they were having trouble understanding law, procedure, or facts, or perceived that their material might create problems in a case. A judge expressed the view that reporters should allow a source to see their filed copy before it is submitted to their editors. He said that when he practised as a lawyer in another town he had such an arrangement with reporters and editors of the local newspaper, helped no doubt by the fact that he had served as a lawyer for the newspaper. 'I would react to it, I might knock out the odd thing because very often when we're talking generally to people, you use expressions that you shouldn't. Now, it doesn't look good for a judge to say somebody is stupid, but you do that every once in a while, so you take it out and say, look, this is unformed. You know it just lets you brush up your language a little bit. But I never really had any trouble with the media.'

On the rare occasions when their margins of intrusion were violated, sources tightened their boundaries and made them more evident. Thus, a trial co-ordinator complained about publicity being given to a publicity ban, and suggested that pressure of this type had the effect of further enclosure as well as consequences for the reporter concerned.

> One instance where there was a particular problem was on bail review, a bail application ... [T]he judge had banned publication and a particular reporter ... made a big fuss instead of just not mentioning it at all, which was complying with the judge's order. There was the headline, 'Why should the judge put a ban on the publication of this story?' ... [I]t was a controversial issue and if the judge decided that there should be a ban on the publication, he didn't make that decision lightly, he had given it serious thought ... [S]he thought [it] would help her with her career [but] it really didn't, it just made a lot of trouble and made administrators and judges more reluctant to mention anything. But fortunately that incident is quite rare and that reporter is no longer here.

FRONT-REGION DISCLOSURE: PUBLICITY

In spite of this structure for front-region enclosure, the courtroom remains the primary region for obtaining knowledge about a case. Prior to the court hearing there is often insufficient knowledge disclosed to make a story, and no official resolution that marks something different from what might have been reported when the accused was arrested or civil action initiated. It is in court, and particularly at trials, that details are given and outcomes announced that seem newsworthy. Hence, in a routine case, the search for a story begins only when the matter starts to unfold in the courtroom. Moreover, unless something dramatic or unusual occurs as the hearing progresses, there is no story until there is an outcome officially decided and announced in court (e.g., conviction, sentence). We observed instances in which reporters, eager to ensure that they would have a story to file, actively encouraged lawyers or litigants to proceed with their scheduled court hearing rather than to have it remanded.

In addition to being the region where detailed knowledge is presented, the courtroom is a place of drama and entertainment. Reporters were as interested in capturing dramatic moments or quotations in court as they were in obtaining the facts of the matter. Indeed, reporters selectively attended those parts of court hearings that were most likely to yield a quotable quote and a touch of colour. Court officials themselves emphasized that court is theatre, and believed dramatics are what reporters are looking for in court. A defence lawyer suggested that news outlets might do better to 'go all the way' and 'send in a drama critic to analyse it as drama, with all the training and history that that particular function has.' Another defence lawyer, well known for his dramatics, discussed how the presence of reporters in the courtroom influenced his presentations:

> I'm smart enough to realize that if I want to get my name in the paper, which I do, I am going to come up with something that has a little zip to it. The type of quote you like to see in the newspaper. Something that has a little humour to it, that is incisive, is to the point ... [Referring to a case in which his client alleged police deviance.] We were out at my house preparing the jury address and in addition to trying to give a fairly effective address to the jury we were not unmindful of the fact that there was mass-media coverage. And caught up in the somewhat carnival atmosphere of the trial, we thought that we would let everybody down if we didn't add a little something to the festivities, if I may put it that way. I am a court jester, I am an actor, in court and around the courts I am a very public person, as soon as the sun goes down you can't find me. It's my theatre ... I really enjoy the theatre of the absurd and I like doing silly things. I mean that's me. I'd like the public out there to know that I'm well and alive and practising law. Every courtroom lawyer is egotistical, as all actors are, and they want to be in the media.

Front-region disclosure was not limited to the courtroom. It also included access to public documents and court officials in public regions of the court building. Previous research indicates that court reporters make extensive use of documents. For example, thirteen or twenty-four reporters interviewed by Drechsel (1983: 101) said they consulted documents daily. In our observations, only basic public documents, such as fact sheets, the list of cases scheduled in each courtroom, and judgments from superior courts, were consulted. It was rare for court reporters to ask for other documents pertaining to a case, such as warrants and investigative reports. It was also rare for them to obtain a copy of the court transcript for a case, cost and time being obvious limitations. Occasionally judgments and case documents were consulted if the reporter was not at the hearing, although the preferred route in this circumstance was to go to court officials for an account of the facts and what transpired in court.

The main source in this regard was the Crown attorney, and to a lesser extent, defence lawyers. However, a number of other court employees were asked for information the reporter had missed in court, and were consulted to 'size up' the newsworthiness of the case. Court clerks, constables, and co-ordinators supplied names, spellings, case background information, and sometimes a summary of the Crown attorney's summation of a case. A judge's secretary was questioned about a judge's reserved decision, and a clerk for a defence lawyer was asked to outline the background of a case. The police were not used as a source for disclosure of this type.

The citizens involved in court cases were rarely consulted outside the courtroom for information or interpretation as the case unfolded. The only exception was inquests, where key witnesses were asked to give interview accounts as soon as they had finished their testimony in court. At one inquest a Crown attorney told a reporter that it was better to obtain a witness's account from her court testimony than from an individual interview outside court. The assumption conveyed was that court testimony had greater veracity because it was given under oath. The reporter followed this advice. As Fishman (1980: 62) has observed, the fact that citizens are typically given coverage only as they appear in the courtroom is another means by which the court story articulates only the official, legal-bureaucratic version of the case.

Defence lawyers sometimes acted as go-betweens for their clients and reporters who wanted to interview them. Whether the client should talk to reporters as part of case strategy, and with an eye to the law of contempt of court, is important advice the defence lawyer can offer her client. Usually the accused was advised not to talk. Most often the reporter did not even entertain the possibility of asking. At most the defence lawyer herself was asked to give an account of the accused's reactions, along with details about what transpired in court hearings reporters had missed; case developments, including their strategies and tactics; and developments in the Crown's case.

Crown attorneys were *the* source for information about case updates, issues, outcomes, and facts. There was a prevailing view among court reporters that if some detail was missed while listening to the court case, or the hearing was not attended at all, the Crown attorney could supply the information most readily and authoritatively (see Drechsel, 1983; Fishman, 1980). Given the inaccessibility of the judge, it was left to the next 'highest' official to give official imprint to versions of reality. Indeed, a Crown attorney we interviewed said it was best if reporters did not report what they had heard in court without a verification check with the Crown attorney. A reporter might have heard only one side of an argument because he was not in court to hear the other side, he might omit the other side, or he might not have the knowledge to judge properly what he saw in court.

Reporters routinely accepted what Crown attorneys said about a case as if it was fact, and reported it without attribution. A reporter who had missed an entire trial scurried into the courtroom to hear the judgment. Based on the judge's statements she decided to do a story focusing on the accused, using testimony of a key witness mentioned by the judge. Since she had not heard this testimony, the reporter contacted the Crown attorney in his office to get an account of this testimony as well as of the accused's background and facts of the case. As she was writing up this story, the reporter commented to the researcher that things reported to her by the Crown attorney are generally treated as factual without independent checks and without attributing statements to the Crown attorney. For example, extensive descriptions of the key witness's testimony and of the accused's background in this story were based on the Crown attorney's account during interview, without any reference to this fact in the filed story. There was no reference to the Crown attorney anywhere in the story, even though he was the primary provider of the accounts it contained; instead, the reporter made it appear that she had covered the entire case.

REPORTERS' SELF-ENCLOSURE

The control of regions and closures is not entirely the making of sources, but is also a matter of journalistic resources and practices. In this section we consider how reporters contribute to their own enclosure, how restrictions on knowledge are partly of their own making.

Reporters contributed to self-enclosure in their initial visualizations of what was newsworthy. Their conceptions of newsworthiness narrowed, shaped, and framed what case was worth attending in the first place, and what aspects of that case should be attended to. Reporters considered only a tiny fraction of the cases being heard in court, and concentrated on the criminal rather than civil courts. Regular court-beat reporters described the trick of their trade as knowing what not to attend. One reporter recalled that in his first two weeks on the beat he 'wasted' a lot of time sitting in courtrooms listening to 'endless details' of cases and almost every facet of a hearing. He soon appreciated that this practice was unproductive, and that he could produce more stories in less time by deciding in advance which cases would be newsworthy and what parts of those cases should be covered by attendance in the courtroom. He said he learned from his court-newsroom colleagues and his own experience that the cross-examination of important witnesses, the accused on the stand, the summing up, the verdict, and the sentence were the things to 'key' on in the criminal courtroom.

These aspects of hearings were mainly important because of their potential for 'quotable quotes' and colour. Otherwise reporters were not particularly bothered if they missed one or more of the key components, since they could obtain what they needed from interviews with the Crown attorney or other court officials, and a scan of their fact sheets. While judges could not be interviewed after the hearing to recount what happened or to add colourful quotations, Crown attorneys and defence lawyers could be called upon to restate what they regarded as their most memorable and quotable moments in court. Moreover, as documented in previous sections, these court officials could offer descriptions of key testimony, the judge's statements, and facts of the matter, which the reporter then wrote without attribution, making it seem *as if* he was at the hearing.

In summary, reporters felt they did not need to attend to most of what was open to them in the front regions. Moreover, most of what they did attend to was based on what key court officials told them went on there. Not only were reporters unable to penetrate the back regions for knowledge about the 'real trials' that took place there in the form of negotiated-plea settlements, they rarely attended enough of the front-region court hearings to form their own summation and judgments about what appeared to be the case. Reporters declined the opportunity to present a motion picture of the process, preferring instead to take snap shots through the words of key sources in interview. Court officials regarded this as *the* locus of inaccuracy and distortion in court reporting. In the eyes of a judge:

> I think in order to report accurately there must be a presence of the reporter for the whole trial. I see a tendency for more spectacular aspects of a particular piece of evidence hitting the reporter's, or drawing the reporter's attention, and that's what gets reported. It may be completely out of context if that reporter has only heard a portion of a particular witness's evidence and I don't think that is accurate reporting or does it give the flavour of the overall crime ... [F]rom up on the bench you can see them coming and going, they'll come in and they'll listen for a while to see whether it looks like an interesting case. They don't appear to have any idea of what the case is about, they've done, in my view, no preparation to see which cases should be covered or would perhaps be newsworthy or of interesting value to the community to know about. They simply seem to come in and gauge for themselves in a few moments whether it's worth staying for.

Reporters also effected self-enclosure by relying upon one another for knowledge about the cases they were reporting on jointly. When a reporter was faced with enclosure from official sources, he turned to colleagues in the court newsroom for what he had missed. For example, some reporters arrived late for a judgment and were prevented from entering the courtroom while the judge was speaking. Reporters from two different newspapers who were in attendance gave accounts of the judgment to their colleagues who were kept out. During a recess at a sentencing hearing, several reporters approached both the Crown attorney and defence lawyer for confirmation of basic facts, such as the amount of money involved in the offence and the home addresses of the accused. These sources refused to give any information, and the reporters then huddled to exchange what they had gleaned from the hearing and arrived at a consensual definition of facts such as the amount of money lost. Specific quotations were also trafficked in freely. Written notes were sometimes exchanged or compared, either to inform the person with the inadequate account, or to reach a consensus on precise wording. Stories were also based on already published stories in other newspapers. A reporter noticed that two cases he should have covered were published by a competing news outlet. With an eye towards editors' expectations about 'covering' the competition, he wrote brief stories on each case, based entirely on the account of the competing outlet. More experienced and well-connected court reporters were the hub of consultation. In particular, reporters who were not regulars on the beat, or who were novices, made extensive use of more experienced colleagues from other news outlets. As introduced previously, resource limitations of a news outlet on the beat produced the conditions for exchanges between its reporter and reporters from other news outlets that also had fewer resources.

Court officials were well aware of these dealings. A judge who was aware of an exchange relation between reporters from two newspapers commented, 'None of the reporters cover the whole trial, they cover bits and pieces ... [I]f [names a newspaper] has to go off somewhere else, they'll ask [names another newspaper] to kind of cover for them during that time and tell them what's happened.' A lawyer expressed his concerns about this practice:

> [I]t's always alarming when you've been in the room, first of all to read
> something that hasn't happened as though it has happened in the courtroom.
> There's a practice that's going on now amongst the reporters, and they do
> this I'm sure for organizational reasons, but they pool their efforts. One
> person will cover the High Court, for instance, who's related to [names a
> newspaper]. Another person will cover the provincial courts whose out of
> [names another newspaper]. And they'll tell each other what happened in
> these places. And that's the child-telegraph problem. And it gets, you almost
> never get the person who's been in the room doing the writing. Which is a
> horrible problem.

Reporters' self-enclosure was required to make the beat manageable. Even some prominent news organizations had only one reporter to cover all of the courts, at the provincial, county, and Supreme Court of Ontario levels, on a regular basis. Reporters could not afford the luxury of sitting in on a case for days or weeks at a time, not knowing whether there might be a 'pay-off' in terms of newsworthy material. They had to decide in advance what was worthy of coverage, and what glimpses of hearings and snippets of conversations in interview were reportable. Meeting a requirement of two or three filed stories a day led reporters to opt for source interviews rather than court observations. The interview was a vehicle for saving time, obtaining colour, adding descriptive detail, clarifying facts, establishing knowledge of law and process, and ultimately minimizing the risk of interpretive error that is inherent in óbservational accounts. Fellow reporters were also good sources in conditions where parsimony took precedence over testimony.

A lawyer commented about 'glaring examples of inaccurate reporting' in a prominent newspaper, adding 'it's really important that these are [this newspaper's cases], because if any newspaper has the resources to get accurate publishing, accurate facts and convey it accurately to the reader it's [this newspaper].' He then went on to explain how reporters' enclosure is a product of both court organization and news organization:

> A lot of ... situations [producing inaccuracy] ... result from the fact that the remands are so unsteady, the fact that so many of the cases do not happen when they should happen – they're remanded for three days, occasionally something will be pulled up earlier and the media will not be aware of it. Often the reporters are covering three cases at one time ... Lawyers have to spend weeks and weeks hopefully applying themselves to learn the facts, and you think that a reporter can come in there and just get the sense by being in there a fragmentary twenty minutes? So you have the limitations on individual reporters covering a number of courts and also handicapped because they don't have specific knowledge about what they are covering. And ... their copy is taken down by someone at the other end who may not understand.

Influences of News Texts

Court officials had sympathetic understanding of reporters and the limitations of the stories they published. This knowledge helped them to appreciate how news texts influence the courts, serve the purposes of the court system, and affect their own careers. The reasons why court officials were concerned about news coverage and devised mechanisms for secrecy, confidence, censorship, and publicity are made evident in considering how news texts play back upon court organization and affect social relations there.

INFLUENCES ON PROCEEDINGS AND PARTICIPANTS

Research on sentencing indicates that judges see élite, informed members of the community as their source for 'public opinion' (Hogarth, 1971; Asworth et al, 1984). Similar to journalists, their reference group is not a general public but authorized knowers of their own choosing. Unlike journalists, judges do not consider the knowledge authorized in news items to be a source of informed opinion that they can use in forming their own opinions, even though the news gives preference to those elevated in the hierarchy of credibility. Apparently they look more directly to community leaders, through social contexts rather than news texts, to decipher what seems to be in order.

Judges we interviewed did not talk of news accounts as an influence on their own decisions. They were more concerned about the influence of news on other decision-makers in the courts. While they thought they themselves were above influence, the influence of news on others, especially citizens called upon as witnesses or jurors, was of concern. A senior judge believed that news

> very often ... may put in the minds of prospective jurors or some prospec-
> tive witnesses, a view which may not be accurate. And if you get something
> fixed in your mind, it's not always easy to get rid of it. A lot of these people,
> through the media stuff if it's not accurate, could come into court with a
> preconceived idea of guilty or innocence in a case maybe and, you know –
> human nature being what it is – you hate to toss out an idea that you think
> you've come up with yourself – but you really haven't, it's been forced upon
> you by the media and you've accepted that. You've accepted their state-
> ments in the newspapers as being factual and you've reached the conclusion
> and you don't like to toss that aside, even when you hear evidence, sworn
> testimony to the contrary. This is why we warn them all the time.

While judges believed they were immune to the influence of news texts, some lawyers believed otherwise. One reason for seeking publicity about a case was to bring outside influence to bear on the judge. A lawyer who used the news media frequently commented: 'There are cases where [the accused] would be convicted in a minute were it not for the publicity attached to cases and the fact that they're high-profile. The judge realizes it's an important case, he can't just dismiss it ... [T]hey're not interested only in what happens in the courtroom. They're interested in what the press says about them. What it says about the issues that are raised. And that is where you have influence. That's a form of a broad effect.'

Accused persons sometimes choose a lawyer known to be adept at gen-erating publicity, and elect to proceed to a trial because it is a vehicle for publicity. In a criminal case in which the accused wanted to introduce evi-dence concerning police wrongdoing, the news media were proactively con-tacted and cultivated by both the accused and his lawyer. In a civil case in which the plaintiff was suing a prominent person for breach of promise, a reporter was contacted and given considerable 'discovery' information, ap-parently in the hope of generating pretrial publicity to force an out-of-court settlement. Publicity was also sought while a hearing was in progress, for example, through demonstrations outside the courtroom by interest groups. Publicity sometimes became a strategy only after certain expectations were not met at a hearing. Thus, a lawyer who was refused standing at a hearing subsequently went to the news media to present his case, hoping to influence the decision-makers who had been denying the legitimacy of his case.

Respondents believed that publicity is especially influential in cases connected to political causes. Referring to a case involving anti–nuclear-arms demonstrators, a lawyer stated: 'If there hadn't been media publicity on the crime itself and on the proposed defence, some judges would just convict them without thinking about it. You know, who cares? So what? But the fact there's been a lot of publicity on the crime and on the fact of a defence being mustered means that case is going to be a very, very difficult case for a judge to convict on, he's going to think about it very carefully. You're going to get a better hearing than you otherwise would have got.'

The benefits of publicity were seen to hinge on the outcome of the case. If the lawyer won, publicity was sought about the issues concerned. If the case was lost, silence was preferred so as not to give further authoritative strength to the other side. A lawyer elaborates:

I'm certainly not above trying to manipulate the media for my own purposes or my client's purposes ... I was acting for a client who was sued by the police for malicious prosecution. After he'd been arrested he went down and charged a couple of police officers with assault causing bodily harm, saying basically that they beat him up after they arrested him. They were acquitted, as is the usual case in charges against the police, and they then, with funding from the Metro Legal Department, sued the guy for malicious prosecution ... I think it went on a five-day trial in the Supreme Court of Ontario. And I decided early on in it, at the beginning of when the thing was actually going to trial, that I didn't particularly want to notify the media to come and watch it because I was concerned that if the outcome were unfavourable to my client, the overall purpose for which the police were bringing the lawsuit would be achieved, which is to scare people out of charging them. As it turned out in fact the jury just didn't believe the officers on anything. The guy was found not liable, the jury found that there hadn't been a malicious prosecution, and the jury found that the officers hadn't been assaulted in the manner that they suggested. Costs were awarded against the police. And I thought that that result and the whole issue of the police being charged and then subsequently suing the people after they're acquitted, is a matter that's fairly important ... [and] I had some contact with [names two reporters].

A spokesperson for a citizens' interest group, whose members had been criminally charged after distributing a publication, explained their strategy in going to trial as a vehicle for publicity, and their disappointment at the publicity received. This experience taught that while the courts provide some opportunity for the presentation of competing facts, values, and interpretations, reporters must narrow this perspective into the grooves of the news genre and provide a partial account. This account gives access to officials and 'names,' while accused and marginals are left with mere *coverage* (see also chapter 5).

> The reason we pushed ahead with trial, I mean why we didn't plead guilty and just get it over with ... We felt the trial was a public forum that could be used to educate the people around the issue the [illicit article] was about ... [A]nd that to some extent determined the kind of witnesses we called and so on and our expectation was that we'd get some of the arguments or points of view of those witnesses into the news and therefore we'd be, however slightly, altering people's perception [of the issue raised in the article]. And that to a large degree shaped the way, what we were pushing at them. Also the secondary issue of our right to publish, you know, what we want to. Now, I think what I learned from that is that we were wrong to think of a courtroom as a public forum, I mean that's a nineteenth-century notion, I think, when trials were entertainment and so on, because what we did find was that the media rarely did pick up on the issues discussed by the witnesses. Instead it would be their titles and a shocking quote. You know, if possible in the case of Crown's witnesses there would sometimes be something to show what right-wing loonies they were, and in the case of our witnesses, there'd be a show of something to say what crazy, irresponsible ... revolutionaries they were ... So I think what I learned was that people looking at the news coverage that we managed to obtain, even with all the efforts we made to provide our side of the story and the willingness of the press to accept that, wouldn't have gotten any idea what was involved.

Publicity was seen to have an adverse effect on some victims and witnesses. This point has been widely debated, and recently brought under legal control, in cases involving sexual assault. Court officials remarked that possible adverse effects of publicity on victims and witnesses were a consideration in their decisions. There were agreements between court officials and reporters to avoid reporting details that might cause a victim or witness undue suffering. Respondents offered contemporary examples of witnesses who suffered greatly from reporting. One person was taunted and had to move to another address. A respondent referred to another case in which, 'Certain of the facts that were reported ... will no doubt damage one of the witnesses for life and [it] could have been reported in a different way.'

For the accused, publicity can be a form of punishment, with lingering stigmatic effects, even if she is found not guilty. A lawyer explained his lack of initiative with reporters as an obvious reflection of the fact that his clients 'are people who don't need to see or hear their names in the papers.'

Another lawyer said, 'Client after client who comes in here, little people ... they're much more frightened of it getting in the newspaper than they are about whether they're going to have a criminal record.' Indeed, publicity can be more painful to the offender than anything the courts might give more directly in a sentence (Feeley, 1979; Walker, 1980). Lawyers spoke of clients who had experienced major trauma, and even committed suicide, as a result of publicity. In a case of indecent assault of a child victim, publicity was described as 'a punishment that's beyond anything the court could do ... he's branded forever, and you can never undo those things.'

In light of its effects, lawyers sometimes work as hard to ensure that their clients do not receive publicity as they do regarding the achievement of an appropriate verdict and sentencing outcome. Thus, publicity is an important consideration in back-region negotiations among defence lawyers, police, Crown attorneys, and judges. From the defence viewpoint, it is sometimes necessary to forgo any formal rights available to the accused, including a trial, to minimize the possibility of publicity. The scheduling of the hearing at a time of the day when reporters are unlikely to be present is sometimes included in the calculus of the negotiated settlement. A defence lawyer discussed back-region practices in this regard, and why they are necessary:

> There's an awful lot that ... goes on in the courts late in the day when the media's gone home ... [V]ery often your client wants nothing more than to get in and get out with a minimum amount of publicity and there are a lot of games played about zipping a case through the courts when the media's not around, deliberately. I'm particularly sensitive to that because of a case ... that involved the issue of whether or not the male who went looking for the prostitute could be charged with soliciting. The Crown appealed, for technical reasons, two separate acquittals. My client did not want to be the test case. He wanted to plead guilty, pay his $25 fine and get the hell out of there. Counsel for the co-accused, or the co-respondent, I guess, in the Crown appeal, moved for and obtained a ban on publication, at least pending the resolution of the issue. Well, the media got so upset about that, that when finally the Court of Appeal ruled that the men could be charged with soliciting, two newspapers published name, age, address, and occupation. Well, my poor client, who was just a gentle little man who lived at home with his family and was a schoolteacher, I don't know if he committed suicide but suffice it to say he was found dead a month later in suspicious circumstances.

Another lawyer described how he used his recipe knowledge of news deadlines, and of what the Crown attorney and judge would find appropriate, to schedule a hearing out of the hearing of reporters:

I've been able to avoid them in rather subtle ways ... I remember for example one particular case ... where my client was a well-known celebrity
charged with a pedophilic act and he had the [good] fortune to be arrested
under his real name and not his stage name ... [H]ad this charge been made
public it would have been the end totally ... of his career ... [H]e was a very
talented man and he was a rather sick man but we had worked towards ther-
apy and all kinds of things like that and through some very nimble-footed
scheduling and timing and holding down on the court list, through a knowledge of the deadlines of the various papers, through co-operation really from
the judge and from the Crown attorney, the final sentencing was held late in
the day when no one was in court and around. Now very manipulative but I
feel it's one of the reasons you come to be a defence lawyer is that he or she
knows how to manipulate the press. It could have been an awful consequence
had the name been known, and I felt I had done pretty well what part of
my job was as his lawyer. Now, I've done that several times, just managed
to deal with things ... at an earlier time in the proceedings than would have
been expected for the plea, and I've used my knowledge of how the reporters
work on the deadlines and everything else to avoid publicity for my clients
and I've avoided ... their being hurt.

The shrewd defence lawyer uses her knowledge of what reporters find
newsworthy to keep things *out of* the news. Knowing that her case will be
newsworthy if discovered, the defence lawyer tries to push everything into
the back regions as much as possible. One defence lawyer depicted his role in
terms of efforts to 'disguise' and 'camouflage' any signs of newsworthiness
that might be given off to reporters, so as to keep the case out of the news. He
described his efforts in one case, including how a key sign of newsworthiness
eventually escaped him, leading to news coverage.

[Having stated he had been proactive with the media about a case only five
times in his long career.] I'm not going to phone the media and say, 'Hey,
I've got a sensational trial,' or get my client a ton of publicity, which he
doesn't want. And in fact I'll do my best to disguise and camouflage this
trial ... I was defending two lawyers who had, through a *kite*, cheated a
bank out of a million dollars. Now [the police force involved] were fairly
sympathetic and we waived the preliminary hearing ... So, finally we had
arranged with the Crown attorney that these two lawyers would get two
[years] less a day [imprisonment], and one of them didn't think that was a
good enough deal and went to another lawyer. So, now the other lawyer was
going to call character witnesses, and I said to the other lawyer, 'Hey, wait
a minute. Look, let's do this nice and quietly. It's in front of Judge [named]
and we'll see him in chambers. We'll iron it out in chambers. We'll go into

court, plead guilty, we'll say they're sorry, announce their age and marital status [but not profession], the Crown will ask for two less a day, and we'll say that's fine, done.' You know, and these lawyers didn't need any publicity and hadn't had any. So, it was arranged that Judge [named]'s court would proceed in the usual way and when the cases were all over, the court would adjourn, the court would close down. By pre-arrangement, then, we would arrive half an hour later, after seeing the judge in chambers, and come in and hopefully the reporters would have gone home for the day. Done our thing in five minutes, walked out, no publicity. But this other lawyer, who was a very well-known lawyer, is parading around the courthouse with about six or seven character witnesses. All fairly high-profile people and all with Florida tans and worth about $25 grand on the hoof; everyone of them, with silk suits, diamonds and everything, and some alert reporter says, 'Now, that's a curious thing, where are they going?' And followed them right into the courtroom. The headlines, 'Two Lawyers, Million-Dollar Kite, Go to Jail.' So I will try to camouflage my client's existence where he doesn't want any publicity.

These examples indicate that Crown attorneys were also involved in out-of-court transactions aimed at minimizing publicity. It is essential to secure their collaboration in back-region enclosure as part of negotiated-plea and sentence arrangements. Moreover, Crown attorneys have their own stake in minimizing publicity that might interfere with investigations or court proceedings. If a reporter publicizes an investigation that the Crown wishes to keep secret, it can have a fundamental impact on when suspects are charged, what they are charged with, and how proceedings develop. Normally reporters wait until a case is officially designated and imprinted before they deem it reportable (Fishman, 1980). At times, however, a reporter makes his own designations in advance of official announcements or proceedings, thereby forcing the authorities into making their official moves prematurely. A Crown attorney described her moves in a case she knew would be newsworthy.

[The suspect] had been located by the police and I had been notified and we were making preparations to apprehend him. I was at the stage when I had to assess the evidence and ... we were trying to find out for certain that he was the right man because, as you can well appreciate, you don't want to arrest the wrong man. I mean his life would be ruined, it would be a thoroughly irresponsible thing to do, had to be certain he was the right man and that you had sufficient evidence, which in my judgment would be sufficient to put him on trial. Somebody ... had we suspect leaked the news that this man had been located to a news reporter and a news reporter called up certain officials ... and said, 'We know where he is,' and actually his address and said, 'If you don't tell us what you're doing ... we're going to announce it on the radio,' and of course then it would be in the newspapers. And they were literally holding the government to ransom ... [T]he government's response, the first man refused to talk to him, which I thought was a mistake, and what this chap was saying was, 'Come to a deal with us.' In other words, 'We want to be the first people in on this story – if you tell us what you're doing and how you're doing it then we're not going to publish it,' which I think is wrong too. But I certainly would have spoken to the guy, and I would have called him in and I would have said, 'Look, I'm not going to tell you anything but I expect you, I'll certainly let you know as soon as we are in a position to release it. Since we'll tell you, and since you're on to it, fine, we'll tell you first, but don't hold a gun to my throat because this is the consequence of what'll happen.' And that was one of the reasons why the suspect had to be arrested so soon. I didn't want to have him arrested at that point because at the time he was arrested we didn't have the evidence in our hands ... [O]ur hand was forced by this particular reporter.

A judge described a case in which she collaborated in keeping reporters out of the courtroom to avoid the likelihood that publicity would result in the accused losing his job. However, her efforts to enclose a front region that reporters were entitled to enter resulted in embarrassment for her, and the extra punishment of publicity for the offender.

[The accused] happened to be a chauffeur who drives those lovely limousines that transport judges ... and he had been wiring judge's conversations ... And because of his job, being a chauffeur ... he wanted the case heard *in camera*. He was unrepresented by counsel. There was nobody in the courtroom and I guess as a matter of convenience I said o.k. Now, the Crown, of course, consented ... just to sort of keep people away from the court ... [A named reporter] has a great interest in all court and somehow he happened to hear about it. So, he appeared on our doorstep the next morning and pointed out to me how this was strictly illegal and I at once said, 'No problem, this court is open. It was closed, so to speak, yesterday, but I understand nobody was kept out of the courtroom because nobody was interested.' So, he wrote a big article about how he had made a hole in the 'wall' that had been put around that particular court. And he, of course, just told everything ... But it was a case that was so insignificant. I think the sentence was like a two-hundred-dollar fine or something like that. It was ... blown a way out of proportion, a harm done at this level, [the offender's] in Calgary now because he probably lost his job ... [A]t the time I knew I was wrong, I mean, the law didn't provide for this, such a relation where a man could have his little case decided in private. But until a newspaper reporter or a member of the public came to the door and said I want in ... you had to let them in. There are very, very rare cases where you can close a court to the public. And it's all set forth in the Criminal Code.

Reporters were taken into consideration as part of courtroom proceedings. One lawyer said the presence of reporters is similar to the presence of citizens in a jury trial. '[Y]ou've got a real audience that are locked in there, you've got to make it interesting for them. I mean it may not be interesting but it's got to be interesting for them. And what interests the jurymen will interest the press.' For another lawyer, the interests at stake influence how he responds to reporters' presence. If publicity appears to be the most severe punishment, he reduces and tailors his submissions in court, even though it might lead to a more severe sentence from the judge. 'If there are media there, for example, I'm pleading somebody guilty to diddling some little child, I'll be very careful to give absolutely no data that makes the story interesting, in an attempt to encourage non-publication. If there are no press present then I will tell more things about the person that makes it interesting so that the judge is more likely to give me a favourable result.'

Court officials felt further constrained by their perception that there are no easy or obvious remedies for unreasonable coverage (see chapter 6). Some felt it is as improper for them to complain about news coverage publicly as it is for them to seek coverage in the first instance. Judges in particular stressed that it is not proper for them to seek a correction or retraction directly by contacting journalists concerned or writing letters to the editor. 'I don't perceive that conduct as proper for a judge, to call any newspaper and give them hell for something they've written about the judge ... don't feel that is good for the office of a judge, to get personally involved in something [where] there may be points of view. [B]ecause it's unfair to the other party, because of your judicial office, or because it might get the office involved in a conflict in some way. And perhaps lead the public's regard of the office of a judge in a way that is harmful to the office ... One must think of the system rather than the person.'

This judge represents a view that was pervasive among officials on the court beat. They were most concerned with the authority of their office. They did not want to use the news to bring that authority into question or to make it appear they were stepping outside of their authoritative enclosures. Usually, the value they saw in news was not in terms of what it would do for them in the particular case. Rather, news was conceived as a valuable means to accomplish wider purposes: enhancing their authority, influencing other branches of government, and serving principles and goals of criminal punishment.

SERVING THE PURPOSES OF THE COURT SYSTEM

Court officials believed the news is important in conveying the purposes of the court system to audiences beyond the courts. While they had no direct evidence to support this view, it was what they visualized the function of the news media should be. This visualization influenced what they took to be newsworthy and their decisions to co-operate with reporters.

News was considered to be an agency for promoting and sustaining the legitimacy of law. One respondent expressed a view similar to that of Atiyah (1982), who argues that the more mystery surrounding the law, the greater its powers of social cohesion. This lawyer asserted that it is the *duty* of reporters, as part of the court system, to promote public confidence in it. The place of reporters in the court system is 'the job of keeping the administration of justice respectably in the minds of the public. And, instead of dealing with the story, somehow keep in mind that the public has to be kept confident in the legal system ... [G]enerally the system has to be promoted and the press have a real responsibility to promote it.'

Many respondents conceived this as a matter of professional legitimacy. Their goal was to have the news media portray their office and their work in a way that made them appear as 'competent professionals.' Thus, a Crown attorney referred to news as 'being helpful from the point of view of raising the consciousness of the people to the fact that we are professional ... we're trained lawyers, we're specialists in fact, and we are concerned about the welfare of the community ... [A] group of professional people who are really affecting the quality of life that you enjoy on the street.'

In this connection court officials were even appreciative of news accounts that focused upon procedural deviance in the court system. A bureaucracy that deals in the procedural deviance of other bureaucracies is also sensitive to its own procedural strays. Hence, the news media were depicted as the 'eyes and ears of the public,' 'the court of public opinion' having a legitimate watchdog function in the courts. A senior judge commented, 'Our basic philosophy is that the courts are open to the public and most times very few members of the public are there, except those that are particularly interested in matters, so that ... the press really are the public in that sense and they can stand guard to see whether things are being done, in their view, in a fair and open way.' A lawyer emphasized repeatedly, '[O]ur court system only works well when officials, the people who have power, know that they're being watched, they're being scrutinized ... I know from my concern, not what the media's concern is, this is of prime importance, without the press watching what's happening people tend to get haphazard in what they're dealing with ... This to me is the highest function of the press, that eye in the courtroom, if they do it the right way, and generally once they're sensitive to these things, they keep people behaving the right way and it's very important in the justice system.'

Respondents seemed well aware that reporters could perform this policing function without any substantial knowledge of law or court process being conveyed in news stories. The social-control effect of reporters was a matter of the *possibility* of their presence in court, creating a *potential* for critical coverage related to procedural slippage. The reproduction of court-system legitimacy depended on visualizing procedural strays and then using them in news communications to announce that social control had been effected and to acknowledge that a more orderly process was now in place. Legal officials sometimes collaborated with reporters in designating the deviance in order to bring the pressure of publicity to bear on something they wanted changed in the court system. A lawyer described one of his collaborative efforts to effect procedural change through news, a collaboration that had the rather ironic effect of enclosing information previously available to other court officials and reporters:

> I was always distressed ... at the psychiatric reports of people who are ordered for psychiatric examinations ... And I felt that legally there was no foundation for them in the Criminal Code before a preliminary hearing, but also what I discovered was that the confidential reports, when they come back with the person, were then stapled to the information, to the court documents. And you know I was defence counsel then, ... and I was horrified that some clerk in that office who was bored and had very little else to do could just open up and read the contents of those reports ... I'd been interviewed on [another] issue by [names reporter] ... and I called her back, invited her in and said 'Would you mind doing something for me? I'm going to give you the names of four people that anybody would have heard in the courtroom and I'd like you to go to the Information Office at the courthouse and ask for the information. If they ask you why you want them you tell them you're doing it for [me]. If you say why you want them you say it's in connection with a newspaper story he's doing, exposing a lack of privacy for confidential information of this sort. And I took an affidavit beforehand – she had never been in that courthouse before – that she had been given those instructions. She went, she gave the four names, she asked for the four reports. She was handed two of them, the other two were already processed. And with them were the copies of the confidential reports which she was permitted to photocopy and then hand back. That became a [names newspaper] story, and the practice has been greatly changed ... you can't get them unless you're a lawyer or the accused person himself.

Court officials also saw news as a vehicle to pressure officials in other branches of government. Sometimes this pressure was specific to a particular legal procedure or issue, as indicated in the case above. It was also directed at justifying the need for more resources for the court system. Judges, Crown attorneys, and a trial co-ordinator, all emphasized that the news was useful in selling the idea that their facilities were lacking, bringing pressure to bear on politicians to give them more resources. Chief justices had actually begun to hold a news conference at the beginning of the court session each autumn to publicize the problems and 'plight' of the courts, thereby justifying the need for more resources.

The legal rationale for court reporting has traditionally been its value in deterrence (Jones, 1982: 70). In publicizing sentences, news is part of the system of punishment as a source of both individual and general deterrence. In the previous section we discussed how, from the perspective of the defence, publicity is usually to be avoided because it can be more punitive than the sentence of the court. From the perspective of law enforcers, however, this negative effect on the offender can be a positive value of publicity. Publicity is punishment, to be considered along with sentences of the court in calculating what harm is due the offender for causing harm to others (cf Walker, 1980).

Publicity also serves notice to the public of what they can expect if they commit a similar crime. The value of news regarding imagined general-deterrent effects was mentioned by most judges and Crown attorneys interviewed. One judge observed, however, that the general-deterrent impact of news is minimal because of reporters' selection of court cases to report. The tendency to report sentences for sensational and isolated cases of violence, rather than for the routine burglary, means that the message is lost for the vast majority of would-be offenders.

> Now, if the public doesn't know what is happening, for instance, to break-and-enter men, then there's no deterrence. Now, I think some of those cases should get more publicity ... But, you see, that sort of routine case, very unfortunately break-and-enter is a very routine thing nowadays and we just get so many of them that it's just not news anymore. And that's the key word I suppose, it's not *news* anymore. So, you very rarely get any publication say of what's happened in a break-and-enter case and therefore the deterrent effect is lacking. I think that's one of the functions that the press can fulfil is assisting the courts with the deterrent effect of sentencing. If people don't know what's happening then there's no deterrent effect.

It seems that whatever is the imagined role of the news media regarding general deterrence, it provides little practical knowledge for the rational calculation of crime and punishment. Sentencing is accomplished in the context of a tariff operating in the courts of a local jurisdiction (Sudnow, 1965;

Heumann, 1978; Feeley, 1979; Ericson and Baranek, 1982). Only court officials who are regulars in the particular jurisdiction know what the local tariff is and how it relates to the 'normal' case before them. In reporting individual sentences of abnormal cases, the news media give no sense of what the tariff is, or even that it exists. If the local sentencing tariff was publicized, it would likely be seen as too lenient and result in pressure to move it upward. Indeed, if anything it might undercut the general-deterrent effect because it would be clear that the normal sentencing range is well below what is provided for as maximum penalties by legislators in the Criminal Code. The news tendency is to portray individual sentences as too lenient, and sentences are perceived as such by the news consumer (Doob, 1984). If the public is getting the message of leniency in sentencing from news accounts, the result will be to loosen rather than strengthen the general-deterrent effect, at least according to those who believe in this theory.

In this light, it is arguable that the court system benefits from news reporting that does not yield substantial understanding of its process and structure. To quote again from the lawyer cited at the beginning of this section, the news media should do their 'job of keeping the administration of justice *respectably* in the minds of the public.' Whether it is the everyday workings of plea bargaining or the everyday reality of sentencing tariffs, what the people do not know will not hurt the system. As a set of procedures not to know about the court system, the news media enhance that system's powers of social cohesion. In this respect also the news media are an integral and influential part of the system reported on.

SERVING THE PURPOSES OF PROFESSIONALS

Lawyers viewed the news media as a means to communicate their views and opinions in a manner that would enhance both their professional powers and their individual egos. One lawyer cited regularly in the news, and who occasionally published newspaper articles under his own byline, addressed the benefits of news coverage: '[I]t's not really a benefit in a financial sense in any sort of way. It benefits me by giving me a voice much stronger than I otherwise would have had to communicate the types of things that I'm doing regularly and that's a strong benefit.' Other lawyers were more pecuniary in their interests. They mentioned Law Society restrictions on their ability to advertise outside of their professional media, and saw news coverage of their cases and opinions on issues as a form of 'cheap advertising.' In a competitive environment with an increasing number of practitioners, many lawyers struggle financially and view their work in terms of a small business (Macfarlane, 1982). As one of our respondents stated, '[W]hen you get your name in the papers in this business, it's like anything else I suppose, the people in trouble with the law remember the name they read in the paper. And it's a business matter. You know, it's a very compelling business matter. When you get your name in the paper, when you're known as a person who does this sort of work then you're maybe more likely to get other work of that kind ... [S]o to that extent it's vital sometimes.'

Another lawyer emphasized that it is 'the name' that is remembered. Appreciating that consumers recall 'name brands,' personalities, and their images rather than the substance of what is on offer, she was quite willing to participate in news communication for its advertising value rather than educational value. '[I]t's a form of advertising and people know my name. I don't know if they can remember anything of the content, ordinary people who are not interested in the story, but they do remember that you're important, and that's undoubtedly of some assistance.' Court reporters also appreciated the advertising aspect of the coverage they gave to particular lawyers, and saw it as one of the few inducements at their disposal to secure co-operation from lawyers.

The news media are not only a power to harness in the enhancement of professional reputation and the authority it brings within the legal system. Traditionally Canadian legislatures have been very overrepresented occupationally by lawyers and some prominent lawyers seek publicity with an eye towards a second career in politics. Reporters believed many coroners used that office for publicity that would pave their way to political office, pointing to past instances in which prominent coroners became politicians. They also pointed to a particular coroner who called a newsroom when a decision was about to be handed down, saying he was doing so with an eye to political office rather than to inform the public out of a sense of citizenship.

PUBLIC KNOWLEDGE OF THE COURTS

Court officials believed that the news does not provide knowledge about contexts or reasons for decisions in individual cases, or knowledge about legal issues and the court system. They located this lack of understanding in the new-selection process, and reporters' ignorance of law and legal process, rather than in their own practices of enclosure. One explanation of their perception is that they failed to appreciate fully the difference between news texts and their own specialized knowledge embodied in legal texts and drawn upon in the formal legal rationality of the courtroom. A legally trained newspaper editor has remarked, 'I suspect that most lawyers think they do not get fair press and I think that's because lawyers are trained to think in qualifiers' (Keillor, 1982: 16). Reporters express certainty in their use of valued facts, giving unqualified imprint to events in the world. In fulfilling the requirements of news discourse, legal discourse is left out, relegated to its specialized professional contexts and texts. Inevitably, sources will complain they were misunderstood. They are literally correct when they say that in news coverage they are always taken out of context.

News transforms the specialized knowledge of the legal institution into the common sense. In the process it serves to acknowledge order and points to precursors of change. Far from omission, selection, and distortion being problems for the news, they are fundamental to the news process of envisaging order and influencing change. The resultant mystery of the courts and legal institution helps to constitute the public's sense of cultural coherence and consensus, and efforts to document that the reality is quite different might undermine this (Atiyah, 1982). The majesty, justice, and mercy of law is upheld through the myriad oganizational and legal arrangements for channelling reporters into selected spatial regions, and for enclosing on their channels of knowledge. The public knowledge that results helps to reproduce social order, even while it fails to yield understanding of how that order is constituted in the everyday work of the courts.

3

The Police

News Culture and Ideas

THE SELLING OF THE POLICE

Historically the police beat has been a prime locus of news coverage. Early newspaper proprietors in England saw the police as a source of readily available and entertaining material. Newspapers were also seen as an agency of policing; for example, the front page of a newspaper was sometimes prepared as a 'wanted poster' that could be torn off and displayed as such. The first full-time journalist in the United States was a crime and police reporter, imported from England to transplant the police-beat entertainment formula that had worked so well there. Other u.s. newspapers quickly adopted this approach, with the typical newsroom consisting of the owner, a reporter on general assignment, and a reporter on the police beat (Steffens, 1931; Hughes, 1940; Roscho, 1975; Sherizen, 1978; Gordon and Heath, 1981).

As news organizations and media have expanded, the police beat has remained a significant component. Chibnall (1977: 49) observes that in the nineteenth century crime reporting gave emphasis to the coverage of court cases and post-trial developments, whereas in the late twentieth century there is an increasing reliance on the police as the major source. Today nearly all news outlets have at least one reporter who is a police-beat specialist. News outlets that can afford very few reporters – such as most commercial radio stations – typically ensure that the police beat is covered as a stable source for a staple product. Sherizen (1978: 210) cites 'a major nationwide study of American journalists, [which] found that 13.7% of the 70,000 full-time reporters in the United States cover crime or police, with another one or two percent of the reporters covering courts exclusively.'

Contemporary news emphasis on the police is also related to their political centrality. '[T]he police ... play a role in the democratization process of society ... Like the state and the society itself, the police are continually the object and the forum of political conflicts' (Van Outrive and Fijnaut, 1983: 56–7). In Canada the police are a national symbol (Walden, 1982). At the forefront of debates concerning the relation of the state to civil society, the police embody the traditional constitutional concern with 'peace, order, and good government.' There are signs that the police are increasing their political potency, both symbolically and in practice. In the past three decades their personnel and fiscal resources have multiplied dramatically, and they have been taking an ever-increasing slice of the overall crime-control budget in relation to the courts and penal system (Solicitor General of Canada, 1984). They have also become increasingly centralized, with smaller police forces being taken over by larger metropolitan forces, new municipal region forces, provincial police, and the RCMP (Ericson, 1982). Coincident with these trends is the politicization of the police, 'their *overt* intervention into the *public* political arena in order to change the *content* of rules both within the police organization and in the wider society' (Reiner, 1983: 130; see also Reiner, 1985).

The political functions of the police, both instrumentally and symbolically, have parallels in how the news-media institution sees its own enterprise. The police have always been 'a political instrument for the control of social developments and conflicts' (Van Outrive, and Fijnaut, 1983: 53–4). Instrumentally, the news media have had a similar political concern, embodied in their fourth-estate mandate. They are centrally involved in designating deviance and advancing control remedies, and they do so in the name of the general good or public interest. At the symbolic level, the 'primary significance of the police in newspaper ideology lies in their physical and symbolic role as representatives and defenders of the established consensus and its institutions ... Given the notion of "responsible reporting" entails the promotion of the public interest it follows that it also entails the promotion of police interests' (Chibnall, 1977: 142–3). The news media and police have an instrumental affinity in reproducing order and an ideological affinity in acknowledging order.

All organizations control knowledge of their activity in order to sustain the view publicly that they are operating with procedural regularity, and are therefore accountable. Organizations expend enormous resources in this legitimation work, sometimes to the point where it becomes a major goal of the organization (Meyer and Rowan, 1977; Warshett, 1981). Traditionally, the police have adopted a reactive approach to news communication. This approach has entailed either defending their actions when questioned, or simply enclosing on knowledge. More recently they have made an effort to control their environment through a proactive strategy of selectively disclosing knowledge about organizational activities. Parallel to their high levels of proactivity in 'making crime' (Ericson, 1981, 1982; Brodeur, 1983, 1984), the police have become proactive in making their public image. The police now accept that in relation to a particular incident or activity, a proactive approach to the news media is useful in controlling the version of reality that is transmitted, sustained, and accepted publicly. In the long run and in the aggregate, this proactivity can enhance organizational legitimacy (Wheeler, 1986). Ironically, by being more 'open' in news communication, organizational members can close off incursions that make the organization more vulnerable and its environment more equivocal. As one of our respondents stated, the main rationale for the police public-relations unit was control of reporters and their news accounts. 'If you have a public affairs office within a large organization, then certainly ... it's logical for [reporters] to favour that area. But if you don't then they will certainly favour certain areas of vulnerability, which they will prey on, which can cause problems.'

Along with an increase in police personnel, fiscal power, and political power, has come an expansion of police ideologically. In the past few decades the police have become much more involved with the news media, loosening some aspects of their back-region enclosure over knowledge while effecting front-region enclosure through more proactive 'feeding' of reporters. In the process the police have come to appreciate that the news media are *part of* the policing apparatus of society, and can be controlled and put to good use in this respect. The news media are incorporated into the architecture of new police buildings (they are given newsroom facilities there), they are taken into account in police organization charts, they are subject to the regulations in police operational manuals, and they are part of everyday practice at all levels of the police hierarchy.

This realization is well documented in Britain. After longstanding hostilities with the press in London, the Metropolitan Police under Commissioner Mark reorganized their public-affairs operations to channel news accounts in a more positive direction (Chibnall, 1977; Jefferson and Grimshaw, 1984; Reiner, 1985). Mark advanced a policy of unprecedented 'openness,' emphasizing that the media are useful in boosting both public belief in the police and morale within the police force. A prominent former chief constable in Britain, John Alderson, has expressed the view that it is important for 'police to consider ways and means of harnessing the opinion-forming influence of the media' (Alderson, 1982: 7).

In Toronto, police officers of all ranks emphasized that the force was becoming increasingly oriented to the media. During our field research this tendency was marked by the reorganization of the public-affairs unit, which resulted in the addition of staff, including, for the first time, civilians experienced in journalism and public relations. Police personnel conceived of the news media as *part of* the policing enterprise, a resource to be harnessed rather than a threat to be shunned. In the words of a police commissioner:

> The police for a long time have been their own worst enemies with the media. Absolutely no doubt about it ... One of the [newspaper] photographers who received an award today said he wanted to thank the chief and the police for just loosening up in the last couple of years. He said, 'Showing my press card actually will sometimes get me past the road blocks now ... You can get the name of an officer now, or you can get his number, and you can talk with him without having him say, "No, you're going to have to talk to my supervisor back at the Division and the supervisor has just gone on a three-day leave"' ... In this business we've got to deal with the community. We've got to get rid of the *fortress* mentality. Only 15 per cent of police time these days is spent on catching criminals, other 85 per cent is dealing with the public in any one of a number of different ways. It's getting so complicated now that unless we can encourage the community to come forward and report a mysterious thing or get involved in neighbourhood watch, we can't stay on top of the problem of crime by ourselves. Better relations. Better efficiency. I put a lot of it down to the chief, that's just the way he likes to operate. He's put his mark on the force by opening it up a great deal since he's been around.

A senior officer said there was more proactive contact with the news media: 'We initiate more press releases. We try to think out in advance something that's going to happen in the future and how we'll handle the media, so I guess we've increased where we stimulate the media.' This officer was clear about what was intended from this proactivity: 'I mean they know that I'm looking for ink to sell the police. I'm trying to get some free marketing!'

In Toronto the move towards a more proactive and 'open' philosophy was managed through a report by a firm of management consultants, Hickling-Johnston. This report underscored the importance of news to the police. With an eye to greater control of the environment, greater control of news was advocated. '[C]areful channeling of information in a form readily useable by the press and media has not always been the practice at Metro. More professionalism here will yield more gains for Metro's police and citizen relationships' (Hickling-Johnston, 1981: 19). There was a specific recommendation that 'a Public Affairs department be established within the office of the Chief of Police' (Hickling-Johnston, 1982: 32). Among the 'fundamental changes with respect to Public Affairs [that] will be necessary' (ibid: 31) were the following, which were subsequently implemented:

– Consolidation of Public Affairs activities into one organization unit. Currently, these activities are disjointed and a shared responsibility between a number of departments including Information Services, Duty Desk and Community Services.

- Integration of [civilian] professional expertise in the areas of public relations, minority group relations, media relations and public education together with police know-how and experience.
- Improved relationships with the press and media including:
  - better flow of information and communications which are consistent with the legitimate needs of the media
  - more formalized in-house processes for the release of information to the media
  - ongoing liaison to both identify and resolve problems and conflicts.
- Initiation of more formal in-house Public Affairs training programs for police management. Police accountability requirements are increasing and police management will need to be better able to meet these requirements.
- Adaption of a more proactive stance in conveying and as necessary defending the image of the Force to the public.

A police administrator stated that, in the past, 'There was a feeling by line police officers not to tell anybody anything, if you don't tell them anything then you can't be made to either look a fool, insensitive, cruel, ignorant, or whatever, if you don't say anything then they can't twist your words. [Now] there's a realization that the police must respond.' Another respondent emphasized that the previous attitude was a matter of administrative preference, rather than line-officer resistance. Indeed, it was backed up by the Police Act of Ontario, which includes the offence of 'deceit' if any police officer who 'without proper authority communicates to the public press or to any unauthorized person any matter connected with the police force.'

It was only with a change in administrative policy authorizing lower-ranking officers to talk directly to reporters that a change in police attitude could be fostered. The head of a police unit stated that openness with the news media had

taken on a real strong emphasis since the implementation of the Hickling and Johnston study ... So, it is a relatively new role, and in the past, for many years, policemen I think tended to be very closed-mouth to the media about police work ... That was drilled into us from day one when we started the job. And I remember being up at the police college and it was always stressed that you say as little as possible to the media ... I came up as a rookie police officer through the system, that's the kind of training that we were given and as a result naturally that's the way we did it, the way we were told. Now things have changed, and I am totally open to the media now and they phone me on a regular basis and I try to communicate the accurate information to them as readily as possible.

Police respondents gave different reasons for the shift in policy marked by the Hickling-Johnston report. Some attributed it to internal-management factors and the wishes of the chief of police. Others located it externally. They regarded publicity as part of police responsibility to the public: since the police are a public service using taxpayers' money, the public should be kept informed about police activities. Others stressed the 'business' need of the police to sell themselves and their commodities in a competitive environment where public services each face fiscal constraints. They described themselves as professionals in a business, and similar to all responsible and progressive business organizations there is a need to sell their commodities through a constant, positive media image. As one police officer conceived it, 'I think it's a common concept today by most progressive organizations that it's necessary to tell your story and to sell yourself to whoever you see trying to provide a product or a service, and the Metropolitan Toronto Police are quite progressive I think ... Hickling-Johnston ... identified a need for the police force to sell themselves and to sell or put on an attractive image before the public about what the police Force was trying to do, and how they were trying to do it, and I think this is pretty well an accepted way of operating for business in North America.'

On the operational level there was a perceived need to avoid negative comment or an inference that the police had something to hide. Police officers believed that if they did not respond, reporters would turn to sources outside the force who would not express the police viewpoint and who could be critical of the police. Moreover, if there was systematic non-cooperation, it might lead to systematic efforts by reporters to cast negative light on the police. A management officer said he was so concerned that his refusal to respond would make him look bad that he tended to respond even when he was ignorant about the subject. He gave as an example an occasion on which he was asked to theorize about the effects of alcohol on crowd behaviour. He said he offered his theory even though he felt it was vacuous.

Some police officers viewed the mandate to respond more positively. They saw responding as a way to build a relationship with reporters. Over time reporters would reciprocate in the form of positive coverage of police activities (access), and in agreeing to censorship when the need arose. Their thinking was that since reporters can always find someone to respond, it is better to respond oneself and thereby have at least some control of the account.

There are peculiar tensions in the police organization regarding secrecy, confidence, censorship, and publicity. In some respects the 'selling job' is easier for the police than for most other organizations. At the hub of control culture, political culture, and popular culture, the police are ensured a legitimate place on the daily menu of all news outlets. However, because they are in the media spotlight constantly, the police are especially vulnerable to having their procedural strays focused upon and controlled through the pressure of publicity. The tensions arising from this situation are at the core of our analysis of the police beat.

AN OVERVIEW OF POLICE BEAT ORGANIZATION AND CULTURE

Spatial Arrangements

During our field-work the police had a public-affairs unit headed by a superintendent. This unit was responsible for releasing to the news media major occurrence reports on crime incidents, preparing news releases on police issues and events, and organizing public-education programs and speaking engagements for police officers. It was also a clearing house for enquiries from reporters, citizens, and community groups. One member of the unit said that his role was as 'director' – directing knowledge people in the force wanted communicated to members of the public and directing members of the public to people in the force who could give them the knowledge they requested.

This public-affairs unit at police headquarters included a newsroom for reporters, annexed to the headquarters building, along with the police staff cafeteria. Here reporters were provided with desks, telephones, and a loudspeaker system on which officers in public affairs broadcast the latest news releases.

The reporters who occupied space in this newsroom were from popular news outlets exclusively, in particular radio stations and newspapers that had space to fill with crime-incident spot news. This newsroom was the focal point of an 'inner circle' of police reporters, who sustained relations with a range of police sources and reported on police activities sympathetically. Some other journalists who reported on the police, but who were not based physically in the beat newsroom, nevertheless used it from time to time and were also accepted in the inner circle. These included popular televisionstation reporters and newspaper reporters from a popular outlet. Still other reporters assigned to cover the police were explicitly excluded from the inner circle. Their exclusion was marked by the fact that they did not use the beat newsroom. These reporters of 'the outer circle' were invariably from quality news outlets in radio, newspapers, and television. In sum, the police newsroom was the territory of reporters from popular news outlets who were mainly after crime-incident stories and stories of other events and issues that allowed sympathetic portrayal of the police. Reporters from quality news outlets, who were more oriented towards police management, efficiency, and procedures, worked from the outside culturally, socially, and spatially.

With the reorganization of public affairs, a public-affairs officer was assigned to each of the five police districts in Metropolitan Toronto. These positions were established so that there would be a person in each district available to work with police officers in establishing procedures for dealing with the news media, determining how the news media should be seen and used, and channelling information regarding coverage of specific major incidents.

Provision was also made for directing news communications during times other than the regular daytime office hours of the public-affairs unit. In these other times inquiries were to be directed through the duty desk, usually occupied by a duty inspector or staff sergeant. Enquiries at these times typically concerned major incidents that had just occurred or were under investigation.

Regulations

The force's administrative-procedures document pertaining to news communications gave job descriptions for duty officers and information officers:

DUTY OFFICER
Acts as co-ordinator for the dissemination of news releases
When dealing with members of the media:
- Acquaint himself with the individual member;
- Attempts [sic] to create a credibility bond with them;
- Show no favouritism between their members;
- Promptly disseminate to members current information of all incidents;
- Refer members to the appropriate officer when further information required;
- When necessary, act as a liaison between members of the media and members of the Force;
- Assembles essential information of major incidents as it becomes available
Ensures proper operation of the 'Media Broadcast System' by:
- Broadcasting 'bulletin type' information as soon as practical upon notification of
  - a major incident (crime),
  - developments possibly leading to a major incident,
  - emergency or dangerous conditions for the public,
  - developments possibly leading to emergency or dangerous conditions for the public,
  - a human interest story

Seeking public assistance or participation in locating missing or wanted persons or vehicles.

INFORMATION OFFICER

Encourages a good relationship between the Force and members of the media
Encourages media participation in:
- preventative campaigns
- informing the public of services performed by the police on their behalf and for their protection.

Acts as a liaison between the Force and news media:
- On all matters of the media may require assistance or information
- Upon receiving a complaint from a member of the media or the Force concerning actions of the other.

Acquaints himself with members of the media and creates a personal credibility bond with them.

Refer members of the media to the appropriate officer when assistance or further information is required.
- Assists members of the Force when requesting information concerning:
- Public information;
- Members of the media seeking information.

Appreciating the fact that regardless of formal channels, reporters and police officers establish their own channels of communication, the force gave authority to a large number of officers to speak to the news media. This administrative procedure served as a standing authorization of who could speak on behalf of the force, and who could thereby avoid the jeopardy of the Police Act in communicating police matters outside the organizational boundaries. This administrative procedure not only delineated who could speak, but what they could and could not speak about. The core provisions offer a view of the official position on the value of news, how facts are to be valued, and who should be involved in making valuations.

NEWS RELEASE

Obviously a good police/news media relationship is necessary in today's complex society. Police personnel should not adopt a closed-door policy concerning news releases. Association with the media should include the following objectives:
A. To create, encourage and maintain a good police/news media relationship
B. To keep the public accurately informed of current crime and events
C. To encourage media involvement in preventive campaigns
D. To inform the public of services performed by the police on their behalf and for their protection.

No instruction can possibly cover all eventualities. When in doubt, officers must use common sense, keeping in mind that discretion involves protecting the right of suspects to an impartial trial and preserving the right of citizens to know all the facts not prejudicial to a fair trial.

GENERAL INFORMATION
Authorized Personnel includes:

      A Unit Commander,

      An Inspector or Person of higher rank,

      A person acting as Unit Commander or Inspector,

      A person in charge of a unit in the absence of the Unit Commander,

      A person authorized to issue news releases.

Information Officer:

Is the Unit Commander – Information Services.

When conferring with the media, officers:

- Must not speculate or express an opinion that may influence or prejudice a future trial
- Must explain the reason if certain portions of an incident, crime or arrest cannot be divulged.

Police officers having a complaint concerning the conduct of a member of the media, will forward a report containing the particulars to the information officer.

Members of the media requesting information or assistance for feature news stories or interviews other than a general news release, or a medical news release, will be directed to the information officer.

Police Officers, other than Authorized Personnel, will not supply members of the media with information concerning incidents, or crime, unless otherwise directed by Authorized Personnel.

MEDIA PHOTOGRAPHERS AND T.V. CAMERAMEN
Police officers should permit freedom of media reporters, news photographers and T.V. cameramen, except when:

- they are obstructing emergency service personnel
- their presence would disturb evidence

Suspects must not be posed for photographs

AUTHORIZED PERSONNEL
Must respond as soon as practical to legitimate enquiries from members of the media

Treat all enquiries from properly identified members of the media, as a legitimate function of their profession

Must ensure that disseminating news to the media is not:

- Delayed unreasonably

– Withheld unnecessarily.

When requested by members of the media, express an opinion only when absolutely necessary.

When withholding information from the media, obtain confirmation to withhold, or authority to release, as soon as possible from the Duty Officer, Information Officer or person of higher rank

As soon as practical, notify Duty Section personnel of:

- All major arrests, major offences and other newsworthy items;
- Information recently supplied to the media;
- Developments possibly leading to a major incident;
- Emergency or dangerous conditions for the public;
- Developments possibly leading to emergency or dangerous conditions for the public.

Notify Records Bureau of a major news report.

GENERAL NEWS RELEASE

INITIAL RELEASE

The nature or type of incident (crime).

The location

Time of occurrence

Particulars of victim(s) (exceptions below)

At the officer's discretion:

- Weapons used, if applicable;
- Items taken or involved;
- Description of suspects, if any;
- Description of vehicle, if any;
- Further police action.

Investigating Unit

Time and location where further information may be obtained, if possible.

AFTER ARREST IS MADE

Particulars of accused

Charges laid

Particulars of crime, including time and location

Particulars of victim(s) or complainant (exceptions below)

Time and location of arrest

Particulars of arrest

Investigating Unit

Court location

Officers must not release the following:

- Identity of juveniles;

- The victim's identity:
  - in sex offences,
  - when infirm or mentally ill,
  - when next of kin have not been notified,
  - at investigating officer's request, when justified.
- Identity of witness;
  - an admission, confession or statement,
  - reputation or character,
  - previous record,
  - possible guilt or innocence,
  - a test, offered to, taken by or refused,
  - evidence the Investigator feels may prejudice the trial.

This administrative procedure conveys a definite view of the force's hierarchy of credibility. Their 'authorized personnel' are legally inscribed in this document as authorized knowers for news purposes. Thus, the news tendency to cite authorized knowers elevated in the hierarchy of credibility is not simply a matter of the persons to whom reporters 'naturally' gravitate for their own purposes. It is socially constructed and legally prescribed by the source organization itself.

The force members we interviewed underscored the fact that there is a clear hierarchy of credibility for news purposes. A police officer who was not authorized as a spokesperson under these provisions offered a justification of the arrangements as seen from 'below.'

Q: Have you ever issued a press release through your public affairs department?

A: Number one, I wouldn't attempt it. Now we're getting into internal politics. I don't have the rank for one. I may be involved in a situation that subsequently gets into the media but I would never issue the press release. I may have a part in putting it together because of my personal knowledge but it's always presented by a senior officer ... to get authority to talk about it. When I refer it to a senior officer and they don't have all of the information, they'll simply come back to myself or whoever else was involved and get the facts and then talk to the media.

Q: Well, why not let you just talk to the media?

A: I have a feeling they don't think we're capable. That we might say something out of line and maybe give the wrong impression and it reflects on the police department as a whole. They would prefer, as they've now indicated by putting together a public-affairs or public relations section, that they would prefer people with experience in that area, to deal with the public. A little more polished. They know what to say and when to say it. They also know where to get the information, accurately, efficiently, and so on.

Q: What do you think of that?

A: Sometimes I don't like it. I would prefer to say what I have to say but unfortunately that's based on emotion and it's not very professional and so in some cases it's better that a senior officer who has nothing to do with the situation, does the talking because there is no emotion involved ... [I]f the image of the department depends on what you say, how you say it, and the way you present yourself, then the department feels that somebody in a position, number one with rank, who would immediately get respect from their audience or at least attention from the audience, should handle it. They don't feel that a constable should give that kind of information ... I know the majority of officers, on my level, constable level, will not speak to the media. Again, for fear of being misquoted or being too emotionally involved in something so they come across poorly. Some officers will speak to the media, it doesn't matter what rank they hold. They will speak to the media and there's been no repercussions because of that from any of the senior officers, as long as it's been positive. If it's negative you hear about it regardless. If it's positive it's all right.

This respondent indicates that the administrative procedures were not the only source of control over police officers in talking to the news media, and that some talked regardless of the rules. Social scientists studying police (Wilson, 1968; Bittner, 1970; Manning, 1977; Ericson, 1981, 1981a, 1982; Reiner, 1985) emphasize that administrative rules tell officers what not to do but give little detailed direction on what specific action is most appropriate. For such direction police personnel look elsewhere. In this regard one of our respondents said his primary guidance was 'an excellent book, *Guide to the Use of the Media*, provided by the Ontario Ministry of Labour, which I refer to quite often and find to be a very handy tool.' In discussing force guidelines for the news media, another respondent said 'for every rule there's an exception to that rule.' This view is consistent with the police view of rules generally (ibid). Indeed, it is indicated in the preamble to the administrative procedure cited above: 'No instruction can possibly cover all eventualities. When in doubt, officers must use common sense.' At the core of the common sense was the need to traffic in positive images.

The force provided little in the way of formal education to police personnel regarding the news media. Since lower-ranking officers were not normally authorized to talk to reporters, the basic-training curriculum traditionally included nothing on the news media. Senior-ranking respondents said either that they had no formal training or that they had attended a one-day seminar on the news media at the Canadian Police College in Ottawa.

Formal Meetings

At the time of our field-work the police administration initiated another arrangement for news management. They organized occasional meetings between police managers and editors and producers from local news organizations to deal with issues and problems. The first meeting was to explain the reorganization of the public-affairs section planned in light of the management consultant's report. Subsquently it was designed as a 'high level' meeting among news managers from within both the police and the news organizations, although the editors and producers also brought along reporters. The intention of these meetings was to establish and lubricate channels for dealing with problems in police/media relations.

THE TWO CULTURES OF REPORTERS

As mentioned previously, there were two cultures of reporters on the police beat, each with different approaches to news management and different purposes to its work. One culture consisted of an inner circle of reporters, who based their operations in the police newsroom and established close affinities with police officers. The other culture comprised an outer circle of reporters who were based in their own news organizations' newsrooms, and whose relations with the police were marked by conflict and tension.

The Inner Circle

Members of the inner circle were from popular news outlets that gave considerable play to the reporting of crime incidents. These reporters were after primary facts about the nature of the crime, the persons involved, and investigative outcomes. They needed to develop co-operative relations with information officers and investigating officers to obtain factual updates that would allow them to meet story-production expectations of their producers and editors.

The inner circle was thus a haven for spot-news reporters whose news outlets required a large number of stories on the cheap. It was populated in particular by radio reporters whose news format provided little time or opportunity for interviews or analysis. One radio reporter of the inner circle, whom we observed over several shifts, was required to file six or seven stories each day for hourly newscasts. He was therefore oriented to crime incidents that would allow him to 'bag' his quota. We observed him choosing to cover a routine homicide case over a major continuing story that was receiving significant coverage in other news outlets, because that case was better tailored to what his medium and producer provided for. A typical practice was to find a series of routine crime 'fillers' that he could then update hourly over the day or have available 'for anytime use' in case other things he was working on proved unproductive.

Inner-circle reporters also sought stories sympathetic to the police viewpoint, or tertiary understanding. Tertiary understanding, addressing 'what it is like' for a police officer fighting crime, was easy to link with primary factual understanding about crime incidents. It was an inevitable consequence of long-term socialization through close proximity to police cultures. It served the reporters' need to give reciprocity to police officers who routinely supplied them with updated facts. The repertoire of inner-circle reporters rarely included explanations or secondary understanding. In this regard they were unlike the outer circle of reporters, whose frames centred upon the facts of police deviance and the proferring of explanations that would both account for it and foster police accountability.

The core members of the inner circle made the police newsroom, rather than their employers' newsrooms, their spatial, social, and cultural home. Many were set up to operate entirely from the police newsroom, without the need to return to their main newsrooms. One reporter had a scanner radio to listen to police and other emergency service calls, that he shared with others in the police newsroom. Radio reporters telephoned or 'dictated' their stories to their main newsrooms and had no direct working contact with reporters from their main newsrooms except when other reporters were drafted into the beat for a big case or because of an extra workload. Reporters functioned as their own assignment editors, keeping their own clipping files from newspapers, and building a date file for scheduled events. Some reporters kept a 'statistical file' also. This file, updated daily, was subdivided into homicides, robberies, and fire deaths. For homicides, for example, a list was kept on top of the file giving each new incident a number and recording the date, address, and a synopsis of what happened. One reporter had a similar file for each year of the previous ten. This record enabled him to say, 'Today we had the nth homicide of the year, and this is an increase [or decrease] of n over the last year to this date.'

Reporters of the inner circle expressed great affinity with the police. This affinity was cultivated over a long time by both police and reporters. One reporter had been on the beat for three decades, and most of the others for many years. Wanted posters were hung on or by their desks. In accord with the individual police officer, they dreamed of identifying villains and being involved in a big scoop, even though years went by without it happening. Police officers of all ranks and specializations were addressed on a first-name basis, and inner-circle reporters in turn were familiar to these police officers. When a telephone call was made, there was usually recognition without having to say who was calling.

Reporters of the inner circle wrote articles for police newspapers and magazines, sat on a committee to nominate the police officer of the month, organized parties for police and reporters, and arranged for police officers to appear on special broadcasts such as 'talk shows.' Reporters sometimes consulted with police officers about the advisibility of including or excluding information from their stories. They gave police officers tips on investigations in exchange for exclusives or scoops when the timing was right. They gave the police access to their films and videos as these might help identify suspicious persons or culprits. They engaged in helpful editing – for example, blocking the telecast of an item involving a police officer who was now working undercover and did not want to be identified publicly as a police officer. Special effort was made to write stories favourable to the police when there were serious allegations of police misconduct (sometimes simultaneous to these allegations being sustained by reporters in the outer circle). Care was taken to cite investigating officers in stories, playing on their egos in exchange for the play they had given the reporter by revealing the latest update on their investigations. Coverage of police news conferences regarding crackdowns (e.g., on impaired driving and on shoplifting) was given obligingly. In sum, members of the inner circle willingly joined with members of the police force in accomplishing their policing tasks.

Reporters who were regulars in the police newsroom were deemed reliable in the sense that they would espouse the police perspective. Other reporters and their news outlets were judged as not so reliable, and were talked about negatively by many police respondents. The line of demarcation was simple because the judgment was simple: were reporters and their news outlets producing material sympathetic and helpful to the police?

[Names a television station of inner circle] are pretty accurate but I find [names television station of outer circle], I don't know, I think they're very left-wing people. I think they are trying to put a message across, whether we like it or whether we don't. I don't find them as fair in their reporting ... I don't particularly do an interview to entertain the public. I do it because I'm looking at it from a selfish point of view as well. I'm trying to get a message across, something that's going to help me and my job ... [Offering an example concerning newspapers] Every time I get a picture of a bank hold-up suspect where a photograph is taken by a bank camera, I give it to all the media and make a press release. Or if it goes to headquarters then it's given out to all members of the media, the newspapers, the television stations, for publication, and naturally I'm giving it out because I want people to identify them ... and hopefully we'll cut down on robberies and get people arrested that are committing them. I found the best co-operation I've had is from [names newspaper of inner circle]. They've printed every one. [Names another newspaper of the inner circle] has printed most of them. [Names a newspaper of the outer circle] I've seen only one because they like to print, in my opinion, what they want to print. Their reporters will interview you and they're not really interested in what you're trying to tell them. They're after the sinister things, 'What's behind what he's telling me?'

A senior administrator noted how inner-circle members were responsible and trustworthy, which he equated with accepting police 'requests' on what to report or omit. He attributed these qualities to the fact that these reporters were interdependent with the police through long-term relations.

I suppose there's more access, if you like, to those particular people [of the inner circle]. You go in for lunch and they're maybe having a coffee in the cafeteria or you pass them in the parking lot and pass the time of day. So, you've had sort of an ongoing rapport and a closer relationship. It's like anything, if you work with people or see people on a daily basis, you establish a better relationship ... [I]t's like anything, if you want something, it's a lot easier to deal with someone that you're on a first-name basis, or with someone that you know, than with a total stranger ... I think it is more responsible and factual, and rightly so I suppose. One of the things is they're in contact here all the time and I guess their livelihood depends on, let's be realistic about it, on the contacts within the force and the information they could get. But I think the thing I'd like to say about most of those people is that one can discuss a matter with them and if certain issues come up during discussion, to give them a better insight into the whole story, they will use a lot of common sense and are very responsible in the way they report things, which I can't say for some people that have never worked the police beat. So I think there is more of a rapport, if you like, or more confidence and more trust, in those people that work the police beat ... [I]f we request something of them, generally our request would be condoned and accepted by them.

Another respondent pointed out that inner-circle reporters had a good sense of embarrassing or damaging statements that had 'slipped out,' and were willing to keep them from editors. 'I might say something that couldn't be quoted. [I'm] scrambling to, you know, cut the tape off, and [they're saying] "What if my editor gets this?' that sort of thing. So, we've got a pretty good understanding, pretty good relationship.'

Inner-circle reporters had regular, and in some cases daily, contact with senior police administrators, unit heads, and investigators. They had a greater degree of contact with the police hierarchy and élite members of the force than that available to the vast majority of police officers. In this respect the inner circle of police reporters was very much a part of the police organization.

Their cultural spirit was with the police, matching where they spent their time and who they most often related to socially. Reporters of the outer circle, as well as journalists on general assignment, talked disparagingly of police-beat reporters for being more like police than reporters, and for being too close to their sources and therefore unprofessional. Translated, this meant the access to police by inner-circle reporters was based on friendship rather than on professionalism. '[W]hat sets friendship apart from a business or professional relationship is that the domains open are circumscribed by cues as to how far and how much intrusion into private space is possible. The rules of professional conduct and training in professional practice foster personal disengagement and asymmetry or lack of reciprocity' (Reiss, 1987: 34).

Sherizen remarks that 'Crime reporters become more like the police than like other reporters while the police, to a large degree, remain constant to their police occupational identity' (1978: 211; see also Chibnall, 1977). While this may be true, police information officers said they were subject to gibes from their police colleagues for becoming too much like reporters. One police information officer stated:

> I've talked to reporters in a social context who are viewed by their news
> directors as being more police officers than they are news reporters. There's
> a real concern in at least two radio stations in Toronto, who have the im-
> pression that their boys may not be kicking back all the news to the news
> bureau in the stations, because they're here at headquarters and they're so
> closely allied with the police, and things are nice and friendly, very chummy,
> and they begin to think, geez, dealing with these guys is just like dealing
> with policemen. It's interesting when officers out in the field offices, they're
> dealing with me with the same suspicions and at arm's length, as if I am a
> reporter.

By all accounts, then, there was a special affinity between the inner circle of police-beat reporters and police officers. When the values of journalism collided with the values of police culture, the police culture usually pre-vailed. This situation was very different from the court beat, where reporters and sources kept considerable distance. On the court beat, reporters did not become acculturated to the values of the legal culture, or aspire to be like lawyers, Crown attorneys, or judges. They maintained the respect of their colleagues in journalism, and the tolerance of their sources. On the police beat the inner circle of reporters were acculturated into the police culture and acted in accord with police officers. They lost the respect of many of their colleagues in journalism, but gained the trust of their sources. The trust of police sources in turn provided many gains for these reporters. Given what they were after – primary factual information about crime incidents and tertiary empathetic understanding about the police lot – such trusting relations seemed essential.

In talking about his relations with inner-circle reporters, one police respondent stated, 'I'll give 'em anything.' While this was unlikely to be true literally, it represented the sentiment that these reporters were 'on side,' as well as the trust that they had the sense to keep sensitive knowledge off the record. This same respondent said he often gave tips to inner-circle reporters, with mutual knowledge that he was seeking publicity for the good work of his men and his unit. He used the inner circle of reporters to turn the bad news of serious crime into the good news of heroic and efficient police.

[I'm proactive with the inner circle] if I want to sell my men, I guess, to be honest with you. If I want to give a good pinch, because my men have done a good job, then I'll contact them all. And I don't have any preference on how I contact them. As a matter of fact they answer each other's phones ... So, it's to put the police image up good. I wouldn't phone them if it was something wrong! ... [My] men had worked for two years undercover on a large drug case, and thirty million dollars in drugs, and two years ago they got this but we couldn't disclose it until they were before the courts because it would burn the undercover men. I contacted [all the inner-circle reporters], and through Public Affairs, recommended them for the policeman of the month, which the police set up [and inner-circle reporters adjudicate] ... I contacted the individual reporters and said, 'Look, there's one thing you don't know and it won't become public knowledge, but keep this in mind.' I said, 'Both these men, because of their dedication, one got mono and the other got a blood disorder, just strictly from lack of sleep and irregular eating over the last two years, and their families suffered, and I'd like you to keep that in mind.' I guess I was lobbying for my men and they were chosen policemen of the month from that. Plus they got a commendation from the commission just for their dedicated work ... I felt down the road I had to build them up somehow. How do I build them up except lobbying and phoning the press and saying, 'They did a good job here, do you want a good story?'

Inner-circle reporters functioned informally as public-relations consultants. They were asked for advice on proactive strategies and tactics that would result in good news for the police.

Inner-circle reporters were often given the advantage. For example, simply by using his police-newsroom telephone to call his force contacts, a reporter was able to obtain more current and detailed information about a homicide than was available to reporters on the scene. On another occasion we followed a reporter, who was not a member of the inner circle, as she worked on a story about a homicide. This reporter was repeatedly denied information by police. In contrast, as was evident in his hourly update reports, an inner-circle radio reporter received considerable information from police sources, including details in advance of a scheduled news conference. He thereby clearly took the lead in the story over other new outlets. The reporter we observed eventually had to rely on this reporter's broadcast accounts to fill in the details the police did not supply to her directly.

The police also gave inner-circle reporters the advantage of publicity in police publications, including articles or photographs in which the reporter was a source for the police publication, as well as articles authored by the reporter. Within this hermeneutic inner circle, the police were both sources in, and authors of, news items; in turn, reporters were sources and authors in police publications.

The Outer Circle

Journalists of the outer circle were distinguished by the fact that they worked for 'quality' news outlets and did not make use of the police newsroom. They were a very loosely organized group, since they worked from their own respective newsrooms and only met by chance when they attended the same press conference or converged on the same event. Nevertheless they were united culturally, sharing a view that they were what the inner circle was not: professionally and analytically more detached from police sources, with the important mission of policing the police rather than only policing with them.

Journalists of the outer circle expressed their distance from the values and practices of the inner circle. Negative talk about inner-circle reporters typically occurred as the outer-circle reporter was working on a story that brought him into contact with them. The talk centred on the way inner-circle reporters were like the police, supported the police, and were in effect conduit pipes for their bureaucratic propaganda. Similar talk also arose while an outer-circle reporter was working on a story critical of the police and faced problems of access or threats aimed at censorship. On these occasions the reporter justified his mission, and the trouble he was experiencing, by saying what he was doing was of value both professionally and for society, unlike what inner-circle reporters did.

Outer-circle reporters minimized the significance of their exclusion from the inner circle. They argued that a close affinity with police sources, which admittedly yielded insights, was not acceptable if it was at the expense of their professional values. They also emphasized that quality news outlets had relatively little interest in the type of primary and tertiary understanding that popular news outlets gained from their close relations with police. The facts they valued had to be pursued by different means, and in the terms of a different culture.

Outer-circle reporters were backed by their superiors in this regard. A newsroom manager talked derisively of inner-circle reporters, saying they not only collaborated in police censorship but, through acculturation with police, were subject to self-censorship. In contrast, she mentioned three recent incidents in which one of her reporters had published against police wishes, and suffered the consequences of threats as well as actual exclusion by police and inner-circle reporters.

> What you've got in news gathering is a beat system which causes the re-porter, who is the police reporter, to get to the point where he censors him-self. He censors information. That has been an absolute hideous spectre for me. I can't stand it. We've had three instances where the cops have called us up and said if you publish that we'll cut you off, and I've published every time, because I don't wanna be in a position where I'm going to publish what they want me to publish and not publish what *has to be* published, which is the situation that [names four inner circle reporters] find them-selves in. And those four guys give my guys a rough time because we go and publish stuff which they don't publish. So, in a sense, they're becoming members of the police force.

The police literature makes it clear that the police organization is char-acterized by a number of subcultures, formed socially according to special-ization and rank (Ericson, 1981, 1982; Punch, 1983, 1985; Reiner, 1985). Most fundamentally, there is a division between line officers' 'cop culture' and senior officers' 'management culture' (Reuss-Ianni and Ianni, 1983). The cop culture is oriented to the policeman's lot, providing recipe knowledge about how to recognize problems and take decisions without getting into trouble. The management culture is oriented to the public culture, dealing in indicators of police performance, especially efficiency in crime control. Since police managers are unable to directly supervise or control the work of police officers, their work is characterized by ritual and ceremony, with special emphasis given to 'institutional display documentation' (Van Maanen, 1983). 'When little of the actual work of subordinates is seen only the results can be admired or scorned' (ibid: 291; see also Manning, 1977, 1980).

The inner circle of reporters were oriented to both of these cultures of policing. They sought to convey the everyday lot of the police officer in the workaday world of crime-fighting. Through the reporting of crime incidents and their investigation by police, and through cathected scenarios of police-officer heroics for the public good, inner-circle reporters helped the image-building of police managers. As well, they reproduced the police managers' official statistics (e.g., arrest rates, clearance rates) and attended their news conferences to announce policing initiatives.

In contrast, the outer circle of reporters was oriented primarily to the management culture. These reporters focused on questions of efficiency and good management. This orientation was the one their newsrooms took to any organization: searching for procedural strays, the anomaly that displayed the norm, as a way of suggesting control remedies and seeing that they were put in place (Ericson et al, 1987). It was a normal part of their approach to policing organizational life. A news manager in a 'quality' outlet summed this up in the case of the police:

> [A] police force deals in secrecy, they only allow us to know what they
> want us to know as an official organization. They'll only tell us what they
> think is safe for us to know, when it gets down to a one-on-one between
> an individual policeman and the guy that's covering the beat ... [T]here's
> a realization on my part that we can't know everything that's going on in
> the police force. What we want to know is the things they don't want us to
> know because they've screwed up, that's number one. You know, everybody,
> nobody wants to let out a screw-up, right? This organization doesn't, any
> organization doesn't want to let that out. But, you know, that has to be
> published as well because that's in the public interest. Because we have to
> assume that we have to hold the force accountable for what it does, as well
> as the people who are the bosses of the force, they have to keep the force
> accountable.

With this orientation to his work, the police reporter in the quality news outlet had a very different work experience than his counterpart in the inner circle. There was in effect a 'running battle' between outer-circle reporters and the police. In a quality newspaper we studied in depth, the origin of the running battle was deemed to be the newspaper's contribution to the exposure of systematic violence and other wrongdoing by the local police, leading to an official enquiry (Morand, 1976). With each instance of police non-cooperation with this newspaper's reporters, reference was made to this turning point, even though it had occurred many years earlier. Reporters from a 'quality' television station and a 'quality' radio station had a similar experience. They engaged in forays into the police organization to expose mismanagement, injustice, or wrongdoing. They were repelled and suffered derision and exclusion for a while, before attempting another shot.

The derision and exclusion were not just from the police alone, but also from inner-circle reporters. An outer circle radio reporter said there was col-laboration among inner-circle reporters regarding what they would or would not report, and that they attempted to control other reporters to follow their decisions on these matters. He remarked that he was ostracized from the inner circle and the access it enjoyed because of his unwillingness to collaborate with its members. An outer-circle television reporter we studied over several months continually faced ostracism by inner-circle reporters. On one occasion he asked an inner-circle reporter if he could use his telephone in the police newsroom. The inner-circle reporter responded angrily, making a derisive comment about the reporter's stories and telling him to 'get lost.' In his absence, inner-circle reporters talked negatively about him. He was described as a 'terrible man' who did not get along with some police. After a particular news conference, inner-circle reporters returned to the police newsroom and complained about this reporter 'spoiling' their tapes and cutting into their time by asking his own questions, thereby making the news conference too long. They said he should be 'humble' instead of acting like a 'bull in a china shop.' This complaint was as much a matter of their animosity towards what this reporter *represented* as a criticism of the particulars of his working style.

The approach of outer-circle reporters sometimes also resulted in disagreements and conflicts within their own newsrooms. For example, after exposing police-security deficiencies in protecting delegates to a major international conference and turning down police requests not to broadcast the story, a quality news outlet suffered repercussions. Shortly afterwards they were denied access by police on an unrelated major continuing story, and the police in turn 'spoon fed' an inner-circle reporter from another outlet all the essential ingredients of this major development. The reporter who was working on the major continuing story complained repeatedly about losing the competitive edge he had developed through hard work in nurturing sources. He now faced repeated blockage from sources in the police. On one occasion, as his frustration grew after he realized that an inner-circle reporter from another outlet had 'scooped' him again, he complained bitterly to the police reporter who did the security story. He exclaimed that the producers always seemed to 'burn' sources on 'small' stories and thereby missed the 'big' stories. He likened this practice to cutting off one's nose to spite one's face, and argued that decisions to 'burn' the police or any other source should always be taken with an eye to other stories being developed by other members of the newsroom.

While outer-circle reporters experienced many difficulties from several directions, and were experienced by police, inner-circle reporters, and some newsroom colleagues as irksome and troublesome, it was not all conflict and turmoil. It is arguable that their emphasis on police propriety and efficiency through the portrayal of deviance served in the long run to enhance police management. The typical response to police malfeasance is to demand more resources in the form of more laws or rules, more equipment, and more personnel. In the administered society, with its managerialist state, progressive reform politics is typically based on the assumption that more will work where less has not. In the long run and in the aggregate, outer-circle reporters contribute to this reform politics on behalf of police-management. They actually join with the police management culture in the policing of efficiency and propriety (Punch, 1985; Ericson, 1987)

There were other signs of quality news outlets having an affinity with the police. They gave considerable play to institutionalized crime-control strategies, such as the annual Christmas-time crackdown on impaired drivers. A quality television station we studied in depth had an anchor who sat on the committee to select the new civilian head of the police public-affairs unit. This same organization also went to considerable expense to equip some camera-crew cars with radio scanners that could pick up the radio communications of the police and other emergency services. Some of their cameramen spent time cruising the city streets with their radio scanners on. As did officers in patrol cars, they waited for emergency calls they could respond to reactively. Members of this television newsroom viewed this practice as an effort to match a competing 'popular' television newsroom that did the same thing, and as a significant drift in the popular direction. In summary, some quality news outlets were oriented to some popular and dramatic aspects of police news, as well as to policing the police. They appreciated that the crime discourse of the police (Wheeler, 1986) is too central to the essence of news itself to ignore.

NEWSWORTHINESS

One central focus on the police beat is the 'eternal recurrence' (Rock, 1973) of the facts of crime, including, especially, major crime incidents, but also patterns and trends in crime and criminality. This emphasis on primary understanding of crime is supplemented by tertiary understanding of what it is like to be involved in crime as an offender or victim, and what it is like for the police officer to be 'fighting crime.' This genre was adopted by inner-circle reporters, who fancied themselves as being literally 'in the trenches' with 'the boys in blue' as they fought 'the war on crime.' This approach represents crime reporting as popular drama, directed at the traditional goals of the news media to simultaneously entertain, inform, and acknowledge order.

Another central focus is the police organization and vocation as it participates in the political culture. As agents of law, order, and morality, the police have to be shown constantly to be acting in a legal, orderly, and moral fashion. Hence, also as 'eternal recurrence,' the media spotlight focuses on whether the police are acting lawfully, with procedural propriety. Concern is with the orderliness of police operations, especially how efficient they appear to be in the suppression of crime, and whether they are fulfilling the promise, embodied in the Toronto police motto, to 'serve and protect.' Concern is also with the morality of police officers, visualizing whether the moral order they symbolize is demonstrated in their behaviour, whether their deeds match the promise, embodied in the RCMP motto, to 'uphold the right.' This genre was adopted by outer-circle reporters and their quality news outlets, as they searched for procedural strays who could advance the thrust towards more orderliness. This approach is the stuff of fourth-estate or institutional reporting, policing organizational life to effect social control and stability.

The same elements can be revealed by focusing on other organizations and occupations. However, most other organizations and occupations are less dominant than the police politically and culturally, and they are therefore decentred by the news media in preference for the police. No news organization can afford to ignore the police, while they can to a degree ignore social workers, citizens' activist groups, criminologists, teachers, private security personnel, and the many others who give shape to crime, deviance, and social control. 'Many professional groups have contact with crime, but it is only the police who claim a *professional* expertise in the "war against crime," based on daily *personal* experience. This exclusive and particular "double expertise" seems to give police spokesmen especially authoritative credence' (Hall et al, 1978: 68).

External Considerations

The broad nature of the police mandate to reproduce order (Ericson, 1982) and the politicization of the police (Reiner, 1985) ensure that they are perpetually entangled in cultural and political processes that have origins and implications external to their organization. They inevitably become involved when these wider processes are deemed newsworthy, and are called upon to act as experts in both deviant designations and control solutions. Police participation in workers' strikes is illustrative. The police are not only shown literally to be 'the thin blue line' between order and chaos on the picket line, they are also asked for their opinions about the strategies and tactics of the opposing sides and about their own involvement. For example, in a preliminary analysis of television-news coverage of the British coal strike of 1984, Tracey (1984: 43) found 'that the police have been a powerful third force in provoking the issues covered by the television news. In fact, the police have stimulated *more* issues than the NCB [National Coal Board] and MacGregor [the NCB chairman] combined.'

The more prominent the police have become in dealing with major strife and divisions in society, the more politicized they appear and the less able they are to talk as if they are mere legal agents (Reiner, 1985). One of our respondents pointed to this dilemma as significant in dealing with the news media, especially quality outlets that tend to base their judgments of newsworthiness on political criteria external to the police. Taking the example of the abortion issue, this respondent stated, 'We start getting into almost a political playground ... [which] has nothing to do with the law. The law might be mentioned in a paragraph or two but the rest of it is "and the police swooped down," you know, "there were women embarrassed because they were in there," and it all becomes a very emotional issue, not a legal issue.' This respondent believed it is not the place of the police to comment on wider political issues, except in emphasizing their law-enforcement duty. Other police officers expressed similar disquiet with outer circle reporters who did not keep their criteria of newsworthiness within the confines of the role of the police as law officers. Their tendency to shift the police away from legal discourse and the rhetoric of crime control and onto other ideological terrains made it difficult for the police to talk as if they were simply acting within their legitimate confines.

Several respondents indicated that 'quality' outlets were especially likely to judge the newsworthiness of police activity in terms of external 'political' criteria. An information officer depicted a quality newspaper and a quality television station in these terms:

[Names quality newspaper] Their person assigned to cover the police ... is really, from my point of view, interested in the police as a political organization within the municipal-provincial structure ... more interested I would think in politically motivated activities, race relations, [homosexual] bath house raids because of [the] political overtones alleged, policing strategies, theoretical things. Rather than coming in and reporting on somebody's house getting broken into ... [names quality television station], my feeling is that they might have people who'd be more inclined to do the political research, if you know what I mean. They've also got a political director down there, who, I would be commendable toward him, he has some soft spots toward the police force I think, but is also a good political critic and would look at the police force from a political point of view. And granted, being a 7,000-member police force in this province, I mean we are the biggest ... and this being the provincial capital, and the legislature's here, and everything else, we have some political implications and we are controlled by political activity. So, I can see people having the need to keep an eye on that.

In some instances police officers did not differentiate between popular and quality news outlets in these terms. Several respondents made reference to a moral panic about attacks on women. Over several months, four murders involving women as victims, and the brutal rape of a woman, were linked as a news theme. This coverage provided a daily menu of news reports in all

media, fed by a variety of political interests (Voumvakis and Ericson, 1984).
Respondents emphasized that in spite of police efforts to minimize the panic
or extinguish it altogether, all news outlets persisted with the theme and the
political role of the police in it. Several respondents said that reporters were
given trend statistics by police indicating that numbers of serious assaults on
women were no higher during the period of the panic than in recent years, but
reporters ignored this for a considerable time and then gave it only minor play
(this was confirmed in our observations). As one respondent said, this practice
was akin to that of the media of responding to a complaint about inaccuracy by
printing a retraction: the retraction receives less play and has less impact than
the original story – 'the damage has been done.' From the police viewpoint
the damage was creating public fear, especially among women, and bringing
political pressure on the police Force by making it appear ineffective in face
of the inability to clear these crimes through arrest. Respondents used this
as a 'classic' example of forces external to them affecting newsworthiness.
They believed that the main external forces at work were news media interests
('sensationalism sells papers'), and the interests of various groups in society
who used the occasion to obtain media exposure in which they blended their
causal explanation of the attacks on women with their own political causes.
The police perspective on the matter lost out in the process.

Respondents also saw some specific components of the police beat as
newsworthy because of political criteria. In particular they thought the meetings of the police commission were covered in terms of a political agenda
rather than in terms of criteria internal to police operations. This view was
supported by the fact that police-commission meetings were often covered
by reporters on the city-hall beat as well as, or instead of, by police-beat
reporters. Coverage focused on key politicians or other public figures on the
commission, and on high-profile citizens or citizens' groups making representations. Both commissioners and citizens' groups used the regular public
meetings of the commission as occasions for publicity for their own political
causes, of which the police were only a partial component. As seen by a
police commissioner we interviewed, the chairman of the commission, and
the Metro chairman who sat as a commissioner were highest profile. Even
the television cameras were set up literally to focus on them.

The understanding that reporters often cover the police in terms of newsworthiness criteria generated externally is taken into account when the police
want to use the news for their own purposes. When the police wish to lobby
for a reform and more resources, they do not lose sight of prevailing priorities
in the political culture and popular culture, and how the newsworthiness of
these priorities can be converted to police use. Police strategies in this regard
are explored in our subsequent analyses of the influence of news texts.

Internal Considerations

External aspects of newsworthiness, deriving from popular culture and political culture, are entwined with internal considerations of police procedures and operations. In a society obsessed with procedural propriety (Habermas, 1975), and with the police as *the* symbol of what is proper, the news focus on police deviance is inevitable.

The focus on police deviance is of two types. First, there are accounts of police officers violating the law, failing to conform to administrative procedure, and failing to conform to criminal procedure. When the deviance is exposed, reporters turn to police administrators and ask what they are going to do about it. One alternative for the administrator is to put it down to a few rotten apples, using the occasion to show the overall purity of the barrel (Brock, 1968; Ericson, 1981a; Punch, 1985). Another alternative, and one that has gained currency in recent years, is to argue that while police officers did violate the law, they were doing so for admirable law-enforcement purposes in the public interest. Their acts were in keeping with the expectations of their organization, and should be excused for that reason. This 'noble motives' formulation permeated government publications, court hearings, and news accounts regarding the illegal activities of RCMP Security Service officers (Brodeur, 1981, 1983; Mandel, 1982, 1983).

Second, there are accounts suggesting the police organization is inefficient. Crime waves are used to suggest police ineffectiveness in crime detection. In this discourse of organization failure and mismanagement there is no attention to long-term trends or to how crime is an artefact of police organization (Kitsuse, 1964; Ericson, 1981). News focuses simply on whether 'crime' is 'up' or 'down,' and whether it is being 'cleared' by arrest. This focus becomes part of the daily menu of crime reporting: for example, the latest robbery is tallied with others for the year and compared to the tally for the previous year to indicate whether robbery is 'up' or 'down.' The latest arrest for robbery is declared along with reference to clearance rates for robbery to indicate police investigative prowess, or lack of it. A grander occasion for the same thing is the news conference associated with the release of the force's annual report and crime statistics. Police administrators are adept at converting such occasions to organizational advantage, calling for more resources regardless of the direction of the data (Murphy, 1985). News focus on police procedural deviance and administrative inefficiency, while causing temporary annoyance, serves in the long run to enhance the stability of the police organization and the direction for reform it desires.

News-Media Considerations

We have indicated previously that popular news outlets were oriented to crime-incident reports and primary and tertiary understanding, whereas quality news outlets gave emphasis to policing the police. This orientation was not exclusive. Some popular news outlets did major stories investigating police wrongdoing. As on the court beat, they did so by using a reporter from the main newsroom who was not a police-beat regular. Quality news outlets also gave space to crime incidents. This was especially the case with quality broadcast outlets. The visual capacities of television are so attuned to the sensational, dramatic, and entertaining that it cannot ignore crime and disaster coverage. In contrast, a quality newspaper we studied in depth gave relatively little play to crime incidents. It did have a policy of giving at least a 'brief' report on each murder incident in the city, which sometimes expanded into extended reports and features if there was a connection to a favoured theme (e.g., organized crime) or popular issue (e.g., assaults on women) (Ericson et al, 1987, and forthcoming).

In the eyes of police respondents, both crime-incident reporting and the reporting of instances of police deviance and (in)efficiency are part of the news-media bias towards the dramatic and sensational. They saw the dramatic and sensational as predominant in reporters' judgments of newsworthiness, regardless of what they themselves tried to do to introduce other criteria or considerations. As mentioned previously, these elements were viewed by respondents as a dominant feature in the reporting of an attack-on-women moral panic in the city, and there was little they could do to downplay it. A respondent indicated that visions of the dramatic and sensational were also evident in routine coverage of crime incidents and trends. He talked about being interviewed after a bank robbery in the city:

> [T]hey were saying that there had been a bank robbery, that we've had
> 187 robberies of banks this year ... compared with 67 last year ... [I]t was
> more, I don't know if you'd call it gloating or sensationalism, that this is
> getting to be a terrible city ... [T]hey always compare Toronto with Montreal
> and Montreal has always been considered the hold-up city of Canada and
> I always, on every interview, I mentioned that the people of this city don't
> have to be alarmed. In Montreal when there's a bank hold-up, the people
> know it's a bank hold-up, it's a commando-style raid where people come
> with guns, quite often with submachine guns, terrorize the staff ... And
> I said, 'Yes we have had a number of hold-ups this year, there's been a
> dramatic increase in bank robberies but we're not looking, in Toronto, at
> commando-style raids.' And I always have my figures to back up what
> I'm saying. That this year, for instance, I would say 75 per cent of the
> robberies have been committed by people with notes, note passers. So,
> a person goes into a bank here with a note. The only ones that know a
> robbery's occurring is the teller who's being robbed and the person who's

committing the robbery. No gun is seen, it's just a matter of passing notes. It's more like a theft than a robbery. So, we're talking about a different style of robbery altogether than what we used to experience in Toronto and what is experienced every day in Montreal ... [T]here's not the impending danger that there is in Montreal. But it was never printed ... because I think that it's more attractive, more newsworthy to say the bank has been robbed and let the public figure out whether it's been with a gun or a note or whatever ... One of the stations in particular really dramatized it. When it came on the news it showed hooded gunmen rushing into a bank and the music, the drama-type music with the beating drums and everything behind it. And it showed flicks, and these were actual pictures taken during robberies from bank cameras and it almost made them look as if they were moving like a jerking movement with the accompanying music. Very frightful if you were watching it. You know, they were real robberies but they weren't Toronto robberies. These were Montreal robberies they were showing, that they got these photographs from, I think, the Canadian Bankers' Association. They were not Toronto robberies, but they led the public to think they were Toronto robberies.

Several respondents understood that this emphasis on the dramatic and sensational was in turn connected to 'what sells' the news. They appreciated that crime, and police work in dealing with it, is a staple of news production because it is intrinsically interesting and entertaining in popular culture. Police officers believed that the need of the news business to be dramatic, sensational, and entertaining is paramount. While they worked hard to visualize how they could convert such news-business imperatives into their own criteria of value in the selling of the police, they felt that had only limited effect. This impression was conveyed by an officer in public affairs, who saw the main impetus for news demand coming from news organizations rather than the police. In his eyes even news releases generated by the police were tailored to meet news-media requirements more than, or rather than, police requirements. 'We have to react proactively to the needs of the news media, in general that's the whole concept behind it [our operations].' Moreover, among what was generated by police, the reporters controlled selection, rather than simply conveying it in conduit-pipe fashion. 'Now we're in the position where we publicize almost everything and a tremendous amount of it isn't used at all. Unfortunately a lot of the positive areas are not used.'

These statements indicate that the police, in keeping with journalists, are severely circumscribed by media logic and media formats (Altheide, 1985; Meyrowitz, 1985). The police information officer wishing to achieve news communication is much like the novice reporter learning to write well enough to get published (Ericson et al, 1987). She studies news, consults with more

experienced colleagues, consults with reporters, and tests out certain texts to
see if they are published and how they are edited. As understood by a police
respondent, it is a matter of conforming to news-media criteria rather than
simply passing on knowledge as it would be formulated for internal police
purposes. It is the particular news outlet that ultimately controls whether
something will be communicated and how it will be communicated. 'If you're
trying to accomplish something then you've got to sell that particular message
or idea ... you've got to make that seem urgent and interesting to the person
in the media and hopefully you'll be able to phrase it in such a way that
that person will be able to use what you're saying in an enlightened way in
a broadcast or a story. So, you've got to in a sense assist the media person
in getting the message out because you've got to sort of catch their fancy,
whether it be a catchy phrase, or terminology, or whatever, so that they will
get the message out.'

ORIGINS OF STORY IDEAS

It is clear that on the police beat, as Graber (1980: 47) notes, 'Reporters
rarely stray from what their police contacts supply.' However, we differ with
Graber's statement that 'The bulk of stories ... sound like copies from the
police blotter ... [because] that is what they are' (ibid). As we have seen,
police-beat reporters of both the inner and outer circles had a complex web of
police contacts beyond the public-affairs unit, and their stories about police
went well beyond the reproduction of major-occurrence reports. The police
beat in a bureaucratic police force provides a large number and variety of
sources for story ideas, and these were tapped routinely by reporters.

Inner-circle reporters seemed to be subject to little direct influence from
their own editors in terms of story ideas. In relation to their own newsroom,
they were autonomous from direct supervision and control, and yet compelled
to produce the daily menu of dramatic crime incidents and cathected scenarios
of police heroics. Inner-circle reporters shared story ideas with each other
routinely, although there was an expectation that the person who had done
the 'legwork' on a novel item would get the 'scoop' of broadcasting or
publishing before the others; and that anyone who took ideas routinely was
still required to do his own legwork on a story. Those who deviated from
this practice were confronted directly, and ostracized until they 'pulled their
weight.'

Outer-circle reporters operated from their own newsrooms, and hence
were not autonomous from their city-desk assignment editors. They were
typically treated in the same way as general-assignment reporters. They frequently received their story ideas from their assignment editors, who in turn
were dependent on all the usual sources of that role: more senior editors and

producers, newspaper clippings, police releases, scanner radios on their desks that were tuned into emergency services, anonymous tips, and so on (Ericson et al, 1987). Outer-circle reporters exchanged little with each other. Without a common spatial location, they had few social occasions to set up the trust and reciprocity required for this purpose. Moreover, since their stories were often idiosyncratic forays into some deviant practice by police, and in that respect were 'original,' they did not wish to share with others. Often these stories also failed to excite the 'pack' mentality.

Organizations connected to the police function were also a source of story ideas for all reporters. Police-commission meetings were attended regularly. Reporters we observed viewed these meetings as well-framed and -orchestrated 'shows' for public-culture consumption. They were the functional equivalent of news conferences, usually consisting of an enumeration of official policy and congratulating officers on their good work. Reporters noted that the real work of the commission was accomplished in back-region meetings not open to them or other members of the public (cf McMahon and Ericson, 1987). At times individual commissioners were contacted as sources of ideas or background information, as well as for direct citation. Police commissioners joined the police in their affinity with inner circle reporters. As a police commissioner stated to us in interview: 'I have some friends who are reporters and they're more connected with the police-commission activities ... [names two inner-circle reporters] and one or two others that you see up there all the time and get to know ... And if something tends to come up in between meetings that has received a lot of attention from the media, they might call me up and ask me how I feel about it ... it happens quite frequently.'

The office of the Commissioner of Public Complaints against the Police was also an official source of story ideas (ibid; McMahon, 1987). This office occasionally conducted public hearings on allegations of misconduct by police officers, and these were attended by reporters. This operation was of special interest to outer-circle reporters because of their orientation to police wrongdoing and its remedy. Indeed, this newly created office was a means of rationalizing and cooling out the burgeoning political thrust for policing the police that was sustained by publicity given to more serious and systematic instances of police wrongdoing. By providing an official channel for complaints against the police, it served to channel outer-circle reporters into the grooves of officialdom.

The coroner's office was another police source, sometimes of great significance because of the coroner's role in homicide investigations. At times this office was a source of information the police would not release, advancing story ideas that remained enclosed by sources within the force. Victims, and the relatives of victims of homicide and other serious violence, were

The Police 123

sometimes also contacted for the purpose of generating information the police were not making available to reporters.

Regions and Closures

PATROLLING THE FACTS

The police are the primary definers of crime and its control to the public. They generate the phenomenon they subsequently control (Lundsgaarde, 1977; Ericson, 1981); that is, they develop the system of classification concerning what constitutes crime, crime rates, and case clearance. They account for their work in these terms, both within the law-enforcement system and to the public. Indeed, the police expend a considerable proportion of their resources on knowledge control, fine-tuning their account ability in order to achieve accountability in the legal system and public culture (Ericson and Shearing, 1986). There is an elaborate system of internal reporting to the point where officers become 'paper police': they spend more time writing accounts of their investigative activity than in the actual investigative activity itself (Ericson, 1981). Members of the public – including journalists and criminologists – are routinely placed in the position of being secondary definers, having to address crime as classified by police. The discourse of crime and crime control is the prerogative of police, and all non-police accounts of it are treated as less significant (Hall et al, 1978). Publics wishing knowledge about crime, and police activities in constituting it, are therefore placed in a dependent position. They must work within the parameters of police discourse about crime.

Journalists need to communicate in terms of the common sense, which of course has already been established by the police monopoly on public discourse about crime. Journalists' dependency is accentuated by their need to 'fix' quickly on their stories, to provide daily and even hourly reports of police activities. Therefore, they depend on police news releases about major crime, routinely furthering police crime discourse by rewriting police releases as news items (Wheeler, 1986). '[I]n the final analysis the relationships are asymmetrical because the journalist is always in an inferior negotiating position – the reporter who cannot get information is out of a job, whereas the policeman who retains it is not ... [I]t is the reporter's world which is drawn towards that of the policeman rather than vice versa' (Chibnall, 1977: 155; see also Hall et al, 1978; Fishman, 1980).

Police officers were sensitive to reporters' dependency on them. In spite of the new policy initiative, the police culture remained reticent about cooperation, so that there was peer support for being mum. This trend is predictable in an occupational culture that places a premium on knowledge control. An information officer articulated his views on holding the upper hand on reporters: '[T]he media really need us more than we need them ... The thing is [after we deny them something] tomorrow will be a new day and there'll be another new story and I'll be the one with the information and they're still going to have to come back. And we generally are civil again and we reinforce or re-establish the relationship. Some police officers though do clam up. Burned once and that's it, they won't continue the relationship with a given reporter or agency.'

In contrast, there were ways in which the police felt dependent on the news media. Some degree of co-operation with the news media was seen as part of police duty. This co-operation was inscribed in the official policy: authorized personnel are to 'treat all enquiries from properly identified members of the media, as a legitimate function of their profession.' In addition to a notion of duty, other considerations went into the calculus. The police saw direct advantages to media access, ranging from specific help (such as notifying the public of a danger or identifying a suspect), to selling the police image. There was also the opposite side of the same coin, namely the desire to avoid negative coverage that might tarnish the police image or hurt a specific operation or unit. With these concerns police officers felt quite dependent on the news media, and often believed that they had to respond to avoid negative coverage and denial of future news access.

Furthermore, once the decision was taken to co-operate, police officers felt dependent because of the need to respond to particular aspects of news discourse. While they controlled the primary definitions of the subject of address (crime, criminality, and its control by police), they sensed a loss of control over specific terms of the communication. Similar to others who are being pressed to divulge knowledge (Hepworth and Turner, 1982), the police officer experiencing 'interrogation' by reporters feels literally out of control. She knows that questions are being asked to fit the criteria of news-media logic and formats, not her own. She knows that if she does not talk somebody else will. The feelings of dependency and loss of control are difficult to articulate, but are vividly real to those experiencing them. In commenting upon journalistic methodologies used to compel them to respond, police officers did not lose sight of the irony that some of the techniques were the ones police use in the interrogation of citizens (cf Inbau and Reid, 1967).

Sometimes I see them as vultures and I realize that it's a cut-throat business ... You see them working and they're almost in a frenzy because they have to get this out and their job depends on this. So, I'm more coming to grips with this and realizing that that's the way these people have to be. They're not content to receive whatever it is that we have received about a particular occurrence ... [Offering a specific example] It was the third degree ... trying to trap you ... And of course it goes into their words, and you've got to very carefully sift out what is being said here because that's not quite really what I mean at all. And you try to put it back into your own, but you seldom win, when it goes back to what it is you're saying, because you invariably read that what you supposedly said is really what was their terminology. And it's already down and you don't seem to be able to do very much about this. I think it's a pity that they cannot allow us to feed them what it is that we've gotten ourselves because that is all we have ... [Offering another example] I heard a discussion going on at the front desk between this media person and one of my station operators and I thought, 'Where has he gotten all that information from? I don't know any of this.' And I went out and I said, 'Would you mind telling me where you got this?' And this person proceeded to tell me that over at the scene, he knows a lot of the officers who are there and somebody is slipping him a little something out of the corner of their mouth because they are being baited and asked questions. And they give a little bit and then I think a great amount of conjecture goes on and they second-guess things.

Moreover, whatever partial control is gained with reporters can be lost in the editing process. Control of editing was seen as the real power of news operatives. They can take snippets from one's own interview and place it with others to give it a context of their own making. The news text has a new context as visualized by the journalists involved, without much relation to the source's own social context for contributing to it. Thus, a respondent indicated a preference for being a single source; with many sources, the text escapes him even more. 'They have the opportunity, if they're interviewing five people on an issue, they can manipulate the thing to come out exactly what they want. They can edit the tapes and get just the answers they want ... or not even the full answer, so they have complete control on those types of things and they can make the interview come off or bend it almost to suit their particular needs.'

In deciding to co-operate, and in the process of co-operating, police officers felt quite dependent on journalists. The dominant view in the literature, that the police-reporter relationship is asymmetrical in favour of the police, is a result of the fact that previous research has been grounded in the perspective of journalists (Chibnall, 1977; Fishman, 1980; Wheeler, 1986). By failing to ground their knowledge in the police perspective, researchers have ignored the ways in which the police experience the strictures of news discourse just as reporters are limited by police discourse. Ultimately police-reporter transactions entail controls from both sides, and interdependency. Several police respondents expressed this interdependency, including one who stated, 'We need them as much as they need us ... I would never stop granting interviews because I think it's just as much to my advantage as to theirs. I think it's to the advantage of the public and that's who we're working for.'

The easiest way for the police to overcome the ways in which they lose power in their relationships with reporters is to develop a spatial, social, and cultural system of relations that sustains a spirit of trust and reciprocity. We now examine in detail the network of regions and closures that made this practically possible.

BACK-REGION ENCLOSURE: SECRECY

One of our police respondents said that reporters always seem to operate with the assumption that 'there was something hidden going on.' This assumption is not an unreasonable one, because police work is characterized by secrecy. As articulated by the former Metropolitan London police commissioner, Sir Robert Mark, police officers have 'an almost unconscious but natural bent towards reticence and secrecy in all matters' (quoted by Chibnall, 1979: 135).

Police officers are quite secretive in relation to one another. This secrecy is sometimes related to the desire to gain personal or subunit credit for work and/or the need to appear credible and 'cover ass' with superiors (Ericson, 1981, 1982; Punch, 1983, 1985). In relation to the court system, there is a need to control accounts of cases to achieve outcomes the police deem both just and justifiable (ibid). In addition, court officials and litigants must be protected from untimely disclosure. The police cultural value on secrecy is protected in the Ontario Police Act, which prohibits unauthorized communication about police work outside the organization. While there are situational and strategic reasons for this official seal of secrecy to be pierced (Punch, 1985), the norm is back-region enclosure and an effective system of patrolling the facts.

A dominant focus in the research literature on journalism concerns the limited nature of journalists' methodology. Their primary method is interviewing persons representing two sides of a conflict. There is little direct observation, except of staged public hearings and news conferences, and little effort to consult relevant documents or undertake more systematic documentary analyses. What is underemphasized in this literature is the fact that these other methodologies are not routinely open to journalists because of enclosure by sources. Social scientists should recognize this fact, because they too have experienced police back-region enclosure that prevents them from doing long-term and systematic observational or documentary research. While some research has been allowed in the past two or three decades, it remains nascent. Commenting on instances of police secrecy in relation to social scientists, Van Outrive and Fijnaut (1983: 59) state that 'the future of a socially relevant and critical police research does not look too bright. In itself, this is an important indication of the nature of the phenomenon with which we are dealing.'

In our observations, journalists experienced enclosure from more direct contact with police activities. They did not often ask to undertake direct observation of police activities, or to thoroughly and systematically scrutinize police documents. Perhaps their reticence was based on knowledge through experience that such methodologies were not possible. When they did ask to do something other than to conduct an interview, to attend a news conference, or to scrutinize a news release, they were usually refused. For example, at one point during a moral panic about attacks on women, a reporter asked to have access to rape-case files to do an analysis of them. She was refused permission, and allowed only to consult the police major-occurrence news reports prepared for journalistic purposes by the public-affairs unit. Occasionally permission was given for 'ride-alongs' in police cars, or 'walk-alongs' with foot-patrol officers, but these were of limited duration (one shift or less) and were understood to be for sympathetic purposes (tertiary understanding of 'what it is like' for the police officer).

In interview situations, certain facts about cases under investigation were denied to reporters. There were particular policies regarding exclusion of particular facts. For example, according to one police respondent, as a result of pressure from the Canadian Bankers' Association and from retailers, it was decided that the names of victimized employees as well as amounts taken in robberies would not be given to reporters. We observed instances in which there was a denial of information about victimization. It was also understood within the force that certain matters of police practice in deployment and detection, and related aspects of budget and internal priorities, were not for the public record. The predominant justification for secrecy was that disclosing information might jeopardize an investigation in progress by affecting the production and later value of evidence. This concern was stated in the administrative procedure on news releases as a discretionary matter. For example, in the 'initial release' it is 'at the officer's discretion' to give reporters accounts of 'weapons used, if applicable; items taken or involved; description of suspects, if any; description of vehicle, if any; further police action.' 'After arrest is made' discretion is circumscribed as police officers are directed that they 'must not release the following,' including 'identity of witness' and 'information concerning the accused: an admission, confession or statement; reputation or character; previous record; possible guilt or innocence; a test, offered to, taken by, or refused; evidence the Investigator feels may prejudice the trial.'

In keeping with the police rule system in general (Wilson, 1968; Bittner, 1970; Ericson, 1981a), these rules provided for police-officer discretion on what to divulge, depending on the circumstances. As one of our respondents indicated, it was not feasible to make more explicit rules because of the situated and contextual nature of the decisions involved, as well as the need to enable and justify disclosure of knowledge where it might prove of tactical advantage. He stated that, for example, where the weapon used in a crime is a commonly used item 'you could easily identify what the weapon was.' However, if the weapon used was unique, that might figure in a suspect's statement of confession, 'there's no way you can identify the weapon because it's unique and only the person who used it would know what it was.' He used this to illustrate that 'it has to change from case to case on evidence,' and to explain why it has to be formulated in administrative procedures as a discretionary matter on the part of the investigating officer or unit.

The police took these decisions in terms of criteria within their occupational culture, while the administrative rules provided legitimate justifications for their decisions. Thus, a police officer said that 'interference with an investigation or evidence' is not only a real concern, but a really convenient justification for denying knowledge for other reasons. Referring to the 'interference with an investigation or evidence' justification, he said, 'If the police don't want to be bothered with you, I guess they can tell you that ... Legally, you have to more or less accept that. And what can you do? The police have said that's the situation and you're not in any position to take it beyond that, but, quite often it is a "snowjob." I know that. And I suppose the media know that. They're not fooling anybody but they have to accept it.'

Many respondents said they had been taught to give a reason for not divulging knowledge, and the most favoured reason was 'interference with an investigation or evidence.' Although real enough, this justification can also be read as part of the police repertoire of account ability to achieve accountability. As one respondent put it, it was much better to say 'I'm not going to tell' with a reason, than 'no comment' or 'I don't know.' Of course, this type of response did nothing to reduce journalists' sense that 'there was something hidden going on.'

Another reason for maintaining secrecy was sensitivity to the impact of publicity on citizens involved. This sensitivity was directed to victims in particular, especially those deemed more vulnerable (e.g., juveniles) or those involved in sensitive matters (e.g., sex offences).

Secrecy regarding police operational matters was formulated in terms of not giving the 'criminal element' information that would be to their benefit. For example, a decision might be taken not to divulge knowledge about what investigative tactics led to an arrest because it might decrease the value of these tactics for apprehending other criminals. The advantage of displaying investigative wisdom and shrewdness to the public was of less significance than keeping the intelligence advantage over potential criminals.

A more particular reason for secrecy was related to the reporter involved in the story and the news organization he represented. Police respondents gave many examples of 'cutting off' particular reporters who had been critical of police in previous stories, or who were perceived generally as 'anti-police.' In our observational research of reporters, there were many examples of reporters being denied access because of who they were, or because of the organization they represented, rather than because of the nature of the knowledge they were after. In general, outer-circle news organizations and their police and 'investigative' reporters were pinpointed as uncooperative, untrustworthy, and interfering. When relations were particularly bad, it was not even possible for reporters to obtain knowledge that was routinely available to other reporters from other news outlets. For example, in a news organization that repeatedly published stories critical of police procedures and efficiency, it was sometimes difficult for their reporters to obtain ordinary details about crime occurrences. On one occasion, a reporter was unable to obtain update information on two criminal occurrences, and her desk editor planned to write a formal letter of complaint to the chief of police in this connection.

In a bureaucratic police organization with hundreds of units and thousands of members, control of knowledge is always partial. Similar to their crime-control mandate, and inextricably linked with it, police effort to control knowledge is a perpetual struggle. The police devise various formal-organization appearances that they are in command even though fundamental control remains elusive. The work of the organization does not get done simply in terms of where the parties are supposed to connect on the organizational charts. It is accomplished through a complex web of relations, affinities, trust, and reciprocity. Van Maanen (1983: 277) summarizes this aspect of police bureaucracy:

> Bureaucratization represents another more or less remote organizational
> control mechanism. Ordinarily conceived as a faceless or structural matter,
> bureaucratization refers, in part, to the institutionalization of power and authority within the organization ('who can do what to whom'). Because police
> tasks at the lower levels are ill-defined, episodic, nonroutine, accomplished in
> regions of low visibility, and are dispatched in ways that most often bypass
> the formal chain of command in the organization, control over the work itself
> resides largely in the hands of those who perform the work (Banton, 1964;
> Cain, 1973; Manning, 1977). In this sense, police agencies resemble symbolic or mock bureaucracies where only the appearance of control, not the
> reality, is of managerial concern (Van Maanen, 1980).

This statement is as true for police-reporter relations as it is for police relations with any other group. Thus, reporters regularly circumvented Public Affairs and went directly to the police officers involved in the matter. Inner-circle reporters seeking crime-incident facts and investigation updates went directly to the investigating officer involved. Reporters knew many investigators on a first-name basis, and often obtained knowledge from them before it was available to or digested by the heads of investigative units or information officers in Public Affairs. Outer-circle journalists likewise used the size, scope, and porous nature of the police bureaucracy to their advantage. The larger the organization the more accessible it is for obtaining knowledge and using that knowledge for social-control purposes (Reiss, 1983: 86). Outer-circle journalists seeking to police the police used a wide variety of police sources and units. When they had burned one person or unit, and were denied further access in consequence, they moved on to other persons or units to further their purpose.

As elaborated in the next section on back-region disclosure, the co-operative reporter was the one who went along with the police sense of time and place. If the police wanted something to remain in the back regions until they had completed their work on it, they expected reporters to co-operate by not publicizing it. They were after helpful publicity, not the type that would create difficulties. These expectations were no different from those that prevailed on the court beat. However, as we have seen, sources on the court beat were able to routinely avoid incursions into their back regions (e.g., plea-bargaining sessions, judge's chambers, etc.) and to control accounts to the time and place of the court hearing. This avoidance was not managed as easily on the police beat because of the mandate of outer-circle reporters to police the police.

An illustration is provided by a reporter who persisted in giving coverage to an underworld 'hitman,' who had become a police informer in exchange for not being prosecuted for an alleged murder. The reporter persisted in raising the visibility of this exchange and the identity of the informer, in opposition to the police who wished to keep the whole affair out of the public eye. As he became excluded from police cooperation, the reporter used alternative sources, including the informer's wife. Seeking to keep the matter 'alive' in every way possible, the reporter even reported an instance in which the police arranged for the couple to meet in a hotel room, and failed to intervene when they heard their informer assaulting his wife in a 'domestic.' To the reporter, this failure to control the informer's violence was another instance of the general immunity the police were granting him. To the police, this was 'the final straw' in a continuing series of incursions into their exclusive back regions. A police respondent gave an overview of this matter, indicating that trust was defined ultimately in terms of interests:

[Names reporter], we had an incident with him over the guarding of the hit man ... When I first met him, he introduced himself to me and told me who he was, and he was a 'crime investigative reporter,' as he called it. I said 'fine.' He didn't seem to be satisfied with the cooperation all forces were giving, RCMP, OPP and myself. So, he was doing a little bit of his own, through this [informer's] common-law wife. He got an 'in' with her, and he wasn't taking into account of who she was and what she was. And as a result of that he started doing outside articles that were really hindering our investigation, and he was told that. Said, 'Look, it's your story, we'll help you.' But a lot of the people that we're still trying to charge did not know what [the informer] looked like, and we were sending him with an undercover policeman back into this area in order to get the evidence that we required, through body packs and everything else. But no, he wouldn't let up, you see, and as a result of that we had to curtail it. We could [have] pick[ed] up maybe a lot more evidence that we wanted. But it became so obvious that he was making it very difficult for the safety of our undercover men, never mind the [informer].

... [A] headline that really came out way out of context, was where [the informer] met his common-law wife. He wanted to meet her, and she agreed to it, in a hotel room, and our officers were in the next room. And as a result of it, they had a domestic, and he dinged her, and of course the headline came out, 'Police Stand by While Key Witness Assaults Girl,' words to that effect. So, I talked to him and I said, 'You know you just put two police officers' careers in jeopardy. They're under investigation ... that they permitted this man to assault his common-law wife.' And I said, 'You should be on the Ann Landers column because I can give you domestics every night.' And that's what it boiled down to, is a domestic. 'And yet you've blown this out of context ... He's not under arrest. We're only guarding him. If he didn't want to stay with us tomorrow, you know, he could go and take his chances of getting shot by someone. Versus she agreed to meet him and she wanted to meet him' ... It was a misleading headline. It subjected my men to a lot of report writing [internally], anxiety for their families, and the whole bit. And as a result of that ... we had a meeting with the attorney general and the RCMP, the OPP, all up in the attorney general's office. And all because of [names reporter]. And we told him right there and then, right in that room, I said to him, 'You know you have jeopardized the lives of the undercover operation, and not only that you've jeopardized the career of my two officers.' I said, 'Do you know how many seconds it takes to ding somebody? Split seconds.' And I said, 'And they're in another room. They have a right to be in the room if they want to meet and make love or what they want to do together.' And yet, the headline shows that police stood by while this woman gets assaulted. I really, I lost my trust in the man.

According to a senior executive in the reporter's news outlet, this reporter experienced considerable difficulties obtaining knowledge from police during and after his work on this story. The executive said it took him a year to re-establish relations with one police force. From the police viewpoint, the reporter was interfering with their opportunity to clear crimes and convict offenders of greater value than the immunity they had granted to the informer. From the news organization's perspective, it was important to question the value of granting immunity to someone who had allegedly killed and assaulted, in order to get at others. In identifying a procedural stray, the news organization was questioning police values and whether they could be trusted. With the interest of efficient suppression of crime at heart, the police did not appreciate the reporter's values and decided that he could not be trusted.

This example signifies a dilemma for the police in their efforts at secrecy. If they remain secretive about back-region activity of value to reporters, they risk the possibility that reporters will seek alternative sources and other means to raise the issue and force accountability on the matter. In the court setting these options are limited, in part because citizens themselves are excluded from plea-bargaining sessions and other back-region activity. The police have less ability to control the accounts of those who have some access to their back region activity, including accounts from citizens involved, and sometimes from their own police officers. As one respondent stated, in weighing up enclosure and disclosure a paramount consideration is that reporters 'quite often dig things up on their own and print them.' The source must consider the value of the story to the reporter and predict what length he will go to if denied access. If the reporter is attaching great importance to the story, greater control might be achieved by giving her a controlled account in terms of police criteria of value.

Police sources also face the dilemma that disclosure may allow them to portray their work in better light, but enclosure is essential in the circumstances or is a legal requirement. The particular police source favours publicity, but feels organizationally constrained to stay mum. This situation arises when the police have made controversial arrests and laid charges, but cannot speak about matters before the courts.

How can I respond? If something I think is way out of line, I, as a police officer, nine times out of ten, cannot respond because it's evidence before a court of law. I'd love to reply, many times, to accusations. I cannot. And a great illustration of that was ... the bath-house raids, and it was completely out of context [In these raids, several hundred police officers raided four bath houses used by gay people and arrested several hundred for a variety of offences including being found-ins in a bawdy house – see Fleming (1983).]

... I had my phone ringing off [the hook], homosexuals for police, saying, 'Look, don't classify us with those people.' And yet I couldn't respond because I would jeopardize all these people before the courts ... [If] I start showing evidence to reporters ... defence lawyers are getting sharper every day, they'll say, 'How come did he have access to it?' Or, 'He switched it.' There's so many ramifications. They can create a doubt in the courts of evidence today. If I make a quote in the paper, I end up with a subpoena. Down to the courts, 'Why did you say that officer?' ... And that's why I as a police officer will back off, even more so, because I can't reply. How do I reply, to criticisms or otherwise? ... I can give quotes but I'm cautious of what I'm saying from the standpoint, 'Am I going to jeopardize that person's fair trial?' because 'Is it going to be taken out of context?'

Police officers often wanted to explain their activity in organizational and structural terms, but because of the need to sustain particular myths and values, felt the better of it. For example, in face of criticism about efficiency in law enforcement, or wishing to bring credit to hard-working members, it would be illuminating to talk about organizational pressures on police officers. However, there was a perceived need to sustain a view publicly that law enforcement is more or less full and even-handed, not a matter of organizational structures and situational contingencies. Hence, the police officer should not talk about the reality of his work as he experiences it: selective and partial in accordance with fiscal, social, cultural, and political constraints. A respondent said that news coverage 'can help with image, it can present sort of the positive side to police work.' However, some things that might enhance the image in one respect, and assist in arguments for more resources, cannot be discussed because they would clash with public-culture sentiments and perhaps tarnish the image in other respects.

In drug work ... we just don't have the manpower and basically we don't have the manpower because the department can't afford it. We have five district drug squads and the central drug squad, and they give us, for a budget of one year, $100,000 for all units to buy drugs. The current price of one ounce of cocaine is anywhere from $3,000 to $4,000. There is no possibility of getting off street level or intermediary level and getting to importers unless you have the cash. We can't do that. The department's argument is, if we get the information and we can't pursue it because we're financially inhibited, then we should turn it over to the federal RCMP and let them handle it. Not very satisfying for one. Two, if they have the time, because they have ongoing investigations themselves, if they want to lose that kind of money. So, basically you have to sit down with them and convince them that your investigation is just as important and it just doesn't work out on occasion. If

they [news outlets] could print it, if they could actually get the idea across
[it would help mobilize public support] ... If they could understand, in numbers, how many people there actually are in this department who are actively
involved in drug enforcement, they'll find out it's just phenomenally low
in comparison to the quantity of drugs and the people who are involved in
the criminal aspect of it. If they knew what our budget was, if they knew
the techniques that we have to use. Such as rental vehicles too but after six
months into the year we don't have a budget anymore so we don't have
rental vehicles anymore. Now we can't follow them on public transportation
or use regular police cars so now we're in a bind again. Again they say, 'o.k.,
fine, if you can't do it then give it to the RCMP or give it to the OPP.' But what
it does for a drug-enforcement officer on this department is it makes them
wonder why they're doing it in the first place. There's a lot of hard work
involved, and to get it to a certain point and then simply just to be told, 'I'm
sorry, there's no money. That's it. Forget it. Give it to somebody else. Explain it to them and walk away. Start again. Start something else and bring it
up to a decent level and hand it over again.'

Police officers also located decisions to keep things to themselves in
public-culture elements external to the police force. In the face of dominant cultural frames regarding the status of particular groups, it is difficult
to communicate facts that conflict with these dominant values. For example, it was deemed difficult to convey facts about the criminal activity of
members of particular racial or ethnic minorities because of possible racist
overtones. Similarly, a respondent said that during a moral panic about attacks on women, it was difficult to communicate statistics indicating there
was no increase in murders involving female victims because it appeared as
a slight on the dominant media frame of the plight of victimized women in
the more general political context of the status of women. 'Our murders of
women that year in this city were half what they were the previous year. But,
first of all, how do you play a statistical game with a young girl's life? It is
just a dangerous thing to do.'

BACK-REGION DISCLOSURE: CONFIDENCE

The porosity of the police bureaucracy was a significant concern, and subject
to perpetual efforts at discovering better sealants. Several respondents mentioned the frequency of 'leaks' to reporters, and the fact that reporters were
often better informed than police officials who were supposed to know for
purposes of accountability. A senior officer in the public-affairs unit stated,
'There are leaks. In any big organization you will find leaks.' In referring
to a major continuing story that lasted several months, she said, '[I]n some

instances they [reporters] would know more than I did about the incident. Because you must remember that I'm in the position that I have to give the media what is given to me, basically by the investigators and so on, and certainly they would withhold certain facts from me, unless I ask for them, and that too is quite rightly so.'

In this conception a leak is knowledge that has not been screened or processed through official channels prior to release to reporters. Police officers viewed leaks as inevitable because, with such a large membership, there are always some individuals motivated to circumvent official channels. A unit head stated, 'Sad to say there's always somebody out there [in the force] that thinks they're going to make a highlight by telling the press something ahead of time and picking up the phone and whispering in, even if they do it anonymously. Because there's always that little ego in the people.'

One respondent summed up the policy dilemma for the force as follows. He pointed out that the investigating officer is most knowledgeable about the matter, and in the best position to know what formulation of information should be released to the news media without damaging his case and the interests of parties connected with it. However, he tends to be unaware of overall force policy on the release of information and is not a polished performer when in the media spotlight. The senior police administrator as spokesperson is knowledgeable about force policy and an accomplished performer in the public culture. However, he has no direct knowledge of the matter being communicated, and is left to reconstruct the information already constructed by the investigating unit, sometimes leading to distortion and contradiction.

The fact that inner-circle reporters circumvented public-affairs and other official channels was not necessarily a problem. As noted previously, inner-circle reporters were viewed by police sources as well under control because of bonds of friendship and trust. They were known to be supportive of the police, willing to ignore or suppress knowledge they understood to be damaging to their policing colleagues. They helped to sustain the view publicly that the police were doing what they should be doing. Attuned to police culture, they had a fine sense of what should remain the private knowledge of that culture and what should be published. Much more than a formal public-affairs unit, the police organization required good, friendly, trusting relations with an inner circle of reporters. It was the best means of policing the news media.

It's an interesting thing we noticed a while back, was some of our best
media friends never called us in the media office ... [Naming several inner-
circle reporters], they never came in on business. It was always social ...
Because they've toned their trade and their profession to such a fine art

that they don't need we, the immediate organization. They can call up a specific [police] station, they've established a rapport, and a credibility, and an integrity with these [station-level] organizations that they can call up just about any of the people in charge of units in Metro Toronto ... and he gets the information ... [A]s a rule they don't call us. It's all social interaction.

Having proven they were willing to withhold knowledge from editors and the public, and to delay publication, inner-circle reporters gained the confidence of their police sources, as was articulated by one of those sources:

I build a bridge of trust with the reporters I deal with. Lots of times they have learned of something and it's a scoop story to them and I will co-operate with them and say, 'Look, we need four hours 'til we get all the people arrested ... [then] it's your story.' And I build that trust with those people, and as a result of it, that never really backfires in that sense, if you have that trust. Where I lose the trust in a person I've dealt with, once bitten twice shy ... It basically boils down to the trust of that individual versus that unknown editor out there ... By continued exposure to the media, I ... [am] very cautious in my wording and I generalize unless I know the person. If I can trust him, off the record, I might tell him certain things or certain areas to go and look for.

Police information officers we interviewed said that their rule was to treat nothing as being off the record. If it was going to be said at all, it had to be with a recognition that it might be reported because news-culture values might supersede police-culture values. However, in the back regions police officers routinely said things to inner-circle reporters with the confidence that those things would not be reported. They knew that reporters could be trusted in this respect, where trust meant a recognition that police-culture values would override other considerations.

Inner-circle reporters who came to be trusted put themselves in the position of being very knowledgeable about some aspects of police activity, and yet not able to communicate that knowledge through their news outlets. The very methodology they adopted to be trusted and to enhance their knowledge was also a limit to the knowledge they could make public. As Rubinstein (1973: 7) observes, 'The reporter is always an outsider whose access to the police is assured by his pledge not to reveal what he knows of police work.'

A police respondent pointed out that in a large news-media market such as Toronto it is too difficult to control all reporters through gaining their confidence. Therefore, in a big case the police have to enclose information as it suits them, rather than disclose in confidence at an early stage and face the prospect that someone motivated by the competitive edge might break the confidence too early. He contrasted this to a kidnapping case in a small city in which the police maintained control through back region disclosure:

> [The police chief] called the media in, as I understand it, and said, 'Look, guys, here are the facts and you keep it under your hat.' And they all did. I think that was terrific ... If we could be guaranteed that people would keep the information for background purposes – so that they understood and had a true sense of what was going on, so that the minute they were free to go they could go on a sensible fashion, but without jeopardizing any of the investigation, or in that case, someone's life – if we had that ongoing trust that everyone would adhere to, then I say give them everything. I just don't think it's a practical matter, that that's possible today in this particular municipality.

The large bureaucratic police force has difficulty controlling its own members, let alone the news media. Reporters were tipped off about special police operations, targets, and problems, and reported on these, to the dismay of police administrators. A police officer mentioned a recent instance in which his unit and Public Affairs had collaborated to keep secret impending arrests in a major case, hoping to have it revealed for the first time at a well-orchestrated news conference. Instead the matter was leaked to a television reporter, who appeared at the divisional station where the suspects were to be taken before the arresting officers and suspects did.

While inner-circle reporters usually held the promise of smooth sailing in the public culture, on major stories they sometimes joined with outer-circle reporters and represented the threat of a leaking ship. A senior administrator observed that, 'Good police reporters [still] have their pipelines into a police force and have good sources of information ... Yesterday, three hours before the abortion clinic was raided, the press was starting to phone, "We hear that you're going to conduct, get some search warrents today on the Morgentaler clinic." They picked that up on their jungle drums two or three hours before it happened, through their own contacts.'

The propriety of leaked information was of concern to the head of a police district we interviewed. He said that even with decentralization to a district-level media-relations officer, reporters went to individual officers for additional information and accounts. He used the example of a search for a missing child, who was later found murdered.

> It became a very, very high-profile story and the press were very demanding of the police officers who were involved in the investigation. Initially it was a search, and then as the thing sort of broke into the investigation they were demanding information and time from the officers. To their way of looking

at it, it was their right to be able to tell the public what was current about the investigation or the search. To the police, I think in many instances they were looked upon as people who were butting in or interfering and delaying whatever the process was they were trying to accomplish ... [I]t's their job to inform the public what is taking place and there's nothing quite as old as old news. You've got to have something new, something different, the editor doesn't want you to write what you wrote yesterday or even this morning. And certainly the person who reports on the radio must have something that is interesting, because I am sure there are people who listen to every hourly news broadcast for updates, and that's exactly what it is all about, is updates, 'So, what can you tell me that is different now?' ... I am not sure that we are doing it properly at this time. Hickling and Johnston recommended ... that each district have a public-information person. And a lot of recommendations of Hickling and Johnston were sort of broad-brush recommendations, they sort of gave a philosophy or idea about what they thought we should be doing but they didn't really get down to the nitty gritty and say this is how it should actually happen ... Now, when the girl went missing we did in fact bring in the person who was designated in one district as the information officer ... One of the problems that I saw anyway was the fact that the news media had the ability to phone anybody at anytime and ask any question they wished. So,the information was not always coming through [the information officer]. He could call news briefings, and the media would come, and they would bring their cameras, and their pencils and paper, and they would take down what he said and they would photograph him as he said it. But then they could go beyond that, they could go to some other source and get little bits of information. Down through the years they have established contacts within the force, who will give them information, whether properly or improperly ... And there's probably a return of favour or kind on the part of the news media, for they're a source of information themselves, because of this ability to go around the information officer. There was some difficulty and some conflict in the way the press were handled, if that's the proper word, by the police at the time. It would be nice if we had a central location for news and the news media could be told with some certainty that *this* is what would take place, you will get the information from this person here. If you want background material, or if you want some point clarified, this person here will make arrangements for you to speak to the unit commander or whoever. But you are not to interfere with the operational aspect of the police service during the period of the incident.

This police officer represents the insatiable administrative thrust for central-ized control of knowledge, while recognizing simultaneously that journalists can penetrate the bureaucracy by going through, around, and past formal mechanisms of control. This does not mean that the formal mechanisms are of no value, or that the organization is so porous that it is substantially desta-bilizied through news accounts. It does mean that control is more equivocal and problematic than other accounts suggest (e.g., Chibnall, 1977; Fishman, 1980).

Reporters also had access to systematic sources of police information. For example, reporters said that contacts in the force would run criminal-information checks for them, using the Canadian Police Information Centre system. This procedure was seen by reporters as an aid to their assessment of the character of sources they were dealing with. It was also a means of judging a source's truthfulness, since the person could be confronted with aspects of the record to see if she admitted to it. It seems that police officers gave reporters this access for the same reason that they gave them tips about ongoing operations and problems. It was a matter of personal favour and reciprocity, or otherwise individually motivated, and not necessarily related to force interests. Here confidence was in not mentioning the source of the knowledge, rather than in an expectation that the knowledge would not be acted upon.

FRONT-REGION ENCLOSURE: CENSORSHIP

Knowledge police make available to reporters in public settings is often sub-ject to various restrictions on publicity. These restrictions are at times so limiting that they preclude publication, delay publication, or result in the publication of very partial knowledge. In this section we consider legal, for-mal, and informal mechanisms the police used to accomplish enclosure over what they made evident.

Legal Arrangements

The reliance of police reporters on officially imprinted versions of reality is not only a matter of their working ideology and routines (Chibnall, 1977; Fishman, 1980), but also the invisible hand of the law. If the police disclose their *suspicions* about suspects and 'what went on' in a particular occurrence, rather then officially imprinted *evidence*, and reporters publicize these sus-picions, they are collectively vulnerable to charges of libel. The law of libel is a primary justification for police secrecy in investigations of suspects up to the point of laying a charge. Usually secrecy prevailed, although reporters did sometimes learn of police suspicions of who was involved in a crime and their motivations. In these cases the reporters said they were constrained by the law of libel not to report unless the police were able to develop sufficient evidence to lay charges. Combined with reporters' desire to protect their police sources from these same laws, and to sustain their good relations, the law of libel proved to be a powerful form of censorship.

The law of libel serves to limit knowledge, and in that sense is ideological. Resting uneasily with their own knowledge, and sometimes separate from their interests, police and reporters are compelled to accept the limits of legally framed and controlled knowledge that is not of their own making. As Brodeur (1983: 509–10) instructs, difficulty in establishing legal evidence 'should not be confused with plain ignorance about the nature and ways' of the phenomenon under investigation. 'As any police officer can bear witness to, knowledge and legal proof are very different things; the first notion concerns the substance of the facts, whereas the second is largely a question of formal procedure ... To confuse a lack of compelling evidence ... with a lack of reliable information ... only strengthens the tendency to repress knowledge' (ibid).

There is another way in which the law circumscribes the knowledge provided by police officers in the front regions. They feel constrained to speak within the limits of their role as law officers. This constraint makes them less able to enter the political arena than they might otherwise desire, and may be undergoing some loosening with recent signs of the politicization of the police (Reiner, 1985). However, the constraint remains a real one, and a source of deep frustration, as Tumber (1982: 19) found in his study of British television coverage of the 1981 urban riots:

> The police cannot enter into a debate on the law which they are there to enforce, and therefore any occasion when they might be drawn into doing so potentially threatens their whole position within society. Almost inevitably then the police are frustrated at being unable to give their version of why events occur. For example, they were verbally attacked over Brixton but were unable to get up and say what they believe – which is that years of neglect were responsible for the troubles. Quite simply the police felt unable to defend themselves. As one police spokesman commented, 'How can I go on television and say that successive governments are to blame for Brixton and that we [the police] have only dealt with the manifestations of a deprived society? But the community would warm to that.'

As this example indicates, the strictures of legal discourse are sensed in particular when external events and issues become newsworthy and the police become part of political controversy as agents of the state. Our police respondents mentioned this issue in connection with continuing political controversy over abortion, their role in arresting persons involved in operating illegal abortion clinics, and public protests against those clinics. As one respondent stated, when asked as a police officer to address the abortion controversy, there is only one possible response. One must represent the police in the 'very plain and simple' discourse of being a law officer.

> If you're going to be truly professional and represent the police department, you're not there because of your moral standpoint. I may disagree whole-heartedly with abortion but the law states at this present time *this*. o.k.! I may vote for a particular MP because his wishes are what mine are on the abortion issue, but if I get on television and I'm representing the police department, I state what the law is. That's what my function is. I'm a police officer, I enforce the law as it stands, good or bad. The more I enforce the bad laws, the more public outcry and the faster it gets changed. But I'm not there to discuss anything about how I feel about it and, you know, what would I do in this situation if, say, my daughter became pregnant and she wanted to go have an abortion? ... It's against the law. It's very plain and simple.

One should not lose sight of the fact that the law provides some protection to the police in this regard. It offers a convenient justification of the type, 'Because we are doing things the legal way we are doing them the proper way and you have no legitimate grounds for criticism.' This justification includes enclosure over knowledge.

In contrast, the police *experience* less legal protection than other participants in the legal process. Judges can use the laws of contempt and the authority of their office to remain all but impregnable to reporters' incursions. A police officer referred to criticism of the police in the news media, observing 'I guess when everything's running smoothly, whatever that means, there's no interest in it and it's only when there's something [negative] that creates an interest.' He then observed that judges seem to enjoy relative immunity in this regard because of their legal privileges to enclose. 'The one thing I've heard many reporters refer to ... is contempt of court. They'd love to say something about a judge's handling of a trial, or his sentencing, or whatever his demeanour is, and they're always told by their own legal departments, stay away from it, contempt of court.' This police officer went on to observe that, on the other end of the spectrum, legislators can use their legal privileges to disclose unfairly:

> We have the complaint on that cruise-missile demonstration a couple of weeks ago. Well, when you read what [names a member of parliament] said in the House about that, and he knows nothing about it at all. There's been no investigation done and he's standing up in the House talking about the brutal treatment the police gave these men and he doesn't know anything about it because there's been no investigation. It's just started. So that this is

probably where you get the most irresponsible statements coming out, right in the House, because they know they can't be sued for them, that's it.

The police perceive the law as both an enabling device to justify enclosures and a constraining device at the level of discourse. The law has a bearing on how police formulate their news accounts, although it is far from an exclusive determinant of what is enclosed in the front regions.

Textual Arrangements

Similar to the courts, the front regions of police-citizen transactions are designed to structure and control communications so that certain accounts are given and others are enclosed. In particular, enclosure is effected through the organizational arrangements of the public-affairs unit and its preferred forms of communication, and the decentralized district-level public-affairs officers.

Reorganization of the public-affairs unit and policy meant bifurcation in the direction of both centralization and decentralization. The media-relations function was moved into the direct jurisdiction of the chief's office. This effort was directed at control of accounts through the traditional police-command structure, rather than through a public-affairs unit that had been seen as somewhat separate from the rest of police operations. In this traditional command structure of account ability and accountability, senior administrators are to appear omniscient about all facets of police operations. For example, all correspondence goes out on a letterhead with the imprint of the chief of police, and correpondents are directed to reply to the chief of police.

At the same time media relations was decentralized to the district level. This decentralization reflected the reality of police-reporter relations and the inability of the police administration to channel accounts adequately to and through Public Affairs. It also gave officers removed from headquarters, and of lower rank, a greater sense of participation in communications to the public culture and the credit that could bring to them and their units. The new arrangements represented the latest sensibility of how to patrol the facts in a porous bureaucracy operating within an equivocal environment. This sensibility was conveyed by a senior administrator:

> I think that the more we disclose, the more [control]. Like for instance, at
> one time there was a bit of a policy around here, a number of years ago,
> if a policeman was charged with say an offence of break and enter, or an
> indecent assault on a girl, or something, the general theme was well let's
> just try and get his resignation and try and hush it up. That doesn't work
> because with the amount of leaks in an organization this size, invariably the
> press find out about it and once they find out about it, they have to give it

far more coverage to justify the fact that they had to ferret the story out ...
Every time we arrest a policeman now or charge a policeman criminally,
we put out a press release right away. If you've noticed our thrust with our
consultant's report coming in here, we created a public-affairs unit right up
on the chief's staff, and public-affairs people in each district, and we try to
get as much information as we can out to the media as quickly as we can,
but try to put out what we think they should have.

Front-region enclosure is aimed at the production of a unitary account.
The means to achieve it include the early designation of one police person
as *the* source, and the more active use of press releases and news conferences to make it clear and definite what appears to be the case. As a senior
administrator commented regarding the reorganization of the public-affairs
unit, control of communications requires control of the environment.

Like for instance yesterday, knowing that the ———— was going to be raided,
we planned in advance, which we may not have done a few years ago. We
said 'O.K., if we're going to do that Tuesday, now how are we going to handle
the media?' So we got public affairs setting up the initial press release ...
Deputy Chief ———— would handle the press. And that's working. They
used to, say, phone up the deputy and say, 'What do you think about this?'
and then phone up the chief, and then phone up somebody else, and get
people saying different things. So the more we can concentrate on from our
end, saying 'Look, we've set up a press conference for you, we've put out a
release, we've held a press conference and named a person to deal with the
media, well go and talk to the person that's got the answers.' *We've tried to
give them what they want but in a more controlled environment* [emphasis
added].

The main task of the thirteen employees in Public Affairs was to produce
major-occurrence news releases about crimes police officers had selected as
newsworthy, with reference to a strict encoding procedure. There was a particular form, with specific categories as dictated by the administrative procedure. The facts to be reported were only those circumscribed and channelled
into the grooves of the major-occurrence news-release form. Excluded, for
example, was any account from the victims, witnesses, and suspects said to
be involved in the crime incident.

For the purpose of public knowledge, public-affairs employees settled
on the facts of crime, and in the process gave these facts their 'performative
character' (Fishman, 1980). That is, crime was constituted not as it happened, but as it was produced by the force bureaucracy as they wanted it
understood publicly. As Wheeler (1986: 15) summarizes in his observations

of the public-affairs unit, '[T]he purpose of the occurrence report is to construct the occurrence as criminal, thereby making the police action seem
sensible, proper, and officially authorized. In this way, the account provides
"the procedures for not knowing certain events," namely those events that
are not relevant to the bureaucratic organization.'

Wheeler's study of the public-affairs unit also shows that published news
reports of crime incidents are often largely rewrites of the police news releases, even though they appear as if they are not. For example, a citation
of a police source is given without mention of the fact the statement was
lifted from the news release. 'While accounts in other areas of news will
occasionally make reference to a "news release" or "prepared statement" (as
in, so-and-so said today in a ...), I found this to be rarely the case in the
reporting of routine crime news, serving further to constitute the accounts as
real news' (ibid: 40–1).

Constituted in this way, even routine crime-occurrence news releases
have a promotional character for the police. The world is depicted as rife
with crime and deviance, and the police as *the* authority for keeping the
lid on it. It makes the role of the police self-evident, and their efforts at
crime control appear objective, compassionate, and effective. As Wheeler
observes, this 'discourse is fundamental to the work of the police, and its
adoption by the news media means that the news media are also part of
police work ... crime discourse is a tremendous resource, since it makes the
power differentials [in policing] unactionable. After all, who could believe
that the work of the police is anything short of proper, when that is the
message that is conveyed day after day with the production of news release
after new release and their adoption by the news media?' (ibid: 54). Indeed,
this discourse is even more powerful than the 'good news' arm of the public-
affairs unit that champions police heroes and prowess in crime fighting. That
material is obviously self-laudatory, whereas the 'eternal recurrence' (Rock,
1973) of crime news releases is not.

A verbal and visual equivalent to this textual mediation is the police
news conference. The nature of enclosure provided for in the news release
and news conference is revealed in the following case example. During a
major continuing story about a series of suspicious deaths on one ward of
a hospital for sick children, another death occurred on the ward and the
police decided to issue a press release about it. Upon receiving the release
some television stations asked for a news conference so that they could have
some visuals to go with their stories. The police obliged, and a public-affairs
spokesperson at the news conference read out the release as follows:

I have here a news release which was released at 12:15 P.M. on this date and
it reads, 'On Saturday, April 23, 1983, at about 6:35 P.M., a seven-month-

old male infant died in the cardiac ward at the Hospital for Sick Children. Dr Murray Neighbour, a metro area coroner, was notified and commenced an investigation. On Sunday, April 24th, 1983, at about 6:30 A.M., members of the Metropolitan Toronto Police homicide squad were contacted by the coroner and requested to conduct a further investigation. Preliminary reports indicate the infant had elevated levels of dioxin [digoxin] in his system. Further tests are being conducted at the Centre of Forensic Science. For further information contact the public-affairs office of the Metropolitan Toronto Police.

The news conference was then turned into an effort to obtain further information from this spokesperson. However, refusing to stray from the news release, he would not elaborate in response to reporters' questions.

Journalist[s] [J]: What is meant by 'elevated levels'?
Spokesperson [S]: I can't give you that. That would have to come from someone who is [knowledgeable] in that area.
J: Can you give us anything more than just what's on this press release?
S: No sir, I cannot.
J: What did the baby die of?
S: I cannot give you that, I'm sorry.
J: What have the parents been told? Have the parents been informed of their ... ?
S: I'm sorry, I'm in the position where I cannot release any more than what is on this press release.
J: A lot of people are going to be watching this with children at Sick Kids' Hospital and there's going to be a state of panic if we can't clear some of these things up or if you can't give us anything on it.
S: The only thing that I could answer to you in that respect is that these people who are concerned will be contacted and have been contacted by the investigative officers.
J: Can you tell if it's Ward A or B?
S: No, I'm afraid not.
J: But what assurances can you give if I had a child in Sick Kids, what assurances can you give to me that this isn't going to happen again tomorrow? I mean, do you have men on the ward?
S: No.
J: Extra men watching? What's being done?
S: I'm sorry but I have to restrict myself to the investigation because the investigation is ongoing at the present moment and that I can't give you any further details.
J: Can you say it was murder?
S: I cannot.

J: What did the baby die of?

S: Again, I'm in the same position as before, I do apologize but I can't give you the information.

J: When can we expect to get some more information? When can we get some answers to these questions?

S: As soon as it's available and as soon as it's possible to release that information, it will be released.

J: Is it possible that by perhaps maybe this afternoon you'll be able to tell us exactly what digoxin levels were found?

S: It is possible but I can't give you that evidence.

J: Who's conducting the investigation? Under who? Which officers? Is it the same as handled the ... ?

S: The investigation is being conducted by our homicide squad is all I can ...

J: Was homicide called in because it is agreed the digoxin was placed into the infant by deliberate means?

S: I cannot respond to that question because I do not have that information.

J: Will that also be made available soon?

S: If applicable, yes.

J: Do you have the identity to release of the infant?

S: I'm sorry.

J: Do you have the identity of the infant? Can you release that now?

S: No, I cannot.

J: Can you say where?

S: I'm sorry.

J: Can you say where it is?

S: No, I'm afraid I can't.

J: Was the name ————?

S: I'm sorry I can't confirm or deny any names. I don't know the name.

J: But have the parents been notified, is that correct?

S: I don't know.

J: All right. Has the Sick Children's been told or been asked to take additional steps above and beyond the steps recommended in the Dubin report as a result of this incident?

S: You have me at a disadvantage. I'm sorry I can't give you a response.

J: Have there been, has there been meetings held since it occurred?

S: Again, you have me at a disadvantage. I'm merely a vehicle to give you this news release.

. . .

J: [Names spokesperson], when we're deciding in any potential homicides, we're usually, even when investigations are continuing, we are able to release, once next of kin have been notified, we're able to release the name of the victim and the circumstances surrounding it and we do leave open the fact that investigations are continuing. Why is it different this time?

S: I know, I can't answer, I'm sorry.

. . .

J: So all you're saying is that you had a mysterious death at Sick Kids, which
     you're investigating, is that correct?

S: That is correct.

J: So, what is the point, I mean what's the point of a news conference if it was
     strictly to read the news release?

S: At the request of the news media, especially the visual news media. We, cer-
     tainly we're in a position to give you this conference.

This instance is a clear case of the police deciding to give reporters a
news release and nothing more. The spokesperson was not only a conduit
pipe of partial facts, but also a policing agent there to patrol them. His
mandate for disclosure did not go beyond the news release. Sensitive to the
visual imperative of television, he was willing to put in an appearance, but
nothing more. The spokesperson's view of the matter, and its relation to
Public Affairs as a unit for patrolling the facts, is revealed in interview.

A: That was a very, very high-profile type matter, as you know. There was a news
     release on it, with the details given to me by the Homicide Squad, or by the
     officer in charge of the Homicide Squad. Subsequently we received several
     phone calls from the visual news media saying, you know, 'It's very diffi-
     cult for us to present this on television without having some action,' because
     that's what television requires is the action, showing the individual thing.
     'Would you be kind enough to read it?' And as you know, I was very busy
     on that day on several matters but I said, 'Certainly, by all means, I'll oblige
     by reading it for you, to facilitate that.' Inspector ——— spoke to them, not
     I, and imposed certain conditions on them, saying he cannot answer ques-
     tions, he will only read you the news release and I'm asking each and ev-
     ery one of you not to ask questions on it because he will not be able to an-
     swer them. For the obvious reasons that were involved, because we didn't
     know whether it was a murder, or we didn't know whether it was an accidental
     death, or we didn't know whether it was a death by misadventure. The inves-
     tigation was not concluded, it was as simple as that. I didn't know, the inves-
     tigators didn't know. The coroner didn't know, solicitor general didn't know,
     the attorney general didn't know. So, it's impossible, at that particular time,
     to come out and label it one thing or the other because you would look like a
     fool. Not only would you look like a fool but it would be incorrect to do so.
     Hence we had the news conference and you saw the results. Now, you be the
     judge.

Q: Why did you comply with their request to have something visual?

A: Well, why not? I think that they're entitled to have something for the visual media. You're here to serve, really, the wants of the media at large.

Q: Well, they could scan the news release you sent out.

A: Quite so, but it doesn't give the same effect as a police officer giving it over, or what have you, and that's their concern and they voice that quite strongly from time to time.

Q: Was there any advantage for you to be on the electronic media?

A: Not at all. As a matter of fact, from a police point of view, it's a disadvantage because I knew exactly what was going to happen in that we were going to get this great question time. The problem that you do have with situations such as that, if I had of read that news release and said, 'Thank you, ladies and gentlemen,' and got up and walked out, then the cameras would have been zoomed in ... on me saying, 'Thank you, ladies and gentlemen, I have nothing further to say,' no comment, walk out. And it would look terrible. And not only would it look terrible, it would look as if we were hiding something, which we were not. So, the only way that you can do it is to answer the questions, one way or another.

Q: Without giving information?

A: Without giving information.

Q: What is the best way in dealing with the news media to get your information, your message, across?

A: Oh, by press conference. By news-media releases. We have all the vehicles to do so. By broadcasts, everything ... I think the greatest fear that, in dealing with the news media, is being misquoted. One of the greatest fears, and that does occur, and it occurs quite frequently, unfortunately. And being quoted out of context ... You'll also have, from a police point of view, the infiltration by the media into certain areas of policing or into certain areas of investigation that really, in quite blunt terms, is none of their business.

Q: Are there any ways you can overcome being misquoted?

A: Public Affairs.

Q: Is that one of the reasons that this was set up then?

A: Certainly. The consultants felt that the traditional view that the police had in the past of publicizing things to the media without giving them benefit of in-depth look at it was inadequate, and I agree.

What is remarkable here is the depths to which the police must go to patrol the facts, block knowledge, and yet appear to be responsive. It is far better to respond 'without giving information' than to refuse outright. The textual needs of the news media, whether print, audio, or visual, have to be respected for the sake of the images they have the power to represent. In this style of front-region enclosure, it is literally true that 'the medium is the message,' and nothing more. The police control the account through their own textual medium, adjusting only to the performative requirements of each medium of news.

Informal Arrangements

The police also used various informal means to effect enclosure on the knowledge they made available to reporters. These ranged from subtle interpersonal techniques of framing accounts to more direct and active efforts at censorship.

An information officer discussed how he tried to shift reporters from covering bad-news topics to good-news topics. For example, there were continuing stories on an area of the city with social problems attributed in part to racial difficulties. He encouraged a reporter to do a good news story on another part of the city that had a similar demographic composition and yet harmony within the community and with the police. He described this as a strategy of taking the heat off the police in the troublesome area, and at the same time providing positive images of 'multiculturalism at peace with itself' and police. 'The police come out of it looking [good], 'cause the police were in co-operation with this organization, we've diffused any more coverage up in the other area and avoided any conflict on it ... I felt particularly good about highlighting some other activities, and again, promoting the police.'

Previous research suggests that police are attuned to the subtleties of how camera angles can affect the image of police in handling public-order disputes (e.g., Hollaran et al, 1970; Gitlin, 1980; Tumber, 1982). During our field-work there were less-subtle efforts by police to prevent television cameras from taking unfavourable visuals of their activities. On one occasion a television camera crew happened upon the scene of a police raid on a residence and proceeded to visualize the drama. The police intervened and some of the cameraman's equipment was damaged. The cameraman wanted to pursue charges against police officers involved, but he was discouraged from doing so after meetings between police and representatives from his newsroom.

Our respondents indicated that while reporters' self-censorship was preferred, police initiatives for censorship were sometimes required. At times members of the inner circle were relied upon to not disclose sensitive information, and to bring pressure to bear on colleagues to do likewise. This censorship in return for favours was a part of the reciprocal relations between police and inner-circle reporters.

> I don't really think you can limit what the papers, or any other part of the media, are giving to the public. I don't think you should put controls on it, but I do think that they, out of the public interest, they shouldn't present certain things. Common sense should tell them, it's a matter of ethics ...
> I don't think the police should have to say, 'Don't print that!' I don't think

we should ever have to say that because that gets too, towards a police state, when we start telling them what they can print and what they can't print, and it could soon get out of control ... A short time ago I had a number of buildings staked out in this city ... [Names inner-circle reporter] was aware of it. He used to phone me every day. He was pumping and he would say, 'I was just in the building and I saw a [police officer] sitting in there behind the counter from 52 Division, what do you think of that?' I said, 'Well, maybe his wife works there and he's waiting for his wife to get off work.' 'No! This was ten o'clock in the morning!' I said, 'Don't know, don't know anything about it.' But they knew. It was obvious they knew and they were all fishing. Nobody printed it, to this day, and I thought that was good because I'm sure every member of the media knew that that was going on. And of course if one knows, they all know because they all have their office together down there. I really did appreciate that. That type of thing, I think that's responsible. They know we're in trouble. We're trying to curtail the number of crimes occurring in this city and I felt they were just as interested, as we were. They were playing their part in it ... There are people on this force that are very friendly, personal friends with media people and naturally they're going to go to their friends. I know [names same inner-circle reporter] has access to just about anybody at headquarters ... If I want some help – and I've had to call myself a number of times for things that I knew were going to happen, something was going to be printed and I thought it might hurt something we're doing – I've had him intercede for us and he's done it. So, you know, it's a two-way street.

FRONT-REGION DISCLOSURE: PUBLICITY

The police actively disclose knowledge helpful to their operations and image. They seek publicity about their law-enforcement crackdowns on the presumption it will have a general deterrent effect and, not incidentally, affect the supportive sentiments of citizens. They seek publicity through 'police week' campaigns, police-officer-of-the-month awards, and other bald efforts at self-congratulation calculated to mobilize consensus and consent and to boost the morale of members. They pursue a particular consciousness about crime through their major-occurrence news releases. Publicity is an integral component of the policing mandate and activity.

Publicity is accomplished most regularly and routinely in the reporting of crime incidents, investigation, and capture. The police culture itself symbolizes 'real police work' in terms of criminal investigation and 'the good pinch,' even if most police officers do very little criminal investigation and rarely make an arrest for an indictable offence (Ericson, 1982; Reiner, 1985: chap. 3). This symbolic image is sustained in popular culture to the extent that the news media and television 'cop shows' focus on investigation and arrest to the exclusion of other police activities and other aspects of criminal justice (Dominick, 1973; Hurd, 1979; Garofalo, 1981; Reiner, 1985: chap. 5). From the police perspective, it is useful to have popular thinking mobilized around the notion that the police are primarily crime fighters whose success is underscored every time a 'good pinch' is reported. To repeat the statement of a respondent cited previously, reporters are contacted only 'if I want to sell my men ... If I want to give a good pinch because my men have done a good job ... It's to put the police image up good.'

Reporters sometimes covered crimes from the perspective of victims, or relatives of victims as they were affected by the victimization. The focus was on tertiary understanding from the victim's perspective, in combination with using the victim's plight as a vehicle for encouraging action by the police and other authorities. To the extent such appeals were helpful in mobilizing public assistance and/or public sympathy, the police encouraged publicity in this area. We observed many instances in which police officers went out of their way to encourage victims or relatives of victims to co-operate with reporters by giving interviews and still photographs that would publicize their plight. For example, a radio reporter approached for interview the mother of a child believed to be the victim of foul play. Upon being refused, the reporter had a police officer she knew talk the mother into doing an interview. Apparently the police officer co-operated in the hope that the interview would evoke further public sympathy and thereby assist in the search. The police officer then stalled another reporter so that the radio reporter could maintain the exclusivity of her interview at least as long as her next hourly update.

There were also many explicitly 'hurrah' contexts in which the police sought to publicize their good work. For example, a large number of reporters were attracted to a news conference at which the popular television detective 'Barney Miller' (Hal Linden) was sworn in by the chief of police as an honorary detective, as part of a publicity campaign connected with the 'Police Games' being held at a local sports stadium. Capitalizing on fictional representations of policing, a deputy chief spoke at length about Linden's role in improving the police image. The image of the police in television drama was used to sell the fact that the local police were doing a good job.

The police also have occasion to disclose sensitive private information if it is likely to aid an investigation or discredit targeted individuals or groups (Chibnall, 1977; Leigh, 1982). The police are as capable of using 'leaks' for tactical reasons as are other sources who appreciate the effects of publicity (cf Bok, 1979, 1982). The RCMP Security Service even went to the extent of bogus arrests and false publicity to discredit the deviant individuals and groups it visualized to be threats (McDonald Commission, 1981).

Police publicity is usually mobilized in the name of a force as a whole,

constituting organizational ideology. On some occasions – such as funerals
or memorial services for officers killed in the course of their duty (Manning, 1977; Taylor, 1986) – publicity is mobilized in the spirit of the entire
police vocation, constituting occupational ideology. However, there are also
occasions on which publicity is used by one group within a force to bring
pressure to bear on another group in the force to effect a reform (Punch,
1985). When lower-ranking officers were denied requests to the administration for better resources or working conditions, they sometimes turned to
publicity as a lever. In the opinion of one respondent who had used publicity
in this connection, the administration's need to show harmony and consensus
within the force could sometimes be used to advantage. 'Anything that might
get a little bit of publicity, [management] would rather pay the bucks than
have some controversy in the media ... [The news media] are an integral part
of the chess game, and at least what I've found is, that our board of commissioners, our senior officers, municipal government, provincial government,
doesn't want bad publicity.'

The perfection of knowledge-control is to have reporters censoring themselves, routinely enclosing knowledge that is not helpful to the police and
disclosing knowledge that is helpful. Near-perfection was achieved with the
inner circle of police reporters. Many inner-circle police reporters made explicit statements indicating their affinity with police ideology. For example,
an inner-circle radio reporter repeatedly emphasized the need to tell 'a police
side to the story.' In their daily interactions, police reporters made it evident
to others that they were operating in terms of police occupational ideology. A
television reporter was covering court hearings involving anti-nuclear–arms
demonstrators who had been arrested for obstructing police at the scene of a
plant involved in arms manufacture. A demonstration was in progress outside
the court house, conveying, among other things, the belief that the police had
created and escalated the situation at the arms plant that led to the laying
of sixty-two criminal charges. At one point the television reporter began arguing with the demonstrators, exclaiming, 'The police don't judge the law,
they merely enforce it.' If the reporter had reflected on his own judgments
that day, including his final decision that this demonstration outside the court
house was not worth reporting, he would have appreciated that this was as
vacuous as saying, 'Reporters don't judge the news, they merely report it.'

   Police reporters gave many signs that their nose for news followed where
the police led them. They actively contributed to some of the 'hurrah' contexts staged by the police. Several inner-circle reporters formed the selection
panel for the policeman-of-the-month award, and then did a story celebrating

their choice and recalling the (usually previously reported) heroics of the police officer chosen. Here criteria of value met, as what was deemed most newsworthy was also what most represented 'real police work' within the police culture.

The effect of self-enclosure was also revealed by the thinking not done. For example, an experienced reporter who was 'flipping' through the police major-occurrence news reports was asked by the researcher how the police decided what should be reported on in this form and how it should be reported. The reporter was initially dumbfounded by the question, and then replied that he had simply never thought about that process before.

Failure to think about the police process in providing accounts also leads to failure to ask questions that may be pertinent. A reporter took up the cause of a citizen who wanted the police to release their report on a case involving him so that he could use it in a court case on a separate but related matter. The reporter's persistence paid off as, facing the threat of sustained publicity, the police relinquished the report to the citizen. The reporter left it at that, instead of raising more general questions and issues related to this case. For example, given the police orientation to serving the victim, why is the victim or complainant routinely excluded from receiving a copy of the police report that describes and labels the complaint and states what the police did about it? Is it because complaints become police property, and they exercise their property rights by patrolling the facts *vis-à-vis* citizens? Is it because the police can do little or nothing with most complaints, and do not want to make this evident to complainants? Is it because labels and classifications involve a police interpretation, and often differ from what a complainant has stated, so that disclosure would lead to conflicts over interpretation?

Acceptance of police occupational ideology also entails focusing on particular sources and questions so that the answer will allow the reporter to state the police case. One inner-circle reporter either avoided covering cases involving allegations of police wrongdoing, or called only sources *internal* to the police organization in an effort to discredit the allegations. He also had a practice of eliciting statements from citizens, for example, from the relative of a victim, which expressed sympathetic appreciation for the work the police were doing on the case that concerned them. This reporter explicitly stated that he was out to communicate the police side, and he did so not only through his selection of police sources, but in the careful selection and citation of non-police sources who were 'on side.'

Some non-police sources we interviewed were aware of this selection process, and chose to circumscribe and even shut off inner-circle police reporters because of it. For example, some lawyers and politicians we interviewed, who were sympathetic to a citizens' organization concerned with police wrongdoing, said they had limited or strained relations with inner-circle reporters. One politician said he was proactive with some reporters but not an inner-circle reporter he named because 'he's on the other side of the fence from what I'm interested in. I wouldn't call any of the crime reporters.' Identification as an inner-circle reporter meant exclusion from consideration by some non-police sources, and hence a further source of enclosure on what was reported. It is very unlikely that inner-circle reporters would want the type of knowledge offered by these sources anyway. However, that underscores our point that the inner circle circumscribed the realm of the reportable in terms of police occupational ideology.

Reporters constantly struggled with questions of what was reportable in terms of how it would make the police look. This struggle occurred at all stages of the reporting process, and for broadcast reporters, into the editing stages. For example, a television reporter had film of police dragging demonstrators, who were blocking a road, off the roadway. He focused on one shot that showed a demonstrator being dragged through manure that had been deposited by police horses, but decided to edit out this shot on the grounds that it was unfair to represent police handling of the matter with this visual. He mentioned nothing about demonstrators' perceptions of fairness in how they were handled.

Reporters' acceptance of police authority included taking their facts and using them without question and sometimes without attribution. As with the crown attorney in the court context, the police officer in the context of classifying and dealing with crime incidents could be taken at face value. Facts were not seen as equivocal or contestable, but as whatever the police officer said was the case. A senior news executive we interviewed said that his policy in this connection was to be trusting of police accounts as fact without verification.

[T]he great thing that we believe in, much as the courts believe ... that the police are always right, except in extraordinary circumstances. That is an unalterable fact, that the police are not a bunch of shysters and not a bunch of crooks, but essentially the epitome of the fine, upstanding citizen who has observed and recorded accurately. If we can't take information from them without having to verify, we're in deep trouble. Aren't we? ... What kind of facts are you getting at? That a murder took place at [a specified address]. That's not a fact that's in dispute. The body was there, correct? If the police tell us that the murder took place at [a specified address], do we need to go and get two other people who saw the body in that house in order to verify that fact? No we don't. That a justice of the peace fixed a ticket for somebody, if one source tells us that it's not enough because ... what evidence does a court have to have to prove that? It needs solid eyewitness testimony, probably. It needs documentary evidence. It needs something that proves the case. In a disputed fact the newsroom is no less than a court. When I read my reporters' stories and they come back with facts, I say, 'What's the proof of this? No proof, no fact.' Now it may be right, but then again it may be wrong. So, what is considered a fact in my book has to survive the same test that a fact would have to in court.

Inner-circle reporters also effected self-enclosure by creating their own hermeneutic circle of knowledge sharing. When they had several calls to make to different police sources, they divided the labour and then exchanged the facts that had been given to them. Similarly, details of personal interviews with police sources were shared with others in the police newsroom. Reporters who noted a factual error in another's story pointed it out to him. While on occasion this practice made it evident that facts are contestable, resolution was usually achieved by accepting the authority of a fellow reporter and/or his source rather than doing further checks.

Inner-circle reporters, who were obsessed with obtaining facts and factual updates, often ended up treating facts very casually. For radio reporters, what was required for the next hourly update was the latest account of the victim's condition, the amount lost in the robbery, the number of officers involved in the investigation, and so on. If this account was wrong it could always be corrected at the next hour; indeed alteration helped to give the impression of 'change' in developments and hence of new news. There was occasional exaggeration of the magnitude of investigations, which went along with the tendency towards dramatization. First and foremost these reporters offered a blend of 'cops and robbers' entertainment and 'law and order' ideology, and their choice of evaluative words and attendant construal of facts were attuned to doing so. Suspects were regularly described as 'thugs,' 'perverts,' 'desperate,' 'weird,' and of 'sick mind.' Violence with no preliminary indication of suspects or motives was placed in the context of the worst possible scenario. For example, a middle-class civil servant found shot to death in the underground parking garage of his apartment building, apparently as he was going to work in the morning, was described as a victim of organized crime. The act was described as 'gangland-style execution' and 'an ambush.' The killer was said to have 'pumped several shots at him at point-blank range' and to have 'cut down' the victim. Sounding like popular drama, this account was the most that could be made of all the effort at developing a close affinity with police.

Influences of News Texts

Police recognize that they are first and foremost knowledge-workers (Ericson and Shearing, 1986), and that in all of their communications knowledge is power. As one respondent articulated, 'We're living in an age where information is probably one of the most important commodities there is. And the people who control that information are really powerful people.' In relation to the news media, power entails offensive and defensive strategies that maximize helpful news and minimize hurtful news. Viewed as a strategic commodity news as knowledge is not considered for its truth value, but rather for its value to the policing mandate. In the eyes of a police information officer, news is but another commodity in the social-control business: '[I]n a tremendous amount of ways, I think that the media control our lives ... [E]verything that is portrayed, either visually or in writing in the media, is literally soaked up by the public at large. One way or another it forms opinions, it forms certainly a great part of our society's concept of how they want things to be. And in turn there is a communication backwards ... to the media by the public which also voices their concerns. So, it definitely has a very great influence ... If you look at it from a police point of view, shall we say, the media can be one of two things. It can be very helpful and it can also be very harmful.'

INFLUENCES ON PROCEEDINGS AND PARTICIPANTS

Reporters were seen as an integral part of police activities, affecting the rise and fall of particular cases, organizational units and operations, individual careers, and the proper image of the force.

Interference with Investigations

As introduced earlier, a paramount concern expressed by respondents was the impact of publicity on investigations in progress and subsequent court cases. This concern was related to several aspects and stages of investigation. Through their monitoring of police radio communications, reporters sometimes arrived at the scene of the crime before investigators did, and before the scene had been sealed off properly for the protection of evidence. This physical interference was of great concern to police investigators, and resulted in heated exchanges with reporters. There was also concern that publicity about investigations in progress might tip off suspects about police strategies and tactics. A police officer described how a reporter had asked questions and construed answers so as to piece together police views on the *modus operandi* of a bank-robbery gang, and how they were mobilizing in terms of that *modus operandi*. In spite of having asked the reporter not to publish anything about this aspect of the case because it would interfere with police investigations, a story was published. In the eyes of the respondent, publishing this information had a significant impact on the investigation and considerably delayed the ultimate capture of the suspects. 'The gang that I was referring to, that his article interfered with, when they were captured a few weeks ago they mentioned that article and said that that's why they stopped robbing banks in Toronto, and went outside of Toronto because they knew what we were doing because of his article.'

There was constant concern that specific details of evidence might be publicized, affecting a suspect's confession and the reliability of evidence for court. Detailed descriptions of the scene of the crime, the weapon used, the condition and appearance of the victim, and so on, could be said to confound any later account of these elements a suspect might give, and these confounding elements would in turn be picked up on by defence counsel at the pretrial and trial stages. Similarly, the parading of accused persons and evidence for news visuals was seen as having a confounding influence on witness accounts and unfairly bringing into focus the certainty of the evidence and guilt of the accused before the trial.

Harm to Citizens

The police had a genuine concern for citizens directly or indirectly involved in criminal cases in terms of the influence of publicity on them. They were sensitive to 'the punishment of publicity' on the accused who might be innocent; the impact of publicity on the victim who might want specifics of the victimization and biographical details kept private; and, publicity speculating on police decisions at an inconclusive point in investigations, which might create anxiety for the victim or relatives of victims.

The Image of the Force

The police were not only concerned about the harm of publicity to their actual investigations, but also about how their inability to divulge particular knowledge sometimes cast a negative light on them and the force. While they were trained to say they are knowledgeable but unable to divulge anything at the moment, they knew this could be portrayed negatively in the news. As addressed previously, concern at the level of organizational and occupational ideology, of appearing as competent professionals, at times conflicted with the need to conceal sensitive knowledge. Talking of the need 'for the police force to sell themselves, and to sell or to put an attractive image before the public about what the police force was trying to do,' a police officer said the biggest impediment to presenting this image is the inability to divulge certain information when challenged.

> If the matter is before the courts or if it's very controversial, the police
> are very reluctant. They certainly can't discuss things that are before the

court. And sometimes it's very difficult or unwise to get into some sort
of mud-slinging contest in the media. Sometimes people who represent
pressure groups have free reign because of the fact that they are prepared
to make themselves available to the media. They're available for interview,
they're prepared to supply information and data, or what they represent as
information and data, and sometimes its seized on by the press ... It portrays
us maybe as being overreactionary or vicious, insensitive, when we don't
really have the opportunity to respond at that particular time ... If the police
are portrayed as being particularly bad in an incident, it may come to light
later on at trial, or in an inquiry, or just through the 'watering down' process,
that they are not evil or bad. But the damage is done, or at least it seems to
be done anyway, and this is by a police officer looking out.

Workload Pressures

Police respondents talked of the amplification effects of news coverage on
their workload. 'Crime waves' were seen to have the effect of increasing
public consciousness of the crime problem and hence the level of calls to the
police. A police respondent gave his analysis of an attacks-on-women moral
panic (Voumvakis and Ericson, 1984), and its effect on police workload:

> [F]actually the rate of attacks was down over the year before, but [the news
> media] printed it or created an air that, God, you'd think women were being
> attacked every five minutes on every street corner in the city ... They could
> do it with any crime if they wanted to ... if you wanted to harp on it you
> could have everybody walking around the street looking over their shoul-
> ders ... Anytime the public generally displays a fear of anything, we end up
> getting that fear. People start phoning in with suspicions, everyone's suspi-
> cious. If they saw somebody walking down the street a dozen times a night,
> normally they wouldn't pay any attention to them, but all of a sudden now
> they're afraid and they'll start phoning in about these suspicious characters,
> and perhaps it's just the guy next door coming home from work. But all of
> a sudden everybody's suspicious. So, we do get a lot of – I wouldn't want
> to say they're completely spurious – but they're calls made by people who
> are apprehensive about a certain crime that a week or a month before they
> wouldn't have been apprehensive [about] at all.

Many police officers stated that when extensive publicity was given to
crime waves or notorious crimes, they were forced into avoidance tactics
simply to get the work done. One respondent said she sometimes had to
take her telephone off the hook, while another mentioned that he once found
it necessary to change his office telephone to a private line, and even then
reporters quickly discovered his new number and continued to hector him.

Pressures to Solve Crime

While news accounts may seem fanciful in their visualization of particular police investigations, they can be real in their effects. Of particular concern was the inability to solve a major crime that was in the media spotlight, which tended to bring increasing pressure on the police as the 'culprit' and calls for changes within their organization. One easy way for journalists to visualize police mismanagement is to point to notorious crimes that remain unsolved. A police officer talked about colleagues in another investigative unit who were eventually transferred because of pressure from the news media in face of unsolved crimes.

> [T]hey crucified members of this force that didn't deserve to be crucified.
> The officer in charge of the squad was completely destroyed, as was his
> superintendent in charge of all these squads, they were destroyed by the
> press ... There were editorials, about the incompetence of the squad, and
> they started mentioning people that were on the squad before that who did
> so well. And it was completely unfair because you get this from time to
> time. There's been very few crimes of this type and the squad has had a
> good run since they were on last August, they've had very few crimes of
> this type. But prior to that, around last May and June they did get a clus-
> ter and this comes from time to time. It's always happened in this city,
> and every other city, and it will continue to happen. But the papers, and
> in particular [names one newspaper] made it look as if it was all the fault
> of the staff inspector in charge of the squad and the superintendent. And
> I thought it was completely unfair. And as a result they were both trans-
> ferred out. Our force bowed to them ... [The news media] said for one thing
> they had the wrong people in the squad. They got rid of all their experi-
> enced people. I was on the squad for a number of years and yes, they got
> rid of me, but they got rid of me to promote me. Does that mean I should
> be kept at the same rank to keep up the success rate? I don't know, but
> that's what the papers were saying, that people shouldn't be moved out of
> that squad. That they got rid of all their experienced people and brought
> in inexperienced people and that was their reason. I'm sure people who
> go out and commit these crimes don't say, 'Well they've got a bunch of
> new people in that squad now, I'll go out and commit the crime.' The suc-
> cess rate was low but it always is on that type of crime because there's no
> clues.

Individual Careers

This example indicates that news also has an influence on the careers of individual police officers. A significant fear for the individual officer is that she will be subject to allegations of wrongdoing, and regardless of the truth of the allegations or the outcome of any investigations the stigmatic punishment of publicity will linger. One respondent pointed out that because of their public mandate to 'serve and protect' and 'maintain the right,' police affairs are morally scrutinized much more closely than, say, the affairs of corporate executives. Another respondent described a personal experience in which a lawyer, as part of a court case, accused the officer of sexual misconduct, theft, and conspiracy to obstruct justice. These allegations were covered in the news media, investigated by the police internal-affairs unit, and addressed by the judge in the case. Although it was decided there was no substance to the allegations, this officer felt a lingering stigma publicly. He said the news media did no follow-up to record that the allegations were unfounded, observing that it does not look very good for the news media to dwell on the fact that they gave play to unsubstantiated allegations. This officer also felt there was lingering suspicion among his peers as a result of the internal-affairs investigation, and lingering doubt among members of the legal community.

There was also concern over what police peers think of how one is quoted in the news. Especially for the lower-ranking officer, what mattered was the reaction of the police culture.

> I've had to scramble once or twice in the last year to defend myself with my peers on a few things ... [A reporter] made a remark about a 'fishing hole,' a radar trap ... And at one point after he asked me some questions relative to business, he got onto that subject, and I said, 'Oh, that's the most popular fishing hole in all of Metropolitan Toronto.' Well, the next day he did a feature on getting caught there for speeding, and of course, 'I spoke to Officer —— at Metro Police and he says its the most popular fishing hole ... ' Well, yeah, and my phone lit up the next day, you know, 'What are you doing telling him that kind of information for?!' And I laughed because in my opinion there was no harm done ... But, when losers draw, it's a learning experience.

Police officers' control over news accounts is learned much more at this level and in this way, than by formal training and official directives. Such precedents make them aware of the limits of the tolerable. Some things must be kept private, left to simmer in the pot of recipe knowledge exclusive to the police craft. Other things can be made public, percolating into the melting pot of public acknowledgement that the police are doing what it is they are supposed to be doing, and doing it well.

SERVING POLICE PURPOSES

News is a resource to be mobilized in aid of handling emergencies, investigation, crime prevention, and enhancing police resources. It also serves at the level of organizational and occupational ideology, helping in the creation of a positive image of the police and thereby mobilizing popular support.

Handling Emergencies

The news media were seen as *the* means of mobilizing general public awareness of emergency situations to be avoided and precautions to be taken. While they were well aware of the possible amplifying effects of publicizing dangers to the public, and of creating fear unnecessarily, the police also appreciated the availability of news outlets for announcing particular threats and recommending precautions that would minimize them.

Helping with Investigations

The news media were used as a means of making known the identity of notorious suspects, in the hope that these suspects would be identified by members of the public and the police tipped off. The news media were deemed most co-operative in serving as the contemporary equivalent of the 'wanted poster.' They provided a similar service regarding the identity of some missing persons, especially missing children. On occasion newspaper efforts in this regard went to the extent of preparing special posters for display on street sales boxes and delivery vans.

Television-news outlets joined in police investigations in other ways. Their video and voice recordings were useful in identifying citizens the police wished to involve in investigations. The police made use of news film of demonstrations to identify culprits as well as review their own procedures. This use was a supplement to the increasing use of police video crews at strikes, political-protest rallies, and other demonstrations. News film of funerals linked to criminal investigations was also reviewed with an eye to who was in attendance and who among them might be suspects. On occasion reporters had interview clips in which their source had said something relevant to police investigations. These were reviewed by police as possible witness statements. On one occasion we observed, a television reporter had an interview clip used in this way, and he in turn made a story of this fact, communicating how his news outlet was willing to join with the police in searching for truth and achieving justice.

The research literature includes several examples of reporters willingly providing partial accounts in favour of what the police want, because they are convinced that acting in the police interest is also acting in the public interest. For example, in a well-known English case the home secretary, and separately, officials of Scotland Yard, met with newspaper editors and proprietors to stress the political importance of communicating 'anti-demonstration feeling' regarding an upcoming anti-war march. Two journalists involved later wrote, 'public reaction against the march quickly grew. It was a clear case of the media being manipulated by the Special Branch to serve their own ends. But in our view it was totally justifiable, because the consequences otherwise could have been devastating' (Borrell and Cashinella, 1975: 20; for parallels in the United States, see Gitlin, 1980). Similarly, the policy handbook of a Canadian broadcasting organization points out that deceptive practices, such as hidden cameras and hidden microphones, are only tolerated when very antisocial behaviour is involved and the public interest is at heart. The handbook offers as examples of very antisocial behaviour the selling of illegal drugs to children and street demonstrations. In matters such as these, news-media interest, police interest, and public interest appear as one.

Police officers gave many examples of how journalists joined with them in their investigative tasks, including collaborating in partial accounts that would prove helpful, if not altogether truthful.

> I was in the intelligence bureau ... and there, I'm sure you can appreciate that we have massive undercover operations going on ... [T]here was a large find of drugs in the back of a car ... [and] they had to arrest people, and they had to do something about it ... [But] it ran the risk at that time of blowing a far larger operation sky high, if the whole thing got out and we had to publicize the fact that we had these people in custody for this huge amount of drugs. And they're intelligent people the press, and they smelled a rat, they felt there was far more here ... [W]e appealed to them to hold it until we could wrap up the rest of the case, and there wasn't one word in the press about that and they helped us immensely at that time ... They reported it as we were trying to get it across. And that was that it was a happenstance thing, that we'd happened on that and that it was not connected with anything larger or anything else. And it led the people who were involved in it to believe that in fact they were still quite safe and secure. And it was a whole week later before the rest of it all came out to be.

Deterrence

The news media were also seen as part of the police mandate to prevent crime through a deterrent effect. They participated willingly in police news conferences, which announced particular crime-prevention campaigns and law-enforcement crackdowns. Some of these were sporadic, such as a campaign against shoplifting, while others were regular, such as the annual Christmas-time crackdown on impaired driving. Commenting on the latter, a police administrator emphasized: 'I must give a lot of credit to the media for the kick-off each year of our Christmas campaign on the first of December. TV coverage, the newspaper coverage we get on that is tremendous. I think that the TV coverage on that particular issue, because it's front and centre, there's photographs of police cars stopping people, that has an impact on the public, probably more so than the photograph on the front page that says "Police blitz begins." '

News conferences or announcements concerning the arrest of suspects were seen to have a similar function. They showed the police to be effective investigators, and this certainty-of-capture element was presumed to have a general deterrent effect.

There were varying presumptions concerning what has a general deterrent effect. For example, should the amount taken in robberies be systematically deflated so that potential robbers will think it is not worth it? Should the amount be inflated on occasion in the hope that it will create dissension among the gang members involved and lead them to fall out? Is it better not to report the amount stolen at all, keeping the would-be robber in the dark about the gain side of his calculus, and avoiding the contaminating influence of the news account in any subsequent confession the accused might offer? Regardless of the unlikelihood that criminals are so calculating, respondents believed they are. As with other judgments about the value of news, they saw the determination of what should be communicated as a matter of what is helpful rather than what is informative.

Boosting Force Morale

Displaying the results of superb investigations by a crack team of investigators was also a means of boosting the morale of police officers and their units. Different heads of investigative units said they saw the news as a means of bringing credit to their unit and their investigators. 'I'll always spell out the two policemen that maybe made the arrest ... I want to build them up because they're the guys working for me.' An information officer defined boosting force members' morale as an important function of the public-affairs unit. A senior administrator also emphasized the positive impact on force morale as an attribute of news coverage:

[The] thing that I think I'm consciously trying to do is to use the media as much as they use me. I don't think I'm as successful as they are because they control, but I do look for ways of stroking the young men and women that are out on the street, through the media ... I try and emphasize that more. I try to look for press for people that get created the chief's award for policemen that do community work. Try to stroke 'em publicly, because I think that has a positive effect on the morale of the personnel, that they see themselves, they feel good about themselves, when they're doing a good job.

Pressuring the Administration

This statement indicates only one of the ways in which the police saw the news as a means of communicating to other members of the force. When there was a desire to hand out accolades to members of the force, it could be enhanced by filtering it through the light of publicity and creating a special glow. However, the news media were also used to communicate things to each other that were negative in connotation. The individual police officer under accusation by the administration could use the news media to focus on his cause. For example, a police officer facing disciplinary proceedings he thought were unfair acted on the advice of his lawyer in calling a newspaper editor about it:

> My lawyer thought that the coverage would be good for the case. He thought that it was a unique kind of case that wouldn't hurt us if it was public because we had nothing to hide. And we thought the police commission did have something to hide ... [I chose a particular outer circle newspaper because] They've got good labour reporters, got certainly good political reporters and others. And I thought if it was a story worth following then the other newspapers would pick it up as well ... [I]f things turn out in your favour ... [news] can bring public attention to an injustice. I suppose it can correct certain abuses of the system. They're bringing public awareness to something that some officials know exist, the conditions exist, but they don't want to make these changes for whatever reasons. And I think sometimes by having public awareness these same people are forced to make these changes.

In seeking the positive advantage of publicity, police officers representing a particular unit or level in the force were sensitive to the fact that others in the force might wish to avoid the negative effects of the same publicity. For example, line officers could sometimes pressure the administration by lobbying for particular reforms or working conditions through the news media (cf Punch, 1985). Indeed, they did so with a sophistication about prevailing priorities in the administrative culture, political culture, and popular culture, and how these could be converted to the benefit of line officers, as revealed in the following account:

A: [T]here are quite a few occasions where, and in quotes, 'I use the press to the best advantage ... [for example] protective body armour, and of course with management we had been attempting through negotiation and meeting after meeting to get some movement from them and all they were doing was paying us lip service. I almost think not genuinely concerned enough, or they felt that the expenditure didn't warrant the product that would provide that safety for our police officers. And so that was just at the time that one of our officers was shot, in fact two of them were shot ... And shortly after that ... an Ontario Provincial Police officer ... was killed ... and it was at that point that, well here it goes, we'll give it full volley. And so we got into the area of protective body armour and that every likelihood this officer would not have received a serious gun-shot wound if he had been wearing armour, and blah-blahblahblahblah, and that we had asked the government to become involved in testing different materials, different products ... One thing led to another, and the amount of pressure that was coming on our politicians and our police force! The public, hell, they were, in fact maybe it went a little too far at times but there were different groups donating money and wanting to take up different charitable campaigns and events and all the rest of it to get dollars to provide protective armour for the police officers. And of course about a year down the road it was targeted for another provincial election, and of course the government at that time was in a minority position, provincially. So, everything tied in well and we got some very good coverage, and as a result every police officer in Metro has got protective body armour with the exception of – I shouldn't say 'every' – out of 5,300 over 5,000 have protective body armour ... I'm almost waiting for an issue or something to come up that can be somewhat controversial ... [M]anagement is just acquiescing on almost every one of our proposals. Anything that might get a little bit of light publicity, they would rather pay the bucks than have some controversy in the media ... [On the protective armour matter] I had to, for part of it, maybe tell a little bit of a fabrication as to what government's position was ... I guess what I'm saying is I told a bit of a white lie to effect a particular purpose ... I guess because their plates were so full, they didn't realize where the particular issue was. It certainly didn't have any priority for them, so it was on the back burner and, you know, if this is being quoted and it sounds reasonable, o.k., and they subscribed to it as well. And then of course when they publicly went on record saying, 'Yeah, we want the police in protective armour,' that wasn't a position before. In fact, the most and the furthest they were going to do was to provide two protective vests for each police vehicle, which would have amounted then to ... about seven hundred vests in total. That was what the game plan was from government's point of view, and that would have satisfied the public I think, although it wouldn't have satisfied the police.

Q: Correct me if I'm wrong in what you're saying. Is it that you put a position to the media, of the government, that was a little off target, to more or less force the ministers of the government to ...

A: And our Board of Commissioners of Police and the Ontario Police Commission. I guess ...

Q: To come out more forcefully in your favour?
A: Oh, yeah, yeah.
Q: To be more clear of their own position?
A: Well, they, really it put them in a position where they couldn't do anything but come out favourably, in front, you know, 'for the boys in blue, because we love you.' It makes nice rhetoric but I don't think they really believe it ...
Q: How much do you think the media had to do with you eventually getting the protective body armour?
A: Let's rephrase it and say that if it wasn't for the media, we wouldn't have the protective body armour. They were an integral part of the chess game, and at least what I've found is that our board of commissioners, our senior officers, municipal government, provincial government, doesn't want bad publicity or bad light, or be viewed like that. And they'll respond affirmatively if the issue is right, and of course we wouldn't go to the press with an issue saying that we want, oh maybe some frivolous item, where the public can't identify with it ... Holsters was one issue. What we had was legitimately a 'widow maker.' We had attempted in numerous different ways ... to get a holster that was adequate and that would ensure that for the most part that an assailant couldn't draw a police officer's revolver from the holster. And geez we've had it in negotiations for years and with little or no success. So, finally we said, 'Hey, you know, it's the same strategy again.' And I know the commission is well aware of it now. And so when a situation arises, refer to it, like, 'widow maker,' that's a nice catchy little phrase and people like to go, you know, 'widow maker.' I mean they'll read it and think, 'Why the hell, why have they got an $11 holster when a $50 holster is going to save their lives?'

Enhancement of Material Resources

The body-armour example shows police strategy in using the news media for material advantage. Bad news, the killing of a police officer, provides the occasion, the funeral of the police officer, to dramatically display the role of the police as a core symbol of political culture, generating popular consensus for police authority (Manning, 1977; Taylor, 1986). In turn this symbol provides the political-cultural context for the police to press for what they want, because at such times it becomes politically and administratively difficult to deny them. This situation seems to be common. For example, in the wake of the Toxteth riots in Britain, the police apparently managed to use the instrument of publicity to acquire advanced riot gear and weapons for future troubles (Sumner, 1982). Sumner's analysis of this process leads him to state, 'if it is true, the claim that news is typically descriptive, or that it is merely aimed at description, falls to pieces. Indeed, if it is true, the whole thesis that the growth of the mass-circulation press has meant the reduction of the political propaganda role of the press must be re-examined' (ibid: 26).

While the police may suffer in some ways in the grip of fear resulting from a media-sustained crime-wave panic, they can also convert it to material advantage. This fact has been recognized elsewhere by leading police administrators (Alderson, 1982: 18). During a moral panic about attacks on women in Toronto, in which the police were repeatedly criticized for not solving the murders of four women, the police commission used the occasion of a regular meeting to announce a cure. A police commissioner, facing directly into the focus of television-news cameras and talking to the many reporters beyond, immediately addressed the question of attacks on women and the implication for street safety. He said he had full confidence in the police, and assured that money and manpower would not be spared to keep the streets safe. He announced that the commission had asked the chief of police to follow the 'three Rs': 1 / *reward*, the posting of rewards relating to specific incidents, up to $100,00 for cases such as murder; 2 / *review*, of laws, noting in particular the need to toughen release on bail and release from jail; 3 / *recruit*, ensuring there is sufficient strength on the police force to increase visibility for prevention and to handle troubles. While the occasion was primarily a reassurance that the police were up to their job, it was also informing the people of the need to buy more insurance in the form of more police resources.

Enhancement of Ideological Resources

Reassurance in the form of organizational and occupational ideology is another advantage of the news media for the police. News texts have influence over public opinion about the police, and are a primary aid to police legitimacy. Most members of the public – especially the middle-class public whom the police most identify with (Ericson, 1982) – know the police primarily as they are represented in the media. To continue appearing to be representing their constituency, the police must pay particular attention to media representation.

Police efforts in this regard were directed at good news, along with the favourable control of bad news, presumably on the assumption that there were enough outside forces who would create bad news. As a lower-ranking officer observed, '[T]he police department, if they actively seek interest from the media, it's for something such as a new emergency system we might have or a new program that we're starting ... I have yet to see, either on television or in the newspaper, an officer of any rank going to present his view on a particular thing just to sort of "get the beef off," you know.' This statement is a clear recognition that the police could best purchase legitimacy by relating their activities to consensual concerns and images in public culture. Recognition of prevailing cultural sentiments led to decisions that specific problems in public safety should be announced by police officers who are members of minorities, thus allowing the force to represent itself as representing the demographic composition of the community regardless of the statistical realities of Force membership.

> A warehouse was entered and they stole several hundred cases of snails ... and after the theft of the snails was reported we found out that the snails had been condemned by the federal government, the Ministry of Health and Welfare ... We felt it necessary to issue a bulletin advising the public that cans with a certain label and a certain identifying number on the tin had been stolen and that they were dangerous. And of course this was given out, then it became a rather hot news story and for four or five days it was one of the leading stories in all the forms of media. They had policemen appearing on television holding up tins, and they used a black officer in one instance and they used a female officer in another instance.

The police join with other corporate bodies culturally charged with the task of socialization into the consensus. Considerable resources are expended on police visits to school classrooms for lessons in public safety and for propagating the view that the police officer 'is part of your community, he's one of you.' Students are put to work making pictures or writing essays which reinforce these images of police work. These practices are celebrated further when the news media decide to do stories on them, thus expanding the number who can share in the consensus. An information officer described with elation one such occasion:

> We had hoped to have released this feature information on a Monday ... about two kids who won an essay contest Metro-wide about police. But the *Star* got word of it early, got copies of the essays, and I thought they'd treat it as a feature ... I gave it to them Friday afternoon, the *Sun* was out of operation, we thought we'd go for it Monday ... And they thought, u-huh, no, front-page stuff on the Saturday *Star*. A matter of fact they guaranteed me, they got a middle-management guy on the phone, he says, 'You get this for me and set it all up. And get the people out by the police car and everything else, and make copies of the essay. Front page of the Saturday *Star*.' And 'cash registers,' numbers started to go up in my mind. Front page of the Saturday *Star*, I think, what is it, 575,000 issues, provincial [wide distribution]. And I'm adding this up in my mind, 'cause it was for a benefit and I wanted publicity. So I said, 'Sure!' and I think I set the thing up for them, and they read it back to me. It was front page. I mean you couldn't ask for better coverage. Did you see the front page of the *Sun* this morning?

It's a coloured picture of a mounted policeman, with our horse and with the police museum which is opening up. And I thought to myself, I mean, who can get that kind of coverage on the front page of a major paper like that?

PUBLIC KNOWLEDGE OF CRIME AND THE POLICE

Knowledge of Crime

The police are the fulcrum of the state control apparatus. As the embodiment of 'lawandorder' the police are used to represent the state's moral authority on an everyday basis. They are also used to define the practical contours of that authority through their decisions to designate some things as crimes and some people as criminals. This mandate gives the police a professional expertise in relation to crime. However, their 'positional advantage' (Cook, 1977) in relation to other organizations in the crime-control nexus gives them an attendant practical expertise. This 'double expertise' (Hall, 1979) means that when there is anything to be said about crime, and its relation to social control and order, the police are in the primary position to declare what appears to be the case. All other forms of expertise must address that frame and have their own frames contextualized in terms of it.

Crime rates are an artefact of police organization (Ericson, 1981). They represent what police officers have chosen to classify as crimes, and one must understand this decision-making and classification process to understand the uses and abuses of crime statistics. Yet, news does not provide for this understanding, choosing instead to portray crimes as self-evident objects in the world, lying about to be picked up, polished off, and turned into symbolic gems in the same way as the geologist gathers her rock collection. Police spokespersons themselves have pointed out that the distortion of the relation between the police and the production of crime rates is usually attributed to the police and their desire to show both efficiency and the need for more resources, whereas the news media are often at fault in misreading the meaning of crime rates (Alderson, 1982: 17).

Respondents felt that public knowledge of crime was reduced by reporters' focus on the individual case, dramatized and sensationalized for its presumed audience effects. Far from selling the police, respondents saw this tack as being primarily oriented to selling newspapers and broadcast markets. Beyond the obvious sensationalizing aspects, focus on the individual case was conducive to distortion in other ways. Given their limited time frame and emphasis on updating facts about crime incidents and investigations, reporters are constantly pressing for what the police regard as premature disclosure. The police sense of timing is to carry out a thorough investigation and reveal the facts only when it has been firmly decided what they are. The reporter's sense of timing is to get the facts, with no investigation by him, and little worry if things have changed or require correction for a later news bulletin. Indeed, the reporter demands change between news bulletins so that she can show that on each successive occasion she has done more work and has more news. The problem for the police is that they typically start an investigation with a 'worst possible scenario' orientation, covering a range of investigative possibilities that will provide cover in case someone challenges their interpretations at a later date (Ericson, 1981, 1982). Therefore, the initial accounts to the news media tend to portray an incident in its worst possible construction, and the news media in turn make much of it. When later investigation reveals that the matter was not as serious as initially imagined, the news media either give that final determination less consideration, or ignore it completely: '[There was a serious sexual-assault major-occurrence news release] on the weekend, for instance. From an investigator's point of view, reading it, I immediately thought there's some very serious inconsistencies in this story. And when speaking to the investigators I was able to determine very quickly that my thoughts were correct. But it had been given out as a rape ... serious sexual assault or whatever. That tends to sometimes be a bit of a problem because it quite often turns out, when the investigation's terminated, that it's quite something else.'

Knowledge of Police

News focus on police involvement in crime incidents perpetuates the dominant culture image that 'real police work' is criminal investigation and law enforcement. This image reflects a similar view of police work within the police culture itself (Punch, 1983), although it does not take much reflection for the police officer on patrol to understand that only a tiny fraction of her work has anything to do with criminal-law enforcement (Ericson, 1982). In terms of what she actually does, the police officer is better depicted as a knowledge-worker, dealing not so much in the laws of the Criminal Code as in the laws of social constructs (Ericson and Shearing, 1986).

It is well established that police organizations are characterized by many formal divisions and 'microcultures,' with conflicts among them (Reuss-Ianni and Ianni, 1983; Punch, 1985). However, in the normal news-media presentation of the police the force is united, so that the public does not normally think of its internal divisions. A police officer observed that while divisions exist in any police force – and, we might add, in any human organization – 'I don't think the public perceives differences ... [between police administration], association, commission ... [to them] it's all the same ... it's almost all one and one, unless there is an absolute confrontation situation.' In the example of lower ranks using the news media to pressure the administration for material advantage (pp. 164–6) a difference between line officers and the administration was evident. The administration's need to show internal consensus, that the police are uniform, was the critical point played upon by the lower ranks as a means of getting their own way. Concessions were made to submerge differences and to avoid the appearance that the force was anything but united.

The police talked not so much about the news providing understanding of their work as they did about whether the news helped with their work and the force's image. Indeed, they were not overly concerned about distorting aspects of crime, police organization, and police occupation, possibly because they recognized that these constituted myths upon which their organizational image thrived. This orientation meant that police officers complained primarily about quality news organizations and reporters of the outer circle who tended not to be helpful and who even created trouble from time to time.

Compared to court officials, the police were much more actively involved with, and concerned about, the news. They recognized the power of the news, and wanted to harness it to their advantage while avoiding its negative repercussions on their working conditions and activities. The news has become a significant part of the material and ideological realities of police work, and the police are bound to take it seriously. However, compared with some news-source participants on the legislature beat, the police were not too actively involved with, and concerned about, the news. For some members of the legislature environment, the news is just about everything.

4

The Legislature

News Culture and Ideas

In previous chapters we have seen that the courts and police are important components of the state, and are therefore central to the reporting of politics. In communicating politics the news media also focus on the processes of law-making and policy formation at the legislature and in government ministries. The legislature is the hub of state organization. The kaleidoscope of both private and public organized life converges in matters addressed at the legislature. Journalists on the legislature newsbeat play a pivotal role in shaping those matters and the politics of which they are a part.

Some analysts have argued the decline of political reporting in Canada, 'a decline which accompanies the end of the partisan press' (Royal Commission on Newspapers [RCN], 1981). Rutherford (1982; see also Cayley, 1982, 1982a) has commented upon the transition from newspapers that were organs of political parties and partisan interests to newspapers that have a primary orientation to mass markets where economic rather than political interest is supreme. The Royal Commission on Newspapers (1981) has documented a similar trend, noting that it is only in the past two decades that the partisan press has become extinct. The trend has been accentuated by the increasing dominance of television, which is oriented to audience ratings as a sign of market appeal for advertisers rather than to the explicit promotion of evident political interests. This trend in Canada contrasts sharply with that in other countries, such as Italy, where the major political parties retain their own television stations for the explicit promotion of their respective partisan politics. The democratization of news content through market ratings has led to a bland product, a 'Pablum Canada' brand of news (ibid). Optimistically, it is as if the people are getting what they want, or rather what they think they want after advertisers have had their say, in the market-place of ideas, values, needs, and wants. Pessimistically, it is as if the folks have become depoliticized. Politics has become a spectator sport (Postman, 1985), and interest in it is declining since there are so few teams and one or two teams always seem to win.

Contrary to these arguments, news involvement in the political process has not declined, but rather both the news and the political process have changed. The politically ambitious have always depended on dramatic performances to help constitute their authority. 'One can *possess* the means of power: physical strength, ornaments, and money. But authority must be *performed*. Authority refers to one's ability to gain the trust and willing obedience of others. While power rests on intimidation, authority survives through inspiration' (Meyrowitz, 1985: 62). Before the mass newspaper and broadcast media, the appeal was to the crowd. 'With the mass newspaper was born the politics of the image – the need to perform before democracy rather than argue with it' (Smith, 1978: 169). The performative character of broadcast media, especially television, has contributed further to this image of politics (Postman, 1985; Meyrowitz, 1985: chap. 14). In this, the era of 'politics as symbolic action' (Edelman, 1971), with an array of organized political interests using a variety of communication channels to manufacture images, convey ideologies, and have influence, primary among the channels for communicating politics is the news media.

'[T]he institutions and processes of public communication are themselves a central part of the political structure and process' (Garnham, 1986: 37). In keeping with the historical role of journalists (Boyce, 1978), contemporary journalists are key *participants* in the political process, variously promoting and marginalizing values, interests, ideas, and policy (Gieber and Johnson, 1961; Dunn, 1969; Sigal, 1973; Cox and Morgan, 1973; Dyer and Nayman, 1977; Morgan, 1978; Blumler and Gurevitch, 1986; Golding et al, 1986). Indeed, to the extent that contemporary politics is more a matter of symbolic representation than direct participation, it is arguable that journalistic participation in politics has never been greater. Journalists join with politicians and civil servants in giving direction to social order, and in doing so have an instrumental role in the political process.

Given the dramatic and ritualistic qualities of politics, it is a mistake to try to separate political reality from political performances. That image and reality are interwoven into the same seamless web of political action, too, makes the media of public communication of crucial significance, a resource of political power as well as a vehicle for constituting political authority. 'The work of public officials, of lawmakers and lawgivers, creates an orderly and morally directed society. It is fictive in many ways and a flawed guide to the daily life of its audiences. Yet its consequences for human life and human behavior is by no means slight. The magic of the great statesman has come from his realization that such illusions are also realities' (Gusfield, 1981: 185).

Court officials view journalists as somewhat annoying, although potentially helpful when confined to the correct time and place. Police officials view journalists as alternatively a bane and a boon, although generally appreciating the legitimating symbolic canopy that the news can give to their work. In contrast, for most politicians and selected government officials, journalists' power of communication to citizens makes them a primary reference for their activity. In their everyday world at the legislature, '[T]he press ... *is* public opinion in the eyes of officials' (Sigal, 1973: 135). The public is an 'intangible construct,' and is therefore reconceived as being embodied in journalists on the legislature beat (Hess, 1981). Journalists are the living public for politicians and officials, and therefore their 'public' debates are primarily with them. In consequence, politicians and officials are constantly thinking and watching in terms of another show, that provided in the news media. What they chose to do and say is with constant reference to the news media, and obtaining news coverage is *the* priority. Indeed, as articulated by an officer of the legislature, without the news media a lot of activity at the legislature simply would not make sense:

> The whole purpose of a legislature in terms of question period, the opposition holding the government accountable, and so on, make absolutely no sense without the press. It's a circular system that feeds off the other ...
> [T]hey're not asking questions to get answers for themselves, they're asking questions to embarrass the government in front of the press, and to make the government look bad in the press, and through the press affect the public. Now the question period I guess is a pure type of almost entirely political exercise. But not many things go on around here that aren't political in some shape or form. So, that to the extent that politics are involved in a policy issue, the member's purpose in pursuing something will often be just to inform the public of what their party's doing, what their personal views are, in the long term perhaps to affect things and develop public opinion, and therefore you use the press as that vehicle. But I don't think one should ever lose sight of exactly how important garden-variety politics are to the functioning of anything to do with the legislature. And the implication of that is that the place might as well fold up if the press weren't there.

Politicians we interviewed invariably stressed the crucial role of the news media as part of the process. The need for political 'presence,' for an image that appeals to the heart if not to the head, means that the news media are vital to political life.

A: Ninety per cent of the people in the constituency hardly ever, if ever, have met their member. You try to meet as many as you can and deal face-to-face with as many as you can, but for a very large percentage of the population, all they know of their politicians is what they see in the paper and what they hear and see on television and radio and it's just vital to try and keep as positive a profile in the media as one can ... [It's] important to have a media presence and to be seen through the media to be doing your job and doing it well. And so there is a dependence there. On the other hand, of course, there wouldn't be a Press Gallery ... without politicians, so it's a mutually dependent situation.

Q: Would you say you are more dependent on them than they are on you?

A: I would have to say so, yeah ... As a matter of fact the press, from our point of view, is our life blood and you cannot afford not to co-operate. I would say that more careers of politicians have been made or broken by their friendships with, or ability to get along with, the media. And it's not so much because the media says, 'Oh, you get along with me or else,' but it also has something to do with giving out an image of being able to get along with people, being a warm individual ... I rate the press ... probably at the top, I mean I accord the press higher priority and much greater care than ... my colleagues ... for example, if I say I want a couple of hours and I'm not going to see or talk to anybody, because I've got to get something done, [my assistant] knows that basically there is one category that's always to be talked to and that'll be the press ... [T]hey're important people. Very important to me and my business and I'm very careful when I deal with the press.

Both government members of provincial parliament (MPPs) and MPPs in opposition emphasized that non-cooperation with the news media was out of the question. A cabinet minister said he had *never* refused the news media outright. An opposition-party information officer said any reporter's question was always met with some answer, emphasizing that full co-operation is necessary to sustain the party's and leader's 'recognition factor' with the public.

[News coverage] tells people we're here, it tells people what we're doing, it raises our profile, recognition, and we often used to say ... that even bad news is better than no news ... Better that people, when it comes to election time, they say 'Oh yeah, I heard about that party. I think they raised a lot of noise.' At least that recognition factor that we do *something* ... [because] in this day and age people get most of their information about the political process from the media, and most of their information about politicians, the impressions they form of politicians, come from the media.

This respondent and several others emphasized their priority is to obtain *coverage* first and foremost. While it is better still to obtain *access* – routine play on favourite topics favourably portrayed – even mere coverage or a marginal role in a story is better than no coverage. This emphasis on obtaining *any* coverage is related to the belief that the news media are crucial in forming 'image,' 'presence,' and 'recognition,' regardless of content. In this reasoning, whether one is promoting corn flakes, soap flakes, or political flakes, it is the form more than the content that is paramount.

Politicians find that it is impossible to avoid coverage even if one wants to. The public regions of political life – the House, committee rooms, speaking engagements, election campaigns – mean that one is constantly exposed to the watchful eye of the news media. It is far better to recognize this and learn how to turn the news media to advantage than to remain shy and commit the political equivalent of suicide. In the words of respondents, if you shy away 'you get nailed'; if you do not co-operate 'they then take you and hang you; draw and quarter you.' Thus, the basic operating philosophy is that the best defence is being on the offensive. Parties, ministers, leaders, and individual MPPS develop elaborate information and public-relations units, take training in news-media discourse, and expend considerable time and energy on establishing trust and reciprocity with journalists. On the police beat, and especially the court beat, it is typically reporters who pester sources and sometimes have difficulty getting the story they want. On the legislature beat it is typically the opposite, as a plethora of sources pester reporters and often have difficulty getting the story they want.

While conditions on the legislature beat are conducive to intensified 'selling' of political images, there are equally intensive efforts at securing secrecy (Schiller, 1986: 32–3). Politicians and officials, fearing a refracted image, are sensitive to the policing role of the news media in visualizing inefficiency, mismanagement, corruption, and wrongdoing. The power of the news media to variously underpin and undercut is a force to be reckoned with and something to defend against.

Respondents conjured a variety of colourful phrases to represent the role of the news media in policing political life. A civil servant depicted the news media as a 'watchdog for taxpayers' and 'kind of a surveillance team,' having described a particular instance in which his organization was subjected to stories about procedural irregularities in which 'we really got beaten up by the press,' 'we felt so persecuted,' 'we got scraped up by the editorial pages too.' Politicians referred to reporters as 'police' and 'designated hitters.' Some depicted the news media as an opposition force at least as great as the official opposition. A politician who had experienced an unfounded allegation of conflict of interest in office said the experience had taught him that the news media stand at the forefront as an oppositional force and judges of fact and value. 'The press sets themselves up as the opposition ... I don't think they've been assigned any special privileges to research crime, we have our police departments to do that, we have all kinds of control, but they seem to place themselves as a police department, as a court, and judge, and I think it's wrong.'

ORGANIZING BY JOURNALISTS

Press-Gallery Facilities

A range of news outlets from all three media occupied space in the legislature newsroom. There was one reporter representing each of eight radio stations and five television stations, although in some cases these reporters had additional responsibilities elsewhere, such as the Toronto City Hall beat. A popular Toronto newspaper had one reporter and one coloumnist, a mass-market Toronto newspaper had three reporters and one columnist, and a quality Toronto newspaper had three reporters and one columnist. Various newspapers outside Toronto each had a single reporter assigned to the beat.

Taking the example of a Toronto newspaper, one reporter was designated as the bureau chief and functioned as an assignment editor: matching reporters to stories, checking on their progress, and liaising with the desk editor in the main newsroom. The reporting team had a secretary/researcher available to them in the afternoons to assist as the pace intensified towards the 6:00 P.M. deadline. Word processors with video terminals and a printer were available to enter stories directly, so that the reporters did not have to return to their main newsroom to file stories.

Members of the press gallery elected one member as president. The president was the official liaison person with the House, for example, bringing forward grievances which members of the gallery had against the House. The president was also responsible for using the legislature-newsroom public-address system to announce to members the time and place of upcoming key news conferences and other scheduled events.

In addition to the newsroom facility, the work of gallery members was facilitated by the provision of a press lounge. The lounge included a bulletin board for announcements, and a place of deposit for official reports and other public documents that appeared to be of news interest. Most importantly, the lounge was a context in which to meet with fellow reporters and sources to talk casually. There was prevailing sentiment that whatever was said in the lounge was 'off the record.' Sources said they used the press lounge to lubricate their relations of trust with reporters, to learn things from reporters, and to implant ideas with reporters to the point that it influenced how they framed people and events.

Another knowledge region was the many committee rooms, where MPPS participated in special topic deliberations, usually between 10:00 A.M. and 12:30 P.M. After lunch it was into the region of the House for question period, a one-hour frame in which ministers made short pronouncements and the opposition questioned in denouncement. Sometimes in the hour before question period opposition MPPs briefed reporters on the questions they would ask and provided background knowledge to their questions. Wednesday was 'cabinet day' and question period was not normally held. On Friday question period was held at 10:00 A.M.

These regions constituted the main spatial arrangements for journalists at the legislature. In practice these were only a few of the many locales and instruments through which the newswork of the beat got done. Telephone calls, meetings in the offices of politicians and civil servants, 'scrums' outside the House, corridor conversations, and interviews with people from outside the beat, all contributed to what one politican called the 'great hornet's nest of rumour and information' that made up the legislature.

Relations with the Main Newsroom

Taking the example of the same Toronto newspaper, their legislature-beat reporters enjoyed considerable autonomy from the main newsroom. Their autonomy was enhanced by the ability to file their stories directly without having to return to the main newsroom, and by having their own assignment organization with the bureau chief as the assignment editor. For major continuing stories, or for especially busy periods such as election time, they could draw on the pool of general-assignment reporters from the main newsroom for assistance. However, the autonomy of legislature-beat reporters was circumscribed by their desk editor in the main newsroom. Production expectations were high, with each reporter often filing two or three stories a day. There was a requirement to keep in touch with the desk editor and assistant desk editor regarding story ideas, assignments, and developments. On these occasions reporters were sometimes given direct orders to work on particular stories, to cover a particular part of question period, and to interview particular sources.

Legislature-beat reporters were required to work on stories located elsewhere and belonging to general-assignment reporters. Given that accountability for deviance and control in a wide range of organizational spheres is often deemed to rest with politicians and senior civil servants, legislature-beat reporters were frequently asked to obtain 'provincial comment' from sources accessible to them. These requests represented an ongoing source of friction between beat reporters and the main newsroom. Beat reporters felt this work was an additional burden and interfered with their own work. They were also annoyed that they usually did not receive credit for their work in the published stories of the general-assignment reporters they ended up working for. Moreover, their own beat-based cultural values of what was newsworthy sometimes differed sharply from what they were asked to do on these stories, or on matters the desk editors wanted to cover. Such requests were not only an interference with the way they wished to organize their work, but also an incursion into the beat culture they shared with reporters from other news organizations and with their sources.

Relations within the Legislature Newsroom

Reporters from the newspaper developed specialization on issues, and therefore decided who should work on each particular story according to who had worked previously on the same or related issue (recipe knowledge) and/or who had specialist knowledge regarding the issue. Sometimes the boundaries were blurred, and often assignment was based on who was available rather than on what they knew. When two reporters discovered they had been working on the same story, comparisons were made to determine who was farthest ahead and that person took over the matter as her property.

Among reporters on the beat, property disputes were minimal. They regularly provided one another with tips. They conducted some interviews and attended meetings for one another's stories, expecting balance in the overall distribution of this labour rather than credit for the work done in the particular published story. For example, a reporter covered question period and other aspects of a colleague's story while the colleague was away for a doctor's appointment, but the story remained the property of the colleague and the reporter expected no credit for it in any subsequent publication. We observed a similar co-operative spirit among members of the various radio and television affiliates of a broadcasting organization covering the beat. As long as it was within the corporation and involved regular members of the beat, reporters were willing to exchange ideas, information, and reporting tasks.

Reporters from different news organizations who were regulars on the beat were willing to share particular things in some circumstances. Sharing the same beat culture, they sometimes had more affinity with one another than with reporters from their main newsrooms, and they acted accordingly.

Some exchanges were routinized on a more formal level. There was a public-address system in the beat newsroom used by the gallery president to inform colleagues about scheduled news conferences and other meetings. Other spatial arrangements, such as the press lounge, were also designed to facilitate exchanges with colleagues as well as with sources. The 'scrum' – a herding around a source at a recess of the House or committee hearings – was a semiformal and ritualized context in which some reporters took whatever source clips they could get no matter who asked the questions or how they might later use the clips in their own specific news contexts. The fact that this knowledge was not exclusive made it unproblematic to share it, even if it had to be repeated to a colleague later.

Informal exchanges of more exclusive knowledge fermented among particular groups of reporters, constituting microcultures within the legislature-beat culture. These microcultures were formed on both a personal and social basis. Reporters who exchanged with one another were friends, trusting one another not only in terms of the quality of the knowledge shared but also in terms of the mutual commitment not to reveal to their respective superiors the fact that they were using one another in this way. However, who a reporter could be friendly with was circumscribed by the news outlets involved. If an outlet was seen as direct competition, that is, with the same local market and within the same medium, then exchanges were minimal. Thus, there were few exchanges among members of the Toronto newspapers, and among members of the main Toronto television stations. If the outlet was more distant, exchanges proliferated. Hence, we observed newspaper reporters representing outlets in different cities exchanging details of source interviews and even quotations. Reporters for one newspaper had an ongoing co-operative relationship with a Canadian Press wire-service reporter, exchanging all types of knowledge, including quotations from sources. This co-operation was not seen as surreptitious or problematic by the newspaper reporters. Since Canadian Press had an obligation to file its material with the newspaper, it was simply a means of getting the knowledge in advance and incorporating it into one's story rather than leaving it to the discretion of editors later. Given the practice of news outlets using one another's published stories in their own subsequent stories, the same rationale could be given for 'advance' exchanges with any reporter on the beat.

There was differentiation among news media at the legislature. Newspaper reporters were regarded as having the ability to capture in more depth the ongoing deliberations of committees and the evolution of special issues and topics. Newspaper reporters took the lead in these areas, as broadcast reporters depended on them for tips when to 'pop into' meetings for the most relevent testimony and their 'quick fix.' Television was seen as especially influential in question period, and at election time. Radio was deemed the least significant. In the words of a television reporter, the fact that radio reporters were least active in setting agendas, establishing leads, and asking questions made them 'spit collectors,' that is, they picked up what was left over from source comments framed by newspaper and television reporters.

There was animosity among reporters representing different news outlets and microculture groupings. These divisions were along ideological lines, including what political parties and political forces a particular reporter and her outlet seemed to represent. They were also divided on methodological grounds, with particular reporting strategies and tactics being approved of by some and denounced by others. The support or castigation of methodologies was linked in turn to ideological differences.

In the research literature there is considerable discussion of 'pack journalism,' and how the consensus in reporting it fosters is a particular problem on political beats (e.g., RCN, 1981). However, there has not been attention to the fact that, as in any other type of pack, there are leaders of the pack and an hierarchy. One longstanding member of the gallery was described by many as especially influential. She tried to pressure other reporters into taking her view, which was essentially pro-government and against the two opposition parties. She was said to have the advantage of good government sources for leaks, giving her the power to establish frames and elicit deference and conformity from other reporters. In the eyes of an opposition MPP:

> I feel that the media here is influenced by too much of a pack mentality,
> and that there are certain key spokespeople in the gallery who will tend to
> influence the opinions and the writings and the information disseminated
> by all reporters ... Part of it may have to do with the fact that some of
> the people around here have had very long tenure ... The one that would
> come to mind most, early to mind in terms of longevity and influence in
> the gallery would be [names journalist referred to above], who has been the
> president, who has been recognized as one of the chief spokespeople, and
> she's been around for a long time. So, obviously when new people come
> they look to the leadership to sort of give them the clues as to what's going
> on.

Another opposition MPP remarked on how this journalist repeatedly wrote against the party's leader, and mobilized other reporters in the gallery to do likewise. 'When [our leader] was very popular, [this journalist] and others would really just savagely attack members of the gallery who seemed to be writing, in their terms, non-critical pieces about [our leader] and just glorifying him.' These attacks ranged from subtle nudges in the corridors, through embarrassment in front of colleagues, to published statements. An information officer for an opposition party described this journalist as 'probably the envy of many reporters because she has complete licence to speak her mind and write in whatever way she chooses. I've never seen a reporter get away with some of the things she says, whether it's venomous, or totally personally directed, or completely opinionated, and so she's her own person.'

Aware of the leaders of the pack, the hierarchy of media, and what outlets are best for what purpose, sources develop their own organization for news. We now examine how various types of sources organize for the news, and their attendant accounting practices.

ORGANIZING BY SOURCES

Projecting and Protecting the Image

Sources saw their relations with the news media as a game of snakes and
ladders. They were motivated to treat reporters as a priority to avoid the
slippery slope of negative coverage, and to ascend the political ladder through
positive access. Hence, they devoted considerable time and material resources
to the news media. This expenditure on the news media was also related to
their belief that there was a 'knowledge overload' on the beat, making access
a very competitive matter.

Sources were consumed with the desire to prevent distortion of their
public image. 'It's not a question of what happens just today or next week,
it's the picture the media is giving of you, that's the real problem ... The
problem is that they've developed a pattern into which everything is going
to fit and that's what you want to try and deal with well.' Correction of
information, and especially correction of the image, is extremely difficult
after the fact. When respondents were asked about remedies available for
unreasonable coverage (see also chapter 6), typical responses were 'absolutely
nothing,' and that if you complain to news outlets you 'have dug a deeper
hole ... worse thing in the world you can get [in politics] is a reputation for
whining or complaining.' Since effective remedies for a refracted image are
not available, it is necessary to plan and mobilize before the fact to secure the
proper image. A politician who recognized this fact too late, and attributed
an election loss to poor relations with the media, said that in retrospect he
would have expended much more on good media relations through a more
elaborate public-relations operation.

Because the legislature beat had a competitive 'knowledge overload,'
sources had to go out of their way to sell their symbolic wares. A former
reporter on the beat who had become an information officer for a political
party explained this situation:

> It makes no difference a lot of the time if we put out a press release on
> something. If it's something important you follow it up in other ways, oth-
> erwise people don't even notice it. The bulletin board in the press gallery
> is covered with press releases, most of them trivial, so if you put out some-
> thing important you cannot count on the reporters even reading it that day
> ... They depend on you hyping it and contacting them directly. So, what you
> have to do is, you have to contact their editors downtown, or you look for
> the reporters around here. You pick the most important ones, the ones you
> think will most likely cover it, you 'phone them, you call a press conference

instead of [issuing] a press release, everything you can to draw attention to one item among many.

Sources must develop recipe knowledge about reporters, their media, and their audiences in order to know how to time release of knowledge, how it should be presented and to whom, and the threshold of knowledge that might receive some attention rather than be relegated to more 'buzz' in the 'hornet's nest.' In particular the source requires a sense of the audience she wishes to reach, what outlet will allow her to reach it, and what outlet will have the most influence. If the news media will not do, alternative media become a possibility, or pamphlets, or paid advertising. The news media are preferred because they have the appearance of impartiality, and entail no direct costs beyond the pre-established level of the source's public-relations operation.

In an environment where a variety of interested parties are using a range of communication possibilities to influence one another, a degree of news sophistication and organization is mandatory. This environment was depicted by a political party's information officer in describing how various political interests used interested news outlets to sustain their preferred versions of reality regarding illegal transactions by trust companies:

[The trust company officials] involved in the affair ... got an ally in newspaper A ... [newspaper A's reporter] was constantly writing that this was a straight business deal ... was a close friend of [names trust company official] and was often writing defending him. And they would describe it as just an ordinary business deal, and that pinko government minister had just misinterpreted things and it was government confiscation of private property ...
So, these guys in newspaper A were being fed information from the various participants in the deal so they were getting good leads, or at least newsworthy leads. Newspaper B ... had a couple of people, I believe, who were inside the trust companies who were against the people at the top [of their companies] ... I think they also had to have somebody who was involved in the inquiry, an investigator for the government side feeding them information, and possibly somebody from the government side *per se*. And I think the idea there was to get out the story that there was something very suspicious ... Newspaper C was in the situation where these businessmen hated them, they thought they were just out to hang them. And the government didn't care for newspaper C either because I think they're a bit scared of newspaper C ... They were scared of [names reporter] because he'd burnt them several times, they're scared of [names another reporter] because he had burnt them ... and so they had no one to get information ... I think the primary problem newspaper C had was a lack of sources ... We had on our staff an investiga-

tive reporter who certainly had a reputation, certainly among the newspaper C people and among the newspaper B people and I think they felt they were in strong competition with us. [We were feeding them but] we were getting a bit less coverage on what we were doing ... because they didn't want to give us too much credit ... [They can't credit us too much or their editors will say] 'Well, how come you're relying so much on what the politicians are revealing, why aren't you revealing stories?' So, that comes back to the competition between us and the news media, I guess ... Now again even among TV stations you had a different interest in the stories. [Names reporter] had a lot of good inside information and he was releasing it constantly. He had a good relationship with [names trust-company official] ... and had a long interview with him, and constantly on his evening shows was giving tidbits ... At certain stages of this case there was information overload, and I think that's deliberate on the part of the government. On certain days the minister made announcements where there would be a way too much to report ... There's manipulation by the press, by government, and by us.

In this account, the information officer indicates the instrumental, manipulative role of the news media in the political process. In addition, he stresses that the news media are in competition with other political interests, as they all seek to take the lead in disclosing knowledge and achieving desired control outcomes. A political interest must find an ally among news outlets to communicate their visualizations of deviance and efforts at control, and simultaneously seek the credit for appearing to have done a lot of work in the process. Considerable organization by the political interest is required, even to the extent of engaging their own 'investigative reporter.' Their 'reporter' requires his own key sources to appear to be in the lead with a story. This information officer also said that just as news reporters have their sources, 'so I have strength among certain sources ... our sources are diverse and we pool our knowledge on something.' A public-relations officer for another political party informed us that in the trust-company affair, this information officer and his party 'turned practically their whole research team over to it. They made that as a strategic decision and in a way it worked out for them in that they certainly did a good job on that issue ... We could have done almost as good a job, although they did have inside people in trust companies that we didn't have, contacts that we didn't have, but we could have probably done it if we had turned everybody over to it.'

The Symbolic Hegemony of Government

Cabinet ministers, government MPPS, opposition MPPS, and civil servants concurred that the government held a strong upper hand because of its control over knowledge resources in the ministries, and because of their place as the ultimate locus of accountability and authority. As seen by an opposition MPP: 'We've had so much one-party dominance here that the government party here has understandably come to the conclusion that it's in their interest to anaesthetize the place and create the impression that there isn't much going on. Because against that kind of a backdrop they can, with their forty-million–dollar advertising budget, and scores of news flacks, manage the news in a pretty effective way, which they do ... The resources available to government are vastly better and greater than anything that anyone else has.'

According to estimates by Media Measurement Services Inc., in 1983 the Ontario government had an advertising budget of $27.1 million (Westell, 1984). In 1984 this budget increased to $32.1 million, making the government of Ontario the sixth largest advertiser in Canada (Singer, 1986: 8). Government advertising has been criticized because it can be used as a means for the party in power to promote itself, and because it takes resources that could be used for more specific policy and direct action, thus substituting images for initiatives. Beyond paid advertising is the more substantial and apparently neutral 'free advertising' that comes with daily news accounts of governmental exercises of authority and achievements in accountability. Of course, this advertising is not actually 'free,' as news-information units are another multimillion-dollar enterprise aimed at ensuring that news access is freely available. It is extremely difficult to even estimate the size of this apparatus, because in addition to those who are explicitly designated as public-relations officers are many more who are knowledge-workers in government bureaucracies directed to mobilize an account for the government when the news need arises. Thus, the government is in a hegemonic position as a primary definer, and opposition parties and other interests are left in a secondary or even more distant position. News organizations also become secondary or more distant definers, because they too lack the resources to match the knowledge resources of government. An opposition MPP elaborated:

> The difficulty I have as an opposition critic is that because reporters are
> not that knowledgeable, and they're fairly malleable, they're often times
> much more subject to believe everything that comes out of the minister's
> office. Because the minister has all kinds of staff who can run around and
> get them statistics and give them all the information and they don't have a
> critical background from which to perceive that information. So, in a sense
> the minister gets the last word, if you raise an issue, and then he gets his
> oar in the water and then he'll have all his assistants running around getting
> information to disprove what you say and you don't have the same resources
> to be able to put your position.

Even when initiative is taken by someone outside government, and the government decides to respond, it can take control of the matter and whatever credit it offers in the image stakes. An opposition-party information officer observed, 'The thing that opposition parties are most upset about is that the media and the public have short memories ... So, let's say we had raised an issue for some time and a year later the government did introduce a bill, the government would likely get credit for it and there'd be very little recognition [for us].' Similarly, a spokesperson for a union of civil servants observed that their initiatives often become translated into the good work of ministers, so that journalists, the public, and even union members lose sight of where the ideas and impetus come from and where responsibilities should rest. 'It makes it appear as if it's only the Ministry of Labour that's involved, that has the power to do something about these problems.'

An opposition critic noted that in his area, justice, government hegemony was so potent and routinized that on many issues reporters did not even bother to seek reaction from the opposition: 'The attorney general is a very shrewd and skilled politician and very aware of the media ... I know that he has said things out there that just make me very angry but the press will not have come to [me] ... The government minister gets the attention and not the role of the opposition ... The government minister's got access, we don't have all that access, or staff, to be able to do it.'

Persons whose knowledge was grounded in other roles had the same perspective on the news media and Government hegemony. A clerk to legislative committees observed that control of knowledge resources by government politicians, combined with their long incumbency, routinely leads reporters to the supposition that they must be right. Thus, in their search for procedural strays reporters often focus their attention on the opposition, thereby underpinning further the government's hegemony.

I don't think that very many, if any, reporters here have an overt bias in favour of the government. What they do have is a natural tendency to take the line of least resistance, so that if a minister of the Crown produces a long statement with a very impressive background paper, they will more likely take that at face value and not follow up on it than they will if an opposition member gets up and asks a leading question. Then they call him in the hall afterward and say, 'You asked such and such today, what basis in fact did you have for asking that question? What's your research?' Whereas, if they asked that of the minister, the minister will say, 'Well, it's all in the statement, haven't you read the background paper?' Which for all kinds of reasons they probably haven't ... For a government that's been in power forty years, there may be an unspoken or unrealized supposition that they must be right, in a general sense. That they've been here this long, they must be good, they must be right. You start from that kind of unspoken predisposition. By the same token, the opposition has been out of power for forty years, they seem to be constantly changing their leaders, they're not sure where they're going. Therefore they must be wrong.

Politicians in Opposition

The two opposition parties at the legislature had staffs of specialists to deal with the news media. There was a press secretary for the leader, another person for the party caucus, a communications unit, and a research unit. In addition a few individual MPPS had access to their own media-relations person, and most had a secretary or assistant whose responsibilities included dealing with the news media. While those in the research unit were designated as research workers, there was considerable overlap with communications officers because they were mainly required to write speeches, develop quotable quotes, and otherwise 'feed' symbols to the leader and other prominent MPPS. Oriented to producing news, they also directed considerable effort towards cultivating contacts and good relations with reporters. The communications and research units were staffed by many persons who had been journalists, including several who had been reporters on the legislature beat. These persons were hired for their recipe knowledge of the journalist's craft and of the legislature beat. One such person was described by a respondent as being an experienced reporter, editorial writer, and press-gallery member, and as having 'spent a lot of time at the press club.'

Opposition members and their media-relations staffs said that they learned to deal with the news media through experience. Like reporters they developed a 'vocabulary of precedents' (Ericson et al, 1987) regarding what was newsworthy, and how it should be framed, by doing the work, observing what is published, and obtaining feedback from significant others. As described by a media-relations officer, this skill is a 'social' one, learned by seeing and doing, and is not something that can be made part of a formal body of knowledge and subject to written guidelines.

A: It's that whole process of reading, watching the news yourself, you see what gets reported and how it's being reported ... What you gain by practice ... What I've learnt is by trial and error ... [when I started] I was terrified of the media, I didn't know how to treat them, I didn't know how to react to them. I think I got to know the media socially before I got to know them professionally, as it turned out what I learnt is that you treat them like you do any other person ... it's a social skill ...

Q: Do you have any policy guidelines on how to deal with the media?

A: We used to. I threw them out.

Q: Why?

A: Oh, they were just so stupid.

Q: What sort of things were they saying that were stupid?

A: It was very unnatural. It made it sound like it was a very structured approach
    … I suppose if I took a manual or a course about how to deal with the me-
    dia I think it would sound silly. Anyone who teaches themself a skill or think
    they know a skill that's self-taught has disdain for anybody who will try and
    approach it from a formalized, structured method. So, I guess I found it some-
    what laughable, it was too serious. It was also silly to the extent that it re-
    quired researchers to check with the research director before they spoke to the
    media and that was too formalizing, it was just silly in terms of the manage-
    ment perspective.

Some control was effected at the level of the caucus, where it was established who would be the designated critics (spokesperson for each topic),
and how it was paramount to express unity publicly regardless of internal
differences or divisions. Having said that his party had no guidelines regarding the media, an opposition MPP said 'they leave it pretty much up to the
individual member. There's the unity of the caucus. The leader doesn't have
any particular discipline. He can suggest … because we have to be consistent
with what we're saying … that it would be better that a particular member
answer those questions in a particular area.'

Opposition-party media-relations officers functioned as knowledge bro-
kers between reporters and MPPs. Their job was to maintain intelligence on
reporters and news organizations so that they could keep MPPs abreast with the
most appropriate communication outlets for each specific purpose, as well as
actually feed MPPs and reporters with publishable material. This information
feed was done in terms of the wider communication goal of disclosing things
that would challenge or discredit the other parties, and especially the government, while enclosing on their own activities. As detailed previously, this
task was made difficult for those in opposition because of government hegemony over knowledge. Knowledge-workers for the opposition have to start
with the assumption that the news media are less dependent on them than on
the government. This task was especially daunting for the New Democratic
party, which has never had a daily newspaper that explicitly and consistently
promotes its causes. In the words of one NDP official, 'We can't dominate the
news, we can't have a monopoly on the news because we're only an opposition party. At bottom line, in almost every instance whatever the government
does is news, what we do is comment.'

Knowledge-workers for the opposition said that this inability to dominate
the news had a significant impact on what they worked on as well as the
timing of their work. It was no use releasing something significant at a time

when it would be lost in a flood of government announcements or drowned by the actions of key government figures.

> Recognizing that we're not going to get that much attention ... [we know] we can't afford to overload the press. We have a limited amount of press space we'll get and so let's not go with three good stories on one day. We'll delay questions, we'll delay background news. For instance, it was totally useless to try and do anything significant this week because everyone's attention was on what the premier was going to do. Tuesday, for instance, we know the premier was not going to be in the House for the second day in a row and we determined that the lead story would probably be the premier's empty chair, and so what we should probably do is just comment on the fact that the premier's not there and why is he not. We appreciate he has important decisions to make but this province is now left without a premier. And that ended up being the story and the questions we asked were almost irrelevant. And so we made a conscious decision ... What we did is we went instead on local issues on Tuesday, because the provincial news *per se* is going to be dominated by this one issue ... So, we went with local issues which would invariably be covered. Like we did a Hamilton story on pollution in Hamilton, also because the leader was visiting Hamilton today, so he comes to Hamilton and the Hamilton *Spectator* has a story on the question he asked about Hamilton.

The opposition strategy is to take the lead and compete with government on a single major item, in recognition that resources would be spread too thinly if an effort was made to cover multiple items. The goal in terms of knowledge is to stake a claim to story ownership; that is, to develop sufficient knowledge on the single major item to make reporters dependent on the opposition party's knowledge-workers. The political goal is to sustain an image that the government is not managing competently, and to suggest to the government that public opinion as represented by the news media is moving out of their favour. An opposition MPP who had recently devised and sustained a major continuing story in this mode, stated simply, 'You've got to make the government feel that public opinion is switching, and to do that you need coverage.'

Party knowledge-workers have the task of socializing both politicians and reporters. Regarding politicians, the task is to train them as news sources. Politicians are trained to look for newspaper coverage to deal with major issues, whereas television is the medium of 'recognition.' Television is 'presentational' (Meyrowitz, 1985), and therefore most fitting for the performative needs of politicians. As one person expressed it, television allows one to sell politics like orange juice. An opposition MPP said television is the most important and powerful medium for politicians, 'the medium of personal profile ... they don't remember what you're talking about, or they can't even remember, but they do remember that they saw you on TV.' To this end her party media-relations staff and hired consultants had given her special training sessions

> on how to dress, how to cross your legs like this, you are supposed to cross them like this, or like that, but never at the knee because it looks really awkward on TV. And other things that you pick up, like don't wear scarves because they're really distracting. Or you shouldn't wear sort of flashy jewellery because the people will be looking at your jewels rather than at your face and what you're saying. And you never wear vertical, never wear houndstooth, and never wear white because white has – have you ever seen on TV – that ripple effect. So, it's all sort of physical aspects.

Such is the nature of 'public discourse in the age of show business' (Postman, 1985). Politicians spend much of their lives organizing for the sake of appearances. Their media-relations staff not only coach them on their physical expressions, but also on what verbal expressions will allow them to appear to be in command.

> This is business we're talking, and politics. It's the age of TV ... I recognize the superficiality of TV but ... the impact is on television now. I mean there's hardly an afternoon paper left in North America and the reason for that is everybody is getting their news off TV, six o'clock. So that TV has the impact and that's what you have to try to reach and get through to ... If you really get into a long policy discussion ... you're not going to be able to do it in the paper very often either, that's something that would take a long article and we rarely get it. Therefore given a basically superficial approach ... a very limited approach of time or space by all the media, given that, then TV's better because of its impact ... [A politican has] to say in twenty seconds what it took fifteen minutes to do at the press conference, and a good politician knows how to do that. And so the impact, it's terse, you can do the whole item in thirty seconds of TV, he gets the whole meat of the thing and that's fine.

Party knowledge-workers directed the bulk of their effort to having their leader work at this clip. A party researcher said he spent 60 to 70 per cent of his time working for the leader, especially developing questions for question period, but also supplying knowledge tidbits including quotation 'clips.' The emphasis on the leader was explained in terms of the news focus on leading personalities to represent the party and its political interests. Given the limited nature of news in representing political life, the researcher's job is to ensure that the leader appears as the embodiment of the party's collective sentiments.

Judges do not become news-media stars, nor do individual police officers. On the legislature beat, however, grooming personalities for stardom is at the core of the enterprise. Such grooming requires not only primping the politician, but also resocializing reporters to the politician's image and viewpoint. A press secretary to an opposition leader said, 'Thinking on my part on how to put things in the best light ... [is] done by my daily relationship with the reporters. They have to trust me, they have to know that they can get access [to the leader] ... through me, and I guess in a more subtle way there is a public-relations function to it.' This resocialization function is at the core of the publicist's work. Publicists were described by a politician as 'flacks who are paid to do nothing but encourage the media to be all on their side ... I think it's important to be able to relate to them on a really social basis.' The ideal is to resocialize reporters to the point where they mirror the politician in the image she wishes to present of herself. While appreciating that the news does not mirror reality, there was recognition that it does mirror images. In communicating politics, the mirror is held to the personalities of leading politicians, and there is comparatively little effort to reflect issues of political substance (Graber, 1971).

An important component of this task is to feed reporters constantly with useful knowledge so that they routinely accept one's material. Media-relations officers referred to themselves as 'news junkies' who are not only 'research assistants' to politicians but also to reporters. They tip reporters on stories, give them background details, advise on the most appropriate sources, offer them questions to ask politicians and other sources, offer them actual quotations on behalf of politicians, and suggest story leads. In major continuing stories that an opposition party decides to concentrate its resources on, the feeding of ideas, sources, and story frames is constant. In our observations reporters whose news outlets were partial to the opposition became quite dependent on opposition-party researchers for knowledge that would further continuing stories. They did not hesitate to call these researchers for a possible angle regarding specific government announcements, assuming that the researcher would also supply appropriate knowledge to fit the angle. On these occasions opposition-party knowledge-workers came close to their ideal: they became the reporters, and the news-media reporters were left to be the editors of their material.

Government Politicians and Civil Servants

In contrast to opposition politicans, government politicians had a much greater capacity to make this ideal of knowledge-control a reality. They had similar staffing at the party and leader levels, including a significant media-relations staff in the premier's office that was available for consultation to ministries and MPPS. However, their advantage derived from the ability of ministers to use the media-relations and research and policy personnel in their ministries. Government politicians have literally hundreds of knowledge-workers on hand, and thus, ministers have the advantage in both volume and credibility of knowledge. The capacity to have relevant knowledge available immediately, combined with the authority of the minister's office, secured government hegemony.

In purpose and function ministry media-relations personnel parallel their counterparts in opposition parties. The purpose is to harness the power of the news media to influence specific programs and to mobilize popular consent. A minister's news-relations officer observed, 'When I came in here the feeling was that the ministry was getting burned in many ways because it wasn't explaining itself very well. So, they went looking for somebody who could help them explain themselves to the grander public and to do that you have to deal through the media. The only way you have of explaining yourself to the public is, by and large, through the media.'

In searching for this person, the ministry looked no further than the press gallery of the legislature. What is valued most of all is local knowledge. This person's extensive experience as a reporter on the beat made him well qualified to be a 'reporter' for the ministry and to turn his colleagues in the news media into his 'editors.' 'I can give you a news event today and tell you how it will appear in all three papers tomorrow with almost unerring accuracy. I think that's one of my values to the people here that pay my salary.' His inside knowledge of the gallery, combined with his inside knowledge of the ministry, allowed him to patrol the ministry's symbolic borders, ensuring that those who paid him were seen in a proper light. His office was a knowledge brokerage for the moral authority of the minister and the ministry: 'I am the mouthpiece for the minister and the ministry ... I advise them on public-perception matters.'

As with other media-relations operatives on the beat, ministry officials have a particular concern with the image, above and beyond substantive facts. The facts have to be valued in terms of the image. 'That's politics. It's the politics of trying to influence the public perception and trying to make sure that your version of this event gets through.' Again television is deemed to be the most potent medium for images, and training of ministry officials therefore focused on television appearances and the twenty-second clip.

Socialization of senior ministry officials also entails giving them ongoing intelligence about what to expect from different reporters and different news outlets. Some media-relations officers developed a rating scale for reporters, and offered those ratings to ministry officials in advance of expected coverage.

The nature of this intelligence and its selective aspects are revealed by a media spokeperson for a particular ministry.

A: It's my rule ... I don't return a call from anybody at newspaper A that I don't personally know.

Q: Your staff know not to talk to them?

A: Yeah, yeah ... The deputy minister, by and large, will never talk to newspaper A, the minister will talk to newspaper A people at the legislature and that's it.

Q: And the assistant deputies?

A: About the same?

Q: So, is this something that was decided by a group of you or did this all come about individually?

A: It comes about individually and we wouldn't decide it as a group because it's sort of a conspiracy and newspaper A would love to find out about it and have it in writing. That happens informally here. I go to speak to a conference of our officials ... and they say, 'Look, let's talk about the media a bit.' So, I go off to this hotel, wherever they're having this, and we do ninety minutes on how to deal with the press and that's how they find out who's dangerous and who they might want to talk to and who they might not want to ... [They've] got a stack of pink phone messages there and they don't know the names but it says, 'Joe Smith, newspaper A,' they may call me – I say call me and I'll tell you what I think ... If [an official] called up and said [names reporter from newspaper A] is calling me I'd say, 'My advice is not to talk to her because you'd get burned too many times ... so, it's your decision but the risk is higher with some people.' If they called me and they said they got a call from [names reporter from newspaper B], a guy we deal a fair bit with, and I will tell everybody, 'Yeah, you always talk to him. He's fair ... with your side of it.'

A media-relations consultant to various ministries recommended a clippings file of news stories within each ministry, indexed to systematize knowledge about how each reporter and newspaper covers the ministry over time. Akin to one of the ways in which reporters learn what their editors want, the recommendation to the source-as-reporter was to learn what gets published in terms of who wants what.

The problem for the large ministry bureaucracy is that it is porous. Thousands of employees and the tens of thousands of other people with whom they have transactions make it impossible to exist without a significant degree of equivocality, and vulnerability. Ministers varied substantially in their efforts to control channels. Some adapted a laissez-faire approach, allowing most civil servants approached to talk about policy and programs. Others took an approach similar to that of the police, formalizing it under the minister's office but then developing guidelines for decentralized public-relations units and designated spokespersons. Still others attempted to channel accounts narrowly, at the level of the minister and her public-relations officers. A public-relations officer for one ministry said that they had tried all three approaches in their search for one that would result in the least trouble.

A: When I first came to the ministry ... it was very much a closed sort of operation ... no one was allowed to talk to the media except the minister and myself, generally speaking. And I've very much opened that up and encouraged the opening up, and just recently we've trained all sorts of our staff how to deal more effectively with the media because it is our expectation they will all deal directly with the media.

Q: Why have you changed this format from you and the minister being the only ones talking to the media?

A: [A] ministry has to speak in one voice but in order for it to speak in one voice, everybody has to understand the policies and the practice and ... people did their own thing. And it was necessary first to bring them in and to give them a system in which to work and a set of standards and procedures and everything else ... I think if you have fifty-two [suborganizations] as we have and everybody's speaking with a different voice, then you have all sorts of political problems I suppose for the minister. They're contradictory to the minister, they don't understand, they are ministry employees, but they don't speak for the ministry if they don't understand the policy, if they're not used to it. So, I think there was that kind of problem to overcome ...

Q: But what's the advantage of other employees being able to talk to the media rather than you and the minister?

A: I think it just adds to the credibility of the ministry, you don't look like you're being protective. I have to face the fact that people may very well think of me ... as a flack, of some kind of a manipulator, of always putting the best foot forward, and perhaps there is an element [of truth] in that, in that I attempt to do that. But I wouldn't have credibility if I said everything is sweetness and light and it wasn't.

Prominent ministers tended to channel news communications through their public-relations units so that preference could be given to the minister if he chose to capitalize on the latest newsworthy issue. In general it was easy for prominent ministers to obtain news access, and a few were able to make the news media somewhat dependent on them. A respondent pointed out that more powerful ministries have the luxury of being tough with particular news outlets and reporters.

A: You can do all sorts of vindictive things to make sure that stories [the hostile

news outlet] is really interested in appear elsewhere first. That's sort of the
old Bobby Kennedy school of, 'Don't get mad, get even,' and I often remind
myself that I should do that ... It's really playing hardball and it's fun sometimes. This ministry, we don't have to go around wining and dining and creating media events for reporters to get reporters to come to them ... We don't
have sort of marginal stuff where you've got to hoke up some little event for
a ribbon-cutting or something. We don't do that, other ministries may have to.
We sort of deal in hard stuff that they like, so we don't have to sucker them
out to events ... They need us in many ways, more than we [need them].

Q: So, the strategy of getting even wouldn't be effective for some other ministry
that isn't as high-profile?

A: No. It can be very effective here. And it's fun too.

Q: Would you say the police are in a similar position?

A: They're in a more powerful position [because the news media] would all but
shut down if it wasn't for the police force. I mean where would they get it all?

With such easy access ministries of this type obtain preferred readings
of their activities as a routine accomplishment. This respondent described
some news outlets as having a 'corporate policy' of supporting particular
initiatives of the ministry. For example, the ministry's recurrent crackdowns
on drinking and driving were said to be routinely given major play, so much
so that 'We couldn't buy that [space] with all the money in the world.' In
playing into the dominant ideology of 'lawandorder' themes, ministries can
turn bad news into good news for their hegemonic interests (Gusfield, 1981).
That is *the* rationale of their news work. While the policies and practices
in this regard are accentuated in time of war or national crisis (Glasgow
University Media Group [GUMG], 1985; Meyrowitz, 1985: 137; Mercer et
al, 1987), it is evident that they are also a routine part of everyday news
management by government (Cockrell et al, 1985; Sigal, 1986).

Civil Servants to the Legislature

Civil servants who staffed the legislature had regular contacts with reporters.
Their relation to reporters was substantially different than that of MPPs or
ministry-based civil servants. This difference is illustrated in the role of clerks
to legislative committees.

The clerk to a legislative committee is the overall organizer and co-
ordinator of committee activities. He schedules meetings, handles correspondence, deals with requests from people asking to appear before the committee,
screens requests for documents, offers procedural advice to the chairperson
and members, helps to draft motions, and occasionally assists in the drafting
of reports. The clerk is supposed to be a neutral facilitator of the commit-

tee's business, although the degree of neutrality and actual involvement in the committee's business varies according to the particular clerk and the particular topic the committee is addressing. A clerk we interviewed stressed that he did not have a policy role, but added, 'Obviously I've got my own opinions and depending on the issues and the members I may or may not make those known. Something that's relatively non-partisan, like wife-battering, one doesn't have much compunction about offering views. On something that there are clear party lines on, one keeps one's mouth shut.'

The clerk's official mandate includes responding to journalists and other members of the public. General co-operation with journalists is assumed, regardless of formal guidelines: in the words of a clerk, 'If there's anything written down it's sufficiently vague and innocuous to be meaningless.' In practice some clerks were very active, even proactive with the news media. They provided journalists with schedules, documents, summaries of proceedings, story ideas, and assessments of the importance of witnesses. They also provided committee members with knowledge about the news, including the previous day's newspaper clippings on the committee's activity and a who's who of reporters and news outlets interested in giving coverage. A clerk whose actual relations with reporters went well beyond his official mandate summarized his involvement:

> Officially I'm to respond to questions from the public or the media. I suppose I have some sort of formal liaison role in terms of simply keeping them informed by sending agendas up to the press gallery, and posting them, and responding to questions about them. I like to think that I go somewhat beyond that, more than some of my colleagues do. Partly because I guess that's just my nature, and I've gotten to know some of the press people, and it just makes the job more interesting, I guess, if you're more involved ... [M]ost of the other people in my position will simply send a notice up to the gallery if a reporter comes after them for a document, will do their best to find [it], to give it over. Whereas, as I say, I will actually approach a reporter and say who I am and, 'Can I help you out?' Or occasionally will call people up and say something's going on. I suppose the other thing I do that could fall into the self-initiated category is the situation when reporters wander in, in the middle of a meeting, and they want to know what's going on and, in effect, whether they should stay ... I will often either go to them or they will actually come to me and say, 'What's going on?' I think that they like to think that they can, that I, since I don't have any vested interests in getting my name in the paper, that I will give them a more accurate appraisal of what's actually going on than say some of the members will.

The clerk is thus in a position to influence what is significant for journalists. This position is enhanced by the fact that the clerk is seen as a credible and reliable source. He is also seen as an impartial source because he has no evident party axe to grind. Moreover the clerk has one of the few positions on the beat where being cited as a news source is seen as negative (because of the need to appear non-partisan). A clerk offered her ground rules for dealing with reporters: avoid citation as a source, avoid any bad reflection on the committee, and avoid stealing the limelight from politicians.

This is not to say that clerks do not develop differential relations with particular reporters and news outlets. Experienced clerks learn various techniques to disseminate most widely and effectively the facts they most value. The techniques include knowing what news outlets are most influential in framing the accounts of other news outlets and how to foster contacts accordingly. It also includes knowledge of what different reporters and news outlets treat as newsworthy, and providing them with accounts of significant evidence, documents, and witnesses that fit their respective frames. A clerk stated, 'I've had the very best training in the world, namely watching a lot of very accomplished politicians deal with the media.' She also stressed that the key aspect of what she had learned was not an informal codebook of how to manipulate the news, but how to establish confidence and trust. 'I certainly don't think in terms of techniques, just a case of confidence and trust developing over the years.'

Civil-Service Unions

Civil-service unions use the news to represent the interests of civil servants as employees. This practice can be a contradiction of the role of civil servants as agents of the government's legitimation work. The intricacies of this task illuminate further the complexity of newswork on the beat.

Civil-service–union officials, in keeping with the union movement generally, see power in organization. From this vantage point, news is useful in affecting organized elements of society who have some power to change things in a desirable direction. The goal of news communication is mobilizing particular organizational forces to oppose the force of government on issues affecting union members.

We, I guess, try to put ourselves in the government's position as a political animal, of what it feels the public will tolerate and how the public is going to view [a matter] ... Where we feel that they just are simply overly biased and self-concerned rather than looking at the interests of our members or the public, then we think that the issue ought to be publicly aired and we do this [use the news] to try to influence them. That's the whole objective. We think that an informed public is an important public and an informed public makes

the government responsible ... And I would say we're not just talking about
the public generally, we're talking about the organized public, whether it
be opposition political parties or various other organizations that have some
clout and some force in the society.

The force of news symbols is especially important for civil-service
unions because of limitations on their ability to strike. Similar to that of the
police association in relation to the police administration, the main weapon
in politics of the civil-service union is symbolic action, rather than the instrumental action with material consequences, represented by a strike. As
articulated by a union official, news communications are first and foremost
in this weaponry, providing a means of bringing pressure on government as
well as mobiliziing the consciousness of members on the importance of an
issue.

> We have no power actually on the shop floor because we don't have the right
> to strike, that's been taken away, so the power we exert is usually external.
> Management inside their work-places are fairly secure, they can ignore you
> forever if they want to, they can do all kinds of things to discourage workers.
> And of course they can fire people too, that's always a fear that workers
> have. So consequently, in order to get changes in the work-place, you need
> some outside influence. And the ... two things that seem to work best are
> government pressure to get things changed and press coverage ... I think
> press coverage is more effective because this government's very reluctant to
> enforce its own laws and to pass new laws, so there really isn't that much
> fear of that kind of pressure ... But they are, especially in the public sector,
> very afraid of the press and the kind of stories that can come out ... Of
> course the other thing about the press is that they're ... an educational tool
> for our own workers. We don't do that good a job of education, again for
> the same reason, that we're not allowed on the work-site to educate, all we
> can do is educate externally ... so the media is a great educator and many of
> the issues that we have to get across, the only way we can do it, get to our
> membership properly, is by the media. So, these two things will help to exert
> pressure on changing the conditions in the work-place.

The means to achieve publicity is the same as that used by all other
political forces on the beat: a sophisticated public-relations unit and a network
of conduit pipes to journalists. One civil-service union for example had a
public-relations department, with a director, another full-time officer (both
experienced journalists), a copy editor, and a graphic artist.

Initiation of coverage was often accomplished through another party. For
example, a matter could be brought to the attention of the New Democratic

party, who would in turn have a member raise it in the House. As one union respondent explained, because news access for them was very difficult there was a need to rely on 'friends in the NDP, they ask questions, specific questions. They issue press releases that are picked up much more readily than ours. So through them of course we get a lot of press releases out and we create all kinds of incidences there. The story is then picked up because of the question that's asked in the House. And that's one of our favourite tactics, as a matter of fact. It's a shame we have to do it, well it's not a shame because, what the hell, the NDP get good publicity out of it too.'

This respondent said that the other major tactic is to literally create incidents that fit the criteria of newsworthiness on the beat. For example, matters embarrassing to government politicians who are prominent news personalities can be used to obtain access and score points on other grounds.

> The other thing, of course, that we try to do to get the press's attention is to create incidents. We'll try to involve higher-up officials. For example, it's always good to get a minister embarrassed some way or other. They'll pick up on the story and want to know why, if you catch a minister out ... I'll give you an example where we're trying to create an incident because we can't get to a minister, he won't listen to us. So, what we're going to do is we're going to create a bunch of people in his own riding, union members, that are going to bring the issue up as a local issue. Even though it's a national issue actually, but particularly a provincial issue, and he won't listen to us and he won't give us a hearing or anything. So, we'll do it in his own riding, so we'll create that bunch of people in his own riding to create pressure on him there, because you see they vote for him and he'll have to listen to them. Hopefully the press will then pick up on that and make it a provincial issue and after he listens to them he's going to have to make it a provincial issue because he won't be able to answer it himself ... We'll have to create that in order to get to him, you see. Now, we hope the press will pick up on that because there will be a public meeting. I'm not suggesting go out and saw people's legs off, but they're the kinds of things you have to do. So you create a part of the story to get the whole story in, so that the story in his local area will be, 'Minister attacked at public meeting.'

TRUST AND RECIPROCITY

Trust is crucial for news access. When trust is in place, collaboration and reciprocity are routinized, and assimilation results (Gieber and Johnson, 1961; Sigal, 1973, 1986). However, in spite of its quality of fusion, trust can never be taken for granted. It is something that is built up over time, and always threatens to fall apart as new bonds are established with a different constellation of persons. A public-relations officer for a political party said that most of his time had to be spent in 'public-relations stroking' because relations with journalists were always equivocal and something to be worked at, rather than taken for granted.

[There is constant] thinking on my part on how to put things in the best light ... [I]t's done on my daily relationship with the reporters, they have to trust me ... [and I] have to understand the way reporters work and think ... I've always been close to newspaper A because I worked there for so long and so I'm friends with a couple of those reporters. But on the other hand ... newspaper B sells twice as many papers, so clearly anything that I would be talking over or pushing newspaper A to use, or making a point of explaining to newspaper A reporters, or trying to interest newspaper A reporters in covering, I would have to do the same thing with newspaper B ... because of blunt coverage, I mean you have to try and get as many people as you can interested in something ... [T]he main time I initiate contacts is daily public-relations stroking. Just going out wandering around, listening and being friendly. Hanging around the press gallery is the only way that people who do jobs like this know what the general mood is, what the conventional wisdom is. Conventional wisdom, for that long anyway, of what their view is of something that's happening, of a cabinet minister's performance, of a quote by somebody, by hanging around there you find out what they are telling each other about that, and clearly you have to know that to do this kind of job ... The reason that politicians try to hire somebody who knows something about media – preferably even somebody who has covered this place for the media – is so that it won't affect how they speak. You see I've been here so long, basically, that when I'm up there I'm almost one of them ... [G]enerally people will talk quite openly there if you are perceived to be a fairly realistic individual only, and you're known to them, if you've been there a long time ... I go up and I talk about my days as a reporter ... smart things and dumb things from the past, and I like talking to reporters and I think like a reporter ... I learn a lot from them and they do too.

Politicians themselves talked in similar terms. Trust and reciprocity are subtle and intangible matters: easy to feel, and at least in that sense to understand, even if they are difficult to see. A politician referred to 'a certain unstated relationship evolving there which is going to serve me in good stead at some time in the future ... if he's going to nail me some day, he might nail me a little less hard because I've tried to help him do his work, and vice versa.' Reciprocity is a tacit accomplishment of trust, not a tit-for-tat rational calculus. Everyone recognizes that the exchange cannot be quantified; what matters is the perception of quality in the relationship and what that means for future perceptions. As explained by a politician's public-relations officer, 'You can never expect a return, and anybody who expects, implies, demands anything in return for the good relationship is totally wrong. Reporters do what they want to do, but clearly it helps to be friendly ... you try and give them access when they want it to the politicians and in return they'll call you about things too.'

Quality does not mean that the relationships do not include specific favours and expectations of favouritism. Sources assist reporters in the context of their time and resource constraints; in this connection, trust is itself an important resource because it allows reporters and sources to save time and energy by taking each other's accounts at face value. Sources gave off-the-record tips and exclusives to reporters in expectation of major play and future favour. Exclusives serve multiple functions. They provide the opportunity to take revenge against outlets not favoured. They create the ability to set the story frame in a more controlled setting (because other news outlets are forced to work from the initial single story). Exclusives also have adhesive properties regarding specific source/reporter relations.

In contrast to the court and police beats, there were multiple competing interests institutionalized in the legislature beat. Thus, the politics of knowledge was substantially different. A competitive environment of different interests trying to sustain their versions of the truth is conducive to offering reporters privileged access to material in exchange for privileged access to their news outlets. Sources wishing to offer counterpoints to the government and their ministries needed a good sense of which reporter in which news outlet would respond to privileged access, and what specific privileges would work. An opposition MPP explained his motives and one approach in this regard:

> It's a competitive market out there. And the idea is to have something that others don't have in a highly competitive market ... Just might be information that you're privileged to, that's probably going to come out because it invariably comes out. You know, some kind of a political discussion that's been going on ... [I]t generally builds good relations in the long term ... [I]t hopefully cultivates the impression in the minds of the dealt with reporters that these guys plugged into what's going on, which never hurts in the world of politics ... The point is good press relations, which are extremely important. I'm one of those who firmly believes it's better to have the media on your side or be reasonably sympathetic to what you have to say. They may not agree with you but there's no point in making enemies of people who are likely to be useful down the road in transmitting some of your ideas or whatever.

This sense of privilege is not exclusive to those in opposition. Government politicians and their officials also regularly sought privileged news access through granting privileged access to their own material. A public-relations officer for a ministry talked of favouring a news outlet he had previously worked for as a reporter on the beat:

A: I really believe that you get the best, most complete reporting from somebody who knows the subject. And to that extent I always try to deal with the people who know the subject, who've expressed some interest in it.

Q: You were saying earlier that shortly your ministry will be leaking some information to newspaper A. How did you decide to leak it to newspaper A ... ?

A: This issue involves ———, it's a government report, it's a premier's task-force report. Newspaper A has spent an enormous amount of time and effort on that issue lately and have been instrumental in changing public attitudes ... [Public] attitude is starting to change and it's only the media can change that attitude ... Newspaper A is very interested in that issue, they've asked me repeatedly about it. I've talked to newspaper A senior executives about it, said they can have the report in advance if they honour our release time. They will ...

Q: Do you ever leak information in advance so that a particular organization will get a scoop basically, come out with it in advance?

A: Yes.

Q: And why would you do that?

A: Sometimes revenge against somebody else. Sometimes I think somebody's done a heck of a good job over the last year or so, focusing attention on this issue. And if this report is a result of that, if it's part of that, then that person or that organization will give me the most complete reporting they can get. They might selfishly claim responsibility for this. They have a stake in it too, is basically what I'm saying. If they've taken an interest in the issue they will report this as something they're interested in, and all this goes to not so much 'scoop' as getting the most complete coverage possible on whatever it is you're trying to say or whatever report you're trying to put out. You can affect that substantially, like if this is given to newspaper A in advance ... newspaper A has two full pages on this. That immediately determines how much the broadcast people will spend on it in time and effort and whatnot. So when you influence one you influence them all a little bit ... [A leak also helps] in solidifying a contact with a particular reporter, he owes me a couple then for that. That's all. Nobody keeps score, but that's just like the grease that keeps the machine running.

Journalists have a variety of reserves to pay their debts. The most significant currency is major play and favourable coverage. Such coverage is not within the control of the beat reporter, and must be secured at higher levels, as in the case above in which the respondent met with 'senior executives.' Other types of reciprocity are more in the hands of reporters. Beat reporters often give coverage to news conferences or ceremonials not because they see them as intrinsically important or even interesting, but as a favour to sources. Reporters also maintain a sense of their sources' dignity and decorum by omitting potentially embarrassing material or retaking broadcast interview clips. A politician expressed his gratitude to reporters 'who are particularly close to me in the gallery who will run stories leaving out things that they think might be a little embarrassing and [that I would] not really want to go out.'

A more subtle and less direct value of reporters to sources is their 'intelligence' about the legislature and its key figures. Reporters are sources to their sources, supplying valuable knowledge. Knowledge from reporters is used to help sources formulate their news more effectively. Beyond its specific news value, knowledge from reporters is used to verify knowledge of importance to the source organization internally. It is also a means by which the source can learn how to deal more effectively with political opponents. The senior information officer for a political party stressed that in dealing with specific information, reporters have as much to offer him as he has to offer them.

A: I find it very important to talk to the press not only in terms of promoting the product we're trying to sell, our own politics, but it's one of the tests of the work you do ... [T]he press are generally sceptical to some extent and so I'm trying to convince them, or my argument or my research is being challenged by them and so I enjoy that. The other thing is that in developing relations with the press there is a feed-back process. I mean they have information as well and you trade information to some extent and trade rumours, and developing contacts I find is very important. So, I don't ever turn down talking with the press ... [If I did turn them down] I think the extent to which we can get our information out would be curtailed, and perhaps there'd be a bit less understanding of our work and certainly less sympathy for our work. Finally, I suppose I would have less sources of information ... because every once in a while I do have to call up the press and ask them what's happening. I mean there are times when I need the information from them ... I'll call them up for very straight information. For instance, I'll call up if I know there's something on the wire, I'll call up CP [Canadian Press] and ask them to read it to me. If I know there's a press conference at a certain time I'll call them up if I can't find any other way. A lot of my research is, has been, I guess still is in an investigative field, and there the relationship is a lot more delicate ... [T]here's personal relationships that develop ... I know what they're working on, and sometimes by exchanging an idea they'll say, 'Oh well, why don't you speed that up because I'm working on this to this deadline.'

Q: But they respect the off the record nature of what you're telling them?

A: Yeah, and I respect the off the record nature of what they're telling me and it works because we both rely on each other ... [I]t's usually a background information we get from the press, or a confirmation of something that we've heard that further reinforces our ability to ask a question. Normally when we ask a question or put out a press release we want to be certain of our facts, and if we're a touch uncertain it's always good to know that some other person has verified it independently.

Source organizations lacking their own public-relations specialist, or members without trusting and reciprocal relations with reporters, have the option of buying these relations through hiring media consultants from private firms. There were three consulting firms who offered their services to sources. The consultants were ex-journalists who had gained trust with of journalists and recipe knowledge of their craft. One consultant, who had been a reporter, and later an information officer with an organization on the beat, stressed that what he had for sale was his trustworthy relations and recipe knowledge. 'It's an art, not a science ... What I sell as expertise is the fact that I've had experience in the business ... Having that behind me I went to the private sector and sold that ... I do have some level of expertise in terms of how the Ontario government works and who the players are at any given time and I'm able to counsel clients in their dealings with Queen's Park.'

Another consultant said that his business was thriving because his clients were generally 'scared to death of the media, they have a lot of misconceptions about it.' His most essential task was to change sources' perception of the news media as a negative power to be feared to a positive power to be used to influence others. To the extent sources lacked the trust, recipe knowledge, and reciprocity to use the news media as a positive power, the private consultant filled the experiential gap. As one consultant described it, 'the media is only one outlet for an institution's or a corporation's marketing efforts, whether you're trying to sell the government on new legislation or you're trying to sell a new bicycle.'

NEWSWORTHINESS

External Considerations

Deviance and crime are as pervasive on the legislature beat as they are on the court and police beats. Many events and issues of deviance and control that arise in other spheres of organized life – corportions, voluntary associations, and the courts and police themselves – end up at the legislature. Respondents emphasized the need to tie their political concerns into the latest 'hot topic' being articulated by particular interest groups and expressed in the news media. While these 'hot topics' were seen to have external origins, they eventually filtered into and enveloped the legislature environment. The justice critic for an opposition party talked of having to respond in the frames set by these external criteria:

> Crime is always a news item ... [A]s the justice critic I get quite concerned when certain almost fashions [develop ... For example,] when the Canadian Association of Police Chiefs meet, you can be guaranteed that we will see a lot of stories in the press on a sort of fashion basis about the return of capital punishment or street prostitution ... You could read newspapers for a long time and you could almost chart that at a particular point it would be fashionable again about wife battering and child abuse, but there wasn't any information or anything. It would flare up and then it would die and flare up again. And nothing was done about it until suddenly ... it seems to have become important for the government to be seen to be concerned about this issue ... [although] the world hasn't changed all that much in between ... I wish I really understood why fashions in politics change that way ... Something which everybody knew was there now gets to the point of ... public consciousness, that a government says, 'We better respond to it.' Not so much in a reasoned way, but instinctively. Somebody says we should have a select committee on wife-battering. Why is it that they say no to that for a certain period and then say yes, we will have that? And all the parties get together, no dissents in the report. And they study it and everybody feels they've got to be seen to be up front and centre about it. I don't understand how that gets put together.

One thing that is clearly understood is that when an issue such as wife and child abuse is dominant in the public culture, there will be 'no dissents' and all parties will scramble 'to be seen to be up front and centre about it' (cf Nelson, 1984). At the point of extended news coverage and attendant popular anxiety, it is beyond the realm of the politically possible to even hint publicly that one does not see this as a worthwhile cause, to suggest that other things are more worthy of attention, or to indicate that the problem has always existed and things are no different now. Indeed, the last mentioned – that it is now just a popular moral panic that bears little relation to the history, context, and facts of the matter – is perhaps the most unspeakable. As another respondent observed with reference to a legislative committee on family violence, it was ripe for sustained news coverage over other committees because it was a minefield for deviance and control stories. It provided sensational stories that could be used to engage the reader or audience, and also served as educational bait to inform them about the issues. The topic itself hit home, literally. There was plenty of scope to access witnesses who had been victimized; the problems of law enforcers in bringing offenders to legal justice; and, the concern of members to represent the ability of government to improve care facilities for victims and legal facilities for law enforcers.

At the Legislature the news media take their usual approach to the politics of 'lawandorder.' They stand in for the public, assuming whatever is bad news, such as family violence, should be turned into a public good. Bad news assumes and plays on a consensus: the question 'Bad news for whom?' is inadmissible because it literally does not make sense. Deviance and control frames of this nature are essentially expressions of dominant ideology in moral terms. In becoming a part of public consciousness they also serve to manufacture popular consensus. The news is integral to the construction of consensus in these terms, and politicians and officials are eager to capitalize on its imagery and ideology. They all join in this politics of consensus and its appeal to the public interest.

The need to appeal to the public interest is a related, dominant influence on judgments of newsworthiness. The politician has to be seen to be operating in the public interest, within the consensus. This is one reason why the law figures so prominently in news and political talk; it too plays on and assumes consensus (Gusfield, 1981; Ericson, 1985). By embracing the consensual features of legal ideology in her talk, the politician can 'automatically' indicate what else she has to say is on the right side.

A politician remarked, '[W]hen you're on the wrong side of an issue, enough issues, that the majority are in favour of and you're opposed to, you're paving the way to your own political extinction.' Other organizations too are drawn into the discourse of public interest and its assumed consensus. An official of a public-service employees' union made it clear that his organization had learned 'the hard way' that they could not profitably talk in terms of the self-interest of workers and were better off talking in terms of public interest:

> I think news coverage harms us when it really puts our credibility in question, whether that's just one story that makes us appear as if we're just self-serving and have no other interest at stake but our own very narrow organizational interest ... I think years ago we were prone to make very blustery statements about things, about issues, and had a self-righteousness about it which I thought did not put us in a good light either with the public or with the people in the media. I don't know how this thing comes about consciously, but our organization has become over the years less narrow in its scope in terms of taking on public issues. I mean years ago if a hospital

was closing, for example, if the government was deciding to close a hospital, we would ... try to defend that from the position of losing a hospital as it affects your members and jobs and things like that. I think over the years we've become – I think this is the organization changing itself – much more sensitive to the role our members play as public servants in delivering services to people and seeing themselves as more connected with that, with the larger society, rather than looking at ourselves ... [The news media], probably more than before anyway, view us as a responsible social organization that has a role to play in society rather than simply a group of people that are concerned with their paycheques.

On a different level, external news frames infiltrate the legislature environment because of specific notorious events. For example, reporting on a series of mysterious deaths at a children's hospital eventually fanned out in many directions, including that of the legislature and relevant ministries (e.g., the Ministry of Health, the Ministry of the Attorney General). Police investigations of the events as murder failed to produce a convicted culprit; medical investigations proved inconclusive and problematic; and provincial officials and ministries responsible for law enforcement and health became the locus of accountability. They in turn eventually effected control of the plurality and equivocality by establishing a judicial enquiry into the affair. Over time, newswork on the matter increasingly focused on the legislature beat, which became *the* source of knowledge about investigations and what was being done about it. This coverage included reporters taking their lead from political developments in the matter. For example, at one point a television reporter decided to wander about the hospital ward area where the deaths had occurred in order to visualize that security at the hospital remained lax and that anyone could walk in and commit evil acts. A respondent indicated that this was a political act by the reporter, as it led to opposition-party efforts in the legislature to discredit the government. '[That] was blown out of all proportion by the opposition, who are out to discredit the government. It's too bad they'll sacrifice anything in order to discredit government, which they see as their main objective, and I guess that's to be elected ... [It's] the manufacturing of news.'

Politicians and civil servants themselves are not simply reactive to these external events and 'hot topics' in the dominant culture. Those wishing to be in the public eye realize that the easiest way to obtain news access is to proactively create their own visions of deviance in the terms of the dominant culture. An opposition politician wanted to raise the issue that tens of millions of dollars' worth of fines remained uncollected and the government had no effective mechanism for collecting them. He decided to frame this 'unsexy' issue in the context of popular belief in the depressed or 'crisis' state of the economy, and attendant government efforts to cut back on civil service and other expenditures. He accomplished substantial play by expressing the contradiction that the government took a hard line on cutbacks, and yet was soft on a means of collecting tens of millions of dollars in revenue.

Internal Considerations

Newsworthiness is also constituted in terms of criteria pertaining to the legislature beat itself. In particular, deviance by politicians and civil servants is attended to as part of the wider news mandate to clean up and repair flawed bureaucratic proceedings. Reporters operate with a vision of cleanliness and orderliness in government bureaucracies, a vision that is perpetually shifting and bottomless. So equipped, they are oriented to 'tripping up' the unsuspecting politician and civil servant, using visualizations of their deviance to sketch in the contours of propriety in bureaucratic life. A respondent with decades of experience in journalism and in public-relations work on the legislature beat observed that reporters are oriented to uncover wrongdoing and that sources are too unsuspecting in this regard:

> [T]he way that it exists too often is the reporter comes in and stuffs words in people's mouths or comes in with a bad idea of the program, comes in with an erroneous idea in the first place, preconceived notions, biases, and all those sorts of things ... The reporter doesn't realize that the interviewee is not defending himself, is not really standing up for their own rights, or is not aware of being conned or had or whatever. The reporter doesn't understand that. He expects the civil servant is protecting his behind, but in most cases the civil servant has no idea he's a lamb being led to slaughter.

The nose for news on this beat was especially sensitive to signs of procedural strays. Specific acts of wrongdoing were seized upon, for example, a letter documenting that the party in power had used patronage considerations in appointing someone as a judge. Deviance was observed in the course of covering scheduled events, for example, while covering the hearings of a particular legislative committee a reporter decided to develop a story on the poor attendance and expense claims of committee members. There were also regular occasions for imagining deviance, such as enquiring into politicians' campaign expenses at the conclusion of elections. Whether deviance was visualized as a result of a tip, an observation, or a routine enquiry, it was part of everyday newsworthiness considerations on the beat. Journalists hoped to use these tidbits of deviance to raise questions of government accountability, and to bring it about. Hence, as a civil servant observed, the minor scandal is more newsworthy than the major expenditure and its implications for political accountability. Journalists consider questions of accountability primarily in terms of specific and sporadic incidents of deviance, not in terms of significant and systematic processes of government.

> This morning we had a two-hour meeting [of the public-accounts committee], of which an hour and forty minutes was a very dry discussion of the account-ability of Crown corporations which is really boring, but very important. And some of the press were there because they were waiting for other stuff. I guarantee you there will be nary a word about that in the paper tomorrow. If there's anything ... it will be that the committee chose not to enquire into a supposed minor scandal in Peterborough involving eight thousand dollars. Whereas eight hundred million dollars' worth of Crown corporations, they're never going to talk about that, they're never going to write about that.

As in other organizational spheres, newsworthiness is constituted in part by the place of sources in the hierarchy. In a committee meeting, the MPPS who are more senior and respected are cited. Similarly, party leaders, senior cabinet ministers, and the premier are more newsworthy. While reporters were highly selective in what news releases they would attend to and what news conferences they would attend, if it involved the premier, or the attorney general, they would attend for that reason alone regardless of the topic of their address.

Another internal consideration, peculiar to the legislature beat because it is characterized by multiple organizations and interests, is a notion of 'property rights' over an issue. The MPP, party official, civil servant, or other organizational representative who did the initial reporting 'leg work' on an issue was given respect for this work and deferred to as the primary source for as long as his efforts continued. This was not only a matter of reciprocity, but also of respect and integrity. As suggested earlier, it was all the more reason for each interested organization to have the public-relations resources to devote to taking the lead on an issue. It was also the reason why the government, with its large knowledge apparatus in the civil service, sustained the upper hand.

From the source organization's perspective, especially those in opposi-tion, it is strategic to link this identification with an issue to their leading news media personalities. Opposition parties found news access was en-hanced when their leader or prominent MPP could be identified with a partic-ular issue the party was known to be most knowledgeable about or on top of. An opposition MPP outlined these considerations:

> [T]he leader of a political party [has to be] ... seen to be publicly visible, and I think one of the ways they get that is by being identified with a par-ticular issue which has some follow-up capacity, that you can follow over a

period of time and develop as an issue which will be identified with you ...
The instincts of ——— when he was leader of the party was a very clear
recognition that only an issue that was of concern *to him* would continue to
be news, and to be focused on the government registering a public concern.
[This] was the only way in which he as leader of the opposition could function at that time because he knew that he could talk forever in the assembly
and nothing would happen unless there was some public opinion generated
on the issue outside ... [The issue] which he selected and which he pursued
and which was totally identifed with him on an ongoing basis was the question of occupational health and safety. That became interchangeable with [the
leader], that he was the one who had generated it ... My sense of the media
is they're quite scrupulous, that if that particular political person has made
that his issue, they won't let somebody else sort of tag along or horn in on it
some way at all, they will always go first to that person whose issue it is ...
[The leader of another opposition party] was the one who was on the ———
issue and it didn't matter what we would do – and quite rightly so – we had
to be seen to be in the game but there was no way in which we could, even
if we wanted to, pre-empt the fact that he had made it from the provincial
politician's point of view, his issue ... I have a funny feeling that that's part
of, not a code, but almost an ingrained part of it. It's not a 'you scratch my
back and I'll scratch yours.' It isn't. I think it's just a sense of integrity that
if so-and-so has made this his issue, I'm not going to let someone else come
in on that ... It seems to be indigenous to the press people that I've run into.

News-Media Considerations

To obtain news access in these terms requires more than the discovery of a
topic with which a leading organizational member can be identified. It also
requires a good sense of newsworthiness criteria pertinent to the news outlets
in which access is being sought. The shrewd source learns to market bad news,
and to do so in terms of core ingredients of news discourse: dramatization,
personalization, simplification, conflict, and specific events. In the process
she is precluded from being straightforward, offering generalization, raising
complexities, appearing detached, and making abstractions. The weight of
these news-media considerations was addressed by an information officer for
a political party:

> [B]uilt into media is a severe limitation on detail. I mean by its very nature
> it is usually superficial. So one of the things that politicians have to deter-
> mine is how can you get your basic message out in a reasonable way, that
> answers most questions, in three paragraphs or in twenty seconds. And so all

the time, that's why you try to dramatize it, that's why you use gimmicks, that's why [you do] everything you can think of to try and get the message out in a way that the media can cover it without many inaccuracies. We put out a release the other day, we did a very successful tour of Pickering and Darlington [nuclear generating plants] last Friday. I chartered a mini-bus and we toured Pickering and Darlington, and we argued that Darlington is now at 12.2 billion dollars and it's not worth it because we don't need the power when it's finished and won't in the foreseeable future. Well, one of the things we did – we gave out some ponderous backgrounders and a serious press release – but I also calculated what you could do with 12.2 billion dollars ... [it] would buy ten thousand Canada Day hot dogs for every Canadian! 12.2 billion dollars would buy you a hundred thousand Rolls-Royces, and two million Ladas, if you prefer! What we did is we did some of these funny little comparisons of what kind of money we're talking about. We'd buy a domed stadium for every Conservative member of the legislature and two for cabinet ministers ... It actually ended up in the *Star*. The reason you do that is not because you want to appear silly and superficial, but because you want to show people how big an amount of money we're talking about here, especially when you argue it's unnecessary. The reason that you get into gimmicks is because you're trying to make it marketable within the limitations of media.

Respondents recognized that any one of the core ingredients of news discourse could be sufficient to obtain coverage. As mentioned earlier, personalization of an issue through one of the 'personalities' of the beat was sometimes sufficient to ensure coverage. According to respondents there were thirteen politicians who were the media stars of the beat: the premier, six cabinet ministers, three Liberal MPPS, and three New Democratic party MPPS. Their star status was attributed to some combination of their elevated position in the official hierarchy, their own personalities, their ability to offer quotable quotes, and their skill in translating issues into news stories through their own public personalities.

Dramatization was another element frequently referred to as a basis for newsworthiness. A heated exchange between two MPPS in the House was itself sufficient to warrant news coverage. This was linked to the news emphasis on conflict. Conflict was seen as an essential ingredient for ensuring coverage, and sources wishing to turn their issue into a story acted accordingly. A former legislature bureau chief for a newspaper, who became the head of public relations for a ministry, observed that it is necessary to stage morality plays involving conflicts of good and evil people in order to obtain access, even if it has the unfortunate effect of depoliticizing the process.

If you look at the press coverage of the [development and enactment of the new Canadian] constitution, that's all it was. You reduce terribly complicated, philosophical and political and legal and social arguments down to a conflict between a prime minister and a couple of premiers. That's what it reduced oil pricing to, a fight between individuals, and that just trivializes the issue ... It's not just a personality conflict, but it often seems just a personality conflict if you get your information from the media ... A terribly complex issue is very hard for the media to deal with in comparatively tiny amounts of space and time. You can't reduce those issues to that little bitsy sort of thing, so you set it off in a personality conflict. Then everybody knows there's a black hat and a white hat here, and it's like an old frontier western movie and everybody can follow it, they think ... When I left the newspaper business to come here seven or eight years ago, that was my single biggest impression and probably still is about public life, that everything is terribly complicated ... The public, because it is so trivialized, is just left with a sense of frustration that this seems so simple and if only these people would bury their hatchets and get on with solving it we wouldn't have all this wrangling about energy or constitution or crime ... A reporter doesn't have to spend weeks trying to understand some criminal-justice problem, he can see it as a conflict between different factors ... I'm not saying politicians aren't somewhat to blame for that too ... [They] often trivialize issues, thinking that's the only way the public will understand it ... They know the conflict will get them on the six o'clock news back in Renfrew. That's what'll do it! They won't deal with the issue, but they'll deal with the issue of this shouting match on the floor of the legislature or in a committee or whatever and they'll all be full of rhetoric ... The minister will have hostile public relations with one of his critics in the legislature, for example, but when the shouting has died down, will quietly go over and talk to that person and say, 'Look, I've got this real problem with this,' or, 'We'd like to amend it this way. Here's a draft of it, can you let me know tonight when we come back after dinner what your party's position will be on that?' It's the informal sort of stuff often that makes it work ... It's very hard for public figures to be seen to be backing away, or backing down or compromising. That's seen in simplistic-journalism public-attitude terms to be weak. The person who comes across is the one who's strong and resolute and whatever. Politics really is compromise and you can't govern without it, you can't always run headlong on your own way or you'd just hit a brick wall ... That's what makes the system run, but it doesn't work in terms of the media's sense of it [because] it isn't conflict and clash and drama. The drama is the questioning in the legislature every day, and 'You guys are so corrupt you should resign,' and then answering them back, 'No, you guys are so stupid, you don't understand it' ... It's the only way to use it. I mean the media's not [otherwise]

interested ... Once you're in politics, you come to the view that the media
won't deal with it in a serious, thoughtful way ... Once you realize that's the
only thing they'll deal with, then that's how you play it. And I don't think
there's a politician in the legislature who wouldn't tell you that ... it's very
hard to have serious discussion in the press or in the media. I mean you just
can't do it, because it's always reduced to its most simplistic form. They
think that everybody has to understand every issue, so we'll reduce it to such
a base common denominator that the most simple person can understand it.

Politicians and senior civil servants cannot just throw up their hands
in exasperation and decide not to deal with the news media. Unlike court
officials, and all but a handful of senior police officers, they depend crucially
on news access and must therefore come to terms with news criteria. They
have to learn to use the news media within its limitations, or risk political
death.

The efforts of one politician illustrate how the genre capacities of news
can be converted to personal and party advantage. This politician had been
designated by his party, which was in opposition, as a candidate for media star
status. The party wanted him to be one of three or four MPPs with high profile,
and to help represent them as a 'social conscience' party. This MPP had taken
up the issue of the plight of those on welfare, arguing that welfare income was
inadequate for basic food-and-shelter needs of recipients. However, several
months of effort yielded little news coverage, let alone access, and he decided
that a 'gimmick' was required. The 'gimmick' decided upon was to try to
live on a welfare-level income for a few weeks to dramatize the plight of
welfare recipients.

In interview this politician detailed the considerations that went into making this newsworthy. It was a matter of human interest, playing on populist
sentiments. It was personalized through him. It provided good opportunities
for visuals, for example, buying 'basic' groceries, taking the groceries to a
'basic' apartment to prepare for eating, standing on weigh scales to show over
time how much weight he was losing. Initiation of the story was calculated
for a 'slow' news month, when the legislature was not sitting. The goal was
to make it:

[as] controlled as you can get it, where you are in charge of what's going on.
In that you aren't sharing it with a minister, you aren't just responding, and
you aren't being limited to a ten-second clip. The thing is of your fabrication
and development, and so the focus is on you alone and then a commentary
by somebody who you've had some time with and who is therefore likely to
put forward your idea ... And so the welfare-diet approach, once we got into
being filmed making dinner, being filmed buying food, being filmed when

we moved into a boarding house, that kind of thing, I was much more in control. My scene that we were developing, they shot it from their particular perspective, but they were there for that reason, there was no commentary from the minister or something on it. So, that was the best way, developing your own campaign and getting them to come into it that way.

The politician predicted correctly that, being a populist issue, greatest access would be achieved with the popular news outlets. This idea was so popular with a local television station that its legislature reporter decided to go on a 'welfare diet' with the politician. This secured regular and continual access that the politician recognized neither he nor his party could 'buy' in any other way. In retrospect, this MPP described his strategy as having worked brilliantly, establishing his place as high profile for the party and as *the* spokesperson on the beat for welfare-related issues. He felt this was especially remarkable because of the unpopularity of the topic in a time of perceived economic crisis and political conservatism. The wisdom he gained from this experience was that the opposition could harness the news to advantage by engaging it in its own terms.

Broadcast media were regarded as most responsible for perpetuating the tendency towards personalization and dramatization. The politician who devised and implemented the 'welfare diet' story had his eye on popular television in particular because it could best portray his personal dramatization of the issue. The limitations of broadcast news outlets were also linked to their resources. While all Toronto newspapers had teams of journalists on the beat, no broadcast outlet had more than one reporter. Moreover, many broadcast reporters also covered Toronto City Hall or other beats as well as the legislature beat. Faced with such severe limitations on their time and material resources, many broadcast reporters depended on source hand-outs to ease their work. They allowed their sources to act as reporters, leaving them to edit the source hand-outs as the final copy that was heard on newscasts. This resource limitation contributed to government hegemony. Since the government had to be referred and deferred to for the official word on most issues, reporters from news outlets with limited resources started and ended with government accounts. Government accounts were reproduced verbatim because the reporter had no time or additional resources to obtain counterpoints from sources in opposition, let alone to investigate further through document searches or other independent means. An information officer for an opposition party expressed her exasperation with this circumstance:

Almost all the time you're dealing with media that has little time and little space and that's the biggest limitation … Some media are much better than others, some cover provincial politics much more seriously than others, give

it more space, give it more time ... [names 'cheap' broadcast outlets] if
there is a big press conference they'll cover it, but they will never go out
to cover a speech by a politician, they won't go on tour ... they don't do
anything beyond sort of nuts-and-bolts coverage. And the trouble with nuts-
and-bolts coverage of press conferences et cetera is that what that turns out
to be is government announcements. That's the easiest thing, the government
announces something, they come and cover it, and sometimes they'll get
some opposition reaction, sometimes they won't. To really cover the place
requires reporting what opposition parties are doing and they don't do that,
very, very very little. They cover it as though there were one party and one
administration and no real politics ... They don't want to spend the money,
or the time, that's all ... The reporters generally know they have a crack
at only one story to get in the paper or into the air, and again that tends
to favour the government because ministers get up and actually announce
policy or announce the spending of money or announce a new program.
It leaves the opposition parties in a very difficult situation in getting their
message out or their alternatives. Occasionally you get tacked on as a post-
script to a government announcement, which often just looks like carping and
negativism ... [I]t's the very nature of the place that it is very difficult, given
the sort of complacency of the government, and the government's approach
that there really is just administration and carpers. They've succeeded in
spreading that, and that's now pervasive around here, that if you are too
active in opposition you are a doom-and-gloom person.

In this view newsworthiness is dependent on what is easy to obtain within a
news organization's limited resources and format (Altheide, 1976; Altheide
and Snow, 1979; Altheide, 1985; Meyrowitz, 1985), and the result is political
bias. Respondents saw broadcast media as inherently limited in this regard.
This was observed by an information officer for another political party. 'Because of the nature of the medium, because they have short news, because TV
is more action-oriented than commentary-oriented, the government is more
likely to get coverage because they do more, they have the power to act.
And I think it's not necessarily ideological bias so much as it is the nature
of the medium that they're far more likely to report on the powers that be. I
think probably television lends itself to a conservative ideology, a small "c,"
a status-quo ideology.'

The two newspapers with most resources on the beat were seen as willing
to take up an issue in opposition. The two opposition parties consequently mobilized their knowledge-producing resources to make news for these outlets,
thereby enhancing further the resources of these newspapers. Often 'readings'
were done of whatever issue was the current newsworthy 'kick' of these outlets, and knowledge resources of the party were mobilized accordingly. As

an opposition-party infomation officer explained, 'Newspaper A probably is the one that you can recognize their trends most readily. I think their editorial stand seems to control things much more. For instance ... once they decided that the biggest economic problem that we face in Canada was unemployment, then it was unemployment stories all over the place and all you have to do was ask a question [in the House] on unemployment and you get covered.'

Here the hermeneutic circle of the press gallery and the legislature is fully drawn. The news is read to find out what is the latest problem and, thus, to determine what questions to ask in the House. Asking the right question yields coverage, which is used in turn to develop further questions. Even if knowledge of the problem is lost in the process, the visibility of the party and its personalities is implanted in the public mind.

Regions and Closures

Publicity is essential to liberal democracy, and must include more than what the state wants citizens to know. Recall that the horror of Orwell's *1984* was not only the state's capacity of secret surveillance, but also the omniscience of its Ministry of Truth. Bok (1982: 179) observes, 'if officials make public only what they want citizens to know, then publicity becomes a sham and accountability meaningless.' She poses the question asked by J.S. Mill in *Considerations on Representative Government*: without publicity, how can citizens 'check or encourage what they are not permitted to see'?

However, secrecy and deception are vital to the state in some circumstances. Plato pointed to this in *Republic*, and even suggested it is a privilege exclusive to public authorities: 'Then, it's appropriate for rulers, if for anyone at all, to lie for the benefit of the city in cases involving enemies or citizens, while all the rest must not put their hands to anything of the sort.' Publicity might advance the project of an enemy. It can be used to manipulate public opinion in favour of particular interests and against the public interest. It can be used as a tool of injustice, inflicting unduly harsh punishment on those judged as deviants and hurting innocent persons labelled as deviants. Organizations require shelter from publicity in order to arrive at reasoned choices and to carry them out. Transparency of back-region decision-making can cripple the policy-making process, while secrecy can serve rationality and efficiency. Many policies require an element of surprise in order to be effective. For example, a government's new budget would lose its intended effect if various components of it were leaked to interested parties at different points prior to the date of official release.

Historically states have tended to be secretive and hypocritical about their need to be secretive and hypocritical. This is evident in contemporary Canada, where initiatives to legislate knowledge control lead to titles for Acts that suggest the opposite of what the Act is designed to do. For example, the law that provides for the police to *invade* the privacy of citizens via wiretapping is called the Protection of Privacy Act. The Access to Information Act provides for *no access* to information the federal government receives from other governments, RCMP information, trade secrets, income-tax information, cabinet documents, and material the government decides might affect international relations, national defence, and their work against subversives, to name but a few examples. However, the Privacy Act allows for the *invasion of privacy* by giving out confidential information to any MP or senator, the RCMP, a foreign government, or anybody else if it is in the public interest as defined by a cabinet minister and certified by the privacy (equals publicity) commissioner.

Notwithstanding that Sweden enacted a Freedom of the Press Act in 1766, it is a modern trend to legislate for secrecy and disclosure. This trend is undoubtedly related to the proliferation of more systematized forms of knowledge in the knowledge society, and increased difficulties in controlling it. As Erving Goffman remarked, 'Among all the things of this world, information is the hardest to guard, since it can be stolen without removing it.' The state responds to the daunting task of policing knowledge by constantly innovating and intensifying its techniques for both secrecy and publicity. This policing is always partial and equivocal, and frequently accompanied by the fear that defences will fall apart. As Downing (1986: 170) observes regarding government secrecy and the media in the United States and Britain, 'The art in their strategy must be exercised in picking precise areas for secrecy, delicate mechanisms for controlling the media, reserve powers "for emergencies only," a whole tactical array for ensuring the acceptable longevity of so-called "Centre-Right" administrations. Yet, like tax laws, the more complex the apparatus, often the greater its potential for disarray.' We now document the complexities in policing knowledge in the legislative environment we studied, and how various organized interests kept their policing mechanisms from falling into disarray.

BACK-REGION ENCLOSURE: SECRECY

There are 'two tiers of political debate, the public and the private. The public debate usually starts when the decision has been taken; sometimes it may never happen at all' (Bolton, 1986: 107). All constituencies on the legislature beat emphasized the need for privacy and secrecy while policy options are being conceptualized and formulated. Publicity is appropriate at the time a policy has been agreed upon, signifying a consensus. Until then it is a disruptive influence on deliberations, and likely to expose dissensus. Additionally, control over the release of knowledge pertaining to a policy gives the controlling party the upper hand in obtaining news access. An information officer for an opposition party explained:

[W]e don't give out things that we're working on until we've finished working on them ... [First] because in a way we're in competition with the media
as an opposition party and we're trying to create news ourselves and until
we're finished with it we don't want to be scooped ... Secondly, I suppose
... we're trying to create a certain product and if we feel that product is
not going to succeed we don't necessarily want to publicize that. Let's say
we're working on a project where we want to show that the government has
been negligent in the handling of a certain case and we find out we can't
prove it, we wouldn't put out a press release on that. So, I guess we want
to know what the end result of what we're working on is before we make it
public.

All organizations limit the release of knowledge during the process of
enquiry. They do so in order to appear certain about what they are doing and
to express their final decisions with collective authority. We considered this
premise in the case of the police, but it is more generally true of all those in
the process of sifting facts and trying to settle on them. Governments sometimes allow part of the investigation or enquiry process to appear in public,
for example, through royal commissions, official enquiries, or parliamentary
committees, but like the courtroom these are highly controlled settings in
terms of law and official hierarchy (cf Burton and Carlen, 1979).

Civil servants face bureaucratic and legal restrictions that urge secrecy,
including the Acts mentioned previously as well as the more bluntly titled
Official Secrets Act. These provisions wrap the veil of administrative decency around a wide range of government activity, and across the mouths of
civil servants (cf Black, 1982: 86; May and Rowan, 1982). Civil servants in
government ministries, corporations, and regulatory agencies are much like
their counterparts in police bureaucracies: often they can talk about things
only when they have become public in particular settings – official reports,
courts, the legislature, public hearings – and even then there are legal restrictions and informal controls that lead them to conclude that the greatest
safety is in silence. Moreover, beyond the legal restrictions are the more
pervasive and direct informal controls over those held responsible for undesirable publicity. 'In the Soviet Union, whistleblowers are sent directly
to criminal psychiatric wards. In this country [the United States], we drive
our whistleblowers to the borders of insanity and sometimes over the edge
by humiliating them, taking their jobs, demoting them, or forcing them to
do non-work; slander and character-assassination are frequently used' (Ball,
1984: 307–10).

Many civil servants we interviewed talked in the same terms as line
police officers. They said they follow the law and administrative procedure
on matters of publicity and secrecy. This policy protects their own position,

even if it sometimes entails news coverage only from the perspective of those making allegations against them.

> I'm caught in my position, I'm caught with the Act. So, my conduct is pretty well set by that section of the Act. But I have an easy position in that sense. I'm allowed to talk about things but I'm only allowed to talk about things that have become public. So, all I have to bear in mind is what has become public ... [e.g.,] when we file court documents, that becomes a public matter ... If I was a reporter I could obtain all the information we're talking about without talking to anyone [by] going to court ... [T]hey interview much more readily my opponents than I. Perhaps they feel I won't give them anything, they expect that I will say no comment or something.

This respondent articulates the view of lower-ranking civil servants that it is best to shy away from the news-media spotlight. Far from believing that contributions to government hegemony are in his hands, he sees his situation as giving advantage to oppositional forces outside government who do not have similar legal and bureaucratic restrictions on using the media to impute deviance and offer preferred control solutions. Instead, government hegemony is accomplished through the structures that control him, the legal and bureaucratic procedures that ensure that whatever he has to say is said only when it has been officially routed and imprinted as public knowledge. The reporter too is channelled into these bureaucratic points of knowing, and all else remains a secret unless there is a breach of confidence.

In being secretive about internal deliberations, conflicts, and equivocality in decisions, and offering only agreed-upon products at the appropriate time and place, organizations give off the image of internal coherence and consensus. Many respondents, representing different interests, stressed the centrality of consensual-image production in their work. The source decides how the priorities of the organization are being valued in the public culture and what should be said about that. Certain internal facts and values may be kept secret because they do not accord with beliefs about what is publicly acceptable, and they may reveal internal problems, contradictions, conflicts, and dissensus. As recognized by an information officer, this is the essence of public relations:

> It's a very difficult job for a reporter [because they're] not kept in full possession of the facts. I'm in PR now and there are many times, I do not lie to reporters but I don't always tell them everything ... Sometimes I get conflicting information from people here and then I finally have to arrive at the truth. Because I'm new they can easily bullshit me too because they're covering up sometimes ... A lot depends on the organization and who your

people are. And right now I don't think many of our people are capable of giving in-depth interviews, nor should they. Really we have a very awkward situation because what is reported at the [senior administrative board] meeting becomes the story for the next day ... [But] sometimes the [board members] have a misconception of what's going on in the organization, and they will state something that is not necessarily a fact, and unless we move and have an opportunity to move ... [and] say 'that's incorrect' it goes on record as being correct unless you challenge it. So, there's a real problem. Really big problem ... There are other groups in this organization that handle the media too, and there is more than one source of information, but I'm moving to stop that ... We kick over ideas about how to respond to a certain question, to rehearsing and rehearsing a supposed news conference, and organizing the whole thing and making sure the presentation looks good. I'm not telling them what to say, I'm suggesting. I'm also suggesting what not to say ... I will hope to bring in guidelines ... nobody talks to the media except ... through our department ... Not to prevent reporters from talking to the source, but often as a reporter you might come across the person who's the wrong person, doesn't really have all the information, and I can find somebody who'll give you more background, and better information, who's a better talker.

This respondent indicates that control of incorrect or potentially damaging information requires several *stages* of back-region activity, as well as the *time* to either submerge the information or to mould it for public discussion (cf Meyrowitz, 1985). Another option at a particular stage is to offer a journalist knowledge in confidence, allowing her to understand the source's predicament and why the 'full story' should not be publicized. Often, it is possible to offer confidence in the form of revealing at one stage and time that which can be publicized at a later stage and time.

BACK-REGION DISCLOSURE: CONFIDENCE

Effective mechanisms for secrecy not only prevent knowledge from being made public, they also create the power of selective disclosure. Structures for enclosure are also structures for selective disclosure. The power of enclosure over knowledge is also the power to disclose how and when one prefers (Downing, 1986: 157). The legislature beat thrives on back-region confidence because there are many organizations interested in penetrating one another's secrecy. Organizations have knowledge-workers who specialize in leaking material to reporters in the hope it will force their opponents to disclose knowledge and take action in the desired direction. The trick of the trade is to do back-region disclosure work that will lead reporters to go after disclosure from those one is opposed to, which at the same time deflects the reporter away from one's own back-region activities. Back-region disclosure is aimed at exposing others' partisan interests, showing them to be against the public interest, while simultaneously avoiding publicity about one's own self-interest.

An elaborate and delicate web of relations provides the communication network for back-region disclosure. Conversations in the press lounge, the corridor, the office, the restaurant, and over the telephone, all direct reporters to the 'correct' view of an issue. The head news-relations officer for a ministry talked of her efforts to put things in proper perspective after an opposition MPP tried to blame the Ministry for an act of patronage. Her job was to argue in the back regions that the act in question was not in her minister's jurisdiction and therefore he had no responsibility for it. She described the 'nudge-nudge' world in which she tried to get reporters to change their frame of mind on the matter.

[T]hat didn't all happen in one day, it was over the course of a month or two when it was up and down in the media's minds, I made sure that they understood that there was no way that the minister could answer that, it wasn't his [jurisdiction] ... I'm up there most every day when the legislature committees are sitting, and almost every day, at least for a while, it's just a question of casual conversation in the hall or in the lounge up there ... They all knew that the opposition member was playing a political game, a partisan game, and trying to embarrass. And that he was trying to embarrass the wrong person ... Somebody had to make sure that the opposition member's remarks are put in perspective and the opposition member was making the same informal contacts with reporters ... *That's* politics. It's the politics of trying to influence the public perception and trying to make sure that your version of this event gets through. Whether it's accepted or not is another matter, but at least it gets put in front of the people ... [T]here's always more to a story than what is being said in answer to formal questions in a formal place, like a committee room. You can tell reporters things informally that you can't tell them on the record, publicly ... We establish ground rules, usually beforehand ... Material that I would find embarrassing if I was quoted publicly saying so. It's usually political intelligence material. [Reporters] will tell me secrets, they'll say, 'Jesus, you know, the opposition member said he's just going to play games with you guys,' or, 'No, he's really serious about this one.' And we would treat it differently ... That's part of the grease that makes the machine work ... information is power, people are trading information constantly. I have regular contact with opposition members, including [names the person involved in the patronage allegation] who I've had drinks or dinner with three or four times a year. I understand that he's playing a political game, he knows I know he's playing a political game, and everybody else does, but you're still trying to influence the ultimate public perception of doing that. And you do that sometimes by gossiping about people. Gossiping has big currency in politics. Obviously in all public affairs gossip is big currency, so that's just part of the process.

Gossip 'is an important medium of control and knowledge' (Rock, 1986: 9; see also Shibutani, 1966). Respondents spoke of extracurricular contacts with reporters as part of 'innuendo campaigns' to discredit opponents. Certain damage could be done even if the knowledge could not be published owing to legal and bureaucratic restrictions. The reporter could be subtly urged into a more jaundiced view of the opponent that would affect his coverage in the future. This strategy was described by the press secretary for the leader of an opposition party, as he castigated a particular minister for his practices in this regard.

> I agree with a lot of people who have said that the use of the media by that minister has often been sleazy. Since the day he was sworn in he has used the media for his own ends. In turn he doesn't tell the legislature, he would walk out of the House and then make comments. And he's made gratuitous comments about people on several occasions ... There are officials in his ministry who have been doing the same thing for years. In the sense the media are prone to that kind of extra-curricular usage ... certain people can make comments that determine coverage in a form where they shouldn't be, i.e., in a little conversation in a hallway of the legislature. I think it's deliberate on that minister's part and it works, politically. I think they do get a point of view across ... [Often] what that does, is not that you can run out and write or report what these officials are saying but it determines what's in the reporters' minds ... [Y]ou deal with the officials, and if you start getting this from the very beginning, just between us, without evidence, it determines the coverage, it determines the point of view you go in there with ... This is a very subtle thing I've described. It's in passing, it's at parties, that sort of thing ... [T]here would be two ways to counteract it. One would be a long-term also personal and subtle relationship. That you have credibility with the press, they know you as more than just a name. The other thing would be to actually have the goods. Would be to be able to give somebody, as a point of fact, something that you know that made your own side of it much more credible. That's practically impossible. Neither side can wreck their case by giving out anything substantial, that's why you have to do it with an innuendo sort of campaign.

An information officer for the minister described by this respondent readily admitted to innuendo campaigns. These campaigns are especially important when there is an organizational need to influence public opinion, and a concurrent need not to appear to be trying to influence public opinion.

> It's this minister's wish to take on issues ... He takes a very activist approach to it, and so he in effect likes to lead public opinion in that sense. So, we will do some things that we know are not going to change events over night, but we know in the long term they will start to have an effect ... [The minister] made some comments last week that we were going to have a press conference but we decided against it ... Because – this is always our problem – there are court cases ongoing, the royal commission is ongoing, there is a civil case ... We're sort of intervening ... In the end it was decided rather than making a formal sort of thing, he would just make some remarks to some reporters when they nabbed the minister in the hallway outside the Cabinet. Because formally you leave yourself wide open to complaints that you're trying to influence, in a back-door way, the outcome of whatever proceeding it is. [Informally] you're still open to that criticism, but much less so ... Our problems are almost always ones of perceptional understanding. People will think we're doing one thing and we are either doing something else or our motive is quite different. It's really one of trying constantly to explain yourself. We have a very strong sense of our public accountability here, but there's all kinds of restrictions on it all the time.

Those in opposition to the government responded in kind. Politicians and information officers from opposition parties informed us of their efforts to slip knowledge to reporters that was damaging to the government without an expectation of being cited as a news source. Sometimes this was done because the MPP or party did not have the time and material resources to develop the matter on their own. They hoped that the same effects could be achieved by having a news outlet expend its resources. Moreover, when the news outlet eventually published on the matter, the MPP and party had the advantage of prior knowledge, as well as reciprocity from the grateful reporter.

Reporters variously used and held back knowledge according to the adhesive qualities of the trust and reciprocity they had with the particular source concerned. Beyond this, there were special circumstances in which it was agreed not to report something because it seemed to serve no worthwhile purpose other than sensational effects to sell the news. For example, a death threat directed at two cabinet ministers was not reported. Similarly, it was decided not to report security measures taken to protect cabinet ministers, including the fact that at least one cabinet minister's car was equipped with a machine-gun.

FRONT-REGION ENCLOSURE: CENSORSHIP

The problem with secrecy is that it allows rumours to foster. Speculative interpretations are made about speculative interpretations. As one respondent said, this can even lead reporters to be 'fed their own rumours.' It can create anxiety to the point where the anxiety becomes more of a concern than the problem being kept secret. A MPP said experience had taught him that failure to co-operate means 'bits and pieces' come out, and the resulting distortion requires more accounting efforts than if disclosure was made at the outset.

The way to avoid these problems is to provide a controlled account. Moving into the front regions usually entails closure in the form of disseminating news releases, holding news conferences, or agreeing to be interviewed. The operating principle of front-region activity is not to be 'open,' but rather 'reasonable' and 'co-operative.' In talking about an instance when the organization's internal telephone lines were tapped by a reporter, a public-relations officer said the real danger was 'they were getting unedited information. And the reason for edited information from a source ... is because an initial report is not always the final report, and it's always good to check, and what sounds pretty awful or what sounds very certain at one stage may not be.'

This is not to say that all disclosure is aimed at deceiving the audience. Audiences themselves want a delimited and streamlined account (Meyrowitz, 1985: 30–1), a point no more evident than when the audience is reporters concerned about their own time and resource constraints. Reporters are usually most grateful for a manageable account, even if they know it has been well-managed by their source.

In planning controlled accounts, the spokesperson must keep uppermost the organization's need to show certainty, coherence, and consensus. An information officer for an opposition party said that his biggest adjustment in moving from being a news-media reporter to his current job was learning to present a one-sided, consensual account. Trained in the strategic ritual of objectivity and emphasis on conflict, he was now required to display unity even if there was none.

> The biggest thing that I had to learn is that you can't and should not be
> totally open with everything that's going on. For instance, caucus meetings
> are private ... as you thrash [out] a position on something, as you try to gain
> a consensus and then ... stick to that. I mean, take a caucus point of view
> and not deviate from it even though your personal views may be slightly
> different. That's good politics to do that, but it's often quite tricky to arrive
> at and requires a lot of debate, and that's why it's private. And clearly when
> you then take a public position, that's part of my job is to communicate it as
> best I can to people.

Opposition MPPs emphasized that in addition to caucus solidarity, there is a concern not to transgress on the territory of the party's designated critic or to say anything that contradicts party policy as channelled through the designated critic. As one opposition MPP explained, the government was very adept at 'tracking down' these inconsistencies and using the news media to highlight them and discredit the opposition. There were parallels in ministries. A cabinet minister outlined his twofold consideration in giving a consensual news account: avoid giving the impression of a cabinet split and avoid any sign of conflict with civil servants, even if the reality is that there is a split or conflict. A private public-relations consultant with a thriving business said his primary clients were ministries that wanted their civil servants trained how not to let knowledge slip in contradiction of their minister or one another.

With the need to show consensus paramount, organizations set out to censor their accounts accordingly. Censorship occurs in the context of deciding what topic to 'push' with reporters in the hope of minimizing attention to other topics; in the choice of what official spokesperson will represent the official view; in the selection of appropriate formats for news communication; and in the use of particular techniques within the chosen formats.

It is a matter of ongoing strategy to play up topics that will generate positive coverage in the hope that topics likely to generate negative coverage will be played down or ignored altogether. Reporters were sensitive to this strategy and complained that they were sometimes 'prisoners' of these efforts to frame a story. For example, in covering the attorney general's news release and conference on his annual estimates, a reporter noted that the ministry's plan for expansion of legal aid was highlighted. This reporter believed that the ministry chose to highlight this aspect because the opposition parties were known to be very supportive of legal-aid expansion, and because her newspaper was also on record as being supportive. The reporter felt that in consequence she too had to highlight the legal-aid plan initiatives in her story, and that the ministry had thereby avoided attention to several cases and issues for which they were being severely criticized. She felt this was a very skillful means by which the ministry had achieved consensus and even positive support from political opponents, including the news media, at this critical juncture.

The choice of a spokesperson to best represent the facts of a matter also contributes to front-region enclosure. Preference is given to the person who is credible, articulate, and able to convert reporters' questions into answers that serve the organization's interests. Political parties put forward a few 'stars,' supported by a cast of news-relations specialists. Government ministries and corporations also use news-relations specialists to give preferred accounts and to train particular civil servants in the art. This procedure is not aimed at being open, but rather deciding what persons are relatively safe and useful for particular news 'openings.'

In order to avoid too much coverage on a controversial issue, arrangements are made to have the issue dealt with by an 'appropriate' source rather than the most knowledgeable source. An opposition MPP was given the task of handling particular controversial issues because she was in a relatively 'safe' riding for the party, and therefore among the least likely to suffer electoral consequences for representing the party on these issues. Issues that might taint the leader, or MPPS in ridings that were less secure, were given to this MPP to protect the others.

Along with enclosure in terms of topics and spokespersons, particular formats and techniques are employed to effect enclosure. When a government is faced with repeated leaks, competing accounts, and heightening anxiety about a problem, an established reaction is to create an official enquiry that can channel the accounts and control them legally (cf Burton and Carlen, 1979). Official enquiries provide for controlled disclosure. In the process of giving official imprint to versions of reality, they also enable secrecy and censorship.

Many enquiries are headed by judges. As we learned in chapter 2, judges are skilled in giving controlled accounts and are extremely reticent when talking to reporters individually. A judge who had headed both a royal commission and a judicial enquiry observed the significance of these formats for patrolling the facts. He addressed the 'almost daily' contacts he had with reporters during the judicial enquiry:

> They wanted to know what was going on, what I was doing, who I was interviewing. But in that type of enquiry, because this was not a public enquiry, I wasn't able to tell them. They finally accepted that. 'When's the report coming down? What's in the report?' I couldn't tell them, so really we just bantered about a bit ... I never did it because I was reporting to the minister and he'd be the first one to receive the report and nobody would know that he had it 'til he wanted to release it ... I guaranteed anonymity to all the people ... so, I couldn't even discuss with reporters who I'd seen or what I'd seen or anything else. But there's nothing to them going to a witness and say, 'Did you see Justice ———? What did you tell him?' And if the witness wanted to say that that was up to him. So, reporters did that a bit, that's fair. I didn't put a closure on the witness, I didn't say, 'Don't talk to anybody else but me.' All I said, 'You tell me what's going on or help me with my inquiry and I will not attribute anything to you,' which I didn't. If you read my report there's no attributions to anybody.

The judge contrasted this enquiry to the royal commission he had headed,

in which he had called news conferences at the beginning and end of the enquiry and even 'invited two of the press people to respond to me, so in a sense
I needed their co-operation too.' He saw the news media as an instrumental
part of the enquiry, especially one news outlet and its reporter who was assigned full time to the enquiry from beginning to end. Nevertheless, he noted
that for this enquiry too reporters were subject to secrecy and censorship, as
they were steered into appropriate knowledge channels respecting time and
place. He also observed that changing hats from royal commissioner back to
Judge was convenient for subsequent enclosure: '[The way] we sort of play it,
you see, when you're sitting as a commissioner you're not actually sitting as
a judge ... But when the report's finished is when reporters really want you
on. By that time you're back as a Judge again. So then when you're talking
about the matter you're no longer the commissioner. So then we reserve our
normal reticence of public appearances, we're a very shy lot!'

The news conference is another standard format for sustaining public
appearances. By exposing the selected topic and spokesperson to the 'pack'
of reporters, there is an appearance of openness and participation, and a connotation of accountability – an integral part of the drama of government.
The source organization writes the script, provides the stage and props, and
ensures that the actors are well-rehearsed. A key ingredient of the performance is the impression that there is no calculated performance (Meyrowitz,
1985: 49). Through front-region enclosure news conferences leave reporters
to function as drama critics, to play their part in the production of consensual
images (Gusfield, 1981: 179).

News conferences are called to assert positive initiatives of the organization, to announce good news. If all that one is open to at a news conference
is questions that will bring out the good news, then openness is called for. In
the words of one respondent, 'I've learned that you hold a news conference
if you've got something good to report and you can elaborate.' In contrast,
in the face of events for which her organization and the government were
being criticized severely, 'I've tended to avoid a news conference ... I felt
inhibited in the type of information I could give out ... There are a lot of
unanswered questions ... But then it only gets down into criticism.' If the
organization wants a controlled response in the face of bad news, a news
conference might still be appropriate to offer the least damning view of the
circumstances. However, several respondents noted the risk in doing so is the
ability of reporters to ask questions that can prove embarrassing if the actor
decides to ad lib or there are repeated refusals to answer.

While these possible effects always introduce a sense of equivocality
into news conferences, the intention is to benefit from the glow of the news-
media spotlight. At the legislature there is particular concern to accommodate
television because of the belief that televised images have the most significant

impact in the political process. There was a need to calculate what outlets would most likely cover a news conference on a particular topic, whether that was desirable in terms of the size and characteristics of the audiences for those outlets, and whether a particular outlet had taken the lead in a continuing story and had thereby established 'property' rights that conferred privileged attention.

> In press-conference terms, the real crucial thing is timing ... you can maxi-
> mize it by selective leaking, or giving some people a little bit of an edge, by
> timing. If one particular TV station's made an issue for a week about some-
> thing and you have something to announce about that issue, whatever it is,
> it's just not seen to be fair to announce that at nine in the morning when it's
> their issue in a professional journalism sense ... when they can't come on
> the air 'til six o'clock at night ...
>
> If you really want to get something on TV, there are certain times of the
> day when you should do that. If you want it on the six o'clock news, not a
> lot of point in doing it at nine A.M. because for the six o'clock news it's half
> dead. It's had a shelf life of six or eight hours and it's been on the radio
> every hour, people driving home from work have heard it on their car radio
> ... it's not news to them. If TV's your audience then you should sort of aim
> at three or four o'clock, if you can control the time, if it's something they're
> announcing. You should do it in a press conference and you should do it
> with something visual if you can ... They don't just want a press conference
> with a talking head there, they want something visual. Tell them what it is
> if you don't have the visuals so that they can get it out of their film library
> or go out and film something else to help fill it in. If you want a big impact
> in the *Star* in Toronto, then there are times to announce things so that it hits
> the right edition, that's the home-delivery edition. I keep quite meticulous
> track of when everybody's deadlines are. If you want to get a particularly
> big impact, and you can, Friday afternoon's a good time because you then
> have the Saturday *Star* with 800,000 circulation. If they know in advance
> it's coming, it's good. You then have all the radio people who've got all
> weekend to fill, with five-minute commentaries and long 'feature' sort of
> items. They can all package those up Friday and they run them all weekend.
> So, there's strategies in that sense. You can maximize your impact by timing
> and [giving] some thought to what you're going to say.

In articulating his approach to the timing and placing of stories, this re-spondent refers to one type of direct assistance that can be offered to reporters: the provision of visuals or ideas about visuals. It is increasingly common for sources to provide electronic-media kits, including 'video equivalents of writ-ten press releases' (Schiller, 1986: 28). As with printed press kits, it is worth the time and effort to do the visual work for television reporters because it allows greater control over the account. Some source organizations prepare video and film clips for anticipated television news, and even add dialogue in the package as it might ease the reporter's task and their own access.

> We have arranged to have made short film clips for use on TV about what we do in relation to the regulations ... If we have a program to give out information, it's generally a long time in preparation ... We would prefer that kind of approach, to say, 'Here is the package and we'd appreciate it if you could show it on your television station.' What we have also done in a case like that is to supply the dialogue that a reporter could use ... A lot of the things that we have, although they're short, have been edited right down to almost zero ... I suppose the main reason [for providing the package] is the information. We would be relying on a reporter or an announcer to be knowledgeable in an area, specialized area, which he isn't, or not normally would be, so we're providing an assist.

Knowledge packages were supplied routinely to reporters covering particular news conferences, ongoing hearings, or a specific issue. Packages included primary facts, suitably valued and distilled, and sometimes quotable quotes from the spokesperson. A party information officer said he always included the leader's key quotations in the written package in case the leader forgot to include the quotations in her oral presentation. Packages usually included selected newspaper clippings pertaining to previous coverage of the matter. Knowing that reporters treat certain newspapers as 'the gospel,' it is worthwhile to include clippings from these newspapers if their frames and use of sources are already in accordance with the source organization's interests. Knowledge packages were seen as an especially effective means to enclose on news outlets with limited resources. Most broadcast stations, and many newspapers outside Toronto, were typed as 'stenographic' outlets because they did not have enough resources to go beyond copying packaged material.

Enclosure is also accomplished through the use of wire services. Organizations wishing to be proactive sometimes release initially through the Canadian Press, or other private corporate services such as the Canadian News Wire Service. The advantage of the wire service is that it reduces the account to the source's version of the primary facts, thereby giving the appearance of 'unadorned factuality' (Roscho, 1975: 31). Such appearance is especially important when the organization seeks to disseminate its version of events as quickly and widely as possible because there are likely to be multiple competing accounts that could be damaging. Getting one's primary factual account out first sets the frame for a range of news outlets. In turn, because of the tendency of reporters to work off of other news accounts for subsequent stories, it can set the frame for continuing stories.

Enclosure is also effected through precise wording. A number of techniques are used to ensure an harmonious relation between thought, language, and action. In addition to preparing visual and written accounts, respondents said they prepared mentally for oral accounts by pinpointing a few basic messages they wished to convey. Thus prepared, they entered the interview situation with the idea of being as parsimonious as possible. As stated parsimoniously by a cabinet minister, 'The more you say, the bigger the hole you dig.' Thus, a lot of effort goes into preparing 'one-liners' and 'quotable quotes' in advance, and having an eye for how they can be worked into the interview. Information officers develop ideas and actual quotations for their politicians, and are akin to advertising personnel who write jingles for their product. As with advertising, the quotable quote is used not only to sell the politician or organization, but also to defuse countervailing images from the competition.

Redundancy is also a key to controlling the account. A private consultant, whose major clients were government ministries, offered civil servants his most basic rule: when you run out of basic pre-established points, repeat them. A politician described this as the 'kiss' technique, 'keep it simple ... have a clear message and repeat the same message quite often, don't get into all the technical background.' In elaborating through examples, this politician made it clear that simplification and emphasis on effects provides the best news access, even if it entails enclosure on the knowledge provided.

> I remember doing a question [in the House] one time and the person who put together the question was our environmental researcher ... [I]t was on acid rain ... so he said that according to the statistics, if they approve the sale of electricity to general public utilities in the United States, which is going to be coming from coal-fired generating stations, that it will produce enough carbon monoxide – or is it carbon dioxide? – to, like 2000 million tons or whatever it is, a really big figure. And so he had this question all worked out with all these details and everything, and I said, 'Well, what does that mean?' I got him to make an analysis of the impact of 200,000 tons of carbon monoxide or carbon dioxide, and he eventually was able to translate it down according to some scientific formula, as to the fact that it would kill 70 lakes in Ontario, or 170, I can't remember the figure now ... The question that I went with to the government was, 'Why are you doing this? – blahblah – do you realize this amount of carbon dioxide could kill 170 lakes in Ontario?' So, the story was carried quite far and wide because I had put it in the context of what people could understand and identify with. Had the

question gone as it was before, which was to say that it's going to create 200,000 tons of carbon dioxide, then the press would never pick up on it because they like to have these little snippets that people can really identify with. I think that being able to make that translation is really important. So, that's why I say keep it simple, and just keep reporting your message so that it will eventually come across. Obviously it would be very different if you were making a speech to an environmental symposium where you had a whole bunch of experts. But when you don't, when you have people who are not necessarily expert in any field, you have to keep it really simple. The statistic that I find is really effective in sensitizing people to the urgent problem of family violence ... – to dispel the myth that women call up the police for no reason – is the fact that in London [Ontario] a woman has been beaten an average of 35 times before she ever picks up the phone to call the police ... And I guess the one-in-ten figure also was something that really shocked people because it was quite plain to understand. You have to be careful because that one-in-ten figure also tends to mislead people in the sense that they look down their street and they don't see anybody being beaten so then they turn around and say, oh well, that's not true. So there's a certain danger to it, but at the same time it really does incite public opinion.

This politician's orientation to the news is revealing. She has no direct knowledge of the problems she represents her party on, but relies on researchers to develop the facts for her and to help construe them. She does not even recall the correct scientific terms, nor the specific magnitude of the problem talked about. What is of concern is communicating in a way that will make people believe there is a problem and that the politician and party are correct in saying something should be done to control it. 'Inciting public opinion' is the goal, as it translates into whipping up popular support. In giving significance to problems and their solution, the hope is that it will bear significance for the politician and party.

Political sources simply fit their desired effects with the news genre. The genre too is implicated in enclosure, especially in television (Altheide, 1976, 1985; Altheide and Snow, 1979; Postman, 1985; Meyrowitz, 1985). The Royal Commission on Newspapers (1981b) reported 'a consensus that the growing emphasis on television news had lowered the quality of coverage. The chief complaints were that television expends most of its resources on the key flashy stories and that politicians have adjusted their presentations to the brevity of television coverage, often producing little of substance for the press' (ibid: 64). Among the effects considered in the report is that 'the requirements of television news have clearly helped to make political coverage more superficial,' and that reporters are 'subject to considerable control by politicians' (ibid: 68, 88).

These effects are dramatically evident in the prefabricated spectacles of political-party leadership conventions and election campaigns (Gilsdorf, 1981). They are also a part of staging official visits and ceremonies of political leaders (Epstein, 1974: esp. 252–3; Meyrowitz, 1985: chap. 14). However, as we have seen, they also enter into the more mundane and everyday reporting practices on the legislature beat. This is no more evident than in question period in the House, which consists of a daily ritual of openness for the news media that is actually a highly controlled forum to ensure enclosure on accounts. Question period is the legislature's regular news conference. The only differences from other news conferences are that all the major political parties are able to participate at once, and that opposition MPPS stand in for reporters to ask the tough questions of cabinet ministers. As Blumler and Gurevitch (1986: 86) observe regarding question time in the British House of Commons, it is a forum for the mass media dictated by their format and logic: 'It was dramatic and theatrical, it generated conflict and excitement; and it brought together in regular confrontation the top party leaders of the country. In addition, it had the eminent merit for schedule-conscious broadcasters of being relatively short (20 minutes) and utterly dependable, almost always starting and finishing at the exact time.' MPPS are n-levels removed from the realities of which they speak. They deal in symbols exclusively. Their orientation is not only to these realities per se, but to how these constituted realities allow them to represent who they are and what they stand for. The reality they confront directly and repeatedly is the eyes of the television cameras and reporters. This reality of images is paramount, and they are as enclosed by the news genre as the news genre is by their front-region stages, props, scripts, and actors.

In their efforts to accomplish enclosure and thereby effect the right image, sources are aware of the blurred lines between fancy, fiction, and fact. This awareness includes an appreciation that in all forums of political talk, lying is one possibility, and occasionally necessary (Bok, 1979, 1982). The decision to mislead is viewed as a political necessity when the timing for fuller disclosure is not right, when the event or issue is not seen as the political property of the source, and when the source wants to avoid potential negative coverage.

Considerations of timing and property rights over a policy-program announcement led a public-relations officer to lie to reporters. At issue for this officer was the fact that the right to disclosure belonged in another person's political territory, and that it was up to this person to choose the proper time and place to make the announcement.

The province is going to announce [a policy program] ... Reporters called me up, it's the only time I've lied, but, you see, it wasn't my story. I was privy to it, I knew this was coming down but I had no details at all, I'm not going to leak it at all. And they said, 'Do you know what the minister is going to do?' And if I said, 'Yeah, I know,' then that would have been added. I mean it's tough, so I said, 'No, I have no idea what you're talking about' ... It wasn't my story ... It's not altering the complexion of the story because the story is going to come out [eventually]. I'm not lying or fudging the facts or the information. That's a fine line, I guess is what I'm saying.

In addition to prolonging secrecy and protecting the property rights of others, lying protects one's own interests and enhances one's image. A public-relations consultant on the beat referred to the practice of constructive lying as one of the important things he had to teach civil servants about front-region enclosure. He described a recent training session for civil servants regarding a government housing initiative:

A: The provincial government will give up to $7,000 a unit to people who want to convert some commercial property which is underused or not being used at all to rental accommodation ... There's an $18 million pot of money there to convert. Now, the problem is that hardly anybody is using this program, a very small amount of money has been committed. They expect a total of 2,600 units to be completed within four years and so far they've only had 134 units that people want to build out of 2,600, so that's not very good ... We test them on their ability to deal with controversial or contentious issues ... [So in this case the reporter asked] 'Well, you're looking at 2,600 units but you've only got 134 committed, that's terrible isn't it?' [The civil servant responded] 'Well no, the program is just beginning. We have four years in order to dig up the 2,600 so we're not doing badly we believe.' Which is a total lie but I mean she did quite well lying ...

Q: It makes it sound very cynical, the whole process. I mean the reporter knows she's lying and she just has to lie to convince the public, or?

A: [S]he said it's not too bad when you're looking at four years. To me that's a lie. To her it's escaping the issue. But later on we say you wouldn't be in that difficulty, you wouldn't have to lie or exaggerate it or whatever, had you been able to describe your program properly in the first place and had you been able to carry on some sort of conversation about it ... And had you controlled the interview the questions wouldn't have come out that way, they wouldn't have been, 'Have you stopped beating your wife?' questions. And you wouldn't have had to have been defensive about it.

In the world of political images, the best defence is offence. Hence, the legislature is saturated with publicity. In considering what is publicized, we keep in mind that what is disclosed has been enclosed through the processes analysed to this point.

In other organizations, the major effort is to keep things out of the news. On the legislature beat there is a major effort to get things into the news. The press secretary to a party leader noted how public-relations work elsewhere entails keeping executives and managers, and their corporate procedures, away from the media spotlight. He contrasted this to his current mandate, which was to take initiative and seize every opportunity to have the media spotlight focus on the leader. 'When you work for a politician – as opposed to working for a large bureaucracy – what you try to do is have the politician on TV, or the politician's name in the newspaper, or the politician on the radio.'

In this light, much of the back-region activity involves writing the scripts, constructing the props, and arranging the stage for publicity. The omnipresent goal is to obtain access (favourable publicity), although mere coverage will do. As one politician stated pithily, '*Any* news is good news to a politician.' Another politician observed that this goal is paramount over the means: 'How the reporter got on the trail is less important than the trail.' The proof is in the pudding of publicity, regardless of what recipe knowledge and procedures in the back regions are used to make it.

This emphasis on obtaining publicity leads the politician to conform to news criteria and discourse as an end in itself. Much more than the court official, or even the police administrator, the politician is ready, willing, and able to speak to reporters on the reporters' terms. This conformity to news requirements was made evident in the back-region preparation of scripts, quotes, and staging techniques of politicians and their knowledge workers, as described in previous sections. An opposition MPP emphasized that when an opportunity arises to have contact with a reporter, '[I] talk to everybody and on their terms as much as possible. When they want to talk, not when [I] want to talk. Try to accommodate them.'

The urge to publicity is not entirely proactive promotion of self-interest. As discussed previously, publicity is an important means of pressuring an opponent to disclose knowledge. Opposition MPPs and information officers in particular stressed the importance of the news media in helping them to force the government to disclose knowledge about policies, programs, procedures, and practices. From the viewpoint of those subject to such pressure, publicity is sometimes a defensive move to set the record straight and to polish the tarnished image. Secrecy can breed rumours, and it is sometimes best to quash them with publicity. Indeed, the very fact of non-cooperation can be more stigmatic than responding with something that is negative. As a government official observed, when the issue is significant enough to indicate persistence by the opposition, including reporters, 'I don't think it's helpful just to stonewall people. I think you have to try to help them to get the whole thing into perspective properly and hope that it'll be reported that way.'

Another salient consideration in the politics of publicity is whether an oppositional interest will gain the upper hand by disclosing first. Although an individual or organization may not want publicity at a particular juncture, they seek it in order to establish 'ownership' of the issue and to control the frame. They are motivated to do this because they fear their opposition will beat them to it. Reporters of course play on this fear, thereby enhancing their control of sources and ultimately the type of play they want out of it.

The forum for seeking disclosure from the government is the House. As introduced previously, question period in the House was considered to be the equivalent of a daily scheduled news conference in which opposition MPPS stand in for reporters to ask their questions for them. An opposition MPP said, 'I've never called a press conference here ... because generally I operate on the assumption that the House is my theatre. I want to raise hell, make a point, I will do it in the House. And I have found that having done it there, people come to me.' The news release and/or news conference becomes much more necessary when the House is not sitting, but in session question period provides the best forum for simultaneously representing interests and forcing the government to respond.

Another point of pressure that enhances the prospects for publicity is the proliferation of paper from sources. A range of transcripts, documents, releases, and reports are accessible to reporters in ways sharply different from the court and police beats. The availability of this paper is a means of generating publicity, and forcing further disclosure from those who do not want publicity initially. In relation to the House the record of Hansard makes it easy for reporters to check background detail on debates or obtain specific quotations. Reporters we observed used Hansard on several occasions. In contrast court reporters very rarely bothered with court transcripts, in part because they were not as easily accessed and because they had to pay for them. Beyond the House, reporters frequently wrote stories based partly or entirely on government reports or filed documents. They were also aided by opposition-party knowledge-workers who undertook very extensive documentary research which they passed on to reporters in the hope that the knowledge advantage would sustain publicity that articulated with their interests.

Paper was so prolific that several respondents emphasized the need to control its quality and quantity to ensure that reporters would pay attention to what they did receive from the source. The situation was in keeping with

Roscho's (1975: 84–5) observation that, 'Newsmen rate the competence of press officers, in part, by their restraint in issuing press releases,' which is related to an appreciation of the irony that publicity can also be a form of mystification and enclosure. Bok (1982: 114–5) has observed, 'Motives and actions kept secret or blurred by avalanches of information or by manipulation are often precisely those that go against the public interest.'

The ability to achieve publicity varied by a number of factors beyond the usual criteria of newsworthiness. Respondents believed that some news outlets had definite preferences and prejudices among the political parties. It was therefore strategic to seek publicity through the outlets that were politically sympathetic. These outlets offered more control in framing an event or issue from the outset, as well as the opportunity to defend oneself from imputations of deviance within the preferred political frame. Some respondents were very explicit in this regard. An opposition MPP stated, 'Some columnists I might find aren't sympathetic to my point of view, because I know their orientations. I don't expect a columnist for the [names newspaper] to sing Te Deums in response to some of my public utterances, but that's the nature of ideological cleavage.'

As mentioned in the previous section, politicians preferred television because of its assumed greater impact on citizens. However, when there was a need to have considerable detailed information conveyed, or sustained continuing coverage, newspapers were preferred. Thus when information officers for ministries or political parties in opposition conducted extensive knowledge searches on major issues, it was to initially feed newspaper reporters rather than broadcast journalists, thus contributing to a definite news-media differentiation on the beat: newspapers for major ongoing issues, television for ongoing images, and radio as a residual medium.

Geographical criteria also entered into considerations for publicity. The basic division was between the Toronto media and media in other cities and towns in the province. MPPS from constituencies outside Toronto were concerned to develop access to their local news outlets in addition to what was reported in the Toronto media. News-media access in the smaller community was deemed to be relatively easy because of the MPP's standing in the community, and the relative paucity of competing sources of news. In contrast, MPPS from Toronto faced much more competition for news access directed at their local constituents, in spite of the large number of news outlets in the metropolitan area, not only because there were many MPPS from Toronto competing for news space, but also because there was a plethora of competing local news possibilities in other spheres.

However, because the legislature beat was dominated by reporters from Toronto news outlets, and because of Toronto's dominant place in Ontario's political economy and culture, it was seen as important to have a Toronto locus to raise an issue or problem. A MPP made this point in talking about an issue involving federal-government support for a particular type of health-care facility, and the initial unwillingness of the provincial government to share in the financing:

I know that this will sell: the Birthing Centre in Toronto and how they've been basically held back from proceeding with their three-year study project because the provincial ministry hasn't been willing. The federal government is prepared to pay for it, but they want consideration to be given by the ministry that if it's successful as a pilot project then the province will continue that commitment. And I can almost tell you that when you get into an issue like the Birthing Centre in Toronto that the media will all love it. If I was to talk about the Birthing Centre in New Liskeard, they wouldn't care. One thing I find really quite interesting about the media here is that they're very Toronto based. I mean you could have the exact same situation that you raise occur in Toronto and in Timmins, and generally speaking if it's in Toronto they'll pick up on it, if it's not they won't. It could be the same injustice, the same whatever.

Additional factors in publicity arise in the context of the legislature itself. Chances for access vary by the time of year, for example, whether the House is sitting. Placing stories is much easier when the House is not sitting and therefore the news media are not framing the issues through question period. However, what is gained in access during recess periods is offset by the loss of televised coverage of the dramatic exchanges in the House between the opposition MPP and the cabinet minister responsible. An opposition-party information officer discussed strategy in this regard:

Once you've got the goods together you then talk about how and when you're going to use it. Whether you do it while the House isn't sitting. The advantage of that for some issues is that reporters have less to do, it's less busy and more of them will cover your press conference, they don't have as much news to report so they're looking for stories. On the other hand some of them are on vacation so you may not get many reporters around and you can't raise it in the House because the House isn't sitting. The advantage of doing it while the House is sitting is that you can then ask it in the House where there's TV coverage and where you can get an exchange going with the minister, and where you have somebody right there to accuse, that's more dramatic.

These questions of time and place are connected to the question of vol-ume raised earlier. When there is less activity – less volume of news conferences, releases, government reports, and so on – there is more opportunity for a voice to be heard. In particular opposition parties and interest groups wishing to stake their initial claim to ownership of an issue can obtain more access, and an extended period of control, by timing the release so that the government's organized reaction in the House and elsewhere is not possible immediately.

There is also variation in terms of status both individually and organizationally. Among MPPS for opposition parties, the ordinary MPP has more restricted access than the party critics and the leader. Among MPPS for the government, the back-bencher is more restricted in access than cabinet ministers and the premier. Legislative committees are also a basis for status. Members seek membership on high-status committees because they want the publicity connected with those committees; in turn, of course, reporters attend to high-status committees in part because they are constituted with high-status MPPS. There is also a status differential among the ministries in relation to access for publicity.

REPORTERS' SELF-ENCLOSURE

Reporters' self-enclosure on the legislature beat varied according to the news organizations they worked for. The political affinities and thrust of the news outlet restrained reporters to be selective about their topics, sources, and accounts. The economy of the news outlet also had a bearing. Outlets that budgeted little for their news operations forced their reporters to be especially dependent on selected sources and their news releases. Some believed that the government's place as a leading advertiser circumscribed the ability to be critical of government. There was a fear of not wanting to bite the hand that feeds. Specific instances of not publishing critical pieces imputing deviance to those in power were attributed to not wanting to offend those in control of the advertising budgets. One respondent emphasized that government advertising budgets 'can very seriously affect the positions that they [reporters] take in respect to the people that are in a position to authorize [those budgets].' He went on to describe an instance in which a reporter's filed stories on corruption in office were not being published, and concluded, 'You'll never convince me that they weren't influenced by the fact that they're getting major advertising, and they belong to a chain, and now somebody sets that policy, and it's set on the basis of financial decisions.'

On the level of journalists' methodology, self-enclosure is related to a lack of knowledge, as well as no inclination or incentive to search further. It is frustrating to have to deal with reporters who 'pop' from one story to another, and who therefore have no sense of history or context for the particular issue they are dealing with. However, such a practice often gives the source control of the account because reporters are forced to accept her statements uncritically. When reporters persist with potentially damaging questions, it is often possible to rely on their ignorance of developments to turn the occasion to advantage. An opposition MPP described how a cabinet minister managed this on one occasion:

> The minister came to our committee to talk about child abuse, and we got onto the subject of family violence. The minister was under attack because he hadn't implemented any of the recommendations or done anything about the things in our report. And then he came out of the committee meeting and the press was going after him and attacking him. And then he said he was going to announce that there would be fifteen centres [for victims of wife assault] in Ontario within the next month, or fifteen new centres. So, the story was, 'Minister announces fifteen new centres.' Again the problem being that the reporters who covered that particular intervention did not understand that in fact those fifteen new centres were all on stream before these hearings ever took place. The ministry has nothing to do with organizing them, funding them, getting them off the ground, it's all total local grass-roots intervention. And so, because they're not well informed, when the minister announces that he's going to be building these fifteen new centres, they all went off and wrote stories about how great the minister was building all these new centres, when, in fact, he was merely reporting that these centres were to be built by people out in the community who really had received no encouragement at all from his ministry to date. The reason that that could happen was because the people who were covering the story again were not people who had participated all the way along. I guess continuity is the other thing that would be important because you can come at things: the minister is a pretty strong guy and if a reporter comes at him without all of the facts, then he'll turn around and just throw it back at them, and so they hesitate, and they kind of tiptoe, and then he can just carry the whole thing.

Reporters rarely did extensive checks or research, relying instead upon opposition-party and/or ministry information officers for detailed knowledge and key spokespersons for quotations. Some broadcast reporters admitted that they never did any 'serious' research into their stories. When 'research' was undertaken by any reporter, it typically consisted of searches for past newspaper articles on the topic. Reporters had much greater freedom to obtain knowledge than they actually made use of. The occasions of denial of access to knowledge are sometimes the cause for extensive news coverage and cries about freedom of the press. The norm, however, is that reporters rarely bother to obtain the documentary detail available to them, relying instead on the performative accounts of sources. The head news-relations officer for a ministry observed that reporters 'have far greater access than they know. Most reporters don't know where to look for information, and particularly in the justice system.' A clerk to legislative committees concurred, saying that even the research she did for reporters as background to a committee's work was typically ignored:

> Freedom of information [is] much less significant than most people think because the press neither have the time nor the inclination to read the stuff anyway. It's quite true. One of my functions as a committee clerk is to, as much as I can, supply the press with information to the committee. And virtually everything that comes to a committee is considered to be public information. So, they'll be sitting there, and they'll ask for the briefs, or the submissions, or the exhibits, and so on, and I try to help them out and give them the stuff and so on. And you can just see them, flip, flip, flip, flip. If they find something really good they circle it and it's put into the story, or they'll ask the witness about it later on. Most of the time the stuff is simply left at the press table afterwards and they've not really – they've scanned it. And effectively scanned it, I'm sure, they've become very good at it for what will be a, in their terms, news story. But they haven't really got the full sense of the thing, I'm quite sure. Partially because they don't have the time, they've got to run off and do another story. Some other minister is holding a press conference, or the House will be starting soon, and they have to go off and file on that or something. It's partly inclination and partly it's time. There are very few reporters, for example, who will read the Hansards of committees. Virtually all of them are transcribed and available and in fact they're sent up to the press gallery.

For journalistic purposes, it is often satisfactory to obtain an imputation of deviance from one side and the counterpoint response of the source subject to the imputation, with truth being held to reside somewhere in between the two accounts (Tuchman, 1978). Searching documentary sources leaves the reporter open to interpretive error. It can also offer a more accurate view of the matter that resolves the conflict and hence 'kills' the story. From the journalists' perspective, it is usually far better to leave the documentary realities unknown, giving preference and deference to authoritative accounts visualizing what appears to be the case.

As elsewhere, reporters also circumscribe their knowledgeability by relying upon the knowledge of news to keep informed. 'Pack journalism' has been frequently referred to as a feature of Canadian news, especially in relation to political reporting generally (Black, 1982), and election-campaign reporting in particular (Gilsdorf, 1981; Soderlund et al, 1981; RCN, 1981b: 90). Reporters we observed readily used other reporters as a guide to what was newsworthy, exchanged ideas and quotations with one another, and turned to old news accounts to understand what might be news.

Reporters' criteria of newsworthiness were also limiting on what information they sought and who they sought it from. The need to personalize issues through political leaders was referred to by many respondents as *the* limiting factor. 'Even those who purport to report on politics often get caught in the web of performance and become part of the ritualized drama, just as sports commentators often become part of the ritual of sports' (Meyrowitz, 1985: 277).

As Gilsdorf (1981: 67) comments, 'It may be correct that the only truly Canadian stars are political leaders.' The cult of political personalities fostered by the news media, especially television, and the effects on limiting public discourse, have been addressed by a number of critics. Todd Gitlin observes:

> This is of the essence of advertising, which is the systematic creation of images for the purpose of generating a behavior – namely buying – on the part of people who have no larger, no deeper familiarity ... And in a situation like that the leaders and actions that come to the fore in a sense are out of central casting. Their political identity bears no organic relation to the real political situation, but is a back and forth refraction of media images. What's being done is no longer politics as an exercise in freedom. Really it's the end of politics and politics at that point becomes really a spectator sport in which a few people go out and play demonic roles and other people root for them. (Cayley, 1982a: 171)

It is too simplistic to assert that government presses for enclosure and the free press champions disclosure. Given our analyses (see also Ericson et al, 1987), it is reasonable to conclude that for journalists, more 'open government would sharply alter the practice of their craft' (Downing 1986: 163). There would be a greater onus on reporters to search for documents, read detailed research reports, and so on. There would be more work, not less. In addition to these practical effects on journalism, more open government would affect journalists' occupational ideology. '[G]overnment secrecy has its pay-offs for journalists and their editors. Leaks, individual or institutional (for example, the lobby system), give a journalist status. Without them, without being privy to special information, from where could the journalist derive the necessary elevation over the rest of us?' (ibid).

There are powerful factors emanating from reporters' ways of knowing and the genre capacities of their media that contribute to enclosure. These combine with sources' own cultural and social-organizational reasons for effecting enclosure to produce a product that is severely limited. Ultimately,

enclosure on the legislature beat and the conversion of politics into prefabricated spectacles is a result of the organization of both reporters and sources.
Both sources and reporters use techniques of 'self-editing' to satisfy their
capacities for news. As expressed by a political party's information officer:

> Oftentimes we write the press releases almost like a news story and organize
> them in such a way that there's a lead, the punch is in the lead, then there's
> the follow-up explanation and facts, figures, and quotes, and then finishes
> off with a punch or something ... I must admit we try to make their work
> as easy as possible, we try to make it so that all they need to do is copy
> our press release if they're so inclined ... I think the only thing we could
> do more ... would be to write possible news stories, and have the press just
> put their bylines to it. I mean that's been thought of. That might be a bit
> insulting.

Some sources had made this thought a reality. A reporter was known to
permit officials to see his copy before it was submitted to his editors, allowing
them final editing enclosure in addition to all the work they had done in
advance to effect enclosure. A government MPP noted his 'quasi-journalistic'
style in preparing releases, and his success in having them published almost
verbatim:

> One of my strengths over the years, even before I got into politics, was
> writing. Fiction and non-fiction. So, if I'm drafting a release ... I can draft
> something that will be picked up and that will generally be perceived pretty
> well ... If you're conscious of what you're doing you appreciate that a
> release is more likely to be picked up if it's easy for the media to use. And
> one way to make it easy for them is to put it in quasi-journalistic style
> already, and just let them have it. And sometimes, especially in the case of
> local media – the smaller outlets as opposed to the big metropolitan ones
> – very often they'll lift whole passages out of your release and just reprint
> them as part of your story.

While reporters sometimes reprint sources' material as if they are no
more than a conduit pipe to their news outlet, this does not mean that sources
ultimately control the account and perpetuate their bureaucratic propaganda.
All it means is that sources are as well versed as reporters in the requirements of news, and that they tailor their accounts accordingly. Sources are
as constrained as reporters by the limited capacities of news communication.
If they want the power of the news media, they must visualize their activity
and refract their image in terms of 'media power' (Altheide, 1985).

Influences of News Texts

The Significance of Television

The political imperative to co-operate is based on the knowledge that the news media are extremely powerful. Respondents viewed the news media as the most influential part of the political process, and therefore a force they had to come to terms with. When describing news-media powers of communication, they complained about superficiality, distortion, inaccuracy, and lack of context. However, when describing news-media powers of influencing political processes, they emphasized their respect and even awe for its potency. They recognized the severe limitations of the news media as a vehicle for providing adequate knowledge, but at the same time acknowledged its enormous influence as an agency of social control, reform politics, and institutional power.

Politicians and civil servants wanted to harness the power of the news media to educate their constituencies and to socialize them into their view of the world. The news media are a means of selling one's product, better than advertising because news appears more neutral and objective. The news media also allow testing of one's product in the market-place of ideas, generating feed-back from the general public, interested organizations, and journalists themselves. In addition to these positive powers of news-media signs, there is also the negative power to stigmatize, marginalize, and exclude, that can be used to discredit political opponents.

Political actors give priority to television because, regardless of substance, they believe in the power of its image. While the court beat is print-oriented, and the police beat is print- and broadcast- (especially radio) oriented, the legislature beat offers a special place for television. Television has transformed the official culture of our society from the literate and formal logic of print to its inverse, image and rhetoric (Fiske and Hartley, 1978: 117). It has *illiterately* transformed the political stage (Meyrowitz, 1985). Politicians and officials have joined with advertising executives in appreciating that television is the best for 'getting an image across, imposing an impression of a product or service' (RCN, 1981: 73). 'On television, discourse is conducted through visual imagery, which is to say that television gives us a conversation in images, not words ... You cannot do political philosophy on television. Its form works against its content' (Postman, 1985: 7).

No matter what is done by the politician or her organizers for the people, its political significance is lessened substantially if it cannot be converted into the twenty-second clip, as is evident in the Canadian federal parliament:

Television reporters, in particular, form an identifiable elite in the Gallery,

with incomes and audiences far larger than those enjoyed by print journalists. They have unrivalled access to politicians. Political developments are
scheduled and staged to suit their requirements.

   In a typical Ottawa 'scrum' of journalists besieging a politician for comment, radio and TV journalists usually are at the centre, asking the questions,
while the print journalists scribble in their notebooks on the sidelines. The
politicians tend to answer in short 'clips' tailored for newscasts rather than
entering into substantial discussions with journalists. Researchers for the
Commission found that 'despite the good work of some correspondents and
producers, especially with the CBC, the requirements of television news have
clearly helped to make political coverage more superficial.' (RCN, 1981: 142)

The dominance of television in political strategy comes to the forefront
during election campaigns. 'Television has come into its own, and political
journalism has veered toward total irrelevance, during recent election campaigns. Liberal party strategists in 1980 went so far as to declare that they
did not care what the print medium published so long as the party received
regular television coverage' (ibid: 143). An analyst of the 1979 federal election campaign records that 'key aides of all parties unabashedly admitted the
television orientation. Scheduling, policy statements, speeches, rallies, sleigh
rides, paper mill visits, farm visits and Chinatown visits were all designed
with the visual media in mind. There seemed to be a general ranking order:
television (CBC first), wire service, photographs, radio, wire service reporters,
selected columnists, the *Globe and Mail*, the Toronto *Star*, and, finally the
rest of the print media' (Gilsdorf, 1981: 62). In this same election campaign
the three major parties also signified their media preferences through their
advertising budgets: 55 per cent on television, 27 per cent on radio, and 18
per cent on print (RCN, 1981: 137).

   It is not only politicians and their publicists who have become television-
oriented. Those representing the official views of ministries and Crown corporations are also trained to orient their news talk to the requirements of
television. On the legislature beat a private news-relations consultant to government bureaucracies organized his training sessions around hypothetical
television interviews. He included actual videos of the interviews to play
back to trainees so that they could experience how they appeared. The head
of a ministry public-relations office explained why television was being emphasized in the training of ministry officials as news sources. 'People get
most of their information from it. It's impact, in some events, can be far
greater than the papers can ever be ... We try to get things that are good TV,
as we say, but it's nearly impossible ... It's really tough to explain to people
how the system works when they can't see it at all, and what they do see are
dramatizations of it ... that are very wrong.'

INFLUENCES ON PROCEEDINGS AND PARTICIPANTS

As part of the political process, the news media are seen as having powerful influence on the proceedings of the legislature, ministries, institutions, political parties, and individual careers. The presence of the news media, or the possibility of their presence, means that those engaged in the business of the legislature are always half-watching in terms of another show.

The House

The influence of the news media is most evident in the House itself. The issues and specific questions raised during question period are as much or more framed by reporters than by politicians and their information workers. This situation is parallel to that pertaining in the Canadian federal parliament (Munton and Clow, 1979). The manner in which the news media set the agenda so that it favours the government, and to a lesser extent the official opposition, was articulated by an opposition MPP:

> Under our system here of the way the House is covered, the cabinet ministers
> and the government have the full advantage of getting the coverage, and not
> the opposition. You can expect only one story a day to come out of here in
> terms of TV; maybe several in terms of some radio stations, very short snips;
> and then the two major Toronto papers, two to three stories depending on
> the day, usually not necessarily on prominent pages; and, in the *Sun* maybe
> one story a day depending on the day and their vitriol column. These people,
> then, who are getting one story a day, get it out of question period primarily,
> it means there isn't much research done on the way this place operates.
> Not a lot of coverage of committees and any background work. Then you
> get people looking for the quick fix in terms of a cabinet statement. On
> Thursdays, for instance, when we have cabinet statements galore, which is
> set up for the weekend press essentially, that's what gets covered. You may
> get the opposition reaction to it, but it will be way down in a column, or
> it'll be a couple-of-seconds clip at the end, or mostly just a voice-over by an
> on-camera man saying, 'And the opposition said they didn't like this, but,'
> and away they go, sort-of-thing. And they have that huge advantage then ...
> In third place, you don't get on until there have already been six questions
> asked, essentially. All around two areas, but six, and so what happens is the
> official opposition gets to choose what they think is a crucial story of the
> day. And they get to ask the first questions on it, they therefore get the most
> coverage on it, and you're following up on it. Even that isn't that clear in
> terms of the opposition actually making news. Often what the opposition
> parties do in terms of their own laziness is to choose the story that was in

the press the day before or that morning. So, we already know what the press wants to concentrate on because they've already decided that for you. Then you ask a question on it so you get to manipulate it ... You know the press are interested because they did a story on it, and then you can do the follow-up question, which they couldn't do, they just cover the main story and then you will get some coverage for asking the question.

It is in this respect that the news media are seen as having almost an official place in opposition to the government. The events and issues the news media select to cover were seen by opposition-party politicians and strategists as the events and issues they should raise in the House. Opposition party use of the agenda established by the media was aimed not only at criticism of the government, but more significantly, at obtaining news visibility for the party and the specific politicians who put the questions. The House therefore lost any sense of self-containment, and was subject to continual strong influence by the news media. This situation is quite different from that on the court and police beats where journalists are often conduits for official voices. During question period in the legislature, politicians asking questions were little more than conduits for the news media.

The decorum of the House and its potential for rational discussion is also under the influence of the news media. While the House agenda is heavily influenced by newspaper coverage, the tone and style of discourse is affected by television. Respondents referred to the presence of television cameras as encouraging exhibitions for the sake of public images rather than rational discussion towards the actual resolution of problems. This view extended beyond the politicians themselves to the public gallery. The speaker and other members were concerned about television amplifying and encouraging public demonstrations in the public gallery. There were calls to ban filming of public demonstrations in the public gallery. Apparently the wish was to limit the account to the theatricals of politicians, rather than allow outside political forces to stage events that might lead to communication of their counter-images.

Legislative Committees

Some believed the presence of reporters at legislative committee meetings also affected the process of rational deliberation. A clerk to House committees noted that MPPs become more regular in attendance, willing to speak, and animated when there is news coverage of a committee. Reasoned discussion from multiple perspectives aimed at understanding gives way to fragmented conversation from political interests aimed at grandstanding. In the observations of the clerk:

One of the things that makes members 'go' is the prospect of publicity. A
lot of the work they do here they do because it's the right thing to do, and
that's what they're elected to do, and they get almost no publicity for it.
But a lot of things they do, they do because they get publicity out of it,
it's just the nature of the beast ... Their primary goal is either to defeat the
government or maintain the government, and therefore a lot of times publicity
will have a decidedly negative impact on the workings of a committee.
The committee will be going off deciding issues on their merits or having
reasonable discussions, and the press walks in or the press takes an interest
and all of a sudden people start grandstanding and yelling and screaming,
essentially for publicity reasons. And it just makes the atmosphere much
more politicized, and much more difficult to deal with issues on a reasonable
basis. I mean it's understood there are a lot of things people will disagree on
philosophically and politically, but often those differences are exacerbated
when the press comes in. Which is why a lot of the committees choose to
do their writing of their reports, and deliberation of their reports, *in camera*.
Simply because it's easier to have frank, open discussions when a / the press
aren't there, and b / there's no Hansard transcript kept. So that if you say
something really stupid or something that might be unacceptable to your
party – just by way of throwing out an idea, as just a talking point – it won't
come back to haunt you.

Political Process and Careers

Respondents were haunted by the desire to maintain personal and organizational integrity, while at the same time sustaining news presence. There
was no obvious or fixed means of accomplishing this. It was a yearning in
the abstract, but in reality had to be juggled in the particular instance and
always seemed equivocal. The press secretary for the leader of a political
party suggested that the one thing that could be done was to treat the image
as paramount. While the news media might attack your views or policy, that
can be absorbed if you have given your account in the proper form. His observations bear testimony to the fact that it is the form rather than the content
that makes for effective political discourse.

If news media hurt you by covering your policies in an unfavourable way
and people agree, that clearly has hurt you but they are still your policies,
you stand behind them ... But the riskier thing in the sense that it is more
determinable by us would be the image of the leader or of the party. So that ·
the one thing you would not want is the kind of media that portrayed your
leader as an idiot, or as a person far too radical, or a person far too boring,
et cetera. And in that sense you can try to determine the media yourself

and it's the way you present the leader, who he appears with, what he says
when he's on TV or being interviewed for the papers. And they're things
that aren't directly related to the policies. Clearly if somebody asks a leader
about policy and he answers truthfully, the reader or viewer will either like
it or not. But generally TV interviews are not directly about policy, they're
stylish things. The way you answer, while not deviating from policy, has a
wide variation in how you're perceived. Whether you're funny, for instance.
Whether you're witty. Whether you appear a person of deliberate weightiness
of thought. Whether you appear frivolous. They're all things of style that are
very important in what you convey in the media, and that's where strategies
come in ... *Style*, the message is the same.

Politicians learned that reporters do not seek objectivity as much as political objectives. The point/counterpoint format of the 'strategic ritual of
objectivity' means it is inevitable that one side is portrayed negatively via
an imputation of deviance from the other side. The trick of the trade is to
ensure that one is on the right side as much as possible, making the imputation rather than having to answer for it. A politician who had been a reporter
prior to running for office said that as a reporter he had truly believed he was
being objective. As a politician he realized that reporters are not objective
methodologically, but instead are in pursuit of political objectives:

[The news media have] a very selective role, and I think that unfortunately
if you're in politics you have to accept that. 'You can't fight City Hall,'
only in reverse, as it were! Certainly I probably believed much more in the
objectivity of the press before I was actually a subject of the press. Having
been a subject of the press, now I can see how, in so many ways, they carry
all of their prejudices with them ... [T]hat's the way it is and so you have to
try and roll with those punches. But if you cannot adjust to that, eventually
you will be destroyed, rather than the other way around. I am thinking of
my former leader, who was really very much a purist I think. He never
could accommodate himself to the fact that everybody's motive and goal
in life were not as pure as his, and he never really grew to understand that.
And I think in a sense that alienation both from a policy point of view,
but also from the press, really showed, and it hurt him very much. He was
perceived by many people in the press to be very cold and distant and sort
of intellectual in the negative sense. Removed, personally, and that was the
image that went out across the airwaves. And obviously did not lead to his
electoral victory. So, in a sense you have to co-opt the press, because if you
don't then you cannot win, ultimately they will win.

In political sparring, 'punches' and even 'low blows' are frequent and have to be absorbed in the proper way. A politically hostile columnist, reporter, or news outlet can be a constant source of 'jabs.' Sometimes the leading members of the press-gallery culture collectively 'attack' a particular politician, with selected issues and questions designed to put her to the 'test.' In recent memory one new party leader had passed the test, while another one (referred to in the quotation above) had failed and paid the consequences of a shortened political career. As Adams (1984) observes, 'by personalizing public life, the news media drive people away from public service.' This effect of personalization was addressed by the press secretary for a party leader. Referring to the leader who failed with the press gallery, he said when that leader was criticized in the opinion columns and news items he struck back, criticizing the journalists and even making jokes about them. In contrast, the leader who passed the test simply 'paid his dues' over the first few months, remaining personable and showing he could absorb criticism in the proper way. He was successfully socialized into 'an easy going sidestage, or 'middle region,' style that can bear a great deal of exposure' (Meyrowitz, 1985: 304).

> Several reporters ... felt that ... they would teach him a lesson and not particularly cover him here ... This is a very delicate business with the media. For instance, some people are very good TV and the leader is, he's very good on television: he's incisive, and he looks good on TV, and he thinks fast, he has good lines, and is just good for that medium. Some print reporters here, the more conservative ones particularly, have something against people that look good on TV and sort of resent television, and said, 'O.K., well, we'll show him that it's not easy to get to be a media star here!' It's something that we just put up with for a while until he got to know them and they got to know him ... We're now getting, I think, basically fair coverage. But it's just being an outsider and having to get to know people ... Once you get a personal sort of knowledge so you can chat in the hallways ... there are no longer any points to be made in the coverage or lack of it.

Often what hurts most is the subtlety of text and context. Everyone could recount experiences of having their statements used against them by juxtaposition with others' statements to reveal contradiction. New ministers were shown to be in contradiction with what their predecessors had stated. One organizational member was used to contradict another. In a world where the appearance of organizational unity and consensus is crucial, and interorganizational conflict is the norm, showing something contrary can be devastating. That is why politicians and their knowledge-workers try so hard to get their symbols straight. A party information officer related a learning experience in this regard: 'One of our critics got up in the House and mentioned a figure in the context of some critique of the government. That had not been a figure generated by party researchers. A smart reporter called up and asked for the party researcher in that area, and just asked about this figure, not saying where it came from. And the party researcher tore the whole analysis to shreds! That's because the researcher had only been there for a week. He was forgiven, but he never became good friends with the member.'

The subtleties of interpersonal relations, availability, appearances, ability to take criticism, and reciprocity are key ingredients for access. While respondents found it easy to articulate these in the abstract, it was difficult to say in the specific instance what led to access or resulted in negative coverage. Similarly, in thinking about the influences of news texts, it was difficult to articulate the specifics. There were real effects, but these were more easily visualized than made visible.

> This is a working environment, remember, for 125 members and ... many permanent members of the gallery, there are probably at least 50 that are here every day. So, you get to know people really well, and in that kind of a situation you get along with some people better than others. It may be because you're the same age, the same background, the same ideological predeliction. The converse of that is that you don't get along with others. So, one of the problems sometimes ... there seems to be a little wall between you. You can never prove it, but you just sort of get the feeling that you annoy somebody. Or something you do or something you believe in really has upset somebody ... It's more easily felt than seen. You can't, being forced to prove anything I'd be hard pressed, but you just sort of sit here and say, 'Well now, that's interesting, columnist X has taken a shot at me, beginning to almost look like a pattern' ... The clash, maybe that starts out as ideological and, as a result of that, becomes a bit personal.

The harm done by these clashes is not restricted to being misrepresented or having one's ideology or person slighted. It can also involve being ignored completely. For the politician some coverage is essential for a 'presence' and the image, even if it is not entirely favourable. This finding is based on the assumption – which research evidence shows to be correct (e.g., Jacoby et al, 1980; Stauffer et al, 1981; Stern, 1973; Wilson, 1974; Neuman, 1976; Katz et al, 1977; Gunter, 1980; Salomon, 1979) – that news consumers retain little knowledge from the news but do remember who was mentioned. Citizens are imprinted with the image of the person, including what she represents symbolically, but not the specifics of an event or issue. While surveys indicate that the public prefers political issues over images, they also reveal that a substantial proportion of voters are most influenced by the personal characteristics of candidates and express their evaluations of politicians in terms of their images rather than their policy positions (Greenstein, 1969;

Hahn and Gonchar, 1972). When it comes to having political presence, being 'blackened' in the particular story can be of less consequence than being 'blacked out' altogether. When asked about the negative influence of news, politicians and their publicists referred to the significance of being ignored. One politician responded, 'It can harm you by ignoring you. It can harm you by misrepresenting you. I guess those are the two main categories.' Another politician stressed that news visibility was *the* source of power for him: 'I need to feel that at least my voice is being heard, if nothing else, 'cause I have no other power in me here.'

One aspect of misrepresentation that is feared is the appearance of being self-interested. Research on news media has emphasized the ways in which both news organizations and their official sources are committed to operating in the name of the public interest (e.g., Hartley, 1982). While politicians wish to address issues that ensure their ideological position is well represented, it has to be done subtly in order to appear in the interests of everyone. Otherwise reporters, with reference to their visualization of the public interest, might impute deviant self-interest that could have damaging effects. An opposition MPP spoke of the disadvantage to the opposition in this regard. An opposition criticism of the government, or new program or policy initiative, is seen initially as against the consensus because it does not have the support of the government. Furthermore, because the matter is personalized through the individual opposition critic – often intentionally by the party because it will enhance the possibility of news coverage – it has the consequence of being covered as an isolated, individual critique or initiative. 'In opposition to majority government, you do not have any power. All you have is a voice. We're all very much personalities in a theatre of the absurd, in a daily theatre setting. And we all have the limitations of being characters within the theatre. Which essentially means that I can have the best kind of attack that you can imagine, get some coverage out of it, but it is still just *me* doing this. That it has no [public interest], there's no need for the government to change, why should it bother?' Government MPPs had a similar concern about how they were portrayed. Regardless of noble motives, they knew that readings of ignoble self-interest always lurked. A cabinet minister said that this concern is engrained in the legislature environment: 'There's always a danger in publicizing that you're accused of publicizing the government rather than publicizing the message that you're trying to get across. An example of that was the "Preserve it, conserve it" campaign for energy conservation a while ago. Those were very effective in helping to conserve energy, but regretably they were attacked quite bitterly by the opposition, by the media, and everything, as being subliminal announcements for the Progressive Conservative party.'

News presence is at its best when personal, organizational, and public interest are blended. It is also gratifying even when one is not portrayed so favourably, as long as it is kept to differences of opinion between known oppositional interests, each claiming it is better at serving the public interest. However, things feel nasty when a person or organization is portrayed not only as having a differing opinion, but as lacking competence. When quality is at issue there is a desire to decrease quantity of news coverage. From the politician's viewpoint, this point often spells the beginning of the end. Sustained imputations of deviance are hard to ignore, and it is difficult to submerge coverage. Submerged coverage or being ignored can be equally devastating in terms of the image.

Regardless of their political affiliation, the persons we interviewed seemed always to believe that their opponents were being represented better than themselves. When it comes to news coverage, it seems that that which hurts personally is most easily remembered, whereas that which helps personally is less easily appreciated. In proving the point that news communication is vital to organizational and personal survival in party politics, respondents typically pointed to instances in which they failed to receive the benefit of news coverage *vis-à-vis* their opposition. Similiar to news discourse itself, they signified the negative and deviant to imagine where they stood in the process.

PUBLIC KNOWLEDGE OF THE LEGISLATURE

Our analysis of newswork on the legislature beat indicates that only partial knowledge is produced. It is partial in the sense of being incomplete, and in the sense of representing particular interests to the exclusion of others. In this section we summarize the main factors contributing to the partiality, and their implications for public understanding of the political process.

In the House, topics for discussion are chosen, questions framed, and answers formulated with reference to news requirements. Especially in question period, there is a hermeneutic circle of reporters and politicians who constitute the political agenda. As such, reporters are literally part of the legislature and its political processes. News is a communication among authorized knowers and journalists, with the rest of the population left to be spectators (Tuchman, 1978; Garnham, 1986).

Spectatorship is also encouraged, and knowledge made more partial, in reporting on government administration. The journalist's nose for news leads to where the power is, including the power of knowledge resources. The government achieves hegemony not only through being party to reported transactions from the House, but also through control of literally hundreds of knowledge-workers in its ministries and other bureaucracies. Neither opposition parties nor news outlets can match the quantity of these knowledge resources. Over time this gravitation to official government sources leads to a discourse about administration. Fundamental issues, philosophies, and ideologies are played down in favour of talk about procedural propriety and efficiency. This administrative discourse is at worst a complaint about inefficiency, and can lead at most to calls for tinkering or repair work. It can also lead to the effective co-optation of influential members of the press gallery, and of their editors, who eventually look elsewhere for more significant copy. The hegemonic effects of this administrative discourse were articulated by an opposition MPP:

> I think one of the reasons that politics in Ontario is so boring and so unimportant to people is that the news media in Ontario do not take it as seriously as they should, and do not give it the prominence that they should ... And as a result we have a very *depoliticized* electorate in the province of Ontario. And that, then, makes it very difficult for an opposition party to change [things]. And we basically have elections run here on the capacity to manage, not on political education ... [I mean] management of the province [by the party in power]. It's seen as an administrative capacity, and nothing to do with philosophy or ideology mixed with administration, which it is almost everywhere else. And because of the lack of emphasis on the legislature and what goes on here, it has affected the political process here, and basically is one of the major tools of the Conservatives for continuing to govern. If you don't have any attention placed on this level, then one presumes that everything is going just fine.

When government hegemony is particularly strong – as it was during the period of our field research, with the Conservative party having been in power four decades consecutively – the news media can be particularly influential in underpinning the administration and choosing which procedural strays to target. In this respect they may be more powerful than the opposition parties. Their power is enhanced further by the extent to which they are seen publicly as less partisan than other interests at the legislature. An organization that is believed to be relatively neutral and objective while conveying partial knowledge can be much more effective at mobilizing general consent than one that is explicitly partisan.

An opposition MPP talked about how opposition parties mobilize their information officers and develop their questions for question period in accordance with what is receiving prominent news coverage. He pointed out how the government was a dominant influence on this news coverage and went on to emphasize the implications of this dominance for the place of the opposition. He stated that in effect the opposition were decentred not only by the government, but by the news media, to the point where they were left with only a distant and marginal voice.

Q: During my interviews some people have commented that the media consider themselves the official opposition.

A: I think that's a traditional thing in parliamentary democracy, Canada and Britain. And to some extent there's always some truth in it. The weaker your opposition is, the more they feel that, since that is an indictment on the opposition parties' effectiveness, and on the structural constraints we find ourselves in, and perhaps our lack of creativity in finding other ways to get the concentration on us. And in a majority-government situation I think the longer-standing members of the gallery tend to believe that they then have this role. That because it's majority government, the opposition is obviously weaker in terms of using other structures within the legislature to get things out.

Q: But then why don't they support the opposition parties more by giving them coverage?

A: Well, that's interesting, I've often wondered about that. Partially, if they do the opposing then it's non-partisan and it's legitimate. If we do the opposing then it's for our own partisan goals, of course. And they don't want to be seen to be feeding into one party's point of view.

Q: [Do] you find the media an adequate tool for the dissemination of information that you want to get across?

A: Oh, no, no. Our party has failed miserably in getting its information across. [This] wouldn't seem to be so outrageously dangerous to a large proportion of the population as it would to me ... We've never developed an ultimate form of getting our word, information across that was particularly effective, except during elections when you're already competing with two other propaganda machines and at that point you're fairly limited in what gains you can make.

While the news aperture at the legislature was circumscribed by hermeneutic relations among politicians, officials, and reporters, and narrowed further through administrative discourse controlled by the party in power, it was all but closed when these combined with the emphasis on personalization. Personalization provides for the ultimate form of spectatorship, turning politics into show business and the cult of celebrity. Political 'stars' play on images of what they are supposed to represent, and citizens who care can do little more than root for their favourites. Personalization saves everyone – politicians, officials, reporters, editors, audiences, readers – from having to think in other than a cosmetic fashion. The legislature environment takes on the character of news, consisting more of fragmented conversations than reasoned debates. Personalization has become dominant with the ascendancy of television. In reducing political discourse to fragmented clips of a few seconds each, television can offer only images of political personalities with strobe-light effect. The major requirement of the politician is to preen himself to appear as the middle Canadian. This presentation leaves the citizen to measure variation among politicians according to their shades of pastel and permapress. That is, in accordance with the dictates of good advertising, little or no knowledge is provided about the substance of the product, whether the politician is knowledgeable, fair, and skilled. As Postman (1985: 134, 136) says, only dramatic images are on offer. '[O]n television the politician does not so much offer the audience an image of himself, as offer himself as an image of the audience. And therein lies one of the most powerful influences of the television commercial on political discourse ... [J]ust as the television commercial empties itself of authentic product information so that it can do its psychological work, image politics empties itself of authentic political substance for the same reason.'

This is the politics of consumerism. Politicians, like advertisers, must appeal to the citizen's self-interest and fantasies. Any hierarchy of values and priorities that might be defended politically is levelled by the need to simplify, commodify, and package things into single issues and binary oppositions. The voter chooses a candidate and party like she chooses corn flakes and Kellogg's. Apart from emitting this response in voting, there is little other stimulus for the citizen to engage politics. The citizen watches, amused and bemused even when he is being abused.

> It is a form of politics and political communication which enables both citizens and politicians to live in an essentially apolitical world where all our desires can be satisfied, where we can have higher welfare benefits, higher defence expenditure and lower taxes, where we can strengthen the rights of women without challenging the rights of men, where we can appeal to the majority but at the same time protect minorities. Such a politics is forced to take on the terms of address of the media it uses and to address its readers, viewers and listeners within the set of social relations that those media have created for other purposes. Thus the citizen is appealed to as a private individual rather than as a member of the public, within a privatized domestic sphere rather than within that of public life. (Garnham, 1986: 48)

This politics of consumerism is a product of television, and is a core ingredient of television's ideological role. Television organizes minds and channels activity to the point of directing political consciousness and political institutions. It is implicated in the ways political actors define and regulate their versions of the truth. In the eyes of an information officer for a political party:

> [T]he biggest problem I face with reporters is the problems that they have themselves in the constraints that they operate under. A lot of issues cannot be distilled into a very succinct, single news story ... I don't think it's that

they don't understand. So often when we're dealing with the media, you maybe think they do it because they just want an easy excuse. But they'll say, 'How can we put that in a thirty-second clip?' ... [They] have to mix the news with the form of entertainment and human interest stories ... [T]he biggest culprit of that has been the advent of television and electronic media, the fact that people are used to getting bursts of entertainment and short, intensive pulses of entertainment and news and sports ... We're becoming a society that depends more and more on just short pieces of information, and our magazines and newspapers have started reporting the same way and I think they have to compete with television. I suppose there's something about television as a medium that's so compelling. It's a passive form of communication, people sit back and let it wash over them. It's somewhat addictive.

In television news political discourse becomes blended with the weather-man-as-comedian, advertising, and the pugilistic sportscaster, so that the viewer cannot help but see it in the context of entertainment and treat it lightly. Imagine how seriously you would take the text you are now reading if it was interspersed with advertisements for Molson's Canadian, flights of fancy on Air Canada, and laundry detergents that will dramatically improve your own pastel and permapress appearances?

With reference to television news, a respondent declared, 'If you don't think about it, you think you've been told something. You've been told noth-ing.' From the perspective of the political source as image-manager this must be how it appears, against what she knows to be the issues and complexities that would make something properly understood. However, it is a little ex-treme to assert that nothing has been communicated. In fact television and other news media are highly effective at communicating political myths and rituals, which are the essence of political reality for public purposes.

For amateur political spectators, a small number of classic themes or myths serve repeatedly as explanations of what is shaping the political scene. In contrast to the complicated network of competing influences in the empirical world, the world of the myths is simple. It revolves around hostile plotters and benevolent leaders, and both factions carefully plan the future and can shape it in accordance with their plans. The language of political discus-sion, analysis, and debate frequently evokes these themes by personifying observed, feared, or desired trends into plotters and heroes.

The myths frequently evoke a strong emotional response, seemingly disproportionate to what the observer would expect. This helps account for their ubiquity in political explanations. If a few classic themes are surefire vehicles for engaging the emotions of large numbers of people, leaders will

predictably interpret events in these forms, and their audiences will eagerly
cooperate in creating the world in the same configurations. (Edelman, 1971:
77)

Mythical expression is not limited to the utterances of politicians and
officials. Television itself has achieved the status of myth in Barthes's sense
of being natural, 'a way of thinking so deeply embedded in our consciousness
that it is invisible' (Postman, 1985: 79). As ideology, the 'meta-medium' of
television 'directs not only our knowledge of the world, but our knowledge
of ways of knowing as well' (ibid: 78; see also Meyrowitz, 1985).

Any medium provides a structure for discourse. Marx recognized this
in *The German Ideology* when he asked, 'Is the *Iliad* possible when the
printing press and even printing machines exist? Is it not inevitable that
with the emergence of the press, the singing and the telling and the muse
cease; that is, the conditions necessary for epic poetry disappear?' (Marx and
Engels, 1972: 150, cited by Postman, 1985: 42–3). McLuhan has been at the
forefront of signifying how television has become the dominant medium in
structuring discourse leading others to flesh out the details of this discourse
and its effects (see especially Fiske and Hartley, 1978; Meyrowitz, 1985;
Postman, 1985).

Orwell warned how political speech consists of stale phrases that dull the
critical faculties of speaker and audience. However, as Postman (1985) argues
brilliantly, it may be Huxley rather than Orwell who had the most astute
vision of political tyranny in the contemporary era. Orwell feared tyranny
through concealment of knowledge and infliction of pain, while Huxley feared
tyranny through truth being missed by an implosion of trivial knowledge and
a lack of seriousness in culture. 'Huxley grasped, as Orwell did not, that it is
not necessary to conceal anything from a public insensible to contradiction
and narcoticized by technological diversions ... Big Brother turns out to be
Howdy Doody' (ibid: 111).

We have shown that secrecy and publicity on the legislature beat are
related to the ideology of the television medium as well as to the political
ideologies of sources. When the newspaper was the only medium of politics,
the partisan nature of reporting was explicit and public discourse thrived on
the political ideologies newspapers trafficked in. With the ascendancy of television, it is the ideology of the medium itself that has come to the forefront,
forcing everyone to worry more about form and less about substance. In this
sense it is arguable that news-media influence on politics is greater than ever
before. Clear and detailed enunciations of political ideologies, allowing citizens the opportunity to value the facts they are presented with, have receded.
In their place is the dominant ideology of the television medium, reducing
everything to a matter of style, form, and image. The fact that this ideology

is so entertaining may explain why people are so engaged by it. It is worth asking whether citizens – including politicians, civil servants, and reporters – have become less able to even think about political ideologies as traditionally conceived.

5

The Private Sector

News Culture and Ideas

Social scientists studying news have concentrated their analyses on government institutions and organizations. This emphasis is reasonable given that news itself is framed predominantly within the structures of government. Simply following the journalists they study, social scientists are bound to be preoccupied with news sources in government legislatures, bureaucracies, and criminal-law-enforcement agencies. However, such research emphasis has the effect of limiting our understanding of how private-sector institutions and organizations participate in the news system.

The power of communication includes the ability to choose one's role on the public stage and the audience for the performance. It also includes the ability to stay out of the public eye when publicity is foreseen as having possible negative consequences. An analysis of how private-sector organizations use these abilities to control the news media is necessary for a fuller understanding of secrecy, confidences, censorship, and publicity.

An understanding of news as it relates to the private sector is also important in terms of our analyses of policing and social control. As Shearing and Stenning (1981, 1983, 1987) argue, some private-sector organizations, especially corporations, rival the power of the state in defining and reproducing social order, yet social scientists have relatively ignored private forms of policing in favor of a focus on the state's policing agencies. Shearing and Stenning (1987: 15) also point to the ironic ways in which private corporations can invoke the liberal democratic right to privacy to solidify their positions as 'powerful private authorities whose very existence, and activity, mock the liberal frame.' These considerations point to the crucial role of secrecy and publicity in the ability of private organizations to achieve their social-control interests within the liberal-democratic frame. A central ingredient in private policing is policing symbolic borders through defensive mechanisms aimed at secrecy, and through publicity mechanisms aimed at legitimacy.

While government officials predominate as news sources, '[s]econd only to the government as a news source is the business community, which also showers the media with a vast array of press releases for both individual firms and assorted trade and public relations offshoots' (Herman, 1986: 172, referring to Sigal, 1973; see also Ericson et al, forthcoming). Private corporations multiply their investments in knowledge-control operations that have no direct use-value in terms of the production of goods and services. There are escalating investments in knowledge control because knowledge is so difficult to guard, and because the demand for knowledge is so elastic and insatiable (Warshett, 1981). Policing knowledge becomes an end in itself. This feature is characteristic of the knowledge society, and private corporations, as much as government bureaucracies, are bound to buy into it.

The above considerations point to the need for an examination of private corporate sources along with government sources within the news system. As Downing (1986: 156–7) counsels, 'In so far as the secrecy battleground is a key dimension of the battle for power over social development, the sometimes complex interaction between state power and corporate power should always be kept clearly in view. Too often, the government alone is in focus.'

Corporations have a very powerful role within the news system. Schiller (1986) argues that the classical liberal-democratic conception of the news system as a corner-stone of the citizens' ability to reason and make political choices is undermined as much by corporate interests as by government bureaucratic interests. Corporate sources go to elaborate lengths to maintain secrecy and to provide media packages that will be transmitted in conduit-pipe fashion. Moreover, because news organizations themselves are major businesses that tend towards economic concentration, it is difficult for a new independent interest to enter the business. Existing interests in the media interlock with major corporations in other spheres of business (cf Porter, 1965; Clement, 1975; Royal Commission on Newspapers [RCN], 1981; Dreir, 1982). Additionally, access to knowledge becomes stratified between élite, specialist, informative, more expensive quality products on the one hand, and mainstream, entertaining, less expensive popular products on the other hand.

Within this stratified system of knowledge, corporate offiicals not only have a major influence on media content as sources, they are also a primary audience towards which news is directed. Journalists and corporate sources form a hermeneutic circle for rationalizing business practices and articulating business interests. In the corporate sector, as elsewhere, news is primarily a communication between journalists and their preferred sources, with the remainder of the public left in the position of spectator. As 'major wielders of political and economic power ... business coporations today compose the vital audience for authentic news and information' (Schiller, 1986: 26).

These observations apply especially to quality newspapers, which tend to have substantial business sections that offer the latest data on financial markets and interpretations of these markets. The interpretations offered in this regard tend to be far more elaborate and sophisticated than, say, what is reported elsewhere in the newspaper about reasons for changes in the crime rates. The business-news columns, as well as many of the news and editorial columns elsewhere in the newspaper, are replete with corporate developments, profits, take-overs, and wrongdoing as these might affect business and investment decisions. Most of the reports on the government's legislative, regulatory, and law-enforcement activity can be read as intelligence for the private corporate sector on the state of the political climate as it relates to business interests. Indeed, much of the emphasis on deviance and control in the news can be explained in these terms: it provides the corporate sector with a daily barometer of disorder, how it is to be regulated, and what the implications might be for favourable investment decisions (for elaboration and detail, see Ericson et al, forthcoming).

News of deviance and regulatory controls as these relate to business interests is not of exclusive interest to the selected corporate sources who are the regular authorized knowers in the news. A characteristic feature of the current conservative political climate is economic policies that encourage the ordinary citizen to become a small investor. In Britain, for example, the Conservative government's sell-off of shares in state industries at undervalued prices has sent their most loyal constituency scurrying for a piece of the action, then indulging in self-congratulation at making a profit so easily and offering warm testimony about the value of the privatization policies of the government. In Canada, the middle-aged, middle-class population has engaged in a parallel unseemly rush for the purchase of mutual funds. These folks, for the first time, are buying the business-intensive quality newspaper primarily to have a daily peak at the financial-league tables and news intelligence that surrounds them. In contrast to the public conversation of the previous two decades, which emphasized public welfare through mutual help in the search for community, the public conversation of the 1980s, at least as reflected in business-intensive quality newspapers, emphasizes private gains through mutual funds in the search for self-interest.

Other interests of citizens do surface in the news. Accompanying the 'free market' economic model of the 1980s is a 'free market' model of citizens' interest groups, each ostensibly given a stake and opportunity to have political purchase with the state. The news media pick up on these organized voices of democratic pluralism, but some voices are heard more often and more clearly than others. Preferred readings, aimed at granting legitimacy, are given to organizations whose views articulate with the presumed consensus, and whose reformers are 'insiders' in the sense of being in accordance with state-mediated public interests (Elliot et al, 1982; Paletz and Entman, 1981; Ericson, 1987). Negative readings, aimed at marginalization, are given to organizations whose views do not articulate with the consensus, and whose reformers are 'outsiders' in the sense of being discordant with state-mediated versions of the public interest (Gitlin, 1980; Schmid and de Graaf, 1982; Schlesinger et al, 1983; McMahon and Ericson, 1987). For example, the news media and state will embrace aspects of women's rights, especially as these relate to consensual issues such as violent criminal victimization, much more than they will embrace, say, gay rights (Rock, 1986). Similarly, the news media and state will embrace a citizen-based crime-control organization such as Crime Stoppers much more than they will embrace, say, the Guardian Angels (Carriere, 1987, forthcoming).

The news media are crucial players in processes of political mobilization, and the attendant 'battleground' of secrecy and revelation (Downing, 1986: 154). They provide a daily barometer of interest-group values and activities, potentially useful to the legitimacy of these groups (Goldenberg, 1975; Greenberg, 1985). The orchestration of information by citizens' interest organizations, and its marshalling by the news media, also provide an important source of intelligence to the corporate sector and to government.

> [W]elfarism, consumerism, and economic management are aspects of corporatism, one practical implication of which has been the enormously expanded administrative responsibilities of the state through myriad agencies, on the one hand, and on the other, the pattern of representation of interests from interest and pressure groups that are recognized in and through these agencies. Indeed, I would maintain that so wide, diverse, and complex has the state's remit become, that it is only by encouraging representation in and through interest and pressure groups that it can maintain a constant supply of reliable information, formulate sensible policies and avoid inefficiencies, frustration, and constant sporadic outbursts of protest, which can be politically very damaging. (Clarke, 1987: 288; see also Rock, 1986)

The linkages between journalists and sources in various citizens' organizations remain an underresearched topic. While there have been some excellent case studies, especially the work of Gitlin (1980), there is at present no general model for understanding how the power of these organizations relates to media power and state power. As Blumler and Gurevitch (1986: 67–8) note in their recent review of the literature concerning journalists' orientations to political institutions, 'Lacking ... [is] a more enveloping scheme, stretching across several power domains, and designed to explain differences in the orientations of the mass media to a range of diverse social groups and organizations.' The model we have used in previous chapters to analyse regions and closures by various news sources is a scheme that can also be used to understand the newswork of various private corporations, community organizations, and interest groups.

The family is another institutional site in which the news media become involved in communicating politics. The institution has been addressed traditionally in the 'Family' section of newspapers where good-news items underpinning the consensual values the family is supposed to embody are blended with good advertising items underpinning the consuming wants the family is supposed to emulate. More diffusely, the family has been at the core of political news as a part of the eternal dance between the state and the private sphere. The family is a 'battleground' for playing out core values and beliefs concerning the institution of privacy itself. As such, it is a site for assessing how much the state seems to be intervening in the more sacred regions of the private sphere. The state's activity in these regions serves as a barometer for assessing the moral authority of the state in other exercises of authority.

In these terms, the institution of the family provides a ground for moral crusades and reform efforts by various professional groups, citizens' interest groups, and state agencies, and the news media become embroiled in their politics. For example, in recent years child abuse has functioned as a major issue for articulating core values concerning privacy, rights, and state control and myriad state and private-sector professionals have become party to it. As Nelson observes, the news media 'task is to discover, unveil, and create what is "public." To do so they often wrench "private deviance" from the confines of the home. In the case of child abuse the media also helped to establish a new area of public policy' (Nelson, 1984: 51; see also Pfohl, 1977).

A more recent vehicle for making the private family a site for public conversation concerning cultural values and state control is 'the missing children problem' (Fritz and Altheide, forthcoming; Yanke, 1987). In addressing this problem, as with the child-abuse problem, the media join with government agencies and various professional and citizens' interest groups to make a 'motherhood issue' out of family-related troubles. Private corporations have also joined forces: for example, McDonald's restaurants offer free fingerprinting sessions for children, milk companies imprint their milk cartons with photographs of missing children in notorious cases, and newspapers have photographs of missing children placed on their delivery vans and street vending boxes. It goes without saying that these efforts may on occasion serve good social-control purposes. However, these efforts also provide for good public conversation about core values. As a means by which both state and private-sector political forces can whip up widespread consensus, there seems to be nothing that can equal threats to the well-being of vulnerable victims in the venerable institution of the family.

Our discussion to this point indicates that the state is embedded in, and involved with, the full range of private-sector organizations and institutions in society. Each private-sector organization is part of a wider society of organizations and institutions in both the government and private sectors. Some of the organization's relations are part of the totality and some of the totality is part of the organization. In relation to any issue or event a large number of government and private-sector organizations may operate, codetermining order and change in a system of 'integral plurality' (Fitzpatrick, 1984: 115). Moreover, each news-media organization is itself part of this system, participating actively not only in the communication of events and issues but also in the achievement of resolution, change, and order.

On the state side, the most general and significant concern is regulating and rationalizing activities within the private sector. Particular emphasis is given to regulating the economy, and institutionalized means develop for achieving compliance within, for example, the financial market (Shapiro, 1984) and business operations (Cranston, 1979; Braithwaite, 1984; Clarke, 1987). Compliance mechanisms also dominate other institutions – for example, health, education, welfare, the family, and the media – and the corporate sector is involved here too, as in the regulation of pollution (Hawkins, 1984; Richarson et al, 1982) and occupational health and safety (Carson, 1970, 1982).

In controlling diverse activities in the private sector the state relies much more on a compliance mode of regulation than on a deterrence mode of enforcement (Reiss 1984, 1984a; Law Reform Commission, 1986; Manning, 1987). A compliance mode of regulation is aimed primarily at preventing harm through surveillance or inspection procedures. Prosecution is not the goal and is invoked rarely. In its place, faults, errors, and cracks in the organization that cause harm are sealed at least temporarily by warnings, more intensive monitoring, subsidies and tax concessions to improve technology and internal policing, and/or negative publicity. The concern is not punishment, but reducing risks to an acceptable level so that the operation may foster as profitable, efficient, and reasonably safe. Enforcement is typically at a very informal level of negotiation over requirements of a permit or licence. Enforcement 'often takes place in morally uncertain territory in which values, technology, and business practice intersect' (Manning, 1987: 298).

In relation to most things in most areas of regulation, the government has a limited capacity to inspect, monitor, and correct deficiencies or serious errors, or even to decide the magnitude of a problem. This is true across a range of fields, including, for example, regulation of the broadcast media (Law Reform Commission, 1986), regulation of business (Cranston, 1979), regulation of airline safety (Dagenais, 1983), or regulation of nuclear safety (Manning, forthcoming). The fundamental problem is a lack of knowledge, which entails not simply a lack of legal power or surreptitious imagination to penetrate private space for the purpose of surveillance and detection (Ericson and Shearing, 1986), but also equivocality and uncertainty regarding the level of harm. And there is a need for some secrecy and confidences in order to avoid undue public anxiety or alarm: 'it is not the presence of *knowledge* that leads to the emergence of compliance systems of regulation rather than deterrent ones, but the absence of knowledge combined with a willingness to pursue the level, kinds, distribution, and consequences of harm issuing directly or indirectly from a form of production' (Manning, 1987: 310; see generally Perrow, 1984).

A consequence of these conditions is that resources and effort are expended on the appearance of control via publicity. Public-relations efforts and paid advertising by government agencies, private corporations, and citizens' interest groups are directed at educating people about compliance mechanisms, urging people into compliance, and signalling the appearance of control (Adler and Pittle, 1984). Even on the rare occasion when a severe sanction for non-compliance is deemed appropriate, publicity is recommended as a primary sanction because of its stigmatic effects (Law Reform Commission, 1986). '[I]n the nature of the political and legal organization there is a structured acceptance of economic activities coupled with symbolic efforts to regulate. The potential tension between the economy and the state is replaced by the appearance of control ... Government regulation, therefore, is a dramaturgical peformance, displaying a concern for and marking the interests of the whole in action' (Manning, 1987: 294).

Compliance modes of regulation are obviously instrumental, with very real, practical effects. However, compliance modes are primarily symbolic, with drama and ritual being crucial to their enactment. In the drama and ritual of regulating public problems via law, the state is concerned with signifying its values, meanings, and intentions towards the private-sector organizations concerned. In turn these organizations enter into the public conversation about values, meanings, and intentions as these are grounded in their own social positions (Ericson, 1985; Gusfield, 1981). '[S]ince the matters to be regulated are representative of moral and political concerns that cannot be determined, or are such a potential source of dissent and conflict that precise regulation would dramatically reveal the interests of the powerful and the state' (Manning, 1987: 310), the control arena is circumscribed within the drama and ritual of symbolic politics, to the relative exclusion of instrumental penetration into the private organization to effect change.

The role of symbolic politics in regulating private-sector organizations means that the news media are crucial to the process. In previous chapters we analysed how the news media are important to the courts, and especially to the police, in signifying the deterrence mode of criminal law. In this chapter we analyse how the news media are important to private-sector organizations, and government regulatory agencies, in signifying the compliance mode of administrative law. To this end we draw upon our interviews with sources representing citizens' interest groups, corporations, occupational and professional groups, government departments, and public-relations firms. We also make use of our extensive ethnographic observations of reporters on general assignment and on topic specializations pertaining to private-sector concerns.

ORGANIZING BY JOURNALISTS

Most reporting of private-sector matters is undertaken by journalists working from general-assignment desks. This is especially true of news organizations that have limited resources and therefore few reporters – that is, virtually all broadcast outlets as well as most popular newspapers. Hence, the organization of general assignment reporting that we have analysed elsewhere is salient to our present concerns (Ericson et al, 1987).

A few television stations have a business reporter or specialist to do pieces on each successive 'crisis' in business well-being, trade (especially threats from foreign competition), the financial markets, and government regulation. These specialists use a limited repertoire of corporate executives and government officials to represent business 'health,' and more generally the state of the economy, through signs that it might be deteriorating.

In quality newspapers, especially newspapers that have a major business section, there is a much greater emphasis on selected private-sector activity. A quality newspaper we studied had approximately thirty locally based reporters working from the business desk on various 'industry beats' including, for example, consumer products, banking, and specific 'corporate empires.' Correspondents in other centres in Canada were also specifically assigned to the business section, and foreign correspondents made occasional contributions. The complement of reporters available to the business desk approximated the number working from the general-assignment desk.

The business reporter has a different relation to sources than reporters working on the beat specializations we analysed in previous chapters. While court, police, and legislative reporters have physical spaces (beat offices) within the organizations reported on, similar provisions are not made by corporations for business reporters. There is no office wing for reporters as part of, say, General Motors Corporation, International Business Machines, or the Canadian Imperial Bank of Commerce. Thus, while it is appropriate to be physically ensconced in government organizations that are committed to the public interest, it is unseemly to be situated in private-sector organizations that are committed to self-interest. Moreover, short of having an office in the corporate headquarters of all of the major players in a particular economic sphere – for example, an office for reporters in the headquarters of each of the major banks and trust companies – an image of impartiality would be difficult to uphold.

The lack of physical space at a corporate setting does not prevent reporters from fostering social and cultural ties with key corporate sources in a variety of settings. The relations established between a business reporter and authorized knowers in the corporate sector mean that in any event, selected sources for selected corporations are cited more often and more favourably than others regarding key aspects of their sector and the economy in general (Ericson et al, forthcoming). For example, in the banking sphere a chief economist for a major bank was cited with considerable frequency on a wide range of economic matters. Just as a chief of police can appear as the fount of knowledge about crime control, so the chief economist of a major bank can be used as *the* person in the know regarding economic control.

The business reporter differs from counterparts on public-sector newsbeats in having added interpretive latitude in reporting. The business section mandate is to marshal expert opinion and analysis about various sectors of the economy. This expertise includes that of the reporters themselves. Some business reporters have weekly columns on specializations such as the commodity markets, bonds, and stocks. They offer their opinions not only about the general state of these markets, but also concerning what are good buys and what should be sold or avoided. Moreover, since these reporters may also be investors in the businesses and markets reported on, there is the potential for conflict of interest, and any pretense of an 'arm's-length' relation to what is being reported on is extinguished. In columns offering investment advice in one newspaper, a statement was included indicating the reporter's interest in the matter; for example, at the end of the 'Stocks' column was the statement, '[reporter's name], a [newspaper's name] reporter, invests in securities and may hold shares in companies mentioned on occasion in this column.' One would not expect to see at the end of a police reporter's story the caution. '[Reporter's name], a [name of newspaper] reporter, is committed to law and order and may hold views supportive of the police forces mentioned in his stories.'

One newspaper had policies and rules for reporters who participated with a vested interest in the business sector. These were summarized in a publication of the newspaper concerning the activities of its business reporters.

The Ethics of Business and Reporting the News
'I'll write the story as soon as I have finished talking to my broker,' is a
quip business reporters occasionally use when they're being harassed by an

editor at deadline. But whatever one might imagine, business reporters don't often get a news tip that can make them money in the stock market; they are almost always on the outside, not the inside. But there is a potential for conflict of interest, so [our newspaper] has a written policy for its staff on investing.

Reporters and copy editors are permitted to invest in stocks and other equity investments, such as warrants, options, mutual funds and fixed income securities, but there are constraints on equity investments – and there is a reporting process. The policy was established by a management-staff committee.

Those responsible for an industry beat, such as forest products, are not permitted to invest in equity-related securities of companies in that industry. And reporters and copy editors who have access to news that may affect any stock are not to act on that information until it has appeared in the paper, equalizing their opportunities among investors.

Trades by staff members in all equity securities are reported to an outside auditor who maintains a record of staff holdings. The auditor also reads [the business section] with an eye to ensuring that reporters are not writing stories that present conflict-of-interest problems. Since such conflicts come in many forms, there is an onus on reporters to tell a senior editor whether a potential problem exists with any story, such as family member involvement, so that the story can be reassigned.

In summary, business reporters are part of the organizations they report on, but in ways differing from reporters on the beats analysed in previous chapters. They do not have the same physical presence in beat locations so they are less obviously enjoined with their sources in mutual social-control tasks and reform politics aimed at consensus within the public interest. They use selected sources to form their own expert opinions, which are often made explicit in their news items and columns. These expert opinions relate to where resources are best placed for personal profit and private interest. In the business section, *a* public's interest, but not *the* public interest, is served. The admitted specialized interests involved in business reporting give the news organization an admitted interpretive latitude that does not surface in beats specializing directly in governmental operations.

Many news organizations also have topic specialists oriented to private spheres apart from business. For example, a news organization we studied had a specialist in welfare matters who focused in particular on issues of child welfare and the family. The same organization had a labour specialist who focused on the union movement, and legal and health specialists who addressed the professional-association interests of related professions. In reporting these topic areas, as in reporting business, there was no specific physical location for the beats outside the newsroom. Each reporter made a range of contacts with key informants in the professions, unions, citizens' interest groups, and government bureaucracies concerned with the sphere in question. Typically reporting was grounded in the government department concerned, and focused on governmental reaction to, and regulation of, trends and developments at issue within private-sector organizations. For example, in focusing on the activities of a particular union the labour specialist would tend to use the Ministry of Labour as the ultimate hub and repository of the story. Similarly, in examining how the Children's Aid Society was handling a particular instance of child welfare, the welfare specialist would tend to ground the response in the reaction of the Ministry of Community and Social Services.

These reporters rarely separated private-sector activities from the regulatory and compliance enforcement-processes of government. Reporters typically understand business, welfare, labour, professional, and all other institutional action in private spheres to entail government reaction. Hence, more than anything else, news stories about private-sector activities are framed as designations of deviance requiring the invocation of governmental compliance mechanisms, including the controlling influence of publicity itself. In turn, it is compliance enforcement that is at the forefront of concern to private-sector sources as they negotiate the news with reporters.

ORGANIZING BY SOURCES

Private-sector organizations develop public-relations units as a key component of their policing operations. Hence, some of the general goals for maintaining private security operations (cf Braithwaite and Fisse, 1987) also pertain to investment in public-relations units. There is a need to generate and sustain a reputation as a moral actor that will enhance the public reputation of the corporate product. This reputation is achievable through defensible strategies and tactics for handling publicity and securing secrecy in relation to invasions from outsiders, whether individual citizens, organized citizens, corporate competitors, or state regulatory officials. It is also achievable through advertising and news publicity campaigns that manufacture positive impressions.

The importance of publicity varies among types of organizations. However, all persons who are in the news regularly are compelled to take it seriously. Regular sources feel dependent on the news as one source of corporate intelligence. As one respondent observed, 'Even the greatest critics do rely on various forms of the media for their primary sources of information.' Regular sources also take the news seriously because they know its social-control effects: on internal operations, in bringing pressure to bear on others in the process of change, and in selling the virtues of their activity in the market-place of public opinion. Another respondent stated sharply, 'Something written in the *Globe and Mail*, four or five column inches long, can have just as much impact as your latest two years' work.' The fact that news bears such significance means that it is treated with awe. It is not only the politician whose career rises in the media spotlight and falls in its shadow, but also the corporate official faced with publicity because something has gone wrong. A public-relations consultant to corporate sources voiced the fear of his clients:

> [News coverage] can kill you more quickly than it can make you. Ten times as fast as it can make you. The news business is by definition more interested in crisis, agony, problems ... Most corporate people feel that the news media are after dirt, bad-news stories ... And to a large degree that's true ... [T]here's a tendency to go run and hide by a lot of executives, just hope it will go away ... Often you'll find at the corporate level ... a fear of the media, loathing for the media and reporters have a field day with the people who don't understand the limitations on the media ... I find myself, almost invariably, there is a crisis situation, trying to talk them around it [their fears]. The media are there and if you don't get your side of the story across the other side will surface.

The corporate official must be vigilant about the possible harmful effects of publicity from multiple sources. One significant area of concern to businesses is consumer advice columns, media ombudsmen, and action lines (Palen, 1979; Mattice, 1980; Abel, 1982; Pfuhl and Altheide, 1987). In these forums news organizations supply to individual citizens the power of negative publicity against businesses engaged in deviant practices. Recent research indicates that satisfactory remedies are often achieved through the sanction or threat of negative publicity brought by these forums, even if they do not address more systematic and structural defects of the businesses in question (Pfuhl and Altheide, 1987). These forums can also mobilize the consciousness of consumers, serving 'as a bulletin board and routine warning system' and reminding 'viewers that we live in a legal-rational society' (ibid: 25).

Consumers also mobilize through consumer-protection organizations that feed the news media with selected stories of business error or malpractice. This practice is part of the general role of citizens' interest organizations in joining forces with the media, and also on occasion with the state, to pressure corporations into improved products, and the morality, justice, fairness and safety associated with the distribution and use of those products. The more sustained the publicity, the more citizens are sensitized to their stake, the ways in which they have been aggrieved, and how they may in turn use the news media to make demands.

Some researchers concerned with the regulation of private corporations have indicated that a coalition of the news media, citizens' interest organizations, and state regulatory agencies can be effective in the control of corporate power. For example, Fisse and Braithwaite (1983) are of the view that publicity is at the hub of multipronged political strategies aimed at corporate compliance. Elsewhere Braithwaite (1984: 380) observes that 'The best guarantees against the abuse of administrative discretion are provided by diligent investigative journalists, active oversight committees of elected representatives, vocal consumer and trades union movements, aggressive industry associations which are willing to use the political process to defend their members against such abuses, freedom of information statutes with teeth, free access of the scientific community to the raw data on which regulations are based, and a requirement that regulatory agencies publicly justify their decisions and publicly hear appeals against them.'

The use of publicity in economic regulation is politically sensitive. The economy is buoyed by faith as well as fact. Therefore, when the sting of publicity is injected as a sanction in response to a particular instance of corporate wrongdoing, there is a concomitant need to convey the impression that the wrongdoing was an exception, thereby exhuming overall confidence in the financial system. In observing that the financial system floats on images that instil public confidence, a compliance officer in a government department concerned with economic regulation underscored the significance of news accounts that put matters 'into proper perspective.' Imbued with a belief that the news media can create a 'self-fulfilling prophecy' (Merton, 1957), she said she went out of her way to stress to reporters their responsibility to make citizens confident of economic order. This belief is akin to that of police about the need for public confidence in their crime-control capacities as a key to maintaining social order. In the words of the compliance officer:

We are afraid of how information [is] interpreted. We find that among the public generally, including members of the media, there is a lack of sensitivity to the fact that the whole financial system in this country, or in the whole world for that matter, just floats on the confidence that the public has in it. And we are afraid of the damage that can be done to the financial system by misinformed or ill-informed or badly interpreted information. With respect to a major financial institution, or a group of financial institutions, how a misinformed story can result in a loss of confidence in the system ... [When talking to a reporter] if I feel it's necessary I'll wander off into a bit of a sermon on the sensitivity of the whole sytem, the confidence issue, and just try to make sure that they are aware of the complications of the thing if it has the potential of being serious.

Sensitive to the need for public confidence in the financial system, the compliance officer can become an ally of the private sector by collaborating in private confidences and enclosing on publicity so that only partial knowledge is revealed. The compliance mechanisms of the state are not simply vectors of punishment directed at errant private enterprises; rather they are tools to achieve a workable level of damage control and a high level of public confidence. In policing organizational life the task of journalists is to clean up and repair flawed corporate proceedings. The primary task of corporate officials in conjunction with the state's compliance officers is to ensure that corporate proceedings appear clean and in good repair in the first instance.

Business competitors pose a greater threat than the state's compliance officers. The common denominator in all corporate public-relations efforts is keeping private any information that may affect 'the competitive edge' if disclosed. A public-relations officer with experience in several large multi-national corporations remarked, '[I]t doesn't matter whether it's banking, or automotive methods, or natural resources, public relations is pretty much the same wherever you are. It's just a different subject. You quickly understand what is competitive information and what is confidential information.' Secrecy is crucial to corporate officials. Without sophisticated mechanisms for managing secrecy, the corporation may experience serious threats to its survival. Thus, corporations invest considerable private policing resources in guarding their own knowledge while procuring useful knowledge about competitors.

In this connection, and recalling our previous discussion of the role of the state, it is remarkable that the vast majority of users of the Freedom of Information Act in the United States are 'Corporations bent on acquiring each other's secrets ... [D]espite the explicit exemption of trade secrets from the Act's scope, both corporations and newly-established contract agencies were heavily involved in using the Act to acquire apparently general information which would none the less be highly revealing to someone in the business "know." In the year 1979–81 three agencies frequently probed – the Food and Drug Administration, the Consumer Product Safety Commission, the Environmental Protection Agency – received less than 5 percent of their inquiries from media and public interest groups combined' (Downing, 1986: 156; see also Casey et al, 1983).

Many respondents referred to the news-relations officer as a specialist in 'running interference.' She was seen as a significant chink in the organization's private policing armour, used to defend secrecy and to guard disclosures. A news-relations officer with extensive experience working for various large private corporations said she was employed to deal with the periodic 'bashing' inflicted on such corporations by citizens' interest groups, state, and news media. In very large and sophisticated corporations, prominent experts may be engaged to assist in damage control on a continuing basis. Thus, Stone (1975: 190) reports that a utility company hired a respected environmental-engineering scientist to report to the vice-president for public relations. In contrast, we interviewed participants in smaller business who said they were not in the news enough, or did not face enough potential for harm from news coverage, to justify having even a single news-relations specialist on staff. Typical were comments that having a specialist is 'not going to make any money for the company,' and 'I'm not about to pay somebody to run interference for me.'

Regarding the legitimacy of the corporation and its products, respondents took the view that the best defence is offence. This view was in keeping with the sentiments of other private-sector sources, and has parallels in the image-making politics emphasized by sources on the legislative beat (see chapter 4). One private sector source said the best he could do was 'make an impression.' 'The impression is that you are knowledgeable, and responsible, and know what you're talking about, and it seems to make sense, and maybe that's as good as you can get.' Others talked of doing better. They saw news as a form of advertising. A representative of a citizens' organization concerned with victims of violence stated bluntly, 'I'm in the marketing business,' and added that he would not be in business if it was not for the ample 'free time' he had managed to achieve through news access.

Several corporate executives said that in their organization and thinking, news and advertising are together as part of consumer marketing. In a typical public-relations branch of a corporate bureaucracy, news, advertising, and trade and employee communications are covered simultaneously. A senior bank executive talked of news and advertising in the same breath, and went on to argue one way in which news is superior: 'It's essential to get constructive news coverage as far as possible ... You're trying to attract customers. It's like any other business. Why do people advertise? When they ask that and stop, they find that that's why they advertise ... [T]here's a difference between public relations, good public relations, and advertising, in that advertising is what you say about yourself. The result of good PR is what other people say about you. And that's much more convincing.'

A public-relations consultant to both public and private bureaucracies observed that just as his clients paid news outlets directly for advertising space, they paid him to obtain news space. He said his livelihood depends on those occasions when news space is more important than advertising space because it appears less self-serving. News, like advertising, is directed at profit, and he in turn was able to profit from it.

> I gather information, usually from a marketing standpoint, from within a
> client's interest area. If I'm dealing with the news media ... I tailor it in such

a way – because I've worked in the news business – that I think will attract attention ... And then lobby by phoning and sending notes, and the rest of it, to the various media ... Public relations is a component, like advertising is a component of marketing ... They both set out to do exactly the same thing. If they advertise, and public relations is done on behalf of a company which is producing something, basically they both, hopefully, contribute to sales and profits ... The public-relations effort often is considered to be a superior way to go because the credibility of [such] an 'ad' is never in question when an editor has decided that what you are offering is of general interest ... If you read a paper about my revolutionary new bicycle, you're inclined to believe the story ... If I design an ad which makes claims about a revolutionary bicycle which raise some doubts in the minds of some people, then I guess the ad is perceived to be a little self-serving ... Some PR efforts are straight advertising really, or advertising attempts. You're obviously looking for free publicity. And some editors will say, 'Why don't you buy an ad?' But if you package it the right way – one of the secrets is to try and find someone else to endorse what you're trying to do. It's called arm's length or one-step–removed PR. If I can find a scientist at University of Toronto to say that this product has fewer known health hazards than the existing products ... and certainly from an environmental aspect is a better thing ... If you can use that sort of clinical endorsement in some way ... That's why, for instance, if you can get church people or environmental people to support you on something then you go ahead and do it. It's all a question of subtleness, degrees.

These comments signal a major function of public-relations officers in private policing. They are mandated to proactively engender publicity that creates a favourable organizational environment. Among the thirty private-sector sources we interviewed, all but two said they made proactive efforts to publicize good-news aspects of their organization's activities, and half of them said they were proactive regularly or occasionally. In comparison, while sources on the legislative beat maintained a similar level of proactivity, police and court officials interviewed were proactive to a significantly lesser degree: among the twenty-five in this criminal-justice group, none said they were proactive regularly, and twenty-three said they were proactive 'rarely' or 'never.'

The large organization with an established publicity machine is not only geared for regular news releases and media events, it also publishes annual reports, newsletters, newspapers, magazines, and so on that are distributed proactively to the news media on a systematic basis. In these formats the chain of proactivity is long, complicated, and subtle. Knowledge given to journalists for trade and specialist magazines and used in their stories is read in turn by news-media journalists and converted into news stories. Sometimes the stream of proactive work within the source organization is channelled through specialized wire services that cater to corporate bureaucracies, such as Canadian News Wire Limited, and journalists pick up on this packaged material. When proactive contact is made with a particular journalist in one news organization, that journalist's published story may be used by journalists working for other news outlets who contact the source for further knowledge. In this respect the proactive-reactive distinction is blurred, for an initial proactive contact can mushroom into dozens of calls from journalists and a spiralling exchange of knowledge over time as a continuing story evolves. Respondents indicated that when a publicity campaign is started there is a need to be very proactive, but as credibility, constituency, and newsworthiness grow, journalists pursue the source and news-media contacts are predominantly reactive.

As with news-relations specialists in government sectors, the private-sector specialist is knowledgeable about how to 'place' proactive materials. Most news-relations specialists have experience as reporters. What the news organization is buying in a news-relations specialist is someone with recipe knowledge of what will sell to whom. They are also buying the specialist's credibility and trust with reporters, something other employees of the organization are less likely to have through occasional and limited dealings with reporters. In turn the specialist has detailed recipe knowledge of the credibility and reliability of different reporters and news organizations. This knowledge can be used to screen journalists, and to warn prospective sources about them. This screening and warning capacity makes the news-relations officer especially valuable to the private policing operations of the organization.

The public-relations unit of a private-sector organization is not limited to policing the external environment. The parallel mandate is to police knowledge internally to ensure that it doesn't escape except when it seems propitious as defined by senior executives. The news-relations specialist must establish trust and credibility with regular sources inside the organization, increasing their confidence in supplying him with knowledge they know will be dealt with responsibly. He also learns who are the appropriate sources regarding particular issues and events, actively structuring source selection with an eye towards both organizational interests and the requirements of news. As articulated by an experienced corporate public-relations officer, '[W]e are not the specialists, we're the generalists, but we know where to go to get the information. And it doesn't matter what area [of the organization], they have their instructions to open up to Public Affairs knowing that we will use our discretion as to what we can put out ... We're getting the information from people who they [reporters] might otherwise be talking to ... We're not diluting it, but we're taking it under consideration and giving out what is pertinent.'

In chapter 3 we documented the elaborate and detailed set of guidelines aimed at controlling who could say what within the police organization. However, police officers were much more able to deal with reporters than were employees of certain private-sector corporations. Public-relations officers for several private organizations stressed that publicity about the organization was prohibited for all but a few employees. One private corporate respondent said that all publicity pertaining to the company or using the name of the company, even scientific publication, required authorization.

> It's just one little section in our standard rules and regulations which says
> that the public-relations department is the official contact with the media ...
> [A]n employee cannot just talk to the media without authority and cannot
> write an article for publication. As long as they are shown as employees
> of our company we reserve the right to review what they write. Some of
> our employees ... write ... semi-technical articles in areas that don't relate
> to their work here, but they may be shown as a project engineer of our
> company. We have the right to review that article before it is submitted. Not
> that we object to them doing it, whether they do it for free or for funds.
> The article is submitted to me and then it's my responsibility, I'll review it
> simply from a company overview. But if it's a technical article, which the
> majority of them are, I'll submit it to the vice-president of engineering, or
> somebody, for him to review it to see whether it is something that we want
> our name associated with.

Other private-sector organizations were also very restrictive in designating spokespersons to deal with reporters. In organizations concerned with the care of deviant, victimized, or disadvantaged populations – for example, halfway houses and shelters for victims of domestic violence – there was usually a stipulation that residents or clients could only conduct interviews with reporters in the presence of staff members. An official for an organization that assists criminal offenders emphasized the importance of selecting the right spokesperson from among the offenders. Union officials identified the need to have union leaders speak for workers because most workers are unable to represent their collective interests in news discourse. One union official observed, 'Talk to the people that are the front-line leadership, not the guy on the street. The guy on the street is out of touch ... every damn worker should know what's going on but he doesn't, you've got to be realistic about it.' Three lawyers in private practice each stipulated that articling students and secretaries working in their office were excluded from making comments to reporters.

In all organizations, in both the private sector and government, there are élite members who are authorized to participate in the public conversation while all the rest are to remain silent. As articulated by a corporate public-relations officer, 'The only real rule is that there are certain people who talk to the media and no one else.' Thus, it is not simply the resource constraints and professional imperatives of journalists that force them to rely on a limited number of authorized knowers. Even organizations of minimal sophistication and scale know enough to limit their corporate face to a few select people.

The fact that the private-sector organization has so few designated spokespersons means that it does not require detailed guidelines regarding who can speak to reporters under specified circumstances, unlike a public bureaucracy such as a large metropolitan police force (see chapter 3). A private corporate public-relations officer accounted for not developing a guidebook on news relations for the corporation's employees by saying, 'I don't think you can set it down in that way. You have to have a general understanding of what's required and the discretion that you're obliged to observe.' He went on to observe that only a few senior employees were authorized to talk to journalists on behalf of the company anyway, 'Otherwise it gets out of hand.' Corporate interests are better served by ongoing deliberations among a handful of employees regarding precedents, principles, and objectives, rather than by the provision of written rules.

Apart from news-relations specialists, very few private-sector sources said they had formal training in dealing with the news, nor did they see much value in it. Regular sources are like journalists (Ericson et al, 1987) in seeing the production of news as an intuitive, situated enterprise learned by experience rather than in detailed and abstract training settings. The sources we interviewed made it clear that in making news judgments they preferred to rely on their own personal criteria and on the recipe knowledge of their collective experiences with reporters. Respondents spoke proudly of such facts as 'I'm learning it by trial and error' and 'The training that I've had ... has just been my experience in working with the media over thirty years ... developing an appreciation of their needs.' This was seen as *the* way to learn because of the contextual and situational nature of news judgments for sources as well as journalists. 'I suppose it [training] wouldn't do any harm but I don't see it would be any great help. I mean, each [person] has to make up his own mind ... what to do in specific situations.'

At best more formal training settings allow a general appreciation of the constraints on reporters, why reporters should be taken seriously because of the potential impact of their reports, and therefore why the source should learn to control knowledge in interview situations. As a corporate executive said of a college course in communications she had taken, 'You learn ... to control yourself and control the situation ... Unless you are ready and set for it you can very easily say the wrong thing, create wrong impressions, so it's a very serious thing and it shouldn't be taken lightly.' At worst, training is a means of controlling sources. One respondent summed up the view of many in saying that news-relations training is an infringement on professional autonomy.

> I can just see us somehow or other being ordered to attend some room where some person brought in from [the media] would be instructed to tell us how to deal with the media. First place, I don't think very many people would go. Very few of us go to anything that is laid out like this. And in the second place, we would feel resentful, figuring we know how to deal with these kinds of things and, thank you very much, we'll make our own decisions anyway. So, I don't think it would be a very big success. Most of the people that are likely to get tangled up with the media are not only likely to be able to make their own judgments, but see themselves as being capable of making their own judgments about what they want to do. And they would consider this to be a gross infringement of their territory.

To this point our analysis of organizing by private-sector sources has focused on large, established, and legitimate organizations – in other words, those that have an institutionalized place in society. Organizing for news access is very different in the case of smaller, grass-roots, minority-interest organizations searching for identity and legitimacy. While these groups may be small in registered membership and power, they can represent very substantial groups such as women or people of a particular race or ethnicity. Indeed, the term 'minority' is not a reference 'to the small number of people in the group, but rather to the limited degree of access the members feel they have to the larger society' (Meyrowitz, 1985: 132).

Minority groups have their consciousness raised by the mass media and its pluralistic political discourse of constitutional rights and equality. This discourse makes these groups more acutely aware of their minority status: their place in society in terms of exclusions and restrictions from various experiences and rights enjoyed by others.

> Ironically, the sense of restriction felt by many minority group members may be the result of the sudden *increase* in access to a larger, more inclusive information environment. For to know about and be constantly exposed to places you cannot go and things you are not allowed to do makes you feel more isolated than you were before ... Information integration makes social integration seem more possible and desirable. Distinctions in status generally require distinctions in access to situations. The more people share similar information systems, the greater the demand for consistency of treatment.
> (ibid: 133)

Given knowledge of their place by the media, and encouraged by the constitution of the pluralist and managerialist state, minority groups pursue greater political purchase. This pursuit requires access to the news media, but, of course, such access is not freely available. In striving for news access the minority group faces the concrete reality of a stratified society. It does not take long to discover that the space available for participation in the public sphere (Habermas, 1979) has been effectively bought out by the public-relations machines of the corporate and governmental conglomerates. Those without similar clout in the production of mass symbols are variously denied access, given only sporadic coverage, or given sustained coverage over a limited period in a process of delegitimation and marginalization. They come to realize that the publicity machines of the conglomerates are not geared to rational discourse, but to manipulation.

The restriction on some citizens' organizations is not limited to news access for the dissemination of helpful information. There is also the problem that political mobilization requires access to and use of specialized knowledge and expertise. Expertise, too, is more within the power of corporations and governments who can afford it. The rich utility company can hire a prominent environmental-engineering scientist to report to its vice-president for public relations (Stone, 1975), but the citizens' group concerned with pollution is less able to afford such access to scientific knowledge and such a representative of its cognitive authority. '[M]obilization without meaningful information is very hard' (Downing, 1986: 165). Moreover, in spite of wishful thinking in some quarters, new technologies of communication are likely to increase rather than decrease the news and information monopolies of the private corporate and government conglomerates. 'The new technology is less likely, in the present conjuncture, to offer opportunities to small, well-intentioned, high-minded groups than to highly organized business interests ... [Analysis] should start from the question: If deregulation offers freedom, to whom does it offer it and on what terms?' (Hood, 1986: 66).

The academic literature has tended to focus on the failures in political mobilization that are associated with restricted news access or negative news coverage (e.g., Gitlin, 1980; Golding et al, 1986). However, some minority interest groups are successful, even to the point of eventually joining the ranks of the large conglomerates with substantial media resources. Success is exemplified by several evangelical organizations that have manufactured huge corporate empires through strategic use of television supplemented by print-media mailings (Harrell, 1985; Straub, 1986). By playing on an assumed consensus, this minority can actually claim it represents the 'moral majority,' what all right-thinking people believe and do. While joining the multinational corporate ranks has entailed inevitable exposure to allegations of scandal and corruption, as well as sustained critical attention (Gardner,

1987), these organizations are nevertheless a power to be reckoned with. The Christian Broadcast Network, owned by the Pat Robertson organization, is now the largest cable television network in the United States. This network includes international outlets filled with political messages, such as the 'Voice of Hope' in Lebanon, which offers a continuous stream of anti-Arab rhetoric.

Successful evangelical organizations have used modern technology to advantage. For them the television medium is perfect for the message. Playing on the bad-news formula of fears about evil threats to society and guilt about disadvantaged populations, these organizations mobilize support from vulnerable populations. There are about five million committed donors to televised evangelism in North America, predominantely women aged fifty to seventy-five, with seventy-one as the peak age. 'Many live alone on social security, some in nursing homes. Many are too disabled for church-going' (ibid: 17). The policy of broadcast regulatory bodies is to 'sell air time to the highest bidders, and the highest are the bible thumpers. They are the only preachers so fired by the Holy Ghost that they are not ashamed to engage in the perpetual blatant money hustling so necessary to stay on prime time' (ibid).

More modest citizens' interest organizations can be successful by fitting their work into the consensual and controlling interests of the large conglomerates that form the deviance-defining élite. For example, several citizens' organizations have developed to participate in the control of crime and to promote the cause of crime victims. In Canada, organizations that have failed, such as the Guardian Angels citizens' patrol organization, have been unable to accord with police and media hegenomy regarding what is in the public interest. In contrast, the Crime Stoppers organization has joined forces with the police and media in the process of crime detection and control (Carriere 1987, forthcoming). In collaboration with the media, Crime Stoppers serves as an additional means by which the normal crime discourse of the police is legitimated (Wheeler, 1986). Similarly, groups organized around the problems of criminal victimization (Rock, 1986, forthcoming), and those seeking to crack down on particular crimes such as impaired driving (e.g., the Ontario-based People to Reduce Impaired Driving Everywhere or PRIDE), are simply emulating an ideology, and attendant law-enforcement targeting, orchestrated by government officials, media, and the police (note that the Ontario police law-enforcement program for impaired-driving control is 'Reduce Impaired Driving Everywhere' or RIDE). These organizations achieve legitimacy through being accorded a place in the established media and state policing agencies they work with. They may well have an influence within these media and police agencies, but it bears the cost of virtual absorption by them.

TRUST AND RECIPROCITY

There is no collective news culture among private-sector organizations. There are some common grounds for meeting, such as press clubs, and some common values and practices in producing newsworthy material. Nevertheless, the values and relations are not the same as those detailed in previous chapters regarding regular newsbeats. The private-sector organization is more explicitly self-interested than the public-sector organization. The relations with reporters are generally more distant, and less often face to face. They are more likely to be mediated by texts – news-wire releases; video, audio, and written news releases; annual reports; newsletters; company magazines – than by the everyday chats, luncheons, press conferences, and formal meetings and hearings that characterize the regular newsbeats covering governmental activity. Each private-sector organization has it own news microculture depending on its peculiar organizational needs for secrecy and publicity, and the particular media outlets it prefers in this regard.

Personal relations between sources and journalists are significant none the less. Public-relations units for large organizations are typically staffed with persons who have extensive previous experience as reporters. This experience means that they are articulate in the vocabulary of precedents of the craft, that they have pipelines to particular journalists and news organizations, and that they can gauge more precisely who is to be trusted in exchanges of valued knowledge.

Public-relations officers must display that both they themselves and their authorized spokespersons within the organization are trustworthy. The task of appearing responsive, honest, and reliable can be difficult because the source represents an explicit private interest. Unless the private interest can be construed in accordance with the public interest in the reporter's mind, there is a tendency for the reporter to assume that the organization is simply trafficking in self-interested propaganda or free advertising. This assumption is articulated in the expression, 'It's *just* PR.'

Hence, there is a particular onus on a private-sector source to establish that she is responsive, honest, and reliable. These attributes are crucial to the credibility of the news organization that conveys the source's material, since it derives much of its influence from the authority of the source. A news outlet cannot afford to use a source without these attributes, and will eliminate those who show they lack them. Indeed, a lot of news is directed precisely at negative labelling and discrediting of unresponsive, dishonest, and unreliable people and organizations. At the same time that these people and organizations are pushed to the margins, the responsive, honest, and reliable sources are reinforced and *bolstered* as authorized knowers. For the private-sector source in particular, a good relation with reporters is something to be worked at and can never be taken for granted. As seen by one respondent, 'The more you can deal personally with journalists the better. I mean the more personal contacts you have ... Always try to answer then within terms of honesty ... Everybody expects its an advocacy situation and you're there to be an advocate, but not dodging questions because if you are responsive to someone on something they ask then you have a right to expect the same, and they'll respond by listening to something you want to say.'

In turn sources develop recipe knowledge about who are the responsive, honest, and reliable journalists for their purposes. As emphasized in our studies of newsbeats, this knowledge is the lubricant of the entire news-production process. Nevertheless, many respondents said they always warn others in their organization to avoid being lulled into a comfortable, trusting relation with an individual reporter. Just as the source's interests are embedded in her own organization, so the reporter's loyalty ultimately resides within her news organization. The easiest way to be 'burned' is to be lulled by the comfort of trust into what is an irresistible story for the reporter and an irreversible embarrassment for the source.

Respondents spoke of various means of 'tying in' the individual reporter to their perspective. The most obvious means is to do the reporter's work for him: providing good kits, photographs, exclusives, and so on, in the hope of reasonable coverage. In essence, the reporter's lack of time and material resources are converted into a source tactic. A public-relations officer observed, 'I'm doing my job by helping them, so obviously they're going to be a little more positive and responsive to me.' Another public-relations expert observed that the smaller the news outlet the less resources they have, and the more the individual journalist will accept the source's material at face value. The journalist from the small outlet will publish releases verbatim or broadcast cassettes unedited. A common practice in small outlets is for the journalist to agree to do a good-news story, feature, or editorial about the source in exchange for a paid advertisement by the source to accompany the story. In the larger news operation the individual reporter usually has to be offered something else, such as an exclusive. An exclusive can be made to look as if it is the product of an extensive investigation by the reporter, bringing credit to him and to his news organization's image of having 'the competitive edge.' It also brings contentment to the private-sector source who has managed to communicate what she wants through a controlled channel to the competitive advantage of her organization. At the forefront of relations between the private-sector source and the journalist is the realization that they both have corporate interests to serve. The trick of the trade is to establish a relationship of trust that can enhance their reciprocal interests in each news communication they make.

NEWSWORTHINESS

The newsworthiness of private-sector activities is determined within the prevailing criteria of general-assignment reporting (Ericson et al, 1987: chap. 5). In particular there is a focus on significant developments in corporations; significant advances or declines in the political fortunes of citizens' interest groups; events having a major impact on a large number or significant group of people (employees, investors, members of a profession, members of a minority group); any involvement by a prominent authorized knower; and elements of deviance and efforts at control.

In the interviews conducted with thirty private-sector sources, the criteria of newsworthiness mentioned most frequently were the dramatic and sensational (fifteen), conflict and controversy (fourteen), and wrongdoings (twelve). Thus, sensitivity to deviance and control were prime criteria. As stated in a *Globe and Mail* business-magazine article on newsworthiness in the corporate sphere, 'That a company is successful does not necessarily make it newsworthy ... The most interesting companies are those in trouble, undoubtedly with hopes of getting out of it. They provide lessons to us all. Most speeches by executives, industry awards, corporate anniversaries and plant openings should be applauded or celebrated by those who participate – but rarely do they make news.' As expressed by one of our respondents, 'I can *tell* what's newsworthy ... I've been in this business for nineteen years ... you can *sense* what a story is ... Some sense of conflict, some sense of excitement. A strike between union and management causes a better story than a five-year agreement that we've patched up our differences and everything is going to run smooth. It's just common sense if you're in this business long enough. I could go through any agenda any day of the week and I'll have seventy-five items there and I can tell you which one that the story's going to be on.'

Nevertheless private-sector sources we interviewed seemed less sensitive to news of deviance and control in their organizations than did government sources, and especially criminal-justice–system sources. For example, criminal-justice sources (76 per cent) were much more likely than other government sources (40 per cent) and private-sector sources (40 per cent) to mention 'wrongdoings' as a criterion of newsworthiness (a χ^2-test revealed that these differences are statistically significant at the 0.05 level). Moreover, criminal-justice sources (36 per cent) and other government sources (24 per cent) were much more likely than private-sector sources (7 per cent) to mention 'the unexpected' as a criterion of newsworthiness (a χ^2-test revealed that these differences are statistically significant at the 0.05 level). The policing of organizational life by journalists is, on this evidence, much more a concern of news sources in government than of those in the private sector.

Private-sector sources tended to emphasize the publicity value of their newswork. They were after good news with good effects more than education of the public. In conjuction with the advertising arm of their public-relations operations, this goal entailed the production of enticing images devoid of detailed information. Thus, in another tabular analysis we discovered that criminal-justice sources (76 per cent) and other government sources (82 per cent) were more likely than private-sector sources (47 per cent) to mention the provision of information for public education as a function of their newswork.

Private corporations are less vulnerable to journalistic policing than many other organizations and individuals. Some explanations of this fact can be uncovered by examining how corporate activities are regulated through administrative law-compliance procedures, and why this is less newsworthy than how individual citizens' activities are controlled through criminal-law–enforcement procedures.

There are several characteristics of administrative law-compliance procedures (cf Hawkins, 1984; Reiss, 1984, 1984a; Manning, 1987) that make stories about them unattractive to journalists whose parameters of newsworthiness include simplification, dramatization, conflict, and personalization. First, compliance procedures are operable in morally uncertain territory in which values, technology, and efficient business practices intersect. The moral ambiguity, and the possibility that it might yield dissensus if publicized, makes reporting of corporate regulation unattractive compared to the moral certainty and the 'obvious' need for severe punishment characteristic of major criminal-law–enforcement stories. Second, the activities regulated through compliance procedures occur in conditions of privacy. It is difficult enough for the state's regulatory officers, backed by a degree of legal authority, to penetrate private domains to establish reasonable compliance procedures; for the journalist, penetration is virtually impossible. Third, regulatory enforcement itself is less visible than criminal-law enforcement. The standards to be applied, the norm and the anomaly, are much less clear-cut in regulatory enforcement than in criminal-law enforcement. The standards usually appear in administrative guidelines and guidance notes, in contrast to the codified criminal law and casebooks. Moreover, regulatory enforcement takes the form of subtle, interpersonal bargaining over a long period of time. Fourth, the element of time in seeking compliance – with inspections and negotiations ongoing over months and even years – means that continuing news coverage is unlikely except in the most unusual and serious case. Fifth, it is often impossible to isolate an individual victim and the level of harm in compliance regulation. The continuous nature of violations and of their control complicates any effort to visualize the harm through a particular victim. Sixth, prosecution is rare in compliance regulation. Hence, there is often no formal, official context in which to produce news stories routinely. Seventh, and connected to each of the previous points, there is usually no final and dramatic outcome in compliance regulation, only graduated outcomes based on more tolerable levels of violation negotiated over a long period of time. Given all of these characteristics of administrative law-compliance systems in relation to private corporate activity, and given the prevailing criteria of newsworthiness among journalists as well as their time and material constraints, it is understandable why journalists gravitate towards the 'quick fix' of crime, capture, and punishment as officially provided.

Another consideration in the newsworthiness of private-sector economic activity is that the news media are mainly concerned with the public interest. Thus, they focus primarily on signs of procedural deviance or wrongdoing that might affect collective goods and services (cf Samuelson, 1954). However, they relatively ignore problems related to private-consumption goods (ibid) unless some aspect of their production, distribution, or use has serious ramifications for public safety, the public good. Relative to government officials, private entrepreneurs are either ignored by the news media or left to promote the good life through a blend of advertising and news. This course appears to be the most profitable one for the news media.

Regions and Closures

BACK-REGION ENCLOSURE: SECRECY

'A paradox of the understanding of power in classical liberal theory is that it assumes a free flow of information in the political realm, a free flow of goods in the economic realm, but carefully restricted information flow in the economic realm' (Downing, 1986: 155). Private corporate officials we interviewed were in agreement that the capitalist system mandates a special place for corporate secrecy. Their bottom line was that freedom for private capital requires restriction on freedom of knowledge. A public-relations executive for a large corporation observed, 'The media very often don't acknowledge or understand that certain information is competitive, that in this free society, capitalist society, there is competition and certain information just is not their business.' All respondents who worked for private corporations underscored the necessity of concealing knowledge that might be helpful to competitors.

While 'the competitive edge' was *the* standard justification for enclosure over corporate news, several additional justifications were deemed salient. Given the uncertainty and equivocality of product development, and associated scientific and technological development, there is a concern not to make premature claims or false promises that may not only ruin the success of a particular new product, but also taint the corporation's other activities and products.

Given the uncertainty and equivocality of the standards used by the state in the legislation and enforcement of compliance regulations, and the corporate view that these standards are subject to political pressure from unions, reform groups, and politicians seeking popular support, the prevailing sentiment was that it is better to be secretive than sorry. When the media spotlight focuses on a questionable practice that has been accepted privately for years by both regulated and regulator, trouble may ensue. The inability to rationalize and justify the practice publicly may force the state to intensify regulation and the state's regulators to change face (see Hawkins, 1984; Manning, 1987).

The private corporation is often in collusion with the state to maintain secrecy over product development or production. This collusion is especially evident when the corporation is engaged in scientific and technological development or production related to the military, nuclear energy, and similar areas of 'national security.' Thus, a public-relations officer for a weapons manufactory said he maintained tight controls in publicity related to 'national security' considerations. He noted that manuscripts by the company's professional researchers that were considered suitable for scientific-journal publication had to be scrutinized and approved by his office prior to publication.

Among citizens' interest organizations in the private sector, there is a need to maintain secrecy over matters that might alienate their sources of ideological and financial support. The membership of these organizations may even decide to keep secret values and commitments that are shared within the organization and that are at the core of their raison d'être. They conceal viewpoints and knowledge that might jeopardize their cause, even if these are crucial to their internal cohesion and sense of purpose (McMahon and Ericson, 1987; Ericson, McMahon, and Evans, 1987).

A representative of an organization concerned with sexual assaults on women said that it was imperative to avoid questions that entailed a 'no win' situation for her organization. A person who had been convicted of rape, and who was judged dangerous by correctional authorities, was kept in prison beyond the normal expiry date of his sentence, with statutory and earned remission taken into account. A reporter asked for the organizational representative's opinion on this apparently illegal action by the authorities, but she said that she had to 'skate' around it. She said that the organization's members were in accord that prison is not the solution to the problem of sexual assault against women, but they did not want to state this publicly because they believed it would diminish their credibility in light of a dominant cultural view that rape deserves severe punishment.

Public relations, especially in the private sector, is typically conceived as a proactive enterprise, blending good news and advertising to manufacture favourable images that sell ideologies and products. However, public relations includes a substantial, and perhaps even greater, emphasis on defensive strategies to prevent leaks, and to control damage when a leak occurs or a crisis erupts. Indeed, some observers (e.g., Blyskal and Blyskal, 1985: esp. chap. 8 and 9; Meyrowitz, 1985; Singer, 1986) suggest that the defensive and reactive aspects of public relations are becoming predominant.

> [T]he major role of public relations and advertising, in general, was once that of getting information *to* the public. The intent was to make certain aspects of people, institutions, ideas, and products visible. Other aspects were kept invisible through simple neglect. Now, however, public relations is becoming more and more an attempt to restrict information or to counteract information that is already available, as in recent oil and chemical company public relation campaigns ... 'News' is a combination of substance and image, just as all social interaction involves controlling what is revealed and what is hidden. What has changed in recent times is not necessarily the 'truth content' of political news, but the ... [source's] control over information, and the control over the control. (Meyrowitz, 1985: 165)

BACK-REGION DISCLOSURE: CONFIDENCE

With a perceived organizational and political mandate to be secretive, corporate sources are not disposed to offer confidential knowledge about their own operations to reporters. Even if the corporate source has trusting relations with particular reporters, she is not motivated to make disclosures to them in the back regions. Unlike the government official who may offer reporters a confidence in the hope it will aid their understanding and therefore result in a better story, the private corporate source has no particular commitment to the value of public education. She is paid to release information helpful to her organization, and nothing else.

Corporate sources therefore emphasized the need to avoid off-the-record comments as a matter of common sense. A respondent emphasized how dealings with reporters have to be undertaken in the same manner as other business transactions: having paramount concern for your organizational mandate and private interests.

> If you're a policeman and I say to you, 'Now, don't use this, but I committed a horrendous crime,' that's pretty dumb isn't it? If he arrests me, he is breaking our friendship. But if he doesn't arrest me he's not doing his job and he may feel terrible ... [I]f you have some story to tell them you'd better get it straight the first time. Because the media does not protect your own butt, that's up to you, and the media does not do you favours ... These are all things that you have to take care of yourself. In effect you have to watch

out for yourself. And you're not going to walk into a cop and admit breaking into a bank; and you're not going to walk into a bank and admit to the bank manager that you haven't got any money and no chance of making any but you want a loan; and you don't walk into a used-car lot saying I'm desperate to buy a car, give me any junker that you've got in the lot. You don't do those things!

The control of knowledge for private advantage is not always absolute or permanent. Policing knowledge often entails consideration of when it is advantageous to release particular knowledge to select audiences. As emphasized previously, a crucial component of organizational power is the ability to control roles and audiences for one's performances. From the vantage point of the corporate power structure, 'Secrecy is considered its birthright, with the result that the impact of major corporate decisions may be practically inaccessible by the time they become public knowledge' (Downing, 1986: 155).

Confidential exchanges are much more likely between corporate officers and government officials, than between corporate officers and news-media journalists. The tacit, low-visibility conditions under which state officials seek compliance from officers of private corporations provide a continuous exchange of confidences that rarely percolate through journalists into the public sphere (Hawkins 1984; Reiss, 1984, 1984a; Manning, 1987). Moreover, private corporate work that is conducted under the rubric of state secrets involves complex interpersonal and legal devices for the control of confidences. The law permeates many private-sector activities to provide at once a requirement and a justification for limiting knowledge. Several respondents pointed out that they sometimes wished to disclose knowledge to reporters to avoid adverse inferences being drawn in published reports concerning their corporations, but were prevented from doing so because of legal restrictions. A simple example was given by a bank executive, who indicated that legal restrictions concerning confidentiality of data about customers meant knowledge could not be disclosed to reporters even though disclosure would provide a more balanced account from the bank's perspective.

Public-relations officers provide confidential knowledge to reporters when there is a corporate advantage in doing so. Back-region disclosure to reporters can be aimed at discrediting a competitor's procedures or products. It can assist in controlling news accounts of a crisis involving the corporation. It can be useful in anticipating and offsetting changes in government regulations and compliance-enforcement strategies as they might affect the corporation.

A public-relations consultant to a company embroiled in an inquest regarding a fire death described how he worked the back regions to influence news frames in a direction favourable to the corporation. He said that reporters' acceptance of his back-region disclosures eventually led to a shift in news reports that helped the corporation avoid imputations of a cover-up. The change in the news frame also had the effect of shifting the blame from the corporation to government regulatory agencies.

> [I]t's how you get the information out that really matters, not the information that comes out ... The first word in public relations is you don't admit corporate liability. But the reason you wouldn't want the media to know about it [e.g., safety defects] is several-fold. You wouldn't want them to know about it because obviously it would give you a bad image. Secondly, you wouldn't want them to know about it because then that would get into the hands of the people who bring the lawsuits. [But] because it was an inquest, most of it would have become public anyway. To be seen to be hiding information would be worse than having the information come out ... The lawyers in those cases take the tack that, don't say anything, don't create waves, don't open your mouth at an inquest ... I went in with an entirely different premise. I said you've got to get in there and you've got to say you've spent a million dollars to fix your fire system because of the fire, that these things were wrong, these things were right, and so forth and so on ... And it worked beautifully in the end. All of the information came out. It was decided by the end by the coroner and by the jury and by the media that [the corporation] had been let down all the way along the line. And mainly by government inspectors who were supposed to catch the thing that resulted in the fire and didn't. So, as a result of that inquest, seventy inspectors [from one branch of government] were transferred to the fire marshal's office. An admission by government that it was the government's fault that the fire ... occurred.

Members of citizens' interest groups recognized the corporate advantage in selectively enclosing and disclosing to reporters in the back regions. Organization is power. It is the corporate officer and the public official who have the resources to cultivate reporters, establish trust, and sustain ties. So cultivated, corporate and official sources are more knowledgeable, more craft-like and crafty, in the ways and means of news access. When this knowledgeability is combined with the authority of their corporate or governmental offices, their power over news communication is ensured. A member of a citizens' interest group elaborates:

> [T]here's a perception quite often in our society that the media somehow reflect the public and they can be made to stand in for public opinion. And of course if you think about it, even for like thirty seconds, you realize

that's simply, crudely not true ... When the media themselves refer to 'the public,' what they're really talking about, what they mean is the respectable public, respectable members of our society, which again means business leaders and probably a few politicans and other public figures ... Quite often you'll see little announcements in the newspaper, so and so was in town today to meet with the editorial board. Well, I don't get to meet with the editorial board ... it's an expensive thing to do, to constantly ply the media with information and background and contacts. That's what the press club is for, it's maintained by businesses ... Press clubs always have two kinds of membership: one for reporters which is really cheap, and one really expensive one for representatives of companies. And so, in effect, all those companies are paying for the press club and that gives them privileged access to the reporters ... Then there's another layer, officialdom, which has automatic access basically.

FRONT-REGION ENCLOSURE: CENSORSHIP

In the management of appearances it is important not to appear to be hiding something. As the public-relations consultant quoted above observed, 'To be seen to be hiding information would be worse than having the information come out.' He advised that if the source reveals negative or deviant aspects of his activities himself, he has better control over the facts of the deviance, his preferred justifications of it, and signs that positive steps are being taken to remedy it. Thus, in addition to the straightforward good-news gloss, private-sector organizations allow reporters a degree of access to selected front regions to give the appearance of openness even when things have gone wrong. If handled astutely, such access may yield good news.

In the eyes of public-relations specialists, when front-region access is granted it must be tightly controlled. A respondent emphasized, 'The thing about talking to reporters is what you say is very final, so you better be sure you're right ... It's foolhardy to plunge right in unless you're really very, very familiar with the territory they've got.' This sense of trepidation, of having to say something yet knowing that what is said is final and potentially damaging, puts sources in a position similar to that of those who make confessions (Hepworth and Turner, 1982), including the criminally accused (Ericson and Baranek, 1982). The wording of the statement must be chosen with the greatest care.

Public-relations specialists and executives censor the accounts of their own organization's spokespersons. A respondent said that once the decision is taken to participate in publicity, the entire process is one of editing-as-censorship. In his words, anyone who seeks to publish 'information is also a censor, just by virtue of the fact that there are an infinite number of facts in the universe and not all of them are going to get published. Someone has to decide which ones are going to get published and which ones are not going to get published, and that is every bit an act of censorship as it is an act of editing.' Executives and public-relations officers edit and thereby censor material from within their own organization, and journalists in turn edit and censor the source's material as they see fit. The very act of publicity is simultaneously an act of censorship.

A priority in censorship is the choice of an appropriate spokesperson to represent the organization. When there are serious imputations of deviance against one's organization, and there is the possibility of prosecution through the courts, the need for a skilled and responsible spokesperson is especially acute. The spokesperson must have account ability – the ability to provide excuses and justifications acceptable to journalists and other important political constituencies – to sustain accountability in the public sphere.

Research on corporate deviance indicates that some corporations have a system for designating who will take responsibility for wrongdoing within the public realm of the media and the courts (Erman and Lundman, 1982). Braithwaite and Fisse (1987: 227) report that three large American pharmaceutical companies each have in effect the position of 'vice-president responsible for going to jail.' The top offices in some corporations, similar to senior civil servants and politicans in some governments, are insulated 'from the taint of knowledge should the company later end up in court' (Gross, 1978: 203). That is, designated spokespersons must 'take the heat' when something goes wrong. For this delicate task they require a fine-tuned response ability to sustain the appearance of responsibility in the public sphere. Failure to show responsibility in the media spotlight may result in their responsibility being more seriously interrogated in the legal searchlight.

The medium of communication is also an important choice in considerations of front-region enclosure. Defensive communications aimed at getting a jump on the dissemination of preferred facts, as well as proactive good-news packages, can be handled by the use of private wire services and electronic press kits. For example, the PR newswire service advertises that it contains 'the full, unreduced text of press releases from more than 7,000 sources' (cited by Schiller, 1986: 27). Private wire service and electronic press-kit material is used extensively, and it sometimes achieves even greater dispersal by being picked up and transmitted through established wire services such as Associated Press (AP) and United Press International (UPI) (Sandman et al, 1982: 154).

The source faced with sending out a news release directly, or with granting interviews to reporters, chooses the medium most tailored to her purposes. The approach taken by the private-sector source is not fundamentally different from what we have documented in previous chapters regarding government sources. The private-sector sources we interviewed seemed concerned to offer a very circumscribed factual account, especially when they faced imputations of deviance. This concern meant that they had a preference for broadcast media, especially radio, because they saw those media as more 'factual' and 'fairer' than newspapers. This view was related to an understanding that newspapers have more scope for decontextualization – longer stories using multiple sources, and recalled rather than verbatim quotations. A private consultant on news relations said his clients almost invariably preferred the broadcast media in these terms.

> The only reason that radio and television are perceived as being more fair
> is because they're much shorter in their content ... The demands are on the
> reporter to do the stuff on the scene, right there, without thinking about it at
> all. So, the biggest opportunity for the manipulation of the news is certainly
> in television, by the [source] people on the scene. Television – and radio to a
> large degree, but mostly television – is a business of parody ... The reporter
> has very little option but to go out, then, in front of a camera and spout into
> the camera exactly what he's just been told. So that naturally the interviewee
> thinks he's been treated fairly because whatever he has said is just parroted
> by the reporter ... Newspaper items, of course, are longer and the reporter
> gets to go back to the office and write them. So, he gets more time to think
> about them. He says, wait a minute, that guy was lying to me. Or wait a
> minute, I'll go to the [clipping file] and check the real story. So therefore, the
> interviewees who don't get their own way and aren't able to totally control
> the item get mad at the newspaper and accuse them of taking them out of
> context, or misquoting them.

In addition to the choice of a spokesperson and preferred medium, censorship is effected by controlling the context of communication. The public aspect of the news conference allows an organization to monitor its designated spokesperson, as well as control the news media through her. The news conference provides for the channelling of organizationally relevant and accurate knowledge through staging techniques. These techniques include the use of actors carefully selected and cast for the role, the marshalling of suitable props, and the choice of an authoritative setting. Some members of citizens' interest organizations said the news conference is crucial to them because it gives the public a sense that they are indeed *organized*. They observed that private corporate and government officials usually have regular, scheduled meetings and contexts for routine news coverage, but marginal organizations have to create the equivalent in the form of a news conference.

The choice of a context reflects preferences for the best conditions to avoid the appearance of being 'on the spot.' A respondent said he preferred the news conference because it allows a succinct presentation, and because a difficult question can be avoided by turning to another reporter eager to ask a question. In contrast the one-on-one interview allows the individual reporter to ask penetrating questions that expose the source's lack of knowledge or unwillingness to respond. There is an analogy in teaching formats. The lecture allows the most teacher control because the format provides for one-way communication. The seminar loosens teacher control because part of the format allows questioning that can expose ignorance or worse. The one-to-one tutorial minimizes teacher control because the teacher not only tests the student's knowledge but can be interrogated by the student.

The news conference is explicitly designed to allow the source to maintain the upper hand. Reporters generally defer to this format in exchange for the convenience of obtaining their material in a scheduled, organized manner. However, respondents indicated that even in one-to-one interview contexts the source must take the lead, literally. Specifically, the source should not leave herself open by asking the reporter what he wants to know. This practice simply invites the reporter to take the lead and become creative, which entails gravitating towards deviance and negativism. Instead, the source must learn to implant the lead and essence of the story so that the reporter comes to see, and write, it her way. As recommended by a public-relations specialist,

I'm telling them to put at the bottom [line] a message – the one single thing they want to leave in the public's mind ... Nobody – certainly not the media – they're not capable of dealing with a complex issue. They're not capable of dealing with more than one single issue at a time. They're not capable of dealing with even one, more than one straightforward, single fact. And that's not being terribly negative, that's not being detrimental to the media at all, that is saying that that's the way it works ... And you as the interviewee should have some say, being the expert in the public's mind. You should have some say in what the headlines will be, some say in what the lead of the story will be. And, of course, you can't say to the reporter, without being accused of manipulation, that this is the important thing and you will go away and write this in your headline. You can't do it that way, so you have to have in mind a very clear message that you want to get across to the public, and you have to put that message in, and if possible repeat it, and if possible almost club the reporter over the head with it to make it apparent that this is the message that you would really like to get across.

This is easier said than done. Under interrogation, a lot is required to control the account successfully. Respondents stressed the need to have recipe knowledge of reporters and news organizations. There is always equivocality because each news organization has somewhat different rules of the game, and even different sections of the same news organization can have different expectations. Ultimately, specific decisions to limit access to information and control the account are taken situationally and contextually. A public-relations specialist said, 'They're all judgment calls ... you can't write a textbook on it ... [It's] an art ... There is a general seat-of-the-pants feeling that when you're getting good PR you know it, and when you're not getting good PR you know it.' This respondent went on to offer an example of his artistry in making judgment calls.

> I've sworn on television, into the camera, on purpose, to void the whole shot. Because I was getting what I felt was an unfair line of questioning. And the interviewer just laughed ... she realized we were going to start again and we were sort of on heated ground ... I was getting into deep water on something and I was starting to talk too much ... Reporters will try to set you up ... but to deal with the media you should see that coming and know how to handle it. And the best way to handle it is a very aggressive, assertive way, and they'll back down ... Then you try and let them save face by laughing it off and starting again. You don't want to ever have them go away mad at you because you're going to have to deal with them once again. It's a no-win situation arguing publicly in the media, or with the media.

The ability to gain news access and to control the account, either situationally or via staging, varies substantially among different types of private-sector organizations. Citizens' interest groups, especially those that fail to articulate with the official view and popular consensus, have great difficulty obtaining representation in the news. Rather than controlling enclosure and disclosure as they see fit, they are confined to enclosure on their statements by both the news media and the preferred cast of authoritative sources.

Two respondents affiliated with a citizens' organization concerned with police wrongdoing stated independently that one newspaper often used their organization's material in its stories without attribution to the organization. This practice was interpreted as an effort by the newspaper to avoid any appearance of affinity with the organization, because of the organization's stance in opposition to officialdom. Even though the newspaper sometimes took up individual cases and the causes represented by this organization, it could not voice its support of this organization and thereby accord it legitimacy. If the newspaper elevated this organization to the position of being a legitimate voice of opinion on police affairs, it would upset the newspaper's relations to established official voices, including especially the police themselves. In effect, when this organization's members made efforts at front-region access to reporters, they had their information 'stolen' and used without public acknowledgment of its original ownership. Instead of being given front-region access leading to publicity, they were in effect returned to the back regions and silenced.

News interpretation is entwined with news access. A source representing an organization committed to the rights of gay people said that reporters typically refused to take their perspective, and operated instead within official interpretive frames. For example, when the police raided bath houses used by gay people, the news focused on the procedural propriety of the police actions during the raids to the exclusion of asking whether it was proper to conduct the raids in the first place. He observed that news interpretation is a matter of construing facts within standard frames, resulting in 'very little explanation ... They never stop long enough to ask why it's upsetting people and they tend to substitute their own reactions for those of the people they're observing.'

When the unauthorized are called upon, it is typically to challenge the authorities. There is usually a risk to this, because the authorities have already established their ties to news outlets so that their knowledge is treated as relatively unproblematic and factual. However, the unauthorized or marginal spokespersons and their organizations are likely to be portrayed as troublesome, and their talk is depicted as self-interested. They may achieve coverage, but not access (Gitlin, 1980). A representative of an organization concerned with particular minority rights articulated how his group faced this situation constantly:

Police news releases always get a very high priority, it seems to me. Free information from corporations often does, too, although they're a little more suspicious, of course, of free information from them. What we print and send out in press releases is not regarded automatically as information, whereas the output of the police force is regarded as information. That's because we are perceived as an outside group, outside of society, and therefore our information is likely not to be information but propaganda. Whereas what the police print is merely the truth, or a series of facts at the very least ... Obviously this gives the police a special access to the process of forming public opinion ... As long as there are these great institutions in our society which can churn out reams and reams and reams of stuff that's called information or news, we're competing with this huge machine, right, and journalists have a space to fill ... Often, from our point of view, about the only way we can ever get into the news is when in fact there is a conflict between us and one of these more reputable sources of information or of action ... By and large it gives you a much greater advantage, more likelihood of having a sentence or two of your total world-view appear in the paper ... Usually what happens, of course, there is *the* side, which is usually an official one of some sort. We're always the other side. It's interesting, they talk about getting the other side of the story, not getting both sides. We're the other side ... *The* side, by what it's doing or saying, defines what the other side is and that's finally how, journalistically, it gets represented ... There's an order in these sides, a prioritization. Usually what we get to do is react to something that's already happened.

Several representatives of citizens' interest organizations expressed vulnerability in these terms. Lacking regular contacts with reporters, they are at a disadvantage compared to government officials or corporate officers. The reporter can portray them negatively without risking an ongoing relationship based on trust and reciprocity. Indeed, the reporter can often enhance her relationship with powerful and official sources through negative portraits of marginal organizations and individuals. One respondent suggested that the only remedy to this structured enclosure and its consequences would be the establishment of newsbeats focused on unofficial and non-corporate community groups.

Some respondents from marginal groups recalled efforts to counteract this blockage by hiring news-relations specialists, or by engaging prominent authorized knowers. Hiring an established authorized knower, however, can serve to intensify marginalization because reporters frame their stories in the context of the authorized knower's personality and career as a 'media star.' An example was offered by a representative of a minority group whose membership had been accused of distributing an illegal publication. The group decided to engage a 'star' lawyer, mainly because he could serve as a vehicle for enhanced publicity. However, this strategy 'backfired' as group members were marginalized when they appeared alongside the lawyer in news conferences and other front-region encounters with reporters. The lawyer was featured as the leading actor while group members were at best allowed to express their tertiary feelings concerning what it was like to be involved.

[Reporters asked] questions that didn't seem to penetrate to the heart of the particular issue. The usual ones, like, you know, How do you feel? The great question of modern journalism, How do you feel? ... I do remember being very frustrated at the press conference after our first trial, mainly because that was my first hint of something, which I've become quite used to now, which was that the media seemed to see the main actor on our side as being our lawyer. That is, most of the questions were directed to him, even though the three people who were actually on trial were sitting right in front of them. I mean, it was as if we weren't there in many ways, or else we were exhibits, rather than real, live, thinking, talking people. And they seemed to regard our acquittal as entirely his doing and it was in the frame of, sort of like, clever lawyer gets these creeps off. I mean it wasn't entirely like that, but they do seem to be really hung up on the established structures. And it was very difficult from my point of view, because from my point of view we told our lawyer what strategies he could use in the courtroom and what ones he could not. And we came, we provided the witnesses and so on, and so, I was quite shocked to discover that these people think that somehow we were just sitting there asleep during the whole proceeding, and it was some sort of dumb show on our part, and that the real accused somehow was our lawyer ... [O]bviously we weren't going to attempt to conduct our own defence. It's always been our politics to try to be as mainline as possible in terms of society as a whole, i.e., we weren't going to go out and find some sort of left-wing crazy, who happened to have scraped through law school, to defend us. We wanted someone with a reputation, who can attract media attention. Someone who would understand our case from our point of view and how we wanted it presented. I mean we've never wanted to be acquitted on technicalities, you see. We always wanted it to be on the substantive issues involved. And third, we wanted someone who was a good lawyer, and he filled the bill ... Most defendants are probably overwhelmed by the authority of the lawyer, or whatever, and do whatever he suggests. But we had many, many arguments with our lawyer. Rejected his advice a couple of times. You know we were offered deals about three times by the Crown, to do various things in exchange from them dropping the charges. And he always advised us to accept those deals and we always refused. So, it wasn't a case of us just accepting whatever he recommended as our course of action and he's always been very good at accepting our instructions in terms of what he can do and what he can't do, and we decide that in terms of our overall political situation. And the media, see, have no insight into that whatsoever. They, well I was just astounded at that press conference that they hardly asked us anything at all and then when they did ask us questions, they were the most incredibly stupid things.

FRONT-REGION DISCLOSURE: PUBLICITY

In contemporary knowledge society the public-relations unit has a legitimate place within industry, including the news-media industry. With a place established, the corporate publicity machine is naturally pervasive and persuasive in the public sphere. As made evident in our analysis of secrecy, confidences, and censorship, all publicity is enclosed to a degree. The private corporation with a substantial public-relations unit can routinely purcolate good news through 'free advertising' into the public sphere, and relegate bad news through 'damage control' into the private sphere.

State efforts at regulating private corporate activity have the potential for damaging publicity. On the rare occasion when the state decides to prosecute a private corporation, publicity about corporate wrongdoing may surface and even form a significant part of the punishment (Erman and Lundman, 1982; Fisse and Braithwaite, 1983; Braithwaite and Fisse, 1987). However, as we have argued previously, in the everyday world of compliance enforcement, publicity is of little relevance. Compliance officers do not relate to public opinion in the same way as public police officers (Law Reform Commission 1986; Manning, 1987). Compliance officers are more concerned about expert opinion and how it is to be weighed in long-term negotiations over compliance. These carefully controlled negotiations are conducted in conditions of low visibility, or invisibility as far as the news media are concerned.

The situation is different for the private-sector organization representing a particular citizens' group's interest. With the previously noted exceptions of religious groups and a few other organizations that have become corporate giants with sophisticated publicity machines, the citizens' interest organization struggles to achieve access to the news and must work at it constantly, as is illustrated in the case of an established organization concerned with the welfare of criminal offenders. At the time of our field research this organization was just 'waking up' to publicity as a tool for enhancing its place in the public sphere. An executive of this organization said that for the first time in the organization's long history it was becoming proactive with the news media.

> It's really related to getting our story across, getting our message across ... Our position is that crime is really a community problem and that to deal with it citizens really need to be informed and to be involved and our objective is to have some sense of community responsibility ... At one time we had a person who was a co-ordinator of community education. We had to cut that position because of financial cutbacks in resources, and so ... this is what's resulted ... What we've been doing in the past has not been high-profile publicly, it's been publishing scholarly papers ... pamphlet materials and so on ... But we haven't really been moving much beyond the converted in many ways. This is an attempt I think to reach out more.

The organization reached out with a range of proactive strategies and tactics. A 'media week' was launched by providing a special 'kit' to journalists dealing with the organization and its concerns. The kit included a letter from the premier of Ontario, signifying to journalists that it was worth their attention. During media week the same influential people the organization hoped to reach through news communications were contacted by letter: 'That awareness week we also sent out to 30,000 people in Ontario a letter, which again said what we did, what we felt the issues were ... and asked them if they could support us, and to get members and so on ... In that sort of thing you buy lists ... I think the lists included people who were civil-libertarian groups that could be identified, people who received certain [serious and up-market] magazines ... that's a whole other industry I'm becoming aware of.'

A liaison was established with a member of the editorial board for a prominent newspaper, whose position on at least some issues was the same as that of the respondent's organization. Media 'kits' were prepared on specific criminal-justice issues the organization decided to address and, it was hoped, influence, leading to 'talk show' appearances and feature coverage. News conferences were called in relation to specific legislation being considered in parliament, something the respondent described as 'new for us.' Four journalism students were hired for a summer term to make good news for the organization in local community newspapers.

> They're going around and getting as many stories as they can about individuals who've been involved in our service in various branches, success stories, interesting stories. We hope to have a whole dossier of vignettes, kind of thing, that we can use in articles, in newspaper stories, and provide them to newspapers. We think there's a great market out there in small-town newspapers that will run our material slanted towards their community. Using the kind of stories that we have and are familiar with, and properly disguised and so on [to make it appear it is the newspaper's story] that will tell our story ... We've wanted to do this for some time, provide them with an article, maybe even picture, whatever, and they can run it. They apparently do that sort of thing.

Other respondents indicated that they were well aware of 'that sort of thing,' but said they lacked the resources and/or credibility to manufacture it successfully. At best they received sporadic coverage by achieving one-shot access to a preferred format, or by inventing an original format that attracted the attention of the news media.

Three respondents observed that as politically radical or marginal sources, they preferred live coverage. Live coverage allows greater control over communication and lessens the chance of being discredited through juxtaposition with journalists' voice-overs or other sources' statements that create a new context for discrediting them. As one respondent said regarding live coverage, 'You get to say something they probably wouldn't put on the air in recorded coverage.'

Marginal groups sometimes feel compelled to be inventive, even though this practice may accelerate their marginalization. Public demonstrations are staged, complete with theatricals that will attract the journalist's ear and the television cameraman's eye. The contemporary political demonstration owes just about everything to news-media coverage, especially to television. It is the marginal organization's news conference. In visualizing their own deviance – for example, through extreme statements on placards or by burning someone in effigy – marginal groups try to visualize the deviance of the authorities or others they are opposing.

The same approach may be taken by the poor-but-respectable organization. A representative of a citizens' organization concerned with victims of violence described how they orchestrated a full week of demonstrations at a site where there had been several separate incidents of violence. These demonstrations received extensive news coverage, which the respondent attributed to their shrewdness in making it a 'visual story': 'When there's specific demands that we have and they depend on public pressure to see them enacted then we'll try to make the story visual.'

REPORTERS' SELF-ENCLOSURE

In complaining about their exclusion from the public conversation, less powerful sources addressed the tendency of reporters to gravitate to where the power is. The fact that reporters favour regular authorized knowers is very evident to the unauthorized. Sources who are at once highly organized and powerful serve to routinize the news process for reporters, and in turn receive routine access for their own purposes. The reporter gets the job done and the source sustains media presence. This situation was parodied by a respondent:

> If you went through the newspaper we'd have a list of about 112 people and that would be the only people who exist! ... There are only 112 people who count, you know ... Because the media in Canada never goes beyond this little conclave of sources ... It's like the Johnny Carson show. Those who have been sources in the past and proved that they're good sources will, of course, be the best sources again ... [These regular sources] are products of the media in the first place and they have used the media to get their name established ... You always get the same story ... You never have a resolution of problems because the same people are always commenting on the same resolution in order to foster their own cause.

Less powerful sources blamed more powerful sources, specific news organizations, and the media institution for exclusion. In contrast, sources representing powerful organizations tended to blame individual reporters for coverage they did not like. Complaints abounded about the bias of particular reporters, reporters' inexperience, the low standards of vocational qualifications for reporters, reporters' lack of specialist knowledge in the specific fields they are reporting on, and the all-round poor calibre of the reporting corps. In making these attributions respondents showed a lack of sensitivity to the nature of news production and purpose. Their concern about reporters lacking specialist knowledge indicates a failure to appreciate that news is not a vehicle for communicating such knowledge. Rather, reporting entails the *translation* of such knowledge into the simple and literal terms of common sense (Ericson et al, 1987). Even well-staffed quality news outlets prefer non-specialists who can be shifted from assignment to assignment as the organizational need arises. They are after good story-tellers, not technical exactitude (ibid). The respondents who expressed an appreciation of this fact tended to be ex-reporters or experienced media consultants and analysts. In offering her insights in this regard, one respondent indicated that most of her colleagues lacked such insight:

> I think most administrative people have real difficulties ... with the media. I mean real difficulties in understanding that they have problems. I would say I still think that within the kinds of discussions we have among our [employees], that there's still a fairly profound suspicion of the media, really to move very quickly to feel that they misreport or misrepresent or are inaccurate or stupid. And I think a lot of this comes from the fact that many of them have not thought through the ... production processes in which, neither in print nor in radio and TV, is really in the hands of a single individual ... A lot of ... reactions to the media are based on expecting the media are there to carry on this cool, analytical, thoughtful, rational, logical presentation of factual material, and of the hypotheses about the factual material. And, of course, there's no way the format, or the time span, or the nature of the financing, or the mixture of entertainment and information ... permits that kind of thing occurring except in the occasional long, detailed story. I've seen very good stories in the press - not stories, I mean in-depth articles – and I think there are a number of quite intelligent journalists in Canada. But obviously there are limits placed on them by the medium in which they have to work. I think it's a frustration they recognize.

Most respondents also failed to recognize that many of the reporters they identified as having a penchant for a negative slant were in fact mandated to be negative by their senior editors. Many respondents trafficked in a 'rotten apple' theory of bad reporters, saying that certain reporters just did not seem capable of 'getting a story straight.' The reporters they identified were almost always those who were mandated by their superiors to 'twist' stories, usually with the goal of revealing some crooked practice in the source organization. Moreover, the reporters identified came from news organizations that defined their role in terms of the fourth estate.

Reporters are rarely inclined to police organizational life in private corporations. Their lack of motivation in this regard stems in part from the absence of a mandate from their news organization to pursue corporate wrongdoing. With the exception of the CBC, the news organization is itself part of the private corporate sphere. It is therefore more likely to express a corporate affinity against government interference than to join with government officials in the policing of private corporations. Moreover, a symbiotic relationship with corporate sources is often necessary to sustain advertising revenue. Rather than bite the hand that feeds, the news organization is likely to join hands with corporations in the pursuit of mutual interests, which includes doing biting stories about governmental interference in the private sector.

It follows that news organizations are unlikely to allocate substantial resources for the journalistic investigation of wrongdoing in private corporations. While there are rare exceptions – such as the considerable journalistic resources expended on investigating Cadillac-Fairview Corporation and several trust companies involved in 'flipping' rental properties in Toronto (Ericson et al, 1987) – the typical response is to avoid investigating such complicated matters, or to report on them only through official eyes.

An additional limitation is the institution of privacy itself. If the legal rights of private-property owners are potent enough to circumscribe the activities of the state's police and compliance officers, and to allow corporations to organize private policing as they wish (Shearing and Stenning, 1981, 1983, 1987), these same legal rights are surely even more potent in keeping out meddlesome reporters. Policing for compliance depends on the social organization of information-gathering, and news reporters have even fewer data capacities than government officials. Again the reporter is left to rely on official accounts, or to ignore the area entirely. The net effect is that reports on the policing of private corporate activities are rare, and involvement by reporters in such policing is rarer still. The news consumer is left with stories about isolated, major, individual crimes, and with journalistic policing of governmental wrongdoing and procedural deviance.

Influences of News Texts

INFLUENCES ON PROCEEDINGS AND PARTICIPANTS

While there was considerable dissatisfaction with the news media among all types of news sources we interviewed, private-sector sources were the most critical. Only 10 per cent (3/30) of private-sector sources indicated that the news media were fulfilling their mandate *in general*, compared to 18 per cent (7/38) of government sources and 40 per cent (10/25) of criminal-justice sources (the differences are statistically significant at the 0.05 level). Moreover, only 20 per cent (6/30) of private-sector sources indicated that the news media were fulfilling their mandate *in the source's particular field*, compared to 24 per cent (9/38) of government sources and 60 per cent (15/25) of criminal-justice sources (the differences are statistically significant at the 0.05 level).

Private-sector news sources, similar to government and criminal-justice sources, expressed concern about being misrepresented in the news. However, their concern was not simply a quibble over getting the facts straight, but a realization that a lack of balance and distortion were aimed at having particular social-control effects. As indicated by one private-sector respondent, quality news outlets with an institutional news focus can be especially powerful when they blend fact and value for the purpose of social-control effects.

> Journalists do not have very big obligations, because they have this unique niche in the information business of taking information from a source and translating it for mass readership or listening audiences. Their obligation is to give a fair, reasonable accounting of what is going on. What perhaps too often gets blurred is the distinction between what is news and what is commentary. And there has been a tendency over the last few years I think for reporters to encroach themselves or to inject themselves into the story ... [Names quality newspaper] is the worst offender I can think of ... That is why it is the most inaccurate paper ... [But] it is the paper that's read in high places ... It does not make it the best newspaper ... I've always been leery of this activity which brings them to final account within a story.

This respondent went on to say that in his business he always read this quality newspaper and treated it as the most important, while in contrast he almost never bothered to read the popular newspaper he identified as the most accurate. This is another sign that those whose business it is to have influence through the news have to take it seriously regardless of whether they feel it provides a reasonably fair and objective account. They are more concerned about authority and influence than accuracy and balance. They are more concerned about the social-control effects of the news media than about its value for public knowledge. When the news media are seen primarily in terms of their social-control effects, they are evaluated in particular terms: Are they likely to damage our reputation? Do they convey an ideology that is not consistent with our own? Do they portray us in a way that marginalizes rather than enhances our reputation and legitimacy?

On each of these questions private-sector sources perceived more negative effects than either government sources or criminal-justice sources. In addressing how news coverage can harm them, damage to reputations was mentioned by 83 per cent (25/30) of private-sector sources, 71 per cent (27/38) of government sources, and 56 per cent (14/25) of criminal-justice sources (note however that the differences are not statistically significant at the 0.05 level). In contemplating why the news media were not fulfilling their mandate in general, ideological differences with the news media and/or the profession of journalism were mentioned by 40 per cent (12/30) of private-sector sources, but only 18 per cent (7/38) of government sources and 12 per cent (3/25) of criminal-justice sources (the differences are statistically significant at the 0.05 level). And, in addressing problems in dealing with the news media, the problem of not being taken seriously was mentioned by 27 per cent (8/30) of private-sector sources, but only 16 per cent (6/38) of government sources and not a single criminal-justice source (the differences are statistically significant at the 0.05 level).

Corporate sources are especially sensitive to the possible negative effects of publicity about wrongdoing. The 'informal justice' of mass-mediated disputes between the aggrieved citizen and the offending corporation can have financial and legitimacy costs for the corporation (Pfuhl and Altheide, 1985). While the media ombudsman or 'action line' method of dispute resolution individualizes problems to the single special case (ibid; Palen, 1979; Mattice, 1980; Abel, 1982) there can be more fundamental organizational and even system-wide effects on a particular industry. The consumers' movement is organized, not limited to the formats of consumer-advice columns and the media ombudsman's 'action line.' While all sanctions may be relatively weak in their impact on offending corporations, adverse publicity seems to be more influential than legal sanctions in gaining compliance from private enterprise (Fisse and Braithwaite, 1983).

Some citizens' interest groups experience a combination of not being taken seriously, ideological differences with journalists, and damage to their organizational identities. As detailed earlier, the marginal group that does not articulate with a consensual issue is alternatively granted no access; given coverage only in deviant contexts and formats, such as the dramatic public demonstration; and given coverage in other contexts and formats that simply underscore its status as marginal. The net effect is to be treated as unimportant, at best a source of tertiary understanding of the type 'What was it like to be involved?' and at worst marginalized even further.

As political agents of social control, journalists regularly use the source in political opposition in 'straw-man' fashion. Whether it is reporting on international politics or on local priorities in government, weak or already discredited sources can be used as 'straw-spokesmen' for positions the news organization is opposed to. For example, a respondent outlined a story involving a man who went to the authorities to say that he was not receiving enough money from welfare sources and therefore was unable to look after his two children. A television crew visited the man's apartment and visualized *his* deviance by showing beer cases stacked beside a colour television set.

The reporter used these visuals with a voice-over to indicate in no uncertain terms that the fault rested with the father's spending priorities rather than with the welfare system.

Citizens who organize into political movements, like politicians and their supporting casts, become creatures of the news media. Political movements have mushroomed with the ascendancy of the electronic media, constructing their roles in accordance with the formats and frames of those media. Citizens prominent in political movements therefore face the same fate in the public sphere as politicians and their party operatives. They are obliged to speak to the consensus, in turn, and at a good clip. As such, they are readily absorbed in the market of commercial culture. '[T]he current fashion for movement politics ... which is in itself in part a response to the decline of political parties induced by existing patterns of media dominance, in part a product of ... consumerist ideology ... , in part an expression of dissatisfaction with the programmes of existing parties, in no way provides an alternative to the political party, as indeed these movements are discovering. You cannot develop a realistic and realizable movement towards disarmament or women's rights unless it is integrated with other social and economic objectives into some structure and universal program of political priorities' (Garnham, 1986: 51).

The news media can benefit political movements by making the public aware of their cause and willing to contribute financially and through membership and by making governments respond symbolically, legally, and materially. The news media provide the public with the 'view from no place' that can foster groups broadly concerned with human rights, the environment, nuclear safety, and so on. As Meyrowitz (1985: 144) observes, 'Such issues require an "overview," an overriding of traditional group concerns and a bypassing of needs as seen from one's particular place.' However, the '"liberalizing" effect of the multiple-perspective view may still give a political advantage to conservatives, reactionaries, and special-interest groups. After all, multiple perspectives often lead many people to an overabundance of empathy and, therefore, to political ambivalence and inaction' (ibid). This effect is considered further in chapter 7.

PUBLIC KNOWLEDGE

The private-sector source views the news as a promotional activity. The news format is used in conjunction with advertising, entertainment, and public relations to convey images that have social-control effects serving the particular interests of the source. The results are measured by how many members of the public buy into the product. All significant private-sector organizations must invest in political communications that are attuned to commercial culture. This imperative applies equally to the corporation selling goods and to the citizens' organization doing good.

The citizen is given little understanding of the corporate world. Corporations are rarely penetrated by journalists themselves, because they are excluded spatially, distanced socially, and absorbed culturally. Journalists are able to penetrate corporations via official investigations conducted by state regulatory agencies, but this penetration, too, is limited by the filtering of official accounts. Stories of governmental compliance efforts and regulatory enforcement are prevalent in the news, but the prevailing view is the official one.

The corporation is able to reach the citizen with a barrage of entertaining news and advertisements, while the citizen has little access to the corporation to understand what she is consuming. We do not contend that the citizen is a mere cultural dope, invariably taken in by the images. However, the citizen usually has little choice but to act on the images since other knowledge is either unavailable or requires considerable effort to acquire. Corporations spend hundreds of millions of dollars a year in newswork and advertising to ensure that this is the case.

> What we are witnessing, then, is a double movement whereby corpora-
> tions are able to restrict access to strategic information about their activities
> while at the same time gaining unparalleled control over the flow of positive
> images to the public at large. The result is to intensify still further the im-
> balance in the information system. An avalanche of managed material flows
> from the boardrooms to the citizen, but it is increasingly difficult for citizens
> (or the journalists who claim to act on their behalf) to gain access to the
> information on which an independent assessment could be made. The news
> media are therefore less and less able to fulfill the historic liberal ideal of
> acting as a Fourth Estate. (Schiller, 1986: 31)

The private-citizens' organization can negotiate control over images and knowledge about itself if it articulates with a consensus and the public interest. It, too, can become a corporate giant, and even a multinational, if it can show itself to be a public good. Its success is very dependent upon whether it is supported by news organizations that can use it to express their own ideological preferences. However, success in these terms entails failure as an autonomous political movement: it signals absorption into established institutional frameworks, including news frames.

The citizens' organization that refuses to articulate with the consensus is dismissed, usually summarily, always painfully. If it is given news coverage, it is in a deviant cast. It, too, is used to articulate the ideological preferences of news organizations, but in opposition, and usually to the long-term detriment of the citizens' organization. Here, too, the news organization thinks it is acting in the public interest.

The news understands private matters in terms of the public interest. In transforming private matters into public goods, the news inevitably blurs the distinction between private and public, and between state and non-state. This blurring is characteristic of contemporary society. It is evident not only in society's media, but in its economy, politics, and law (Fitzpatrick, 1984). The analysis in previous chapters regarding image-making by politicians, government officials, and law enforcers applies also to private-sector sources. The news functions the same whether the sources represent the state or the private sector, and whether the source is promoting a political product or a commercial product. News is a mosaic of images filtered by commercial and political culture. While this gives news an unreal quality, regular news sources are the first to appreciate that it is nevertheless very real in its effects.

Possible remedies for overcoming these effects, when negative, are analysed in the following chapter. That the news organization is no different than any other organization in having to patrol its spatial, social, and cultural regions, and in having to effect enclosure on its accounts, is revealed in an analysis of how news organizations deal with sources who seek various remedies for unreasonable or harmful news coverage.

6

The News Media

In previous chapters, and in *Visualizing Deviance* (1987), we analysed the role of journalists as designators of deviance and contributors to control in various organizations. We also showed that as participants in the organizations and activities they report on, journalists themselves are subject to imputations of deviance and mechanisms of control.

In addition to the deviance and control mechanisms journalists experience within source organizations, news organizations are subject to efforts at penetration by particular sources, and by government. News organizations experience imputations of deviance and demands for remedy from sources aggrieved by unreasonable coverage, and from government officials interested in compliance regulation. How news organizations deal with these potentially disruptive imputations and intrusions is the subject of this chapter.

In the first three sections of the chapter we examine the remedies potentially available to sources in the face of unreasonable news coverage. This analysis is grounded in the perspective of sources. How do they perceive the remedies potentially available? What are the implications of their perception for understanding their power and relative autonomy in relation to the news media?

In the final two sections of the chapter we examine the major forum in newspapers for redressing unreasonable coverage, the letters-to-the-editor format. This analysis is grounded in the perspective of the newspaper organization. How do its members perceive and deal with material critical of their reports and operations? What are the implications of these perceptions and dealings for understanding their power and relative autonomy in relation to news sources? In addition, the analysis of letters to the editor provides a systematic basis for understanding the criteria that are most influential in granting news access to sources. It is a useful vehicle for summarizing the major components of news judgment addressed in less systematic fashion in previous chapters and in *Visualizing Deviance*.

Limitations on Seeking Remedies for Unreasonable Coverage

The news sources we interviewed emphasized that the preventative devices of regions and closures, as analysed in previous chapters, provide the best hope for minimizing unreasonable news coverage. This perception was based on practical knowledge that remedies available after the fact of unreasonable coverage are extremely limited and very much in the control of the news media. In answering a general question asking them to identify available mechanisms for obtaining a remedy for unreasonable news coverage, the most frequent response (one-third of the ninety-three respondents) was that there is *no* remedy. The most succinct statement was provided by a public relations consultant quoted in the previous chapter: 'It's a no-win situation arguing publicly in the media, or with the media.' If you have not taken flight in advance of news coverage, or taken precautions to meet the requirements of news access, then you are left to take your lumps.

The limitations on seeking remedies for unreasonable coverage are not solely attributable to the power of the news media. Limitations can reside within the source's own organization. An important limiting factor is concern for the proper image of the source's organization and occupation within the public culture. A police respondent said, 'As a public servant I can't do anything, personally I wouldn't, I wouldn't. Because I take my lumps and say well, tomorrow it'll be something else. Many times ... I'd love to reply to them and I know if I do I'll be in bigger trouble.' Judges said it is simply improper to complain about news coverage, except in the courtroom context with reference to the law of contempt.

Politicians were unanimous in stating how dangerous it is to seek formal remedies for unreasonable coverage. When asked about the remedies available to her, a politician said, 'As a politician, absolutely nothing.' She said she had once tried to obtain a remedy through the Ontario Press Council, but the only thing she gained from that was the lesson that one has to 'just look to the future because you cannot redress past things that have been in the paper.' She said that when she is dealt with unfairly, 'I treat it more like an amputation; you just cut your losses and go.' Another respondent said that one of his 'few rules in politics is never, never, ever complain ... to the media.' Another politician expressed it more colloquially: 'Having a good relationship with all members of the press gallery, and not bitching about when they screw you, is really important.'

Politicians exemplify sources who are reticent to seek remedies because they are so dependent on the news media. Criminal-justice officials exemplify sources who are reticent to seek remedies because it is improper to the dignity of their official office. Either way, complaints about coverage are reduced in deference to the source organization and its place in public culture.

The belief that effective remedy for unreasonable news coverage is not possible also relates to sources' perceptions about the power of the news media. A court official asserted that the news media have enormous power and 'abuse it quite often,' adding that he and his colleagues are always wary of reporters because 'there's sort of no controls at all.' Another court official said a news outlet is the 'only organization around who can go out and damage somebody's reputation without any fear of internal discipline.' A government official, who saw the news media as crucial to the success of new procedures for review of public complaints against the police, observed that the news media have greater power than the police to neutralize public complaints:

> A great deal of power resides in the media right now. It's incredible. I think the media are more powerful than the government, than big corporations, than big unions. I think they're the most powerful organization ... in society, and the checks, the balances, are really very, very vague ... I worry about the fact that people who make these very important decisions – and who can make them wrong – are really not able to be dealt with in any way, there's really no one that can handle it ... I worry about them a lot but I do not have the answers ... I would like to find some way to retain freedom and lack of government control and censorship – which I abhor as much as anybody else – and still at the same time impose some controls that are reasonable and fair on the media ... It reminds me of the issue that we're involved with, where people say, 'Police still investigate police, I don't like it' ... If the police are still investigating the police, I don't like it but I realize now [simply asserting that is] too naïve and I'm sure with the media it's the same thing. When they scream freedom of the press and censorship, that backs me off right away. But I'm sure if I looked at it closer we could find a way to avoid censorship, ensure freedom of the press, and still impose some sort of reasonable checks and balances and controls on an organization in the community that has become extremely powerful and dangerous, potentially, because of that power.

Similar talk about the power of the news media, and the inability to do much about it, punctuated most interviews. In expressing awe at the power of the news media to cause irreparable harm through negative publicity, an official said, in relation to the news media: 'There's an old principle of law that where there is wrong there should be a remedy, but there is no remedy.' Another government source spoke of the power of the news media to 'absolutely kill,' and when asked what could be done to remedy harmful coverage he replied, 'Nothing! Nothing! Nothing!'

The power of the news media to ignore, offset, or negate efforts at remedy was attributed to a number of elements. Many respondents pointed out that in any effort to achieve a remedy the news organization retains the upper hand because it has the 'last word.' The news outlet can choose to exclude additional comments from the aggrieved source, to edit those comments as it sees fit, or to juxtapose those comments with its own commentary in order to undercut them. Typical statements included, 'You can't fight the media, it's like you can't fight City Hall, they've got the last word,' and it is a 'no-win' situation 'because the press always has the last word anyway.'

Respondents also emphasized the reluctance of news organizations to change the interpretive framework established for an issue. A corporate executive talked about how her industry was subject to sustained allegations of price-fixing, to the point where any evidence offered to the contrary did nothing to change the frame. 'I don't know how you remedy those things, I really don't, because you spend hours and days and people's lives in frustration trying to counter things that get [established in] the press the first time around, that continually get the headlines.' The public-relations officer for a government ministry that was repeatedly 'bashed' in one influential newspaper made a similar point about the favoured themes and frames of that newspaper: 'If the reporter or paper has already established their position in public, if they've written about this yesterday and the position yesterday was that this is evil or whatever, then almost nothing you can say ever after that will back them off that opinion. Because they're very mulish and don't want to have to back down or back away. And [names newspaper] is particularly like that because ... it won't even run corrections when they will acknowledge to you in print privately that they're making mistakes. And [they] won't do anything about it.'

Respondents also addressed the power of the news media to offset or discredit complaints through the way complaints are presented. For example, the letters-to-the-editor section is set up as an expression of *personal opinion*; hence, the source who complains through that section is categorized as an individual complaining about something that was originally written for the more 'neutral' and 'objective' news sections of the newspaper. In typing the person as a complainer, the newspaper is able to suggest the irrationality of the person. If what the complainant seeks is a denial of imputations of deviance against her, her image may be more tainted in the process. Allegations alone can fracture an image, and repair work can still leave the cracks exposed. As one respondent expressed it, 'Retractions just don't help you, they create, in some instances, more of a problem because they say, "Whoops, we made a mistake, she doesn't beat her husband any more!" ... You can't complain continually, you can't afford to because you lose, you appear to be irrational.'

Respondents generally believed that news-media efforts at self-policing function to deflect criticism and enhance power. They said remedies external to the news media (legal action, complaining to the Canadian Radio-television and Telecommunications Commission or Press Council, avoidance, use of alternative media) are ineffective to the point of giving journalists professional autonomy unparalleled in other professions and institutional spheres. Therefore complaints have to be routed internally to the specific news organization, but again, the news organization holds the upper hand through their control of their news texts and the contexts in which the complainant is represented.

This assessment leads many to conclude that they should not complain or seek remedy. To do so can sustain coverage of a matter one wishes to keep quiet and upset co-operative relations with journalists that can have long-term repercussions. Respondents emphasized repeatedly that complaining makes matters worse: 'What you do is underscore the original story'; 'Corrections often harm the individual more because his name gets in the paper twice.' It was seen as virtually inevitable that complaints about negative coverage sustain negative coverage. As captured by one respondent, when you get 'into a certain kind of contest with a skunk ... you get some of it on you no matter what happens.'

Any minor satisfaction that might come from a remedy pales in comparison with the damage done by the original offending article. A respondent who had been an executive assistant to a person who had obtained libel damages against a newspaper said he was explicitly assigned the task of resurrecting this person's media image afterward. He said that in spite of enormous effort the fractured image was never repaired, and in face of blocked opportunities this person was forced to pursue his career in a different sphere.

The recommendation is to keep silent. Silence speeds the process of exhausting the newsworthiness of the matter. Referring to his experience of not complaining in face of sustained negative coverage, a respondent said, 'I just wanted it to go away and it did go away.' Silence is also a means of not giving journalists the satisfaction of knowing that their reports are having an impact on individuals and organizations they seek to control.

Lacking specific remedies after the fact, respondents advocated prevention as the best cure. Typical is the comment, 'You're not going to undo anything that's been done ... you just have to prevent it happening again.' Such prevention entails extra caution in choices about what to divulge and how to formulate it in the first instance. One cannot turn over the 'property' of organizational knowledge and then deny usage rights (Coleman, 1973) to those who have taken possession of it. A respondent stated, 'Our view here is that once you give information, forget it, it's not yours, it becomes the property of that reporter and that newspaper chain.' The source must use all the preventative strategies and tactics available within the regions and closures of her organization. For those without an elaborate public-relations apparatus or system of regions and closures, the best hope is to minimize the loss. A spokesperson for a marginalized interest group stated plainly, 'I don't think there is any remedy. All you're faced with is a constant struggle to get something less damaging. A less damaging process to work than the one that's going on at the given time. I mean when you talk about remedies it suggests like somehow if we could only figure something out, in a year this could all be solved. All I think of is just, what we do is really just like staunching the wound.'

Remedies External to News Organizations

BEING UNCOOPERATIVE

Respondents addressed a number of possible solutions to their problems in dealing with the news media. The most frequently addressed solution, mentioned by 41 per cent of the ninety-three respondents, was to reduce co-operation with the reporter and/or news organization causing the problem. In contrast, only 16 per cent of respondents advocated more co-operation or accommodation to journalists as a solution to problematic coverage. Respondents also addressed the likely consequences of non-cooperation. Four consequences were mentioned frequently: more negative coverage on the matter, a loss of control over accounts of the matter, the likelihood of bad relations with journalists leading to more problems with coverage in the future, and the likelihood that the reporter and news organization concerned would still give coverage by using other sources.

Having described several 'run-ins' with journalists, a judge said he came to the conclusion that he is 'powerless' in relation to the news media except for the power to deny further interviews, an option he was now taking. A professional working in a medical setting said that complaining to news outlets is 'the death penalty,' and that the most viable remedy is to deny the offending reporter and news outlet future interviews. She added that this can usually be done subtly: for example, dealing with future calls by saying someone else is a more suitable expert; or agreeing to an interview on condition that the journalist read a major book or report, knowing that this condition is almost invariably a deterrent to the journalist facing deadlines.

Some respondents believed that their organization ultimately suffers more than the news organization in consequence of non-cooperation. A politician described one of many incidents that had led her to become selectively uncooperative, then observed, 'I think in a sense it hurt us, the party, and we don't get coverage on those kinds of stories in that newspaper very much. I found that the reporter has written some good stories since, but she's also done the same sort of thing since.'

Many sources spoke of efforts to exclude particular reporters and news outlets that had proved troublesome in the past. One newspaper in particular was mentioned by several sources as having a political bias that made its journalists hostile to the sources' interests. They simply excluded journalists from this newspaper. Thus, clearly there is ideological self-selection between sources and news outlets. What appears as the bias of the news organization is partly a matter of sources' collaboration with news organizations with which they have an ideological affinity, and simultaneously, their lack of co-operation with news outlets that quarrel with them ideologically.

It is easier for some types of sources to be uncooperative. For example, an executive for a private corporation said he had a primary responsibility to shareholders. Since any news about the company is usually bad news – for example, troubles with the union, including strikes, or procedural deviance by management – his task is to minimize news coverage through minimal co-operation. He said there is considerable variation even among private corporations depending upon what they manufacture: his company could not benefit from the 'advertising' effect of news coverage, whereas other companies can and therefore are more eager to sustain good news-media relations. Wearing his other hat as vice-chairman of a general hospital, he said the relation to the news media is very different. In this role he sees himself as a public official accountable through the public media. The news media are useful for fund-raising, medical alerts, and general public confidence in their medical facility. Hospital officials have to be responsive to public enquiries, including journalistic endeavours to police procedural propriety.

The salience of non-cooperation varies by the social place of the recalcitrant source and the issue in question. The professor of criminology who refuses to comment on the police annual report indicating a rise in violent crime is unlikely to be subject to a published comment that she was uncooperative. The prime minister who refuses to comment on an allegation of political patronage is very likely to be subject to a published comment that she was uncooperative. Moreover, the costs of being persistently uncooperative are very high for the prime minister, but relatively insignificant for the professor. Indeed, the professor's colleagues may be scornful of her appearance in the news. They may see this activity as an essentially unacademic one, and possibly even as a political step into the territory of the system she analyses and not in keeping with her academic office. In brief, most of those who are uncooperative can afford to be within the expectations of their organization.

Most regular sources simply cannot afford to deny the news media without risking negative impact on their organization. The best they can do is respond in a limited way. A government official was asked what would happen if he refused to co-operate with reporters, and he replied, 'I wouldn't last very long in this job. I'll always co-operate in the sense that I'll always give them an answer; if they don't like the answer, that's tough.' This response is typical of public servants, who stressed their duty to be co-operative. A civil servant said that it would be a 'terrible mistake' if she refused to grant interviews to reporters generally: 'The thought wouldn't even occur to me. It ... [is] not something I would contemplate because this is a public office.'

A concomitant aspect is that news access is required for the purpose of bolstering one's public image. One respondent said that general co-operation with reporters was like 'buying insurance' to protect the image of his organization. Representatives of different types of organizations talked of the need to maintain their visibility via news coverage, in some cases seeing it as important to survival. Some members of citizens' groups representing minority and unpopular causes said that they would receive negative coverage even if they refused to talk to reporters; therefore, they co-operate because there is at least some potential for having their viewpoint conveyed, even if most coverage is negative and superficial.

Fear of negative coverage is a dominant justification for co-operating with reporters. Failure to respond to the specific enquiry of a reporter often means that the reporter will go to other sources, the potential to control and shape the account is lost, and negative coverage in the story is probable. Moreover, there is the risk of affecting future access to the reporter and news outlet in question when events or issues arise that the source wishes to comment upon.

USING ALTERNATIVE MEDIA

In an urban market-place of many news organizations, one response to unreasonable coverage is to go to another news outlet more likely to give reasonable coverage. Given their own competitive obsessions, news organizations can sometimes be played off against one another as a means of overcoming unreasonable coverage and creating the potential for favourable coverage in the future. In this respect we disagree with Gitlin's (1980: 3) absolute statement that, 'Just as people as workers have no voice in what they make, how they make it, or how the produce is distributed and used, so do people *as producers of meaning* have no voice in what the media make of what they say or do or in the context within which the media frame their activity.' Sources are able to join with journalists in creating meanings and affecting their distribution to advantage. When they fail, they can sometimes use media other than the news to communicate what they think should appear to be the case.

In responding to a general question asking them to identify available remedies for unreasonable coverage, the third most frequent response given by our sources (after 'there are none' and 'contacting the reporter') was 'to use other media.' This remedy was mentioned as a viable possibility by one-quarter of the respondents. Furthermore, in addressing a number of possible solutions to their problems in dealing with the news media, using other media outlets was mentioned by 14 per cent of respondents. Obviously the use of alternative media was not on the mind of most respondents as a possible remedy. Many sources are simply not in an occupational role or financial position to communicate through alternative media with wide circulation. For example, a court official was adamant in his opinion that there are no effective remedies for unreasonable news coverage. 'I've no way to defend myself ... I don't have a circulation of 300,000 to say, "By the way, the newspaper is wrong, I didn't say that or I didn't do that."'

When a specific complaint is ignored by the offending news outlet, it is rarely possible to go to another mass-media news outlet and have them publish a direct complaint or counterpoint against the offending news out-let. Competition among news media in a local market does not go to the extent of such criticism of one another, because it would ultimately erode the credibility of the news-media institution and therefore affect the commercial interests of everyone (Ericson et al, 1987). The source who still feels a need to say something must do so through other communication channels. Respondents cited several alternative modes of communication in the face of unreasonable coverage, including advertising; hand or mail distribution of pamphlets; public speaking; participation in school, college, or university courses; contacting other sources cited in the offending stories to ask them to participate in conveying a more reasonable view of the matter; and contacting fringe, specialist, or alternative magazines, newspapers, and cable-television stations.

Those who spoke most positively about these alternative media possibilities were from citizens' groups representing minority or unpopular interests. A representative of a minority group said that they had started their own publication because it is the only means to overcome the systematic topic and source selection bias of the news media and its implications for control of their activities:

> Simply by choosing that certain things are important and others are not
> important is a very strong mechanism of social control going on. And I
> can tell you that's exactly why we publish the paper that we do, because
> very little news about [our type of] people in different parts of the country
> gets into the mainstream media ... If we didn't have our newspaper and a
> few other publications ... [major events that have affected us] might have
> appeared as a little article on page 27 of the mainstream press. And that in
> turn inhibits people from organizing, and that's the important thing. People

don't know that things are wrong, they sort of sit back and let the world go by.

Respondents who had access to alternative media were also aware of their limitations. They are a vehicle more for 'preaching to the converted' and organizing the already interested, than for mobilizing general public support or the support of influential members of society. The mainstream news outlets circulate to millions in the general population and do so on the authority of sources in powerful positions institutionally. Minority interests – even substantial and influential ones such as organized labour – cannot directly cut into this circle of mass audience and authority. As one labour official observed, there is no mass-market newspaper in Canada supported by labour interests, and the New Democratic party as the main labour party in Canada has never had the sustained support of a daily newspaper. 'I don't think we ever will have one, and it's no use us starting up our own newspaper ... You just can't get enough people buying labour newspapers. They won't sell. People [workers themselves] will buy the *Sun* ... [which is] very anti-union.'

Some politicians were strong advocates of alternative media, although typically as a supplement to the free, extensive, and authoritative coverage they could obtain in the mainstream news media. We interviewed a municipal politician long associated with unpopular causes, and currently a member of an especially unpopular citizens' group. He said the longstanding negative news coverage of his activities was offset by his use of alternative media, especially at election time: 'I think that the best thing is an alternative press, basically. That's my strong belief ... As a politician I don't think I was ever endorsed by the newspapers, I was always dumped on. And in a [municipal] election campaign, because it's so intense and restricted geographically, you can do you own media basically. That's how you get elected. You ignore the regular media and you have control over it.'

APPEALING TO THE PRESS COUNCIL AND THE CANADIAN RADIO-TELEVISION AND TELECOMMUNICATIONS COMMISSION

Sources who wish to complain about unreasonable coverage can step outside of the offending news organization and register a formal complaint with the Ontario Press Council (OPC) for newspapers or the Canadian Radio-television and Telecommunications Commission (CRTC) for broadcast news.

There are four press councils in Canada. The OPC was established in 1972, following the inception of a Windsor-area press council in 1971, and coincident with the formation of the Alberta Press Council. A press council for Quebec was inaugurated in 1973. The OPC is based on a British model, emphasizing conciliation rather than arbitration or judgment. With certain exceptions it limits its activities to the minority of newspapers that constitute the council. During the first decade of operation the OPC dealt with six hundred complaints. 'It has had to deliver a final opinion on only a minority of complaints, the majority of complainants having obtained satisfaction from the accused newspaper or having withdrawn their complaint. More than half the grievances concern the honesty and objectivity of reporting, and nearly a quarter the difficulty of access to the newspaper' (Royal Commission on Newspapers [RCN], 1981: 149).

The CRTC, in contrast, is a federal government agency, not a council of members who choose to join as is the case with press councils. It is equipped with more coercive investigative and sanctioning powers, including the power to revoke or fail to renew the licence of a particular broadcast outlet, although these powers are invoked rarely and compliance strategies are the norm (Johnson, 1980; Slayton, 1981; Clifford, 1983; Law Reform Commission, 1986).

The option of complaining to the OPC or CRTC is not usually thought of, or seen as viable when it is thought of. Indeed, many respondents were unaware of the existence of these mechanisms and therefore had never even contemplated using them. In response to a general question asking them to identify available remedies for unreasonable coverage, only 22 per cent of the ninety-three respondents mentioned either the OPC or the CRTC. Only seven respondents said they had actually complained to the OPC, and two said they had complained to the CRTC.

Some reasons given for not seeking redress through the OPC and CRTC were the same as those stated for not making any form of complaint in the face of bad coverage. A court official declared that it is simply inappropriate for any officer of the court to lodge a complaint with a press council. A police officer observed that a formal complaint does nothing to change the harm done by the coverage being complained about, which is akin to saying that hurting the offender does nothing to help the victim.

The press secretary to a leader of a political party said OPC and CRTC compliance mechanisms are less preferable than going directly to the journalists concerned for corrections or retractions. He reasoned that since the decisions of these formal bodies take months, the original concern is dissipated and any correction or retraction at that point is useless. He preferred informal, ongoing reciprocity with journalists rather than formal mechanisms that might turn that reciprocity into mutual resentment. 'I don't know if I've ever gone to the press council on anything. The press council is basically a meaningless organization ... [It] has no power to do anything much, most people don't even know what they're looking at or what they decide ... When you get a ruling from the press council six months later on some story that appeared, or editorial, I mean it's neither here nor there!'

Some respondents believed that, far from leading to the slow burial of their complaints, complaining to the OPC or CRTC would contribute to prolonged publicity that might cause further damage. A government public-relations officer said, 'Listen, if a mistake was so bad that I would go that far, that would just add to the publicity which I was probably trying to avoid anyway ... Once it gets to a certain point, the less said the better – let's just drop the damned subject.'

Another reason for not using the OPC or CRTC is the belief that they have no 'teeth' in investigation, enforcement, and sanctions. A Crown attorney asserted that there is no remedy for unfair news coverage, then added, 'I think the press council ... is really an organization without any teeth, or if they do have any power, certainly don't seem to exercise it.' Regarding the CRTC, he said, 'I only see their presence in terms of issuing licences ... controlling rates, but I don't see them playing any great role in the imposition of standards when it comes to ethics.' A provincial cabinet minister dismissed the OPC as a viable remedy by saying, 'Really all that amounts to is a slap on the wrist to offenders, if they are proven in the wrong, and a short story about it on page 18.' Regarding the CRTC, a spokesperson for a citizens' interest group observed, 'The most they will do is accumulate all these complaints and then when the licence comes up for renewal, chuck them all out – and at the most say "naughty, naughty" – and then renew the licence.' She added, 'So, there is no effective way really to get at the broadcast media except by appealing to their own professional pride.'

A public-relations consultant celebrated the fact that the OPC and CRTC have little capacity, and even less inclination, to police the news. He observed that effective investigation, enforcement, and sanctions would make the news media even more uniform. At least a modicum of diversity is possible in a competitive news market, but this would be extinguished by an effective policing of the news media. In essence he argued that it is functional for the OPC and CRTC to be kept weak. 'We don't want the media to have a press council which will sit on their back all of the time because then it would make all of the media alike and we'd be in a lot of trouble. Because the media's bad enough when it's separated and the only thing that keeps them honest is the competition. Press councils are a laugh, I mean, what can they do?'

Given the perceived ineffectiveness of the OPC and CRTC, respondents concluded that these bodies serve primarily to cool out complainants (Goffman, 1962) and to legitimate the news-media institution. A politician drew a parallel to regulation in some other occupations and professions, concluding the OPC is 'like the Canadian Medical Association, it's there for window dressing.' A police officer observed that certain news outlets are constantly pressing for a better system for external, civilian review of police activities, yet they persistently refuse to develop any effective external system for policing themselves. Research by McMahon (1987) suggests that there are many parallels to be drawn between police and media formal-complaint procedures as 'window dressing.'

Some respondents who had lodged a complaint with the OPC concluded that redress is not possible. From this experience they inferred that the OPC's only value is in cooling out the complainant, thereby reproducing the legitimacy of the media institution. A member of a professional association said the membership had objected to some unfair newspaper comments about the association and they decided to write to the OPC: '[We were] not expecting anything to happen, but just it makes you feel better, I guess, just writing the letter.' Indeed, as noted earlier, over half of the complaints received initially by the OPC are ultimately dealt with informally by the accused newspaper so that the council does not have to deliver an opinion. Again, this situation is paralleled in other mechanisms for citizens' complaints, such as the system for public complaints against the police (McMahon, 1987; McMahon and Ericson, 1987). The OPC is a sign of a responsible and responsive press, even if this signal often is lost on those who must deal with the press on an ongoing basis.

These findings are consistent with what has been said elsewhere about external mechanisms for handling complaints against the news media (Kingsburg, 1981; RCN, 1981c; Smith, 1982; Robertson, 1983; Clifford, 1983; Law Reform Commission, 1986). They are there to secure the autonomy of members more than as a mechanism of control. The OPC and other press councils were established in the contemporary era of the mass newspaper, which needs to appear credible to a broad and varied readership. The mass newspaper requires the legitimating symbolic canopy of a press council to help with its efforts to be seen as representing the masses. Hence, it is not surprising that a newspaper such as the Toronto *Star* has been at the forefront of the OPC, while others such as the *Globe and Mail* have eased into it more reluctantly and gradually, and still others such as the Toronto *Sun* do not participate at all. 'It is those newspapers with a large advertising market to protect and with a readership representing all social classes of society that have taken the initiative of setting up existing press councils ... The various press councils established in Canada until now are seeking to perpetuate the social consensus which has ensured the success of the so-called omnibus newspapers ... whose formula is specially designed towards advertising-led consumption patterns' (RCN, 1981c: 139). As one of our respondents expressed it, 'The higher-ups of newspapers aren't interested in reporting news, they're interested in making a profit, and they're not going to do anything through the press council which is going to interfere with the newspapers making a profit. They'll never have any teeth.'

TAKING LEGAL ACTION

Legal action, in the form of a libel suit, is another possible external remedy for unreasonable coverage. However, few of our respondents thought that an actual legal suit is a viable means to solve their difficulties with a particular journalist or news organization. In responding to a general question asking them to identify available remedies only 22 per cent mentioned legal action as a possibility.

The vast majority of respondents said that they had legal advice readily available regarding what to say to reporters, or what to do if harmful things are published. Among eighty respondents who provided knowledge on this question, seventy-two or 90 per cent said they had some form of legal advice available. A suitable lawyer was on the organization's staff for 43 per cent; the respondent was legally trained herself in the case of 21 per cent; a lawyer from outside the organization's staff was available for consultation to 14 per cent; and other arrangements for legal consultation were available to 13 per cent.

Respondents indicated that lawyers were consulted frequently regarding news-media enquiries and coverage. Similar to the use of lawyers by journalists (Ericson et al, 1987), this consultation was primarily done behind the scenes regarding what should not be published or broadcast. Also similar to the use of lawyers by journalists (ibid), there was a prevailing view that lawyers tend to be very conservative, typically advising the source not to disclose for publication anything that seems at all doubtful. One respondent stated, 'If we have anything which appears to us likely to bring us within the realm of legal action, we send off for an opinion and then we make up our minds ... partly by taking into account the legal opinion we get. Now, it's something of a ceremonial actually because the lawyer will always tell you not to print it ... lawyers are conservative by nature and always tend to over-estimate these things.' Another respondent, who was a member of a citizens' organization critical of the criminal-justice system, said he would never use a lawyer for advice regarding news-media relations because a lawyer would be bound to have a conservative effect on him and his organization. A lawyer is part of the system he is criticizing, and therefore 'would not tend to contain the feelings that he had about what I was doing ... [he] may not agree with [my] remedy!'

Several respondents said they had used their legal counsel for advice on whether to take formal legal action against an offending journalist and news organization. Lawyers were said to be very hesitant and cautious, typically advising against legal action. Very few respondents said they had ever actually initiated a formal legal action against a news-media employee or organization.

Among eighty-three respondents who addressed this matter, only twelve or 14 per cent said they had ever been involved in a legal action against a news-media employee or organization.

Most aggrieved parties who threaten a libel action do so as a 'lever' to 'pry' a retraction, correction, apology, or more favourable news item from the offending news outlet. This tack often works, but when it does not the offended source sometimes carries through with her threat. A few respondents said they had filed a libel suit in these circumstances.

Even when formal legal action is taken and a settlement reached, the settlement typically involves some effort to control any further accounts of the matter, which may be to the offended source's disadvantage. Thus, in one case we observed from within the offending newsroom, and heard about in interview with a member of the offended organization, the eventual out-of-court settlement included a stipulation that the source remain silent about the settlement: 'One of the things that was agreed to in the settlement – and this is how they protect themselves – was that there wouldn't be any public discussion of the settlement ... So you see, there it is too, they don't even have the guts or whatever to turn around publicly and say, "We did this man a terrible dishonour." They weaseled behind the scenes ... they had the individual who was slandered sign an agreement that he wouldn't discuss it. So, very few people know that this reporter was sued successfully.'

As with other possible remedies, many respondents said the legal remedy is inappropriate to their official office. It was a general belief among politicians and civil servants, for example, that on the political terrain disputes with journalists should not, and usually could not, be taken to the law. An information officer for a political party said he had twice talked the party leader out of suing a reporter. In his opinion, 'that would have been the kiss of death ... I don't think it's in our interest to attack the media. I think when you sue them it's attack.' A news relations officer for a political party said that she could not recall the party ever seeking legal assistance in dealings with the news media: 'I don't think it has ever come up. We certainly have lawyers we could get to if we wanted to. But I don't think anybody sues the media, I mean the number of times that political people sue the media is very limited, it has to be something really extreme ... If you're damaged individually ... you can win for libel but usually that doesn't happen to you. The quarrel you have with them is usually on political grounds, which is not actionable ... In practice you can't sue the media. Individuals find it very hard to sue the media, it's just very, very difficult to make a case.'

Some respondents believed that reporters take liberties with sources they know will be reluctant to take legal action. A public-relations officer for a government ministry said that as a reporter he had been told to go ahead with a potentially libellous story because politicians and civil servants are especially reluctant to take legal action. He said that as a ministry representative he had ample experience of what he regarded as libellous statements against the ministry's staff and against politicians, but with one exception in eighteen years no legal action was taken.

Non-government sources painted the same picture. The public-relations director for a private corporation said she had twice sought legal advice about news coverage but came to the conclusion that legal action 'wouldn't correct or help what happened.' She said that her experiences taught her that the best approach is to take precautions before giving information to reporters. To this end she had enlisted a lawyer's help. For example, in turning over company-produced film to a television station, she had the station's representatives sign a legal document that they would not use the footage for any item other than the specific one for which it was requested.

Overall, then, legal action is not seen as an effective remedy for un-reasonable coverage. Among our ninety-three respondents, only 13 per cent indicated that legal action could be an effective remedy. Among those who explicitly said it is not an effective remedy, the predominant reasons are that it is too expensive; the wrong is too difficult to prove; it is likely to keep the original libellous allegations 'alive'; and it is likely to create difficulties in future relations with journalists, possibly leading to sustained negative coverage over a long period, even on different matters.

One positive thing respondents said about the possibility of legal action is that it provides a threat they can use to obtain some other remedy. Several respondents talked of past occasions on which they had threatened legal action and, following that, received the remedy they wanted without further recourse to the law. For example, a representative of a minority interest group said she complained to a radio-show host about something her lawyers said might constitute libel. She was immediately offered one-half hour air time on a talk show, which she described as 'the best air time I've ever had in my life.' A municipal politician also attested to the value of threatening a lawsuit, saying that twice in the previous year he had threatened the same newspaper and on each occasion he was given the apology he wanted on the exact page he requested.

Some lawyers we interviewed said that the main goal behind threatening legal action, or actually serving a libel notice, is to obtain a retraction. It is simply a more coercive move to achieve an informal settlement, as is done routinely in other fields of legal practice (Ross, 1970; Ericson and Baranek, 1982). An experienced public-relations consultant said that the *only* move available to the aggrieved source is to threaten a lawsuit, which will at least yield a retraction or apology. 'I've never known a case ... where the media have not caved in to a lawyer's letter.' She reasoned that the news outlet is willing to give a little space and lose a little face in order to save the costs of litigation and to avoid having 'dirty linen' exposed in court. She also observed that it is difficult for the management of a news organization to judge whether their reporter is correct in his reporting.

Another consideration is that once a lawsuit is initiated it does legally restrict what can be reported until the suit is decided. Hence, from the source's perspective, regardless of the final outcome, initiating a formal legal action has the advantage of providing a temporary restriction on what can be published or broadcast about the matter. This form of front-region enclosure was referred to as having a 'muzzling effect.' This effect was seen to be a useful 'lever'; to avoid being 'muzzled' the news organization might offer a retraction or a more favourable news item subsequently. In turn, the news organization can proceed to further its coverage of the matter as a continuing story.

Many respondents mentioned the cost of sustaining a legal action against wealthy newspaper chains and broadcasting corporations. As one person concluded, lawsuits are 'impossible ... if I lose, then I'm responsible for [the news organization's] costs. I'm giving them a blank cheque. I have no real remedies. I mean I have to be very wealthy and very certain.' Another respondent said that the only party to benefit from a legal action is the lawyers involved. For many the cost factor is considered in the context of the belief that one cannot be very certain because 'the law is on their side,' and of the fear that news outlets might retaliate through further negative coverage. A respondent who was a lawyer summed up this line of thinking in recalling a case in which he sued a newspaper for libel and eventually settled informally for '$1,500 and ... a retraction that was worse than the original story.' From this he learned that, as in other legal spheres, 'the process is the punishment' (Feeley, 1979) and it is therefore best to avoid it: '[The rules are]: one, that you'll lose. Two, that even if you win the amount of damages that they award may be rather insignificant. Three, that even if you win and get some damages, the costs awarded don't cover the actual [legal-fee] costs of doing it. Four, you may get into a lawsuit where they manage to dump so much stuff out in the lawsuit that in fact your reputation gets more besmirched than it was originally. You need a pretty clear case and you need some pretty serious damages before you would willingly hop into a lawsuit, or take a lawsuit to completion.'

Several respondents said their organizations had suffered further negative coverage after initiating legal action. A politician talked bitterly of what happened when he only threatened a major newspaper with a lawsuit. He had hoped the threat would force the newspaper to be less hard-hitting in the future. Instead they 'slammed' him even harder.

I've come to the conclusion after a couple of years of being in this game that if you're smart you do nothing. There was one occasion where I know that I was very, very seriously misrepresented by a media outlet and I threatened a lawsuit against that particular outlet and they made my life a misery for three months ... [in] every respect they could. The least thing that I said, the merest gesture or whatever, was just slammed into that paper in a very negative light until it became evident that I was not proceeding with the lawsuit. And since then the attitude of that particular medium has been to ignore, it's as if I don't exist. I came to the conclusion then that because I'd tried to take on such a large and powerful organization, I came out the worst for it. They had more resources to do me harm than I had to do them harm. And as a result – and it doesn't happen that often – but if I'm ever slighted or feel I've been treated unjustly by media, I just let it ride ... I never formally initiated the lawsuit, I threatened it. I went to a very respected lawyer in this city, who is very experienced in these matters, he looked at the particular editorial about which I had a concern and said that indeed I did have cause for a grievance and I was in fact slandered. But his feeling was that first of all it would take about two years to get through the courts, it would cost a minimum of $25,000 in legal fees, and at the end, even if the court found in my favour that I had been slandered, I couldn't even be guaranteed getting my costs back. Now I'm not a wealthy man. I don't have $25,000 to throw away. I don't have two years' time even at ten hours a week to push a lawsuit. It's just not there, and so on reflection I just decided not to pursue it. And in reflection I think that not pursuing it, in terms of expedience, was the right thing to do. Because the thing that upset me at the time is long forgotten, nobody remembers it. I don't remember it, the press gallery doesn't remember it, the premier doesn't remember it. If I had kept it alive and fought a high-profile court battle on it, it would still be an issue today.

In negotiating control of the news, sources opt for a low profile. Maintaining a low profile precludes the invocation of external mechanisms for remedy, except as a threat or a manoeuvre when things go badly wrong. It is considered far better to deal with the offending journalist directly, negotiating a satisfactory resolution at the lowest level in the hope of achieving a higher media profile in the future. Preference is given to the subtleties of everyday contact, trust, and reciprocity with journalists. Going beyond the boundaries of these relations to seek remedy is seen as a sure way to disrupt the trust and reciprocity that are key ingredients of news access, and to compound rather than correct the immediate problem.

Remedies Internal to News Organizations

CONTACTING REPORTERS

The source who experiences unreasonable coverage can lodge a complaint with, or seek a remedy from, the reporter who filed the story. Respondents were not asked systematically about whether they had ever contacted a reporter directly to complain about coverage. However, in discussing this as a possible remedy forty-six respondents did give an indication as to whether they had used it in the past. Among those, thirty-six or 78 per cent said that they had contacted a reporter in an effort to seek remedy for unreasonable coverage the reporter had participated in. Moreover, in our observations of newsbeats and general-assignment reporting, complaining to reporters about problems in coverage was an everyday occurrence. Complaints were made in a subtle, discreet, and friendly manner as part of the ongoing relations between the source and the reporter concerned. Casual comments about what was wrong with previous coverage entered into decisions about what coverage to provide next. We witnessed regular and recurrent direct complaints about errors in primary facts; incorrect use of technical terminology; misquotation; misinterpretation; an unduly negative and critical tone to the story; sensationalism, including its presumed negative impact in generating public anxiety and fear; and interference by the reporter and television crews in the activities they were trying to become a part of. Usually the complaints were put in a subtle and friendly manner, although in cases such as alleged interference in the source's activities it was sometimes quite hostile.

Respondents addressed a number of advantages to contacting reporters as a means of seeking remedy. The most frequently cited advantage was that it is the best way to achieve a retraction or correction to the original story. Thus, a respondent said she found a personal chat with the reporter concerned to be the most effective way to rectify problems of context and accuracy: '[T]here may be occasions where one of them would report something that was out of context or was not right, and on those occasions I would phone the reporter and say, "Lookit, you've put something in there that I think should be changed ... I didn't like that, the way it was put. I wonder if you'd mind rectifying it." I can't think of any that they didn't [rectify].'

Many respondents believed that working problems out on the personal level improves the prospect for better coverage in the future. They stressed that in any process of making a complaint, it is best to start at the lowest level in the hierarchy. Achieving a solution at that level ensures indebtedness from the offender for not going 'over his head.' This indebtedness is especially important since the reporter is the 'front line' person one is likely to be dealing with in the future. A respondent talked of his organization's practices when coverage is deemed unreasonable:

In the initial instance we go to the individual who did the story ... basically
to point it [the problem] out. And basically say to them, if this is a beginning
of something that is going to go on for a while it would be appreciated if the
next time you write on this topic that you keep these things in mind and then
get an appropriate balance. If there are recurring inaccuracies and they're
related to an individual reporter, or if there are continued manifestations of
bias on the part of a specific reporter, we will then go to the editor. Before
we do that, we will tell the reporter, 'Look, if something like this occurs
again ... we feel we've got no recourse but to go to the editor.' We do it
that way because in our experience in dealing with individual reporters ...
very often it's a very honest mistake or naïve mistake that the reporter had
made. And frequently he or she is very grateful that we've brought it to their
attention initially rather than go to his boss and in effect say, 'You've got
this stupid idiot working for you, look what he did!' And they appreciate
that, and quite honestly that makes them more sensitive and more likely to
contact us in the event they get some item that they know involves us.

For some, complaining to the reporter concerned was the first and last
resort. One respondent said she would not go beyond the reporter because
'you can't afford to make an enemy with reporters ... you just have to forget
it and let him get away with it.' The recommendation was to appeal to the
reporter's professional pride, and to previous trusting and friendly relations,
in order to convert the bad experience into more positive experiences in the
future.

A substantial majority of respondents did not mention contacting the
offending reporter as a viable remedy, and many explicitly recommended
against doing so. In response to a question asking them to identify available mechanisms for remedy of unreasonable news coverage, 31 per cent
of respondents mentioned contacting the reporter concerned. Although mentioned by only one-third of respondents, this remedy was nevertheless the
one most frequently cited as viable. In response to another general question
asking them to state the available solutions to problems in dealing with the
news media, 38 per cent of respondents said one could complain to members
of the news organization concerned (reporters, editors, or management), and
17 per cent mentioned the possibility of meeting with the reporter causing
the problem. While it was a minority of respondents who imagined these as
viable solutions to problems, these solutions were addressed more than any
other except for reducing co-operation, which was mentioned by 41 per cent
of respondents.

A predominant reason for thinking it is inadvisable to contact the reporter is that she might be offended, even to the point of affecting one's
relationship with her or having her retaliate. Respondents talked about past

experiences in which they complained, did not receive any remedy, and lost their previous good relations with the reporter. Respondents also mentioned their frustration in complaining to reporters because of the ease with which reporters displace responsibility for problems to someone else in the news organization. Reporters have a ready-made vocabulary of excuses: blaming the headline writer, editors in the context of space and time, and the news organization's policies, which 'compel' them to write for their editors. Respondents generally seemed to appreciate these pressures on reporters, and the fact that a given news story is actually the product of many people and many processes. Hence, for many it was difficult, and perhaps unfair, to identify the reporter as the culprit. This reasoning led them to not bother complaining at all or to shift responsibility in keeping with the reporter's accounts, seeking a remedy at the level of editors or management.

COMPLAINING TO EDITORS

Respondents were not asked systematically about whether they had ever contacted an editor directly to complain about coverage. However, in discussing this possible remedy forty-two respondents did give an indication as to whether or not they had used it in the past. Among those respondents, thirty-two or 76 per cent said they had contacted an editor to complain about news coverage. Nevertheless, very few respondents mentioned complaining to editors as a viable route for seeking remedy. In responding to a general question asking them to identify possible mechanisms to obtain a remedy for unreasonable news coverage, only 15 per cent of respondents mentioned contacting editors in the news outlet concerned. In the context of responding to this general question, complaining to editors was mentioned less often than any of the other mechanisms for remedy we address in this chapter.

A few respondents asserted that if they decided to lodge a formal complaint at all, they would go where the power and responsibility lies, namely with editors. While informal friendly complaints, cajoling, or hectoring might be done at the level of reporters, a serious complaint is a matter for the news organization's more senior representatives: 'Any kind of misinformation we would direct usually to the editor of the paper, [with television] it could be the news director, but then again it could be the president of the television station, or the vice-president in charge of television news ... I think we need to get that high because that is consistent with our traditional reporting order within the police force. I think that's the way we look at other organizations.' This routing of complaints not only reflected the police organization's view of the hierarchial order of things, but also a desire at the level of the public-relations unit to displace responsibility for complaining and effecting remedies to others so that public-relations officers and reporters could continue in their friendly ways: 'I think part of our style is to be as diplomatic as possible, and ruffle as few feathers as possible, while yet still getting our point across. Because we do realize that we want to continue the relationship with them.'

Other respondents indicated that going to senior levels in the news organization to complain was not so obvious or automatic. A public-relations officer for a political party said that the choice of whom to complain to depends on the nature of the problem. If there is an unreasonable headline, a call is made to the city editor because responsibility rests with her. If the party's news conferences are being ignored systematically by a particular news organization it is a policy matter with which the news organization's senior management must be confronted. If it is an error or unfairness at the reporter level – for example, improper attribution or inappropriate credit to party sources – then the reporter can be contacted directly.

One of the advantages of having public-relations specialists in an organization is that they have recipe knowledge of who to contact regarding a complaint, and how to approach that person tactfully. In commenting upon the reorganization of their public-affairs unit and the hiring of civilian public-relations specialists, several police officers said an expected advantage is having an effective conduit to news outlets to lodge complaints. Hiring a civilian public-relations director with extensive media experience and contacts was seen as a vehicle for taking a stronger stance regarding unreasonable coverage.

A private consultant on news-media relations specialized in offering clients his ability to transform unreasonable coverage into acceptable access. As an ex-journalist and ex–public-relations officer in large bureaucracies, he had established extensive contacts within various news organizations. These contacts were willing to listen to his complaints and adjust coverage in subsequent stories. He was not required to make formal complaints to editors, only to use a gentle telephone call to nudge them to at least consider a different frame. He was usually hired to deal with 'bad press' of a company faced with a sudden disaster (e.g., an industrial accident, an industrial strike with violence on the picket line, or sustained allegations of procedural deviance).

In talking about the advantages to contacting editors for remedy, the reasons given were similar to those for contacting reporters. Predominant was the desire to obtain an apology, correction, or retraction, and creating the prospect for better coverage in the future. In relation to the hope of better coverage in the future, several respondents referred to the need to shape the attitudes of editors about the source organization or a specific issue. Their experience taught them that supplying senior editors with documents, or talking to editors to 'put things in perspective,' was more effective than a loud or vociferous complaint. One respondent said that he had occasion to contact senior editors in one newspaper to request reassignment of an offending reporter, and that such requests were usually obliged.

Among those who spoke against contacting editors to obtain a remedy, the predominant reason was that it would offend the reporter concerned. Offending the reporter could affect future relations with her and she might even decide to retaliate. Indeed, twelve respondents related past instances in which they had lost a relationship with a reporter after complaining to the reporter's editor about unreasonable coverage. As considered in the previous section, the fear of upsetting the reporter by going 'over his head' was given as a major reason for not complaining at all, or at least keeping the complaint at the level of the offending reporter.

Some respondents feared retaliation from editors in response to a complaint. This apprehension was sometimes based on bitter experience. Among the experienced was a politician who said he had lodged complaints with senior managers in two prominent newspapers and a television station after very negative coverage surrounding an election. Some minor concessions were made – such as a subsequent television item allowing him to state his case more favourably – but in the main the negative coverage persisted. His ultimate barometer of his lack of success in achieving a remedy was the fact that he lost an election and felt forced to terminate his political career.

Others spoke of editors 'closing ranks' to protect their reporters, which entailed less access for the source. Some respondents had long-term and systematic problems with particular news organizations, a situation attributed to the senior editors and their editorial policy towards the source organization that was experiencing the difficulty. A respondent said that in face of recurrent difficulties with reporters from a particular newspaper, various approaches had been attempted: 'cutting off' particular reporters, appealing to management, even refusing to respond to anyone from that organization. However, the newspaper's editors had consistently refused requests for corrections and retractions, and eventually it was deemed futile to contact them for possible remedy.

REQUESTING CORRECTIONS AND RETRACTIONS

Respondents were not asked systematically about whether they had ever sought a correction or retraction. However, in discussing this possible remedy forty-one respondents did give an indication as to whether or not they had sought a correction or retraction in the past. Among them, twenty-three or 56 per cent said they had sought a correction or retraction. Few believed a specific request for a correction or retraction had much potential for achieving a remedy. In response to a general question asking them to state the possible remedies for unreasonable coverage, only 18 per cent of the ninety-three news sources we interviewed mentioned corrections and retractions.

Respondents had little to say in favour of corrections or retractions as effective remedies for unreasonable coverage. The advantage most frequently mentioned was that at least the record is corrected in case reporters consult their files on related stories in the future. In this regard sources respected the internal nature of journalists' knowledge, recognizing that they treat previous news accounts as factual. Correcting the facts at least keeps open the possibility that in future stories the corrected version will be taken into account. Having described an instance in which a reporter co-operated in retracting an erroneous statement, a politician said, 'I was being a [self]-protective politician and I've saved those [news clippings] because I know very well in the next election – and this is totally wrong – it will be raised.' Indeed, it was especially politicians and government officials who saw the advantage of corrections to the record, which may account for their being much more likely than other source types to have actually sought corrections or retractions in the past.

A few respondents said they found journalists to be most obliging in making factual corrections, and accounted for this in two ways. First, if the news outlet prides itself on being a newspaper of record, it has a mandate to record a corrected fact. A corporate executive said, with reference to the business section of a particular newspaper, that a satisfactory correction is easy to obtain 'because this is their bread and butter, to report the financial news accurately.' To negotiate a factual correction is to accede to the news organization's 'web of facticity' (Tuchman, 1978), to its parameters of factuality, range of opinion, and interpretive framework. It therefore contributes to the power of the news organization and its preferred reading of the matter, rather than being a challenge to it. Second, any news outlet can benefit from publishing or broadcasting the occasional correction and retraction because it indicates that such errors are indeed only occasional, thereby giving greater factual legitimacy to everything else. A representative of a citizens' interest organization observed, with reference to the same newspaper mentioned by the corporate executive above:

Of course it's ludicrous for them to propose that there were only two or three errors in yesterday's edition. I think that if they were honest about it, and if in fact they had the apparatus for responding to perceived inaccuracies, it would probably be nearer to half a page [needed daily to print corrections and retractions]. But that would be getting to the point of exposing too clearly the subjective nature of news. And so what you get is this business of admitting the one or two more serious mistakes, or mistakes most likely to damage the newspaper, and that of course lends credibility to all the rest of the things.

Most sources said obtaining a correction or retraction is of little value.

The predominant reasons for saying this remedy is not an effective one included the following: that the statement of correction or retraction does not receive the same news prominence or play as the original story that gave offence; that the damage is already done through the original story, and that a correction or retraction will not remedy it, and might even exacerbate it; and that the complainant has no control over the form and substance of whatever is eventually published or broadcast in correction or retraction.

The typical complaint of respondents was that enormous play is given to inaccurate, misinterpreted, and sensational imputations of deviance, but when these prove to be without grounds, and requests are made to obtain a correction or retraction, journalists have lost interest. Having related one of her experiences in this vein, a government official summed it up by saying, 'Either you ignore it or you handle it informally by phoning the reporter or complaining to the editor ... If it's an obvious case of defamation, normally you'll get your apology and retraction and it will be published. Of course, it's published in a little corner, nobody sees it, and apart from that, even if everybody sees it, it's not remembered. What you remember is the defamation.' Another respondent made the same point by asking rhetorically if there had ever been a front-page headline declaring, 'We Goofed!' A third respondent – who related bitter experiences of unreasonable coverage and insignificant play in retraction with no apology – said the correction or retraction 'gets placed with advertisements about laxative remedies.'

Respondents offered various explanations for the fact that errors are played down. Some surmised that by the time the correction or retraction is negotiated for publication, the story is 'old news' and therefore is of low priority in the competition for news space. Less kindly, some believed that journalists are unwilling or unable to take criticism or admit mistakes because it affects their personal pride and professional legitimacy. Least kindly, they saw the journalists concerned in opposition to their interests, sometimes out to punish or control them, and therefore unwilling to do anything that might lessen the barbs of publicity.

A related consideration for many was a feeling that a correction or retraction can do little or nothing to rectify the damage done by the original publicity. A senior police executive said that a correction or retraction 'Doesn't mean a thing. People don't forget what they read.' He gave examples of turning down offers for news space in correction, observing, 'You can't unring bells when something is in the press and it's been said to the public.' The 'ring' of publicity – its emotional impact far beyond the facts of the matter – was at the heart of most respondents' understanding of why the correction or retraction is of little value. They appreciated that what receives major coverage has an emotional impact and urge towards control well beyond whatever knowledge is conveyed, while the correction is placed in the petty context of straightening out a few factual details. As experienced by one respondent: 'People get the message from the headline, it has an impact on them and they feel more frightened and therefore they want everybody locked up ... Newspapers, I guess, are reasonably good about correcting stuff but ... who reads the corrections and where are they, on page 9 or wherever? So, I think it's very difficult because what gets across in the media has an impact on people. It has an emotional kind of impact and that's what sticks.'

A private consultant on news-media relations advised that while primary facts might be worth correcting for the record, problems of misquotation and misinterpretation are beyond effective remedy, because of the 'risk of them perpetuating the nasty, negative story by saying the next day so-and-so denied today what he said yesterday.' Each and every attempt to have something published or broadcast to remedy a previous problem simply puts one further into the hands of the journalists. A respondent related how she had been misquoted to give a wrong inference, and how this created great organizational problems for her the day the article appeared: 'My phone just about went off the line, it was just like it turned red hot ... calls screaming for my resignation and, "How the hell can you do that job if that's how you feel?" She then sought and obtained a retraction, but the way that was phrased brought the wrath of another organizational constituency and 'did me as much damage as the original story.' In obtaining the retraction:

> We negotiated this for a long time and this is not what I wanted. I mean I would have wanted it to be done a little differently ... [T]here's negotiations, but in the bottom line they have the pen and the print machines and I don't, and this is not the way I would have written the retraction ... I would have set out the background and how the error came to pass and what I really meant and set it out clearly. That would have gotten me out of trouble. This didn't get me out of trouble ... Now what happened was, after this article was in the newspaper, about a month later I appeared before [an organizational constituency] on a panel, and there's 300 or 400 out there and one of them had this article. This had been a month earlier, I thought it had died down and had been forgotten. The retraction had been printed, I thought o.k. it was a bad experience but it's over. But somebody had this article and was waving it in the audience and criticizing me for what I had said.

WRITING LETTERS TO THE EDITOR

Another option for obtaining a correction, retraction, or sense of balance in news coverage is to write a letter to the editor of a newspaper. While some broadcast outlets have initiated a letters or 'mailbag' slot, they tend to receive few letters, and to air them sporadically. For example, a television newsroom we studied over eight months received about a dozen letters a week, and read out only three or four once a week. Hence, for our analysis here and in the following sections, we consider only letters to the editor of newspapers.

Respondents were not asked systematically about whether they had ever submitted a letter to the editor. However, in discussing this possible remedy fifty-one respondents did give an indication as to whether or not they had ever submitted a letter to the editor. Among them, twenty-two or 43 per cent said they had done so. Few mentioned letters to the editor as a viable vehicle to remedy unreasonable coverage. In response to a general question asking them to state the possible remedies for unreasonable news coverage, only 16 per cent of ninety-three respondents mentioned letters to the editor.

Predictably, many respondents who said they had never written a letter to the editor and would not do so explained that it is inappropriate because of their official office. Included among these respondents were several who believed that a letter to the editor is probably the best available mechanism for remedy. Restrictions on the office explain why only two police officers, and no court officials, said they had ever used letters to the editor in search of a remedy. A judge said he could not write a letter to the editor, whereas it is appropriate, for example, that a politician does so.

Q: When you've felt that you've been covered unfairly – your decisions – what can you do about it?
A: Not speak to the press.
Q: What about retractions or letters to the editor?
A: Oh, that would make things worse.
Q: Why?
A: ... I don't think it looks well, that's why I have never yet written the editor a letter ... I am not a politician – politicians probably can do that, but I don't think I should write to the editor ... I think it's unbecoming for a judge to be writing and bandying words in the press, with the media; I don't think it looks good.
Q: But if it's correcting a position?
A: If they libel me, you will hear from me, then I will go to court and everyone will know about it.

Sources take into account the contextual meaning given to different sections of the newspaper in deciding whether they might participate in them. Most police officers we interviewed took the view that it is inappropriate to write a letter to the editor because letters are published within the editorial pages and are thereby contextualized as personal opinion. The personal-opinion context is accentuated by the fact that the name of the writer accompanies the letter. Police officers do not want to be seen to be giving their personal opinions regarding public issues or controversies involving their force. They also shy away from letters-to-the-editor columns because that context is explicitly recognized as providing for the expression of ideologies. In contrast, the police offer their opinions freely and have their names cited as sources in news items and features. It is acceptable to espouse ideologies if they are veiled within the apparent objectivity, neutrality, and balance of a news item or feature, but not in a context framed as a forum for the expression of ideologies. This view is represented in the statements of a police officer: 'I've never written a letter to the editor in my life ... I prefer to communicate verbally with someone and express my disapproval or disagreement or misconception. Because I'm a policeman I think I prefer not to be writing in to the editor and using my name to have it quoted or written down in print. To do it on behalf of my job is one thing – I don't mind being quoted and printed in any way – but then I think that perhaps I compromise my position by writing in as an individual to a newspaper.'

Those who said they made use of the letters-to-the-editor columns, and who spoke positively of them, emphasized that they provide a vehicle for corrections. Just as corrections in general are sought 'for the record,' so the letters-to-the-editor column is used to set the record straight in case anyone, especially journalists, consult it in the future. This view was expressed by the many government officials and politicians who made use of the letters column. As articulated by a public-relations officer for a government ministry, 'I regularly do letters to the editor ... sometimes for the minister's signature. We just take a more activist role and if we see something wrong, better try and correct it because if the error happens once it's there forever and it just gets repeated.'

Letters to the editor were seen by some as a vehicle for achieving more balance in a continuing story. One respondent observed that the letters-to-the-editor columns are a vehicle for complaining about the accounts of other sources in a dispute. Since the letters option is not generally available within broadcast news, interested listeners tend to call the source directly about problems with their accounts, while newspaper readers can use the letters-to-the-editor columns to complain about what the other sources have had to say. A public-relations consultant said she viewed letters to the editor as one of many communication techniques to serve the interests of her clients. She said that as a specific way of achieving correction and more balance it is probably the best remedy.

> The whole idea is to mix up your communication techniques, to have as
> many different ways of saying the same thing over and over again as you
> possibly can. So, it's released one day, it's maybe a picture or something
> the next, it's a letter to the editor the next, and you keep this variety going.

Otherwise the sameness will kill you. But if you feel you've been wronged
by a newspaper, the thing is to write a very 'form' ... but controlled letter
... to the editor in about five or six paragraphs, and they'll run it and it's
right in front of the paper usually and it'll be read ... If your writing is good
enough you can plead your case. And the professional obligation of the paper
is to run it. And by and large they will run it. I can't think of a time when
I haven't seen a letter to the editor that I've either written or instigated not
appear.

While a few respondents talked favourably of letters to the editor as
an option for remedy, most felt they are of less value, no value, or even
negative value. The predominant reasons for believing letters to the editor
are an ineffective vehicle for remedy include the following: that even if the
letter is published there is no assurance that important or influential readers
will see it and use it to offset the account in the original story; that there
is no control over whether it will be published; that there is no control over
what changes will be made in editing the letter for publication; and that a
published letter cannot undo the damage done by the original story and may
compound it.

Many believed that letters to the editor have less impact on readers
than other components of the newspaper, since these letters receive less play
than news items or features and are placed in the context of representing
the personal opinions of an individual with vested interests. As stated by a
politician, letters to the editor are not taken 'as seriously as ... the rest of the
newspaper because that's written from someone who has a vested interest in
the issue.' In this respect letters to the editor appear similar to advertising. It
is better to convey ideology within the apparently more neutral contexts of
news items and features than to have to do it on the specific pages designated
for idiosyncratic opinion.

Several respondents emphasized that in submitting letters to the editor
there is still no control over whether something is published, when it is
published, and how it is published. These aspects were emphasized by a
respondent who said her organization had tried many vehicles for remedy,
but never letters to the editor: '[T]here's no assurance that the letter will get
published in the first place. And it's likely to be in the letters-to-the-editor
page, which is often a long way from the heart of the paper that the story
that you're critical of appeared in the first place. And the people that read the
first story may or may not see the letter, which even if it did get published
would probably appear several days or weeks even, after the original.' Many
respondents who had used letters to the editor in the past spoke of the delay
to publication and the fact that by then the issue was no longer salient. The
delay was said to be anywhere from a few days to two months, effectively

cooling out the complainant and dissipating the issue through the element of time.

Letters to the editor were taken as indicative of the ultimate power of journalists to have 'the final word.' In stating that a letter to the editor is no remedy, one respondent observed:

> Everything that you send to a publisher to publish can come back to bite you. I don't know of any guarantee that if you send a twelve-paragraph letter to the editor that they will publish twelve paragraphs. They may publish three paragraphs, and three published paragraphs may not establish the point that you wish to establish. This has happened many times. There is editorial comment on the same page or an adjoining page of a letter that has been received, and if you're the publisher of the newspaper you get the last word because you publish the last word. If you want to make the person look like a fool you can make him look like a fool. And what can he do? He doesn't publish a newspaper.

One local popular newspaper had a practice of publishing a few words of editoral comment following each letter. As one respondent saw it, this was simply 'being more explicit than what the other media do in that it makes it more clear who has the power.' Most sources indicated that they shied away in appreciation of this power imbalance. One source who didn't shy away was a prominent politician who said he was badly misquoted and as a result was lambasted by fellow politicians and some officials who called for his resignation. He contacted a senior executive in the newspaper concerned and asked if he could publish a short article 'on what I really said and to put it all into the context.' The newspaper executive agreed as long as it was an exclusive, and the politician then submitted a thousand-word article. A few days later he received a letter from the newspaper executive saying his article would not be published because it did not add any new dimensions to the matter. The newspaper executive offered to reduce the article and to publish it as a letter to the editor. However, the politician refused this offer because, 'they only print three hundred words for a letter, and they chop up letters, and they have the last comment.' On the same day that he received the letter rejecting his article, the newspaper published an editorial. According to the politician, this editorial called him 'myopic' and said, 'We want [name of politician] to have the freedom to voice his ideas even though we think them wrong and irresponsible.' As the politician exclaimed in our interview, 'This is the day they turned down the printing of my ideas! It's just the most unbelievable editorial you will ever see in your whole life! ... It's just staggering, and the last thing they wanted to find out was what I was saying!'

Respondents generally believed that letters to the editor cannot rectify the hurt or social-control effects of the offending story, and might actually do more harm. If the source wants the glare of the media spotlight to fade it is best to avoid expressing an opinion through a letter to the editor. A respondent said that members of her organization were always hesitant to use the letters-to-the-editor columns because they are contextualized to appear as self-serving, they can amplify an issue one wishes to de-emphasize, and they can invite more criticism of the type one is trying to counter.

In keeping with their views about other sources of remedy, respondents were negative and pessimistic about letters to the editor as an effective mechanism for remedy. As one respondent concluded, 'A letter to the editor is really for the editors.' By this he meant that it is used by editors to serve their purposes: to sustain a story they want to continue; to help them orchestrate public opinion in terms they prefer; to counter another source they want to marginalize; to correct the record on something their journalists might need to refer to again. The editors have control, and it is within their power to do what they want with the letter in terms of their organizational criteria.

In the next section we enter the world of editors to learn exactly what they do with letters to the editor. This perspective allows us to appreciate from inside a news organization how a particular mechanism for remedy is organized and indicates clearly that what seems to be the least mediated, most open, and most democratic component of a newspaper is in practice as highly mediated, closed, and undemocratic as other aspects. These findings validate the conclusion of our sources that one cannot easily obtain effective remedies for factual inaccuracy, factional imbalance, and fractured images, and the news media are all the more powerful for that.

Letters to the Editor: Format and Functions

From the perspective of the regular news source, the letters-to-the-editor format is one more means by which she can attempt to achieve news access: to raise an issue in the first instance, to offer additional imput regarding an ongoing story, to remedy imbalance, to correct facts, or to simply amuse. From the perspective of the newspaper, the format provides another means of using regular sources for news purposes, whether it is to entertain, inform, or reform.

From our perspective the letters-to-the-editor format is significant in several respects. First, as we noted earlier, it is a potential vehicle by which regular sources can remedy unreasonable news coverage. However, as we shall document, this potential cannot be realized unless the letter accords with the newspaper's social and cultural criteria of what is publishable. A study of how letters to the editor are dealt with underscores the power of the news media, that they do indeed control the last word. It shows from back inside the newsroom that the perceptions of the sources we interviewed are valid:

that the news media have the ultimate power to frame the event or issue, to exclude certain sources from the public conversation, and to intrude into the lives of sources and create organizational trouble for them.

Second, a study of letters to the editor allows us to summarize and accentuate the main points we have made about how sources relate to news organizations. This study continues our analyses of source/journalist transactions, but with a difference. The letters-to-the-editor process differs from the situational transactions mediated by face-to-face encounters and the telephone-mediated exchanges analysed in previous chapters. Letters to the editor, like news releases, entail extrasituational exchanges mediated by written texts. A study of these textually-mediated exchanges allows us to document an additional important context and medium of source/journalist exchange.

The letter writer becomes in effect a 'reporter' whose letter serves as the equivalent of 'filed copy' to be used at the discretion of editors. To be a good 'reporter' the letter writer must have a sense of what the newspaper is treating as newsworthy and giving prominent space to; an appreciation of the newspaper's general political sympathies as well as ideological predelictions regarding the particular matter to be addressed; and an understanding of the newspaper's preference for style, length, and mode of address. A 'structured dialogue' (Hall et al, 1978: 120) emerges between the newspaper and its regular letter writers, just as it emerges between the newspaper and its regular sources used in other formats. What the letter writer submits is highly structured by the newspaper, in the same way that the newspaper structures what its own reporters submit. Similar to reporters, letter writers learn what to write by reading the newspaper generally; by reading other letters to the editor; by submitting letters to assess what happens to them (whether they are printed and how they are copy-edited); and, by the feed-back they receive from their associates and from journalists regarding their published letters.

Third, as this discussion indicates, the way in which letters are dealt with by the newspaper is typical of the way in which the newsroom processes all potential copy for publication. In examining the editor's criteria in accepting letters for publication, we can summarize and highlight the nature of news judgment as analysed previously in this book and our earlier work (Ericson et al, 1987). Hall et al. (1978: 120) observe, 'In the Letters' column, readers' opinions appear in the press in their least mediated form. The section *is* ultimately in the hands of the editor, but the spectrum of letters is not (apart, that is, from occasional "plants").' The spectrum of letters is not controlled by the editor through direct assignment to reporters, as occurs on other news desks. However, reporters also generate stories and file copy without an explicit assignment from an editor. Moreover, as we shall document, letters submitted, and especially those accepted for publication, are usually in response to a theme or agenda already set in news stories. They feed into the established frame, offering more facts and interpretations, and a greater sense of balance. Furthermore, as documented earlier, reporters and editors often use verbatim materials written by sources. These include press releases, official reports, and even news items authored by a source. These are no more or less mediated than letters to the editor. Letters are highly mediated by criteria internal to the newsroom, and a study of the decisions of the letters editor is instructive about these criteria.

In structuring what is an acceptable account in letters to the editor, the newspaper circumscribes letter writers in the same way as other sources. However, in this context 'circumscribed' does not mean 'foreclosed.' Letters can be proactive in the sense of redirecting the coverage being given by the newspaper, and even initiating a new issue. A senior newspaper executive agreed in interview that letters to the editor are occasionally proactive in this way: 'We sometimes will address a subject that has been raised by a letter writer; not too often, but we do from time to time because we get good letters to the editor.' Letters to the editor are thus a blend of reactive and proactive elements. They are reactive in the sense that writers are usually responding to ongoing stories. The frame has usually been established in these stories, and the letter writer must therefore address its terms. When the letter is written to add knowledge, provide balance through a different viewpoint, or correct an error, it is also reactive and usually fits with the prevailing frame. Nevertheless there is an opening for the letter writer to propose a new frame for a continuing story, or a new story altogether.

The letters-to-the-editor format provides a means of establishing and solidifying relationships with key sources, who are given 'authored' space to say what they think is fitting. As such the format provides another place in which the newspaper can carry on its conversation with regular sources. The quality newspaper achieves its power in being part of the élite, and structures its dialogue accordingly. Part of this is fostering correspondents who are knowledgeable and influential. As Hall et al (1978: 120–1) observe regarding *The Times* of London, 'In the letters it prints, therefore, it is making public one current of opinion within the decision-making class to another section of the same class.' In contrast the popular newspaper represents the opinions of the people, as political spectators, to those who are knowledgeable and influential. '[T]hey speak *to power*. Their letters, therefore, must principally be of the "ordinary folks" variety; they must show their capacity to pull readers, normally invisible, into the public conversation' (ibid).

The letters-to-the-editor format is also a key means by which journalists join with their sources in trying to effect social control and affect political reform. Just as sources are used in news items to impute deviance and assert their preferred control solutions, so they are used in the letters columns to designate deviance and control and thereby participate in reform politics.

Indeed, in the quality newspaper with an institutional-policing approach to journalism, the authorized knowers it cites in its news items and features and the authorities whose letters it prints tend to be the same people. As we have documented previously, these members of the deviance-defining élite do not give freely of their time and resources simply out of their commitment to the value of the news media as a free market of opinion. Rather, they are instrumental in their use of the news media, hoping to harness its power to shape the opinions of influential others in bringing about particular reforms or sustaining the status quo. This is the case whether access is gained through the news columns or in letters to the editor. Thus, in writing letters sources intend 'not simply to tell the editor what they think, but to shape policy, influence opinion, swing the course of events, defend interests, advance causes ... Whoever writes a letter to the editor means to cash, publicly, a position, a status, or an experience' (ibid: 121).

A fifth significant consideration regarding letters to the editor is their role in legitimation of the newspaper. Three aspects of letters contribute to legitimation. Letters are a sign that the newspaper is an open forum for public opinion, helping to sustain the fiction that it is a free market of ideas. Anyone is free to write a letter to the editor, on any topic of his choice, and to say what he sees fit. Through the letters columns anyone can impute deviance, suggest control remedies, and add a voice to reform politics. As such, the letters column supports the newspaper's claim to be a fourth estate, and essential to democracy. Consider the comments of Wooley (1985), writing in a special magazine to mark the two-hundredth anniversary of *The Times* of London: '[T]hough restraints on freedom and on the freedom of speech are grimly apparent elsewhere, letters still pour in to prove that freedom to argue or amuse, within the bounds of decency or libel, still continues in the columns of *The Times*.' Or consider the comment of a senior newspaper executive we interviewed regarding the letters format: 'We tend toward people who disagree with what we say. That's just *the* great place in the paper for the guy who buys it to get opinion in.' To the extent that the reader does buy into this definition of the letters format, consents to it, and even participates on occasion, the newspaper will appear relatively open and democratic.

To the extent that the letters section is an outlet for criticism of the newspaper, and correction of its errors, legitimacy can be enhanced. It is a special place in which the newspaper can further demonstrate its commitment to democratic values and openness by allowing correction of its own mistakes, faults, and errors. This aspect is especially important for the quality newspaper committed to an institutional-policing approach regarding other organizations and institutions: how can it sustain its daily volley of innuendo, allegations, and defamations without opening itself up to a peppering? The letters columns provide an ideal context because they are defined as *the* opening in the newspaper for less-mediated opinion; and because it is only *opinion*, the attack may be seen as more marginal than if it was featured with a bold headline in the news columns. As outlined earlier, the sources we interviewed were not inclined to buy into this aspect of the letters columns as an agency of legitimacy. Few perceived the letters format as an effective remedy for unreasonable coverage because of the power of the editor to exclude or edit the letter as she sees fit.

Letters can also help to underpin the legitimacy of the newspaper through the legitimacy of those who write them. The quality newspaper depends on those elevated in the hierarchy of credibility to co-operate as sources in order to substantiate its own claims to authority. Letters written by politicians (or better still, cabinet ministers), clergymen (or better still, bishops), company executives (or better still, presidents), police administrators (or better still, chiefs), and university professors (or better still, deans) are a means of indicating that the newspaper is itself acknowledged as an influential source. It is an influential source because influential sources regard it as the preferred outlet for their public conversations.

A sixth and final major consideration in our study of letters to the editor is what it reveals about the relation between news processes and news products. A systematic examination of letters as 'filed copy,' including those rejected as well as those accepted, provides an ideal grounding to understand how news judgments by sources and journalists are translated into what we see in the newspaper. Hence the categories developed here, and our findings, serve as a bridge to the study of news content reported in a forthcoming companion volume.

There has been little empirical research on letters to the editor other than speculative readings of content pertaining to narrow issues and a limited sample (e.g., Hall et al, 1978: chap. 5). As outlined in chapter 1, we designed a large-scale, systematic study of decision-making by a letters' editor in order to assess the significance of letters. To what extent is the way in which letters are dealt with by the newspaper typical of the way in which the newspaper processes all potential copy for publication? To what extent is the way in which letters are dealt with by the newspaper typical of the way in which journalists relate to and use sources as 'reporters,' including their participation in designating deviance, effecting social control, and affecting political reform? How open are the letters columns to sources who desire access to influence public opinion, to correct or criticize the newspaper, or simply to humour their fellows? Are they more open to some than others? Do the criteria of acceptance indicate that factors internal to the newsroom and news business predominate? What do answers to all of these questions indicate about the power of the news media to control the public conversation?

THE LETTERS-TO-THE-EDITOR DESK

The letters' editor we studied had a desk located among others in the features department, which included many of the newspaper's entertainment-section writers. He had been at the desk for four years, having previously worked at the same newspaper as a features writer and entertainment-section editor. He still spent about one-half of his time on a specific responsibility for the newspaper's entertainment section, with the other half of his time devoted to dealing with letters to the editor. This profile of the editor's experience signifies what we have documented elsewhere about the assignment of journalists (Ericson et al, 1987): it is not a specialization that matters but rather a keen eye for good copy. The editor's background and continued participation in entertainment-features reporting was neither a positive nor a negative feature in assigning him to the letters' editor post. It did not matter whether he had been a legal correspondent, Ottawa bureau chief, foreign correspondent, police-beat reporter, or on the sports desk. What mattered was his proven eye to know newsworthy copy when he saw it and his proven pen to tailor it for the purposes of news. Sensitive to the fact that he had a good nose for news his superiors entrusted him with this significant desk.

The editor described his desk as the 'complaint department' for the newspaper, meaning that general complaints about the newspaper by members of the public were directed to him. He said that in this role he was the policeman trying to sort out differing viewpoints on 'hot' and emotional issues. He referred to his superior as the 'appeals court,' since matters that became too hot for him to handle could be turned over to his superior for judgment. He said that he restricted knowledge of this 'appeals court' procedure within the newspaper to specific complainants, because if it became general public knowledge it would 'open the floodgates' causing many 'appeals' and too much work for his superior and himself.

The editor received sixty to seventy letters a day. (In comparison, Wooley [1985] reports *The Times* of London receives more than two hundred letters a day.) The editor made several observations on variation in the ebb and flow of letters to his desk. He observed that 'statutory holidays, long weekends, postal strikes, and even the weather affect the types of letters we receive, and the volume in which they arrive.' He also emphasized that there 'are two dramatic times when letters flow in an entirely different manner':

> One is during the months of July and August, vacation time for most Canadians, and during Christmas. During these months, we get dramatically fewer letters from corporations ('élite authorized knowers' ...) perhaps because corporations favour those months for vacations, and perhaps because those who draft the letters – communications departments, secretarial help, and

senior managers who would approve the content of the letters – are away. Another is during election time. Fewer politicians and fewer corporations write during these periods; I suspect politicians are too busy on the hustings, or will get a far more immediate and dramatic response answering the newspaper during a speech than sending a letter. I suspect that the corporate writers compose fewer letters during elections because they hesitate to endorse any one political party should a contrary outcome affect their relationship with the new government. These, too, are ... 'élite authorized knowers.'

The editor spent a little more than an hour each weekday reading the letters and making preliminary decisions. He commented that with many letters he could tell by the first three sentences whether they should be rejected. As the subsequent analyses indicate, a substantial proportion of letters were rejected routinely, often without reading them through to the end, because they did not accord with one of the basic requirements of the letters format.

A log book was kept with the name and address of every letter writer, the date the letter was received, and if published, the date it appeared in print. All letters were filed by the author's name, and kept for eighteen months and then destroyed. The letters were kept for this period in case the writer questioned the status of the letter, or complained about how it had been dealt with. Other than complaining, those whose letters had been rejected had no recourse within the newspaper. There was no direct option comparable to that which existed in the early days at *The Times* of London, when letters 'rejected as being uninteresting were treated as advertisements their authors paying for the privilege of seeing their name in print' (Wooley, 1985).

Letters were accepted, sent for queries to other desks in the newspaper, or rejected. Accepted letters were copy-edited by the editor, photocopied, and sent to a particular member of the editorial board to be checked for judgment and errors. If they were subsequently typed and proofed, accepted letters were then checked by another member of the editorial board. The editor said about 35 per cent of letters were accepted, but 10 to 12 per cent fewer than that actually appeared in print. Thus, while slightly more than one-third of letters were accepted, slightly fewer than one-quarter were published. In 1980 the newspaper received 14,420 letters, and published 3,393 (23.5 per cent). In 1981 the newspaper received 13,393 letters, and published 3,134 (23.0 per cent). (In comparison Wooley [1985] cites a 1968 study of *The Times* of London by Henderson, in which he reports that 63,963 letters were received, and 4,270 [6.7 per cent] were published.) The main reason for not publishing an accepted letter was space limitations. More were accepted than could be printed in order to give lay-out editors scope for tailoring a pool of letters to the available space. Letters that had been accepted but not printed because of insufficient space went into a 'bank' file. While in the file they were reviewed periodically, and if the situation the letter addressed had altered and the letter ceased to be relevant it was made dormant. After one month in the bank file a letter was made dormant. A letter would be accepted but not printed if it failed various investigative checks regarding authorship and authenticity. Accepted letters were checked to confirm the identity and address of the author, and if the apparent author could not be traced, or if she denied authorship, the letter would not be published.

A letter for query typically involved a contradiction of a published statement, and it thus represented a challenge to the integrity of a reporter. A letter for query was sent to the relevant desk editor. The desk editor had the responsibility of showing the letter to the reporter who wrote the original story, and of checking for any errors. The responses from the reporter and desk editor were then considered along with the letter to determine if further action, including a published correction, might be necessary.

Rejected letters were given to a third member of the editorial board. According to the editor, this person was especially concerned to check whether any letters that pointed to an important correction of fact had been rejected. If he found a letter of this type he sent it back to the letters editor for reconsideration. If there was still disagreement the final decision was taken by the member of the editorial board who checked accepted letters.

The editor said he made a special effort to check the facts when a letter was in correction of already published facts. He said this check was often difficult because of the fact-interpretation problem of which all journalists are painfully aware. He gave an example of a letter that said a government budget calculation was wrong because it used the wrong figures and methods. He said that with this sort of letter he sometimes gave deference to the professional status of the writer, accepting it on faith and hoping other readers would provide further corrections if it proved wrong. Offering another example, the editor referred to a series of letters sent by representatives of a Jewish organization complaining that the newspaper was intentionally distorting news from Lebanon in favour of the PLO. For instance, a letter criticized an Associated Press photograph of a person being hit by an Israeli soldier's gun blast. The writer engaged in a ballistics argument, which led him to conclude that the cameraman could not have had his camera ready to take such a photograph, and therefore it was a fake. The editor said that this argument was taken seriously, but he and some co-editors decided it was unfounded. They reasoned that while the odds are high against obtaining such a photograph, it is possible with particular fast-reflex cameras. The editor noted that they were not about to try to locate the Associated Press photographer in the rubble of Bierut to interrogate him about his camera equipment and the authenticity of the photograph.

Letters to the Editor: The Editor's Decisions

The Letter Writers

The interpretive intricacies of the editor's work, in relation to the character-istics of letters received and to criteria of news judgment, can be appreciated through a systematic survey of decision-making by the letters editor. We begin this survey by considering characteristics of letter writers and their relation to the editor's decision to accept or reject a letter (table 6.1). In this and subsequent analyses we cross-tabulate various independent variables with the editor's decision as the dependent variable. The dependent variable is expressed as a proportion of letters that were accepted (33.9 per cent of the total sample of 366) as opposed to those that were not accepted (66.1 per cent).

The first characteristic of letter writers enumerated in table 6.1 is whether any organizational affiliation of the writer was indicated in the letter, and if so, the institutional sphere of the identified organization. An affiliation was indicated if the author wrote on the letterhead of an organization, or stated an affiliation in the body of the letter or accompanying her signature. As in-dicated in table 6.1, the large majority of letters (282 or 77 per cent) did not indicate an affiliation. Among the 84 or 23 per cent that did, 27 were in the private corporate sphere, 14 were persons representing private citizens' orga-nizations, 11 were people in the field of education, 10 were representatives of federal government, 5 were union or occupational association representatives, and 3 were representatives of the provincial government. The remainder were from a variety of other institutional spheres, including foreign governments (2), political party organizations (2), Crown corporations (2), a hospital (1), a fire department (1), a public enquiry (1), and a municipal government (1). It was not possible to distinguish the sphere of 4 of the letters and they were coded as 'no information' (NI).

In a cross-tabulation of this variable with the editor's decision, we find that letters that did not indicate an organizational affiliation were much less likely to be accepted than those that did. Except for those indicating they were in the field of education, all writers who indicated an organizational affiliation had 50 per cent or better of their letters accepted, whereas the proportion for the entire sample was 33.9 per cent, and for those without an affiliation indicated only 27 per cent. These data support the view in the research literature that the news media, and especially quality outlets with an institutional emphasis, favour sources who are speaking in the name of a bureaucratic organization rather than as individuals.

We dichotomized the organizational-affiliation variable into letters where it was not indicated and letters where it was indicated for the purpose of

TABLE 6.1

Characteristics of writers of letters to the editor and the proportion accepted

Characteristices of writers of letters to the editor	N	Percentage accepted	χ^2	df	p
Total sample	366	33.9			
Organizational affiliation			34.39	7	< 0.01
Not indicated	282	27.0			
Private corporation	27	51.9			
Private non-profit	14	50.0			
Educational	11	36.4			
Federal government	10	70.0			
Union/association	5	100.0			
Provincial government	3	66.6			
Other/NI	14	64.3			
Writer's status			32.07	9	< 0.01
Not indicated	280	27.5			
Business executive/mgt.	17	52.9			
Educator	11	36.4			
Medical doctor	9	44.4			
Government politician	7	85.7			
Lawyer	7	42.9			
Union official	5	100.0			
Civil servant	4	50.0			
Opposition politician	3	66.6			
Other	23	52.2			
Number of sources cited			24.17	3	< 0.01
Letter writer only	102	15.7			
One	185	38.4			
Two	46	41.3			
Three or more	33	54.5			

the discriminant analysis reported subsequently. In a cross-tabulation of this dichotomized variable with the decision variable, we found that where an organizational affiliation was indicated 57.5 per cent (46/80) of the letters were accepted, compared with only 27 per cent (76/282) where the organizational affiliation was not indicated. These findings are statistically significant (where $\chi^2 = 24.68$; df = 1; $p < 0.01$ corrected for continuity in 2 × 2 table).

The second independent variable considered in table 6.1 is the letter writer's status, if indicated. The writer's status was indicated if the author mentioned it at any point in the letter or in signing the letter. Most writers (280 or 76.5 per cent) did not indicate a status. Among the 86 or 23.5 per cent who did, 17 were business executives or management (9 executives,

4 administrative managers, 4 line managers), 11 were educators (9 teachers or professors, 2 administrators), 9 were medical doctors, 7 were politicians for a governing party either federally or provincially (6 cabinet ministers, 1 MP), 7 were lawyers, 5 were union officials (3 national, 2 local), 4 were civil servants, 3 were politicians for a party in opposition either federally or provincially (1 leader, 2 MPs). The remainder held a variety of statuses, including consultant or promoter (6), a member of a specified organization (6), a leader of a specified organization (4), a news-media reporter (2), a senator (2), a mayor (1), a foreign-government official (1), and a landlord (1). (In comparison, Henderson's 1968 survey of 4,270 letters to *The Times* of London found that the writer's status was not indicated in 71.9 per cent; where it was indicated, educators led the list [10.2 per cent], followed by MPs [7.1 per cent], clergymen [4.3 per cent], peers and peeresses [3.7 per cent], captains of industry [1.9 per cent], and bishops [0.9 per cent]).

In a cross-tabulation of the writer's status with the editor's decision we find that, as with organizational affiliation, writers who did not indicate a status were much less likely to have their letters accepted than those who did. Except for individual professionals (doctors, lawyers, and educators), all those who indicated their status had 50 per cent or better of their letters accepted, whereas the proportion for the entire sample was 33.9 per cent, and for those without status indicated only 27.5 per cent. In keeping with the research literature regarding the use of sources in the news columns, it is the authorized knower rather than the citizen without her status identified who is given preference in the letters columns. Organizational affiliation and status can carry authority and give standing. Their absence suggests that the person has no special organizational relationship to be in a position to know.

We dichotomized the writer's-status variable into letters where it was indicated and letters where it was not indicated for the purpose of the discriminant analysis reported subsequently. In a cross-tabulation of this dichotomized variable with the decision variable, we found that where the writer's status was indicated 57.1 per cent (40/70) of the letters were accepted, compared with only 27.5 per cent (77/280) accepted where the writer's status was not indicated. These findings are statistically significant ($\chi^2 = 20.80$; df = 1; $p <$ 0.01 corrected for continuity in 2 × 2 table).

The third independent variable dealt with in table 6.1 is whether the letter writer cited other persons as 'sources' in his letter, and if so, how many. As enumerated in table 6.1, 102 letters (27.9 per cent) did not include any citation of sources, with the author being the only one identified. In 185 letters (50.5 per cent) one source was referred to, in 46 letters (12.6 per cent) two sources were referred to, and in 33 letters (9.0 per cent) 3 or more sources were referred to. In letters citing 3 or more sources, 15 cited three, 8 cited four, 6 cited five, 1 cited six, 1 cited eight, 1 cited nine, and 1 cited ten.

In a cross-tabulation of this variable with the editor's decision we find that writers who did not cite sources were much less likely to have their letters accepted than those who did. Only 15.7 per cent of those who did not cite others had their letters accepted, compared to 38.4 per cent of those who cited one source, 41.3 per cent of those who cited two sources, and 54.5 per cent of those who cited three or more sources. The more sources cited, the greater the prospect for acceptance.

We dichotomized the sources cited variable into letters in which a source was not cited and letters in which at least one source was cited for the purpose of the discriminant analysis reported subsequently. In a cross-tabulation of this dichotomized variable with the decision variable, we found that where at least one source was cited 40.9 per cent (108/264) of the letters were accepted, compared with only 15.7 per cent (16/102) where no source was cited. These findings are statistically significant (where $\chi^2 = 19.78$; df = 1; $p < 0.01$ corrected for continuity in 2×2 table).

These findings suggest another way in which letters to the editor are treated in a similar way to regular news copy. Just as the reporter usually has to find a source or two to say it is so, so the letter writer is better off functioning as a 'reporter' by citing other authorities in support of her view of what appears to be the case. The letter writer is better off not only if she can represent her own authority through organizational status and affiliation, but also if she can in turn cite other authorities to make her case.

CONTEXTS AND ISSUES

In table 6.2 we consider contexts and issues in letters and their relation to the editor's decision to accept or reject a letter. The first context examined is whether the letter deals with government or private spheres of organized life. As indicated in table 6.2, 166 or 45.2 per cent of letters pertained to matters in the private corporate sphere. A further 69 or 18.9 per cent of letters dealt with the federal-government context. Other levels of Canadian government were addressed in 38 or 10.4 per cent of letters, including 24 at the provincial level, 10 at the municipal level, and 4 at multiple levels. Non-corporate private contexts were focused on in 26 or 7.1 per cent of letters, including 11 non-profit–organization contexts, the affairs of 6 private individuals, 4 unions, 4 deviant or criminal organizations, and 1 involving multiple private spheres. Foreign-government contexts was addressed in 22 or 6.0 per cent of letters. A combination of both government and private contexts were included in 16 or 4.4 per cent of letters. There was an inability to make a reasonable categorization in these terms for 29 or 7.9 per cent of letters.

In a cross-tabulation of this variable with the editor's decision, we find

TABLE 6.2

Contexts and issues in letters to the editor and the proportion accepted

Contexts and issues in letters to the editor	N	Percentage accepted	χ^2	df	p
Total sample	366	33.9			
Government/Private			20.85	6	< 0.01
Private corporation	166	45.2			
Federal government	69	23.2			
Other Cdn. government	38	23.7			
Other private	26	34.6			
Foreign government	22	18.2			
Government & Private	16	37.5			
NI	29	17.2			
Fields			30.33	6	< 0.01
Culture	173	47.4			
Regulation/enforcement	39	30.8			
Fiscal	38	18.4			
Legislature/political parties	34	17.6			
Defence/military	15	6.7			
Other	31	22.6			
NI	36	25.0			
Issues			30.09	4	< 0.01
Information control	152	48.9			
Politics	84	21.4			
Economics	80	28.8			
Other	29	27.6			
NA/NI	21	4.8			

statistically significant differences in acceptance in relation to these contexts. Letters dealing with the private corporate context were the most likely to be accepted (45.2 per cent), followed by those dealing with both private and government spheres (37.5 per cent), and those pertaining to private non-corporate contexts (34.6 per cent), in comparison with the total sample proportion of 33.9 per cent. Letters pertaining to the federal government (23.2 per cent), other Canadian governments (23.7 per cent), and foreign governments (18.2 per cent) were least likely to be accepted.

We dichotomized the government/private variable into letters that dealt with the private corporate context and those that did not for the purpose of the discriminant analysis reported subsequently. In a cross-tabulation of this dichotomized variable with the decision variable, we found that where the letters dealt with the private corporate context 45.2 per cent (75/166) were accepted, compared with only 25.7 per cent (44/171) of the letters pertaining to other contexts. These findings are statistically significant (where $\chi^2 = 13.1$; df = 1; $p < 0.01$ corrected for continuity in 2 × 2 table).

This emphasis on private corporate contexts is rather surprising given the prevailing wisdom that most news outlets, and especially qualities with an institutional approach, deal mainly with issues of procedural propriety in government. Perhaps the letters-to-the-editor columns diverge from other news columns in allowing more latitude for private corporate concerns as well as the concerns of private citizens' organizations. It is also significant that the newspaper studied had a very strong orientation to the business community. It published a substantial business section daily, which was used nationally as a major source of business knowledge. This orientation likely explains why such a high proportion of letters addressed private corporate contexts, and why such a relatively high proportion of letters that did were accepted.

The second variable considered in table 6.2 is the fields addressed in the letters. The field of culture – dealing with matters of cultural policy (e.g., language rights), religion, the media, and questions of meaning and control of information – was addressed in 173 or 47.2 per cent of letters. Matters of regulation and enforcement constituted the field in 39 or 10.7 per cent of letters, including 11 in the criminal-justice sphere and 28 in other spheres of regulation and enforcement. Fiscal concerns were the field in 38 or 10.4 per cent of letters. Legislatures at any level of government and/or party politics were addressed in 34 or 9.3 per cent of letters. Defence and military fields were included in 15 or 4.1 per cent of letters. A variety of other fields were addressed in 31 or 8.5 per cent of letters, including 9 in health, education, and welfare; 7 in transportation and communication; 6 in foreign state bureaucracies; 2 in foreign-policy areas; 1 in science and technology; and 6 that were multiple. Another 36 or 9.8 per cent of letters could not be classified in these terms.

In a cross-tabulation of this variable with the editor's decision, we find statistically significant differences in acceptance in relation to these fields. Letters dealing with culture were by far the most likely to be accepted (47.4 per cent). All others were below the proportion of 33.9 per cent for the total sample, although regulation and enforcement was close to the average for the sample at 30.8 per cent accepted. Letters addressing defence and military matters were particularly unlikely to be accepted (6.7 per cent).

We dichotomized the fields variable into letters that addressed the culture field and those that did not, for the purpose of the discriminant analysis reported subsequently. In a cross-tabulation of this dichotomized variable with the decision variable, we found that where the letter dealt with matters of culture 47.4 per cent (82/173) were accepted, compared with only 21.0 per cent (33/157) of the letters pertaining to other contexts. These findings are statistically significant (where $\chi^2 = 24.08$; df = 1; $p < 0.01$ corrected for continuity in 2 × 2 table).

The third variable in table 6.2 is the issue addressed in the letters. Issues in the control of information predominated. These were addressed in 152 or 41.5 per cent of letters. Issues in politics were the subject of 84 or 23.0 per cent of letters, including political actions by authorities (47), political ideology (17), political actions by subjects in relation to authorities (10), and international political conflicts (10). Economic issues were of concern in 80 or 21.9 per cent of letters, including economic practices (45), economic policy (32), and economic aspects of particular social problems (3). Other issues were addressed in 29 or 7.9 per cent of letters, including public health and safety (9), interpersonal violence (5), entertainment (5), sports (4), the means of violence (2), education (2), property crime (1), and questionable morality (1). Another 21 or 5.7 per cent of letters could not be classified in these terms.

In a cross-tabulation of this variable with the editor's decision, we find statistically significant differences in acceptance in relation to these issues. Letters dealing with information control were the most likely to be accepted (48.9 per cent), compared to those addressing economic issues (28.8 per cent), political issues (21.4 per cent), and the total sample (33.9 per cent).

We dichotomized the issues variable into letters that addressed information control and those that did not, for the purpose of the discriminant analysis reported subsequently. In a cross-tabulation of this dichotomized variable with the decision variable, we found that where the letter dealt with issues of information control 48.9 per cent (74/152) were accepted, compared with only 25.4 per cent (49/193) of the letters pertaining to other issues. These findings are statistically significant (where $\chi^2 = 19.11$; df = 1; $p < 0.01$ corrected for continuity in 2 × 2 table).

The letters format is designed to handle debates over meaning, including especially the interpretation of facts and different meanings based on different values and ideologies. It is one of the key forums for public contests in the control of information and cultural meaning. Therefore, it is not surprising that a substantial proportion of letters submitted were related to issues of information control, and that they were especially likely to be accepted for publication. Some separate analyses add to our understanding in this regard. Letters accusing misrepresentation in previous news accounts were especially likely to be accepted (69/135 or 51.5 per cent compared to 33.9 per cent for the total sample). Letters that questioned the opinions of another source were more likely to be accepted (16/36 or 44.4 per cent), whereas those that supported the opinion of another source were less likely to be accepted (10/49 or 20.4 per cent) compared to the total sample proportion of 33.9 per cent accepted.

TABLE 6.3

Levels of understanding and assessment in letters to the editor and the proportion accepted

Levels of understanding and assessment in letters to the editor		N	Percentage accepted	χ^2	df	p
Total sample		366	33.9			
Primary understanding:	Yes	346	35.5	6.57	1	< 0.01
	No	20	5.0			
Secondary understanding:	Yes	52	25.0	1.70	1	NS
	No	314	35.4			
Tertiary understanding:	Yes	37	21.6	2.19	1	NS
	No	329	35.3			
Interpretation:	Yes	24	25.0	0.53	1	NS
	No	342	34.5			
Evaluation:	Yes	310	36.5	5.26	1	< 0.05
	No	56	19.6			
Recommendation:	Yes	107	26.2	3.54	1	NS
	No	259	37.1			

χ^2 corrected for continuity in 2 × 2 tables

LEVELS OF UNDERSTANDING AND ASSESSMENT

Another set of characteristics of letters relevant to the editor's decision to publish is the type of understanding and assessment they offer. We developed a typology of levels of understanding based on Runciman (1983). We made judgments as to whether a letter contained *primary understanding* (descriptive, factual, addressing the question 'What happened?'); *secondary understanding* (explanation, addressing the question 'Why did it happen?'); and *tertiary understanding* (empathetic, addressing the question 'What was it like to be involved in what happened?'). We also developed a typology of levels of assessment, making judgments as to whether a letter contained *implications* (consequences, addressing the question 'What are the consequences of what happened in theory and practice?'); *evaluation* (moral judgment, addressing the question 'Was the thing that happened good or bad?'); and *recommendations* (future action, addressing the question 'What should be done to control, correct, and improve upon what happened?'). We judged whether or not each of these types of understanding and assessment were contained in each letter, and cross-tabulated each type with the editor's decision for each variable. A summary of the results is presented in table 6.3.

The vast majority (346/366 or 94.5 per cent) of letters contained primary understanding. Letters that did not contain primary understanding were very unlikely to be accepted (only 1/20 or 5 per cent), whereas 35.5 per cent of letters with primary understanding were accepted. There is a statistically significant difference between letters with primary understanding and those without in relation to the editor's decision. The need for a factual statement, or at least a factual assertion, about the matter being addressed is as important in the letters columns as it is in other sections of the newspaper.

Most letter writers did not offer explanations of the matter they addressed. Only 52/366 or 14.2 per cent of letters contained secondary understanding. The research literature indicates that the news contains little in the way of explanation of the issues and problems it reports on, and the same can be said for letters to the editor. Indeed the tiny minority of letter writers who did offer an explanation were less likely to have their letters accepted (13/52 or 25.0 per cent) than those who did not (111/314 or 35.4 per cent). However, this difference is not statistically significant at the 0.05 level.

Even fewer letter writers evoked empathetic understanding. Only 37/366 or 10.1 per cent of letters included tertiary understanding, a finding that suggests that few writers felt encouraged to use the letters columns to relate personal involvement in and feelings about the matter addressed in their letters. While reporters use sources to evoke empathetic understanding in their news stories, this seems more characteristic of popular newspapers and of the broadcast media (Ericson et al, 1987, and forthcoming). It is clearly uncharacteristic of the letters section of the quality newspaper we studied. The few letter writers who did include tertiary understanding were less likely to have their letters accepted (8/37 or 21.6 per cent) than those who did not include it (116/329 or 35.3 per cent). This difference just missed being statistically significant at the 0.05 level.

Turning to types of assessment, it is indicated in table 6.3 that discussion of the implications of the matter addressed was rare. Only 24/366 or 6.6 per cent of letters contained an assessment of implications, and those that did were slightly less likely to be accepted (6/24 or 25.0 per cent) than those that did not (118/342 or 34.5 per cent). This difference is not statistically significant at the 0.05 level.

In contrast, evaluation was a predominant feature in letters to the editor. Among the 366 letters, 310 or 84.7 per cent included an assessment of whether the matter being addressed was good or bad. Moreover, letters that did include an evaluation were much more likely to be accepted (113/310 or 36.5 per cent) than those without an evaluation (11/56 or 19.6 per cent). This difference is statistically significant at the 0.05 level. This finding is to be expected given the general news-media orientation to assessments of good and evil, of deviance and control, and given the explicit mandate of the letters columns as a forum for evaluative opinion.

In 107/366 or 29.2 per cent of letters, the writers made recommendations to control and/or change the matter they addressed. This, too, is one of the explicit functions of a letter to the editor, calling for reform in the name of the citizen or authority who writes it. However, those letters which included a recommendation were slightly less likely to be accepted (28/107 or 26.2 per cent) than letters without a recommendation (96/259 or 37.1 per cent). This difference is not statistically significant at the 0.05 level. While close to one-third of all letters tried to use the letters columns to urge some reform, these were given no preference by the editor.

A DISCRIMINANT ANALYSIS

In order to understand the collective and relative influence of all the characteristics of letters we have considered – the letter writers, sources cited, contexts, issues, levels of understanding, and levels of assessment – a stepwise discriminant analysis was undertaken. Stepwise discriminant analysis weights and combines independent measures in a way that forces the two groups of letters (accepted and not accepted) to be as distinct as possible so that one can predict on what criteria the groups are distinguishable. It is a cautious approach to the prediction of group membership without regard to the strictures of time order or causal structure of variables. This approach, along with the nominal measure on the decision variable, means that there are fewer restrictive assumptions necessary than in some other statistical techniques. We simply wish to classify what characteristics most strongly predict whether or not a letter is accepted (on discriminant analysis, see Morrison, 1969; Tatsuaka, 1971; Greenberg, 1979: 165–7).

The results of our stepwise discriminant analysis are presented in table 6.4. This analysis is based on the Wilk's lambda criterion, although we also used the Mahalanobis distance criterion and obtained the same results. We excluded 36 letters from the analysis because they had at least one missing discriminating variable, which left 330 letters for the analysis, including 115 accepted and 215 not accepted. We initially entered all twelve letter characteristic variables considered previously, dichotomized as follows: writer's organizational affiliation not indicated/indicated; writer's status not indicated/indicated; letter writer only or other sources cited; private corporation/other; culture/other; information control/other; primary understanding yes/no; secondary understanding yes/no; tertiary understanding yes/no; implications yes/no; evaluation yes/no; recommendation yes/no.

Five characteristics are significant predictors of the editor's decision. The best predictor of the acceptance of letters is the field (culture/other) the letter pertains to. Some additional predictive influence comes from adding in turn whether the writer's organizational affiliation is indicated, whether there is tertiary understanding, whether the writer's status is indicated, and whether the writer cited sources. Accepted letters are those grouped as being in the

TABLE 6.4

Stepwise discriminant analysis of contexts, issues, characteristics of writers, and levels of understanding and assessment in letters to the editor and whether or not a letter was accepted

Step discriminant variable		F	Discriminant function coefficients
Field:	*Culture*	17.01	+0.624
	Other		
Organization represented:	*Indicated*	3.59	+0.365
	Not indicated		
Tertiary understanding:	Yes	2.89	−0.254
	No		
Writer's status:	*Indicated*	2.17	+0.290
	Not indicated		
Sources cited:	*Sources cited*	1.11	+0.163
	Letter writer only		

Centroids: Group 1 – acceptance (n = 115) +0.547
Centroids: Group 2 – non-acceptance (n = 215) −0.291
Percentage correctly classified: 63.9%
Wilk's lambda = 0.8618: χ^2 = 48.12; df = 5; $p < 0.001$

field of culture, indicating the organizational affiliation of the writer, without tertiary understanding, indicating the writer's status, and including citation of sources.

In this section we have used external signs of the letters and related them to the editor's decision to accept or reject. This is one significant means of knowing about what criteria seem salient in the editor's judgments. Missing from these analyses is more direct knowledge of what the editor was thinking in justification of his decisions. Our understanding of the letters format, of news criteria, and of the relation of journalists to sources can be advanced further by enumerating and analysing the editor's own reasons for non-acceptance and acceptance of letters.

THE EDITOR'S REASONS FOR REJECTING LETTERS

In keeping with what other journalists told us and practised (Ericson et al, 1987), the letters editor emphasized that his knowledge of the role was learned on the job and based in precedent. Attuned to the vocabulary of precedents in the newsroom, he could quickly recognize whether a letter was acceptable, and if so make it more acceptable through copy-editing, at the same time accounting for his decisions to superiors. While he described this process as making judgments in accordance with 'gut feelings,' it was less personal, intuitive, and arbitrary than suggested by this expression. As an experienced

TABLE 6.5

The editor's reasons for non-acceptance of letters

Editor's reasons	N	As a percentage of all responses	As a percentage of non-accepted letters ($N = 239$)
Total sample	343	100.0	143.5
Incomprehensible	40	11.6	16.7
Stylistic	31	9.0	13.0
Adds nothing new	30	8.7	12.6
Untrue/unfair	29	8.5	12.1
Copied letter	26	7.5	10.9
Regular crank	22	6.4	9.2
Too long	15	4.3	6.3
Anonymous writer	14	4.1	5.8
Too many this topic	11	3.2	4.6
Not focused on issue	11	3.2	4.6
Jurisdiction of another desk	10	2.9	4.2
Too emotional	9	2.6	3.7
Writer untrustworthy	8	2.3	3.3
Too many from writer previously	7	2.0	2.9
Too inflammatory	6	1.7	2.5
Requires complex response	6	1.7	2.5
Columnist cannot respond	5	1.5	2.1
Irrelevant	5	1.5	2.1
Unsubstantiated allegations	5	1.5	2.1
Hate mail	5	1.5	2.1
Too many from writer printed	4	1.2	1.7
Reprint from other media	4	1.2	1.7
Correction to relevant desk	4	1.2	1.7
Criticizes competing newspaper	3	0.9	1.3
Lacks specificity	3	0.9	1.3
Too praiseworthy of newspaper	3	0.9	1.3
Too dull	3	0.9	1.3
Too simplistic	3	0.9	1.3
Doesn't add balance	2	0.6	0.8
Not for publication	2	0.6	0.8
Too theoretical	2	0.6	0.8
Involves solicitation	2	0.6	0.8
Other	13	3.8	5.4

journalist, the letters editor made his judgments situationally and contextually, in terms of the prevailing social and cultural criteria in the newsroom. Thus, he had the sense that his judgments were based on having a 'nose for news.' Nevertheless, as the following data indicate, this nose for news was sensitized by the system.

The editor's reasons for not accepting letters are enumerated in table 6.5.

This table pertains to all letters in the sample of 366 that were not accepted, except 3 for which no reason was given for rejection. Thus, 239 letters are included in this sample. Multiple responses were allowed for and coded, and the editor gave a total of 343 reasons for not accepting these 239 letters. Table 6.5 includes the frequency of each reason given, the percentage of each reason given in relation to all 343 reasons, and the percentage of each reason given in relation to the 239 letters.

It is evident from table 6.5 that a large number of considerations were deemed relevant by the editor in accounting for why a letter was unacceptable. No single reason predominates, and the number of multiple responses indicates that often several factors were deemed relevant regarding a particular letter. However, if we abstract these responses to a more general level, we can delineate the major concerns of the letters editor and how these relate to the typical concerns of journalists in fitting their copy to print.

Unsuitable to the Format

A substantial proportion of reasons can be summarized by stating that the letters were unsuitable to the format. Included in this categorization are letters that were incomprehensible (40) and written so poorly that they could not be made fit to print even with substantial editing (31).

Fifteen letters were said to be unsuitable to the format because they were too long. The letters editor said that he was under general 'pressure' from his superiors to shorten letters and thereby publish more letters, and in consequence had become more conscious of length. He also said that if there are several letters in the 'bank' available for publication, the longer ones are likely to be omitted simply because of length. Hence, it was incumbent on him to accept shorter letters, or at least to shorten them through copy-editing. We decided to undertake a separate analysis on the matter of length, and found that for all letters received on the day we sampled, rejected letters were 50 per cent longer on average than accepted letters. In many respects the ideal letter was seen in the same terms as the ideal interview clip from a source: the more pithy and amusing the better.

Another 10 letters were not accepted because they were deemed to be within the jurisdiction of another desk. These were sent for possible use by the relevant desk. Possible uses included checking on fact and interpretation, initiating further investigation, or even printing part or all of the letter in the desk's own section.

A range of other reasons also indicated the editor's view that particular letters were not fitting of the format: they were too emotional; too inflammatory; required a response that would be too complex (regarding the news requirement of simplification); required a response from a columnist criticized in a letter but the columnist had no means of responding; irrelevant; hate mail; a simple correction that could be sent for information only to the relevant desk; lacking in specificity; too dull; too simplistic; too abstract or theoretical; and not intended for publication as stated explicitly in the letter. Taking these reasons along with the others we have categorized as being unsuitable to the format, we find that 149 reasons or 43.4 per cent of all reasons given fit this categorization.

Newsworthiness

A considerable number of responses given by the editor indicate his concerns about newsworthiness. The editor explained the non-acceptance of 30 letters by saying that they added nothing new to the matter they addressed. In rejecting 11 letters he said there were too many already published on the topic. Typical was his comment that, 'The shelf-life of news, as you know, is very brief.' The non-acceptance of 11 letters was said by the editor to be a result of his judgment that they were not focused enough on the newsworthy aspects of the issue they addressed. In relation to 4 letters, it was the letter writer who was no longer newsworthy because too many of his letters had been printed in recent memory. These reasons we have categorized as being related to newsworthiness considerations number 56, or 16.3 per cent of all reasons given.

News Values

A smaller proportion of responses indicate the editor's consideration of news values in accounting for his decision to reject letters. The editor gave as a reason for rejecting 29 letters that they were untrue and/or unfair, indicating his concern for accuracy and balance. The justification for rejection of 8 letters was that the writer was known to be untrustworthy. In relation to 5 letters the editor said that serious allegations were made that could not be substantiated. Finally, 2 letters were rejected because the editor was looking for new opinion to add balance to a matter but the letters failed to 'take a stand' and provide a different perspective. These 44 responses we have categorized as relating to news values constitute 12.9 per cent of all responses.

Newspaper Policy

Several reasons for non-acceptance given by the editor indicate that he was acting in accordance with established newspaper policy regarding certain features of letters. He said he rejected 26 letters on the ground that they were copies of originals sent to someone else. These were problematic because they were less authentic, and because many of them bordered on self-serving statements no different from the daily avalanche of news releases received in the newsroom. The letters editor explains:

> A mass-mailing is not read because it is, in essence, a press release (we do not differentiate between a mass mailing authored by one individual from that written by a large corporation); we do not reject them merely because we 'demand exclusivity.' Many correspondents simply do not know to whom they send their statements, and so send them to 'the editor.' These can include news of a new development in widget manufacturing or an individual's opinion on the death penalty ... In the case of individuals who send a copy of their letter to every newspaper they can think of, it does not matter what the content or opinion is: the letter is not designed to add to a debate, but to print the writer's name all across the country, enhancing the image of the writer.

There was also a ban on letters that appeared to be reprinted material, already published in other media. The editor said he rejected 4 letters of this type. In doing so he pointed to the fact that non-exclusive material has no place in the letters columns. He also noted that there would be problems of copyright if he did want to publish material of this type.

Another established ground for rejection was the letter-writer's anonymity. A letter was rejected outright even if an organization was named but not an individual author. The editor gave this as the reason for rejecting 14 letters, although there were occasions on which considerable effort was made to identify the author because the letter was otherwise deemed worthy of publication. In spite of our data showing the importance of organizational affiliation in the decision to accept a letter, there must be an individual to identify with the organization. This reason appears to be related to several considerations, including the news tendency towards personalization, and the notion that there is a responsible person in an organization who can stand behind her accounts and therefore be held publicly accountable. While this practice of naming sources is also characteristic of other news formats, it is less stringent elsewhere. Unnamed sources are used and even referred to in the news and features columns. In the letters format there was a requirement that every author, as source and 'reporter,' had to be identified at least by name and city of residence. The letters editor said that ultimately, 'It is a legal matter – we cannot print letters from anonymous correspondents or those who cannot be traced for fear that if a legal action occurs, we would lose our credibility, which is what we sell to our readers.'

The editor perceived an expectation among senior editors that he should not accept letters that are too praiseworthy of the newspaper. He said he was turning down 3 letters on this basis. Another 3 letters were said to be unacceptable because they were critical of a competing newspaper. This finding is in keeping with our observations of journalism in general. To avoid a war of fact and interpretation, and the semantic disorder and loss of legitimacy that would result, news organizations do not directly correct or rebut the accounts of their competitors in the same medium (Ericson et al, 1987). The editor said he did accept on occasion letters critical of particular broadcast-media organizations, but there was a taboo on letters complaining about other newspapers.

Another cause for rejecting letters is if they are in effect solicitations for particular political actions or products. The editor gave this as the reason for rejecting 2 letters. For example, a letter calling for citizens to sign a petition against the way criminal-justice officials were treating a notorious criminal was turned down on the ground that the newspaper does not accept any letters calling for petitions.

Summarizing the reasons for non-acceptance relating to newspaper policy, we find that 52 reasons (15.2 per cent of all reasons given) were given within these terms.

The Writer's Characteristics and the Editor's Inclinations

Two of the editor's reasons for non-acceptance can be categorized as related to a combination of the writer's characteristics and the editor's personal inclinations. The editor immediately rejected 22 letters on the grounds that they were written by 'cranks,' 'crazies,' 'hysterics,' and 'monomaniacs.' There were regular writers who were categorized in this way, including one person who usually submitted two or more letters each day and accounted for a substantial proportion of letters rejected on these grounds. The editor observed, 'We cannot entertain letters from obviously unbalanced writers for legal reasons, as well as reasons of taste and reasonableness. But reasons of taste and reasonableness are irrelevant to the primary reason, because we are legally responsible for what we print and we cannot begin to be responsible for the results of fevered imaginations.'

The letters editor also employed a sense of frequency of submission. A writer who was seen to be submitting too many letters in recent memory was subject to being rejected for this reason. The editor gave this reason in relation to 7 letters. This consideration was a rather arbitrary one related to other considerations, for as we learn later there were also favoured regulars. These were high-status regulars who were able to write in a manner fitting of the format and who were almost as assured of being published as the 'cranks' were of being rejected. In total, we categorized 29 reasons (8.4 per cent of all reasons given) as related to the writer's characteristics and the editor's inclinations.

In reviewing these data and our categorizations, the letters editor emphasized that a substantial proportion of letters are rejected without even bothering to read them. 'Certain letters, for instance, are not even read before they are rejected. These include unsigned letters, mass mailings, clippings from other newspapers, unbalanced arguments from known and unreliable correspondents, and copies of letters sent to other people.' Any one of these signs was sufficient for an 'automatic' rejection of the letter. The letters editor also emphasized that it is almost exclusively the individual citizen, rather than regular sources representing established organizations, who sends in letters within these categories for automatic rejection. Authorized knowers, as *organized* representatives of their bureaucracies, know precisely what will be acceptable within the letters format, whereas most individuals are less attuned to the basic requirements for consideration: 'The majority of letters that are not even read ... come from private individuals with no affiliation given (approaching 100 per cent); the acceptability – in terms of legally usable letters, not counting their expressed opinions – from corporate sources ("élite authorized knowers") is vast (approaching 100 per cent). If we show a bias toward these "élite authorized knowers" it's simply because we begin with a far larger proportion of their letters.'

During the course of our research observations the letters editor admitted to a particular bias. He said he rejected any letter in support of capital punishment because of his personal view that capital punishment is immoral. While observing the letters editor on a day not included in our survey sample, he rejected 2 letters in favour of capital punishment that were in response to a previous letter against capital punishment. One letter was rejected without reading it through to the end. However, the letters editor has since eliminated this bias. In his words, 'Newspapers change, people change, and a letters editor – the same one since the survey was taken – can change. Hence ... my statement that I do not entertain letters favouring capital punishment at all is now irrelevant; I have recently accepted letters favouring it.'

THE EDITOR'S REASONS FOR ACCEPTING LETTERS

In table 6.6 we enumerate the editor's reasons for accepting letters. This table pertains to the 124 letters in the sample of 366 that were accepted, except 4 for which no reason was given for acceptance. Thus, 120 letters are included in this sample. Multiple responses were allowed for and coded, and the editor gave a total of 228 reasons for accepting these 120 letters. Table 6.6 includes the frequency of each reason given for acceptance, the percentage of each

TABLE 6.6

The editor's reasons for acceptance of letters

Editor's reasons	N	As a percentage of all responses	As a percentage of accepted letters ($N = 120$)
Total sample	228	100.0	190.0
Fair comment	56	24.6	46.7
Hot topic	26	11.4	21.7
Humorous	19	8.3	15.8
New viewpoint	17	7.5	14.2
Well argued	17	7.5	14.2
Correction of newspaper	17	7.5	14.2
Response to criticism	11	4.8	9.2
Short	10	4.4	8.3
Easily illustrated	10	4.4	8.3
New information	7	3.1	5.8
Provocative	5	2.2	4.2
Journalist advised	5	2.2	4.2
Superior advised	4	1.8	3.3
High-status contributor	4	1.8	3.3
Majority viewpoint	4	1.8	3.3
Editor's viewpoint	4	1.8	3.3
Writer involved	3	1.3	2.5
Of interest to the newspaper	3	1.3	2.5
Editor needs letter	3	1.3	2.5
Final word on matter	2	0.9	1.7
Writer trustworthy	1	0.4	0.8

reason given in relation to all 228 reasons, and the percentage of each reason given in relation to the 120 accepted letters. In most instances the criteria used by the editor to accept letters were the reverse side of the same coin used in rejection decisions. However, analysis of the editor's reasons for accepting letters raises additional considerations in his decision-making.

Reasonable Opinion

Regarding the majority of letters he accepted, the editor made reference to his assessment that they expressed a reasonable opinion about the event, process, or state of affairs they addressed. In relation to 56 or 46.7 per cent of accepted letters, the editor said they expressed 'fair comment' on the matter addressed. The 'fair comment' reason constituted almost one-quarter of all reasons for acceptance of letters. In relation to 17 or 14.2 per cent of all accepted letters, the editor remarked on how they were 'well argued.' This reason is 7.5 per cent of all reasons for acceptance stated by the editor. Overall then, there were 73 letters categorized in terms of reasonable opinion; these constituted 32.1 per cent of the editor's reasons for acceptance.

Newsworthiness

Also predominant were reasons related to the newsworthiness of the material in the letters. In keeping with the view that letters are like press releases from important sources, or like filed copy from sources-as-reporters, the editor made frequent reference to the value of letters in the context of ongoing themes or issues in the news. Thus, he said he accepted 26 or 21.7 per cent of all letters on the basis that they fit into a 'hot topic.' This is 11.4 per cent of all reasons for acceptance. Another 7 or 5.8 per cent of letters were said to be acceptable because they added new information to a continuing story. This is 3.1 per cent of all reasons given.

The editor made several distinctions regarding what he regarded as topical. He said that one gauge of whether something is a 'hot topic' is the volume of letters received on the topic. He said he kept in his head a sense of the volume of letters on each topic, rather than recording the actual volume, and used this knowledge to judge topicality. When the researcher suggested to him that volume of letters might only be indicative of a small group of vocal, activist people with an interest in an issue, and not something of general concern, the editor replied that those who are unconcerned can always write a letter to say so. The researcher said that the unconcerned are unlikely to make the effort to declare it in a letter to the editor. While admitting the point, the editor still insisted that an issue becomes 'hotter' when more people write letters to him about it. The knowledgeability of the letters editor, in keeping with the journalistic craft generally, was not based on knowing his readership through survey evidence of what they regard as newsworthy.

The editor pointed out that the determination of topicality also emanated from the echelons of senior editors. At the time of the research the issue of surrogate mothers was a favourite of a particular senior editor, and he took the initiative to organize several features on the topic, which in turn stimulated the submission of letters on the topic.

The editor noted that what was topical in the news had a great bearing on what became topical in the letters columns. However, he made the distinction between the 'currently topical' as being what was newsworthy and hence likely to be accepted, and the 'eternally topical,' which carried on for so long that the range of opinion and information had become established, repetitive, dull, and unnewsworthy. At the time of our field-work he regarded the abortion issue as 'eternally topical,' and he said he had an 'unofficial ban' on all letters concerning abortion. He said if he accepted just one letter on this topic, it would 'open the floodgates' and create problems for him.

He said the only thing that might lift the ban would be a major change in law or policy concerning abortion; that is, the impetus for more opinion and discussion about abortion would have to come from a significant action by the authorities, not from citizens wishing to express their actions in words through the letters columns.

If a letter was deemed 'currently topical' it could of course also serve to make more news, and in turn that might make more letters. Thus, in relation to 5 or 4.2 per cent of letters accepted the editor said he was accepting them because they were 'provocative.' By this he meant that they were written explicitly to stir up opposition and controversy, which was good for his column and good for news generally. His primary concern seemed to be a desire to generate more letters and opinions therein, although direct action was also at the heart of some decisions.

Direct action is indicated in the case of a manufacturer of wood heating stoves who said they were tax exempt because they fell into the category of 'energy saver.' A revenue official had, however, decided that while a stove with one door was an 'energy saver' and thus tax exempt, a stove with two doors was a luxury item and therefore taxable. The stove proprietor wrote a letter to the editor expressing his outrage. He claimed that two-door stoves were simply bigger and required the extra door for efficient operation. The newspaper investigated the matter, and eventually published a story on the investigation. This story was followed by a sequel in which it was reported that tax officials no longer regarded two-door stoves as a luxury item.

Contrary to the process in this example, virtually all letters accepted for their direct relation to topical or newsworthy issues were responding to frames that had been established in the news by key sources and journalists. As Hall et al (1978: 122) observe in the specific continuing story they analysed through letters columns, 'letters – like features, "take off from" the points of newsworthiness first identified in the *news* treatment. *News* defines what the issues are, for letters as for other parts of the paper.' To the extent that this occurs, it is the newsmakers – journalists and their key authorized knowers – who circumscribe what is deemed publishable in the letters columns as well as other news formats. The fact that the same criteria of newsworthiness are used in judgments about letters as in the other news formats means that the letters columns are similarly enclosed. 'For it is the awakening of lay public attitudes, and their crystallising in forms which underpin and support the viewpoints already in circulation, which help to close the consensual circle, providing the lynch-pin of legitimation' (ibid).

In summary, 39 letters were judged to be acceptable in terms of their newsworthiness or 'current topicality,' 16.7 per cent of all the editor's reasons for acceptance.

Fairness and Balance

The editor also made frequent reference to the news values of fairness and balance in stating the reasons for his acceptance decisions. This is in keeping with the role of the letters format in providing for alternative opinion. Letters are to provide counterpoints in the construction of meaning and reality about public issues. Obviously these considerations too were enclosed by what was already in the news.

The editor's concern for balance was expressed in saying that he was accepting letters because they added a new viewpoint to something topical (17), were a legitimate response to criticism (11), represented a majority viewpoint (4), and provided the necessary counterpoint opinion for the final word on the matter (2). Taking these together, 34 letters were said to be accepted for reasons of balance, 15 per cent of all reasons for acceptance stated by the editor.

In most instances the editor did not view balance in systematic or quantitative terms (cf Hall et al, 1978: 121). As with his knowledgeability about the volume of letters on what was topical, the editor sensed balance from his memory of what was in the news and what letters he had received and accepted in the past. The one major exception was regarding election campaigns, during which the editor accepted letters in proportion to the number received in support of each political party. The editor himself noted that this, of course, still provided an overrepresentation of letters in favour of the Progressive Conservative party, since the newspaper was known among its readers to be more supportive of that party than of the Liberals or New Democrats. There is no clearer evidence that the letters columns did not reflect a random sample of opinion in the community. Rather, they were framed by the known political agenda of the newspaper and used disproportionately by particular citizens who had an affinity with this agenda.

The letters editor defined his role as making fair *representations* of writers' opinions, as opposed to making sure writers' opinions were *representative* in a statistical sense. Hence, in commenting upon our statistical analyses of his decisions he underscored that he had no pretensions of being democratic. He saw himself as a referee or judge: ensuring procedural fairness in the process of managing a debate.

> In fact, I have never heard the word 'democracy' applied to the letters section; it was never our intent to be democratic, nor is that indeed a desired outcome. What we are doing on the letters page is managing a debate. We attempt to reflect all views, not a statistically representative sample of them. If we tried to be statistically correct, we would end up printing endless streams of letters, all saying the same thing, we would present letters that

misinterpret facts, we would print letters that are libellous. None of this is acceptable, as it would be in a statistically correct sample. We also feel that corrections of the record, or a defence of a person attacked in our pages, deserves quick printing of a letter. The moment we print one letter like that in, say, one year, we are no longer democractic. The reason why that letter was pushed to the top of our list of priorities is not statistical representation, but a sense of fairness. It is certainly not democratic.

This statement indicates that the letters editor makes judgments with an eye to how sources are being represented elsewhere in the 'pages' of the newspaper. In effect the letters editor is part of a team of debate-managers within the newspaper. Individually and collectively these debate-managers decide what themes and issues will be played out with sources in various sections of the newspaper. The debate-managers are committed to equality and due process, but these conceptions are procedural rather than statistical.

Accuracy

In relation to 17 or 14.2 per cent of letters, the editor said he accepted them because they were correcting something that appeared in the other news columns or in previous letters, 7.5 per cent of all reasons for acceptance. Corrections obviously relate closely to notions of accuracy, and also to balance and fairness.

Citizens who called to complain about aspects of a particular news item were sometimes encouraged to submit a letter to the editor. As the editor explained it, citizens who were persistent, credible, and made their point well were likely to have their letters of correction accepted. If the newspaper itself was the subject of complaint and apparently responsible for an error of fact or interpretation, the basic decision was whether to publish the correction as a letter to the editor or in a special column on page 2 of the newspaper. The decision to publish the correction in the letters columns was taken to make it appear more as a viewpoint in the stream of opinion about an ongoing story. Publication in the special column appeared more as a straightforward admission of primary factual inaccuracy. Acceptance for the letters columns thus seemed to be more appropriate when the problem was both factual and interpretive, with attendant implications for fairness and balance. When it was simply a figure or name that had been cited wrongly, the letter could be listed in the special column.

Letters of complaint urging correction were not accepted routinely. As stated earlier, investigation was often called for, and the editor had to make further interpretations of facts about the previous fact-interpretation problem. This procedure was often delicate, as there was the omnipresent possibility of compounding rather than correcting the problem. Furthermore, the editor ruled as out of bounds certain types of complaint. These included corrections of advertisements (which constituted over one-half of the total space in the newspaper); complaints pertaining to substantive editing; and complaints about any coverage being given to disreputable individuals, groups, and organizations.

Suitable to the Format

The editor made some reference to how the letter fit into the format or lay-out in accepting 20 letters, which is 8.9 per cent of all the reasons for acceptance. In relation to 10 or 8.3 per cent of accepted letters he remarked that the letter was easy to illustrate with a photograph or sketch he had in mind. For example, in accepting a letter about how a group of citizens in a small town had saved a historic building, the editor said he 'loved' it because the author had included a photograph of the building's clock tower. He noted that he was now relieved of the need to find a picture for the letters columns on the following day.

Humour

The letters editor and his superiors felt that humour was essential to the letters columns. Along with good headlines and attractive photographs, humorous letters provided a means of drawing the reader's attention, it was hoped leading her into more serious material, in keeping with the historic mandate of all news to entertain as well as to inform and reform. The editor's own background as an entertainment-section journalist undoubtedly gave him an especially keen eye for visualizing letters in this way. He said he accepted 19 or 15.8 per cent of all letters at least in part because they were 'lighteners,' entertaining and humorous, 8.3 per cent of all the reasons he gave for accepting letters.

Interests in the Newsroom

One pervasive interest in the newsroom is to associate the newspaper with élite and influential persons. In relation to 4 or 3.3 per cent of letters accepted, the editor said he was accepting them because of the high status of the author. Talking generally, the letters editor said the status of the author is always salient as long as the letter is relevant to the topic. One of his supervisors went further, stating in interview that status can be a sufficient interest for the newspaper to justify publication, especially if the letter is from a prominent politician in power. 'You feel an obligation to run letters that are written by cabinet ministers. The mayor really doesn't have much trouble getting his letters in. We figure that if they write letters they have something they want to say from their particular position.'

The editor's reason for accepting 5, or 4.2 per cent of accepted letters, was that he was asked to do so by the reporter and/or the desk editor who had produced the original news item the letter writer was responding to. In relation to 4 or 3.3 per cent of accepted letters, the editor said he decided to accept them because one of his supervisors had asked him to after he had initially rejected them. In this handful of cases the review procedure, as described in the previous section, led to a decision differing from the letters editor, and it was resolved in favour of publication. Regarding 3 or 2.5 per cent of accepted letters, the editor said he accepted them because of specific preferences within the newspaper hierarchy for letters of the type. In these instances he was deferring to perceived organizational rather than personal priorities.

The Writer's Characteristics and the Editor's Inclinations

In relation to 4 or 3.3 per cent of letters accepted, the editor said he was accepting them because the viewpoint was in accordance with his own. More generally, he spoke of regular writers he 'stroked' and put on a 'reinforcement schedule' to provide him with a steady supply of material. These writers usually produced pithy and/or humorous material. The editor noted with delight how one 'regular' had obviously been studying the letters columns and what was happening in the editing of his own letters. He said this regular was now trained in being witty and concise. He lamented the passing away of another trained regular. It was evident from these comments that the editor had established a dialogue with a chosen few, and that they served in effect as regular reporters or opinion columnists who filed reliable copy.

The editor also made reference to accepting letters because the writer was directly involved in the event being addressed and was therefore in a unique position to comment. This participatory-knowledge advantage of the writer was given as the reason for acceptance regarding 3 or 2.5 per cent of accepted letters. Also in relation to 3 or 2.5 per cent of accepted letters, the editor said he accepted them because he had an idiosyncratic need for them. In relation to 1 or 0.8 per cent of accepted letters, the editor said simply that the author was trustworthy and on that basis the letter deserved publication.

SUBSTANTIVE EDITING AND PLAY

Substantive Editing

Many accepted letters were judged to contain negative aspects that required removal. The negative features were not pervasive or bad enough to make the letter unacceptable. Instead they were literally 'ruled out' by the editor. Our observations of the letters editor, and our inspection of the letters edited, indicate that the criteria used in the decision to accept or reject letters were also applied in substantive-editing decisions.

While we observed the editor as he marked up the copy of accepted letters, he only articulated specific reasons for his substantive editing in relation to 22 of 124 accepted letters. In relation to these 22 letters he gave 32 reasons for the alterations he made to the letters. The majority of reasons pertained to aspects of the letters that did not fit the format: there was a problem of length (6), and/or of parts being too emotional (6), too theoretical (3), incomprehensible (1), or lacking stylistically (1). In relation to 7 letters the problem was that the part edited out did not articulate with news values: it lacked balance, was unfair, was incorrect, and/or could not be confirmed. The editor removed segments of 4 letters on the ground that the material contained therein was not newsworthy. Another 4 letters were subjected to substantive editing to remove a contradiction evident within the letter.

In observing the editor on other occasions some additional considerations were brought to light. A federal cabinet minister wrote a letter to correct a story about a ministry program. The editor expressed his annoyance that the letter was dated almost four weeks after the publication of the story and that it was quite long. He said he would accept it nevertheless because it was written by a cabinet minister and because it was a reasonable correction. However, he edited out a long paragraph dealing with what the ministry program was designed to accomplish, saying that he was not going to give the minister 'free advertising.'

The editor acknowledged that the boundary of acceptable rhetoric was linked to the status of the letter writer. If the letter was from a citizen without an organizational affiliation or role specified, or from a person of known lesser status, then the boundary was contracted. If the letter was from a high-status person with some direct involvement or interest in the matter, then the boundary was expanded. Moreover if a high-status person expanded the boundary in a news story, that also widened the territory for rhetoric in the letters columns. For example, the editor said he had rejected several letters pertaining to the Israeli–PLO conflict in Beirut that drew parallels to Germany and the holocaust in the Second World World War. However, once Israeli prime minister Begin was quoted in a news story making reference to the PLO leader as a 'Hitler' and saying that Beirut was now like Berlin, it became 'fair comment' to make such comparisons in the letters columns. The editor acknowledged that this is one way in which key public figures set the agenda for his own determination of the boundary of rhetoric.

Unlike some newspapers, such as the Toronto *Sun*, there was no comment or rebuttal from the editor in an end-note below the published letter. A senior editor recalled that it had once been a practice to write end-notes, but he had changed the practice because he felt it discouraged good and serious writers from submitting letters. He said that instead, very occasionally, journalists involved in the editorial and news columns are asked to rebut the claims of a letter writer who strays too far from what a senior editor deems acceptable.

> Sometimes we'll support what the letter writer has said ... More likely, if we're going to say this is a 'crock,' it will be a cabinet minister or someone like that who has written the letter. You'll feel obligated to let him get away with his weasely ways [in the letter], and then say, 'Look here buster, you don't know what you're talking about!' ... The chairman of the Ontario Energy Corporation wrote us a long letter on how dividends from Suncor would pay for all the costs of launching Trillium, a new corporation for exploration. So, we wrote an editorial saying well, that's true, if you take all the dividends, and the dividends are as good as you say they're going to be (because they haven't been paid yet). But if they're as good as you say, that would take care of that item but what about the interest on the $650 million you borrowed? Whose going to pay for that? You didn't bother to include that in your arithmetic. So, that's a case of stomping on the letter writer ... We used to run editor's notes almost after every letter, it seemed to me, before I became editor. This is one of the things I thought I'd change. We seemed to be always having the last word. And so we just about eliminated them; we will run maybe two footnotes a year now. And that's where there's a question of interpretation, of exact fact, and we'll use the footnote. No, the temptation if you use footnotes is to use them too often. You discourage people from writing letters. They say, 'Why am I going to write them if they've got control and they can write whatever they want at the end of it and make me look foolish?' ... We've got a lot of serious letter writers, if you go through, who feel it's a very valid forum. Use perhaps the best known of them all, ———, who rates fair treatment. And I don't expect people like that are going to keep writing to us if we're going to make, have fun with them every time they write in. It's all right to be clever ... If we feel strongly enough about it we'll write an editorial ... Otherwise we just leave it.

The letters columns provide a major forum for rebuttal and correction by prominent news sources offended by coverage elsewhere in the newspaper. It is a two-way street between the editorial staff and prominent sources, and both are given space on the editorial pages to offer their competing accounts. Indeed, in one instance fairness and balance was determined by the arithmetic of column-inches. A federal cabinet minister wrote a letter complaining about an editorial that criticized him. He said the editorial left out some important

TABLE 6.7
The researcher's reading of the editor's reasons for editing

Researcher's reading of the editor's reasons	N	As a percentage of all responses	As a percentage of letters copy-edited ($N = 121$)
Total sample	171	100.0	141.3
Stylistic	118	69.0	97.5
Too long	22	12.8	18.2
Irrelevant information	8	4.7	6.6
No editing required	6	3.5	5.0
Too emotional	6	3.5	5.0
Redundant information	4	2.3	3.3
Accusations against the newspaper	3	1.8	2.5
Too detailed	3	1.8	2.5
Too theoretical	1	0.6	0.8

points, and he wanted to have these points communicated via publication of his letter. The letters editor sent this letter directly to his superior. His superior checked with the author of the editorial, then came back to the letters editor and said it had been decided that the letter would be printed if the minister agreed to reduce his remarks to the same length as the original editorial (17 column-inches). The letter was eventually reduced in accordance with this agreement, and was the lead letter on the day it was published.

In a separate analysis we scrutinized the accepted letters and made our own assessment of the substantive editing of them. As indicated in table 6.7, 121 of 124 accepted letters were analysed in this way, and we discerned 171 reasons for the editing that was done to them. Predominant was routine copy-editing to clean up stylistic problems, which was done to virtually all letters. Length was a problem in 22 or 18.2 per cent of letters. Other tailoring of the letter to the format included removing irrelevant information (8), emotional segments (6), redundant information (4), detail (3), segments that included unacceptable accusations against the newspaper (3), and theoretical or abstract segments (1). Only 6 letters were not subject to any editing, indicating that the author had perfected her writing style to the point of fitting the format.

Play

The letters editor was also responsible for preliminary decisions about the play that would be given to each letter, and attendant aspects of the layout of the letters pages. He designated each letter in terms of which of the two editorial pages it should appear on. Page 6 letters appeared below the editorials. Page 7 letters appeared along with opinion columns and editorial feature articles by invited writers from outside the newspaper, except on Saturday when all of page 7 was given over to letters.

The letters editor also designated the headlined and lead letters. He said he did this on the basis of what letters were on topics that were especially newsworthy at the time. If he wanted to publish two or more letters on the same topic at the same time, he had to decide which would be the lead letter and what order they would appear in. He said he tried to put the most neutral (less strongly opinionated in terms of one side of a dispute) first, hoping that readers with divergent views on the topic addressed would not be 'turned off' and fail to read the subsequent letters. This is yet another indication that criteria used elsewhere in the newspaper also pertain to the letters format. Even in the format that is supposed to accommodate opinionated strays, a concern for the appearance of neutrality is salient.

The letters editor was also responsible for selecting photographs to accompany letters. As in other sections of the newspaper, he said the inclusion of photographs was calculated to draw the reader's attention and sustain interest. He said he tended to visualize photographs to accompany letters in terms of what photographs were likely to be readily available in the newspaper's files. Letters were also deemed acceptable and edited in accordance with an accompanying photograph the editor happened to have available. As indicated earlier, the editor expressed particular delight when a letter writer submitted an appropriate photograph along with the letter, because this made the editor's work easier.

Letters that were not designated for either of the editorial pages were put into a 'bank' for possible future use. These were considered by the editor to be less important, but possibly useful if a senior editor subsequently turned down one of the designated letters, or if they were needed to fill out the extended space available for letters in the Saturday edition. The fact that in the Saturday edition all of page 7 was available for letters meant that the editor felt he should save some letters during the week to ensure that he had sufficient copy: 'I just want to ... reserve a whole bunch of letters that are either good, light, or interesting, or ones that I can find illustrations for because I have a whole page to fill up. And that page has a dynamics all of its own. Like it needs at least three pieces of art on that page and it needs some good heavy letters because it's an awful lot of type to read. You don't want to read just the trash letters that may come in on Friday. Friday does not always bring you good letters. And you may have used up a whole bank of good letters on previous days.'

This practice is similar to that of editors on other desks who saved features in a bank for days when space was plentiful. For example, the Monday edition usually had extra space for which features in the bank were used because the regular newsbeats were closed for the weekend and the available filed news copy was reduced. In play, editing, and publication decisions, the letters editor acted like any other desk editor. He tailored his best available filed copy to the requirements of his news organization and format.

CONCLUSIONS

Letters to the editor provide an important format for the regular source-as-reporter. Sources see the letters columns as one of the options in obtaining news access, sometimes preferable to authoring features or opinion columns, having their press releases published, or being cited in the fragmented conversations of news stories. Especially in quality newspapers such as the one we studied, letters to the editor are a means by which the news organization can carry on a public conversation with knowledgeable and influential authorities. Authorities who write letters regularly function as star reporters. Indeed, in 'signing off' with their name, status, organizational affiliation, and place, these sources-as-reporters are largely indistinguishable from the journalist who signs off with her name, news organization, and place she is reporting from.

Citizens who write without indicating an organizational affiliation also contribute to the letters columns. Indeed, most letters submitted are from individuals who do not indicate their status or organizational affiliation. However, we have documented that letters that do indicate the author's organizational affiliation and status are much more likely to be accepted for publication. Moreover, the letter writer who in turn invokes the social standing of other authorized knowers by citing them as sources is much more likely to have her letter accepted. Just as the journalist usually has to find a source or two to say it is so, so the letter writer is better off functioning as a reporter by citing other authorities in support of her view of what appears to be the case. The letter writer is not only better off if she can represent her own authority through organizational status and affiliation, but also if she can cite other authorities to make her case.

Letter writers use the format for cultural contests over facts, interpretation, and meaning. Letters submitted address the field of culture and attendant issues of information control more than any other, and such letters are much more likely to be accepted. The vast majority of letters submitted include an account of the primary facts and an evaluative assessment, and those that do are more likely to be accepted for publication. Given the strong orientation to the business community in the newspaper we studied, the context most frequently addressed by letter writers was the private corporate one, and letters dealing with this context were more likely to be accepted than those dealing with any other context.

While letter-writers seem willing to submit a perpetual and abundant supply of copy in furtherance of these meaning contests, the matter is far from being equally contested. The matter is fundamentally in the control of the editor and the newspaper. This is the case not simply because the editor, as he himself described his role, functions as a police officer among various citizens communicating oppositional interpretations and viewpoints. It is also because letters to the editor are treated in the same way as all other filed copy available to the newspaper. They are rejected, or accepted and edited, in accordance with criteria internal to the news organization and news-media institution. They must be suitable to the format, or at least be capable of being made suitable through editing. They must be newsworthy, in accordance with an agenda and priorities already established in the news. They must articulate with the editor's sensibilities about news values such as fairness, balance, and neutrality, and with his assessment of the standing and character of the author in relation to the matter addressed. They must be in accordance with the newspaper's policies about letters, some of which relate to legal considerations. They may be used or ignored in terms of the particular interests of influential people within the newsroom.

We quoted a senior editor who said the newspaper had ceased long ago to write editorial notes to letters because they 'turn off' writers and lead to complaints that the newspaper always has the last word. However, it is evident in our study of the editor's acceptance and editing decisions that the newspaper controls words in the letters columns as elsewhere. Three-quarters of the letters are not published and therefore no word is expressed at all. The one-quarter that are published have been assessed and tailored within the newspaper's criteria of rational acceptability. The best the source can hope for in the letters format is the same she obtains in the broadcast-news clip: that her exact words are published, albeit in an edited and recontextualized fashion. The sources we interviewed were cognizant of the fact that the newspaper only publishes the words it approves of, in the letters format or any other news format. This is so whether it is last words, or words intended to perpetuate meaning contests and make more news.

While the letters format may seem relatively open and democratic, and even allows a measure of criticism of the newspaper, it is highly controlled. Letters to the editor have a legitimation function, bolstering the newspaper's image and public acceptance. The newspaper is able to reproduce its legitimacy because it gives preference to writers who are most authoritative in knowledge, status, and organizational affiliation. In the letters columns as in other news formats, sources underpin the legitimacy of the newspaper through their own legitimacy. To the extent that the newspaper thereby sustains its reputation as legitimate, the source can in turn seek his own enhancement through the letters columns. This reinforcement among journalists and élite authorized knowers solidifies their hermeneutic circle. Closure to others secures the élite status of authorized knowers within the knowledge structure of society.

7

Negotiating Control

News is a product of transactions between journalists and their sources. The primary source of reality for news is not what is displayed or what happens in the real world. The reality of news is embedded in the nature and type of social and cultural relations that develop between journalists and their sources, and in the politics of knowledge that emerges on each specific newsbeat.

There are many levels of 'sign-work' within a source organization, through which suitable symbols are processed and prepared for possible use by journalists. These symbols are worked on further in newsrooms, where they are made appropriate for publication or broadcast. Once made public, news symbols in turn play back into the source organization and become incorporated into subsequent signwork there. The process is complex, with many stages, and news cannot be understood adequately by enquiry into an isolated stage, a particular process, or selected items of content.

What is at stake in news production is the meaning attributed to events, processes, or states of affairs. As much as the news itself is light reading, listening, and viewing, the process of assigning meaning is not a light matter. It is crucial to the constitution of political culture. There is perpetual conflict over preferred signs and appropriate meanings. This conflict is evident within a particular source organization, as well as across source organizations as they interface with news organizations. Negotiation of control over signs and meanings occurs at every stage: among members and units within a particular source organization; between members of different source organizations; among reporters and editors within a particular news organization; between members of different news organizations; and between news organizations and source organizations.

There is a dual meaning to this negotiation of control. Sources and journalists are involved in a struggle over the control of accounts. The accounts they struggle with concern the control of organizational life: imputations of deviance and recommendations for control to achieve preferred versions of order. The control of signs and their meanings is crucial to control of the organizational environment. Vigilance is required to keep other organizations in their place, and to reproduce the legitimacy of one's own organization.

Regarding the negotiation of control between source organizations and news organizations, it is not a straightforward matter to answer the question 'Who controls?' Much of the recent research literature has argued that the news media are very dependent on source organizations. Journalists are portrayed as little more than 'conduit pipes' and 'secondary definers' in relation to their sources (e.g., Chibnall, 1977; Hall et al, 1978; Fishman, 1980). However, as our research documents, from the perspective of sources the news media are very powerful, in possession of key resources that frequently give them the upper hand. For example, sources who realize they can only respond within an established news frame, or who are ensnared in a news context such as question period in the legislature, or who are limited to a twelve-second clip, feel that it is they who function as conduit pipes and secondary definers for the news media. There is considerable variation in who controls the process, depending on the context, the type of sources involved, the type of news organizations involved, and what is at issue. It is a matter of who wants to control whom via news accounts, and how all the sources and news organizations involved see themselves fitting into the picture.

The process operates within structural pressures and power imbalances. Some source organizations are more powerful than others in routinizing news access and shaping the public conversation. As we saw in the relationship of *some* parts of the police organization to *some* journalists and news organizations, the news media do function as a conduit pipe for the bureaucratic propaganda of preferred sources. Just the same, there is a hierarchy of relatively powerful and influential journalists and news outlets from whom everyone else takes their lead. At their disposal are powerful resources that have to be respected if one wishes to have a position of authority in public life. Moreover, all news outlets have some fundamental assets that put them in a powerful position: the power to deny a source any access; the power to sustain coverage that contextualizes the source negatively; the power of the last word; and, the power of translation of specialized and particular knowledge into common sense.

In facing up to the power of the news media, and in hoping to benefit from it, the source must deal with the dual meaning of bad news. First, she must appreciate the bad-news emphasis in the media, recognizing that if she is to participate in the public conversation she will be subjecting herself and her organization to the discourse of deviance and control. That is, she must come to terms with the fact that the news formula for translating the local knowledge of her organizational activities into the common sense is to focus on procedural propriety in her organization, and to offer moral assessments of her as an authorized knower. Second, she must learn to handle the fact that the news accounts themselves will be routinely experienced as 'bad': inaccurate, distorted, unfair, biased, and wrong. It is imperative to handle this fact because, as bad as the news might be in terms of quality of knowledge, it is a powerful force in society. It must be taken earnestly by all those who wish to be represented in public conversations, and even more so by all those who are compelled to engage the news as an essential component of control over their organizational environment.

For the source who feels compelled to seek adequate representation in the news, the trick of the trade is to turn bad news into good news for hegemonic effects. By appreciating that bad news is a public good that can be traded on for organizational advantage, the source can benefit from its power. The bad-news formula – with its related core ingredients of dramatization, sensationalism, personalization, and focus on the unexpected – must be accepted as the limitation of news discourse. Working within that limitation, it is still possible to derive powerful benefits. To repeat the pragmatism of one source, 'Once you realize that's the only thing they'll deal with, that's how you play it.'

It is hard work to get one's symbols straight, and even more difficult to keep them that way. Part of the problem is that, in spite of all the self-interest at stake, neither sources nor news organizations can afford to appear to be too self-interested. While recognizing that he is really embroiled in the power politics of meaning, the source must appear in the news as a team player who acknowledges the public interest. That is, even while he imputes deviance to others and seeks to control them, he must do so in terms of the popular consensus that is at the heart of news discourse. Failure to do so puts him at risk of being down-graded in the hierarchy of authorized knowers. Persistent failure will lead to displacement beyond the fringe of those deemed significant enough to participate in public conversations.

Policing Knowledge

All organizations – the police department, the family, the multinational corporation, the newspaper – need to keep some matters secret and to ensure that what becomes known about them publicly is construed favourably. Hence, to a degree, all organizations are compelled to police knowledge about their activities. Patrolling the facts is especially difficult for bureaucratic organizations with a specialized division of labour and a large number of employees. Bureaucracies experience the porosity of their symbolic boundaries, and feel compelled to devote considerable resources to reducing the equivocality and threat to legitimacy it entails.

Among the sources we studied, there was a pervasive belief that the best approach to policing knowledge is through preventative or compliance strategies, rather than by seeking remedies following unfavourable publicity. A substantial number of sources believed there are *no* effective remedies to unfavourable publicity. Most believed that at best the formal remedies available can serve as a threat to achieve a degree of compliance. Sources catalogued a large number of reasons why efforts at after-the-fact remedy usually compound rather than correct the problem of unfavourable publicity. For some, such as judges, it is inappropriate to seek remedy for unfavourable publicity for the same reason it is inappropriate to pursue publicity in the first instance: it is unbecoming to their professional office. Even if some remedy is possible, such as a published factual correction or a retraction, there are problems: there is usually considerable delay from the initial story and its perceived harm to the published correction, making the impact of the remedy less immediate and less salient. The impact of the remedy is nearly always perceived to be substantially less than that of the original damaging story. In publishing a correction or retraction, the news organization still controls the text and context. As when the source gives the reporter knowledge in the form of an interview or documents in the first instance, knowledge given to remedy harmful coverage can be used by journalists in *their* contexts for *their* purposes, including further negative construal of the source and her circumstance. This is true even of the ostensibly open and democratic letters to the editor, which are selected and edited within the news organization's criteria and contextualized as personal opinion. As one respondent recognized, echoing the sentiments of many, 'A letter to the editor is really for the editor.' Indeed, by showing that errors are occasional or exceptional, the news organization can use retraction and correction to display its commitment to factuality and differing opinions, and thereby enhance its legitimacy. Meanwhile, from the perspective of sources, it is the 'ring' of publicity – its emotional impact well beyond the facts of the matter – that is at the heart of why corrections and retractions are of little value.

Seeking a remedy for unreasonable publicity carries other risks. The news organization retains the ultimate power, the last word. A complaint may antagonize the journalists concerned, leading to retaliation in the form of negative coverage and/or no access regarding other matters of importance to the source. Moreover, if the journalists intended all along to control or hurt the source, complaining can give them a clear indication that they are having the desired effect. Remedies that keep the matter alive through more publicity carry the real threat of further damage to the source. Knowledgeable in this regard, most sources believe it is better to be silent than sorry.

In searching for a remedy after the fact of unreasonable coverage, the source also runs up against the institutional hegemony of the media. One mainstream news organization will not normally publish particular complaints about the coverage of another mainstream news organization. The aggrieved source can contemplate the use of fringe or alternative media, but this contemplation typically yields the assessment that this is an ineffective route because these media lack the circulation and institutional-authority impact of mainstream news organizations. Paid advertisements are limited, because they are costly and are contextualized as self-interested. The OPC and CRTC are not seen as viable sources of remedy: in face of a source who has been victimized, they are structured to 'cool out' the complainant and to seek his compliance with journalistic routines.

These impediments to achieving remedy for unreasonable coverage are testimony to the institutional power of the news media. Knowledgeable about these impediments, the experienced source seeks alternative routes to achieving reasonable news coverage.

Since news access can be important to control over their organizational environment, most sources do not have the option of not co-operating with journalists in general. The silent source loses any control over accounts of the matter at issue. The journalist can usually find alternative sources only too willing to co-operate, and that co-operation may include visualizing impropriety on the part of the source who remains silent. A source organization that is expected to engage the public conversation but fails to do so sews the seeds of long-term hostile relations with journalists, and sometimes with members of other source organizations.

Clearly for most sources the only approach is to co-operate with the news media while establishing preventative mechanisms for policing knowledge. As detailed in our analysis of newsbeats, this preventative work is accomplished through an elaborate organization of regions and closures to suit the purposes of the particular source. It is through the physical, social, and cultural mechanisms of regions and closures that sources police knowledge and achieve some autonomy in the news process.

The key to a preventative system of policing knowledge is trust. The bureaucratic organization with a specialized division of labour must trust its employees, who in turn must trust journalists to maintain secrecy and confidence when it counts. Trust takes the form of having the good sense, and common sense, not to publicize something at a time when it might affect the organization negatively. It is thus inextricably bound with confidence: being able to take for granted that confidential knowledge will be restricted to the time and place of back-region enclosure.

Knowledge is extremely difficult to control because it can be taken without removing it. Moreover, as we have seen, after-the-fact remedies for damaging leaks are not especially helpful because the organization has been harmed already. Indeed, the organization may be damaged further if it tries to patch up the damage through further publicity. The best recourse is to try to achieve compliance of employees and journalists through networks of trust and reciprocity, even if these are as elusive and equivocal as the control of knowledge itself.

> All organizations are vulnerable to the disclosure of their secrets. The greater the harm that can result from the disclosure of a secret, the greater the investment an organization has in preventing its disclosure. The punishment of violators for disclosing secrets is of limited value since it takes place only after the secret is disclosed and the organization harmed.
>
> Secrets are integral to trust since the capacity to keep secrets is a condition of trust. Paradoxically, then, secrets are vulnerable to the very conditions that make them possible. The society that exists by surveillance and direct control is essentially without secrets whereas the society built on trust will maintain secrecy and individuality (Durkheim, 1947). The greater the division of labor and the larger the scale of its organization, the more trust must be substituted for direct surveillance. Yet the larger the organization, the more vulnerable it is to the breakdown of trust relationships and disclosure of secrets. Where such secrets are vital to the organization, it cannot, as noted, rely upon deterrent strategies. The resolution to this seeming paradox is to combine control by compliance surveillance with trust. (Reiss, 1984: 29)

As we saw in our analysis of newsbeats, there are contexts in which sources and reporters develop a high degree of trust and reciprocity. Sources can sometimes say things casually and off the record that they know would ruin their careers and seriously damage their organizations if publicized. They can contribute to a reporter's background understanding of a matter by disclosing knowledge they know will not be made public until the source decides the appropriate time and place. They can provide tips about things in process knowing that the knowledge will not be processed as news until journalists are given the performative documents that officially confirm it.

Trust is entwined with interests and values. The source feels she can trust a journalist or news organization when she can take for granted that regardless of what she says it will be construed reasonably, even favourably, in the news, that is, in accordance with the source's values and interests. Thus, police officers felt they could trust 'inner circle' reporters to be helpful both instrumentally and symbolically. When there is a high degree of trust in this regard, the source can become more proactive in her use of the relationship. She can make confidential disclosures to put journalists on the trail of others, and use innuendo to discredit her opponents or to influence public opinion when she does not want to appear to be doing so. Again, she can only do this if she has built up her credibility and trust with reporters. Reporters must feel confident that the knowledge the source gives can be taken for granted as factual, and as in accordance with mutual interests.

Policing knowledge is not limited to secrecy and confidence in organizational back regions. Sources must also devise strategies and tactics of policing the knowledge they decide to make public. Censorship is a part of publicity.

Censorship occurs in the selection of topics to publicize. Sources know that organizational constraints on journalists are such that they will tend to use material that has been prepared for them rather than pursue other matters independently. 'Pushing' one topic is a means of having journalists ignore other topics that the source does not wish to have publicized.

Censorship occurs in the choice of a spokesperson. The spokesperson is typically several steps removed from the matter being addressed, and he therefore lacks direct knowledge of it. This fact is of little concern organizationally. Indeed it is an organizational convenience. The role of the spokesperson is not to provide analysis and understanding. Rather, he is there to represent his organization through the use of authoritative symbols that provide a sense of accountability. Especially when the spokesperson is a media regular, a known news personality, he can use the news method of personalization to delimit the knowledge conveyed to what is represented by his authority.

Censorship occurs in the choice of format for communication, and in the use of particular techniques within a chosen format. Formats such as news conferences, and political and governmental advertising, provide dramas of participation and accountability even while they enclose on political analysis and substantive knowledge. Sources learn to provide partial knowledge through the use of quotable quotes, which are the equivalent of advertising jingles. They also learn techniques of redundancy, limiting the public conversation to their point in order to avoid opening up the proverbial can of worms. There are many techniques of 'canning' one's account: news releases with the primary facts, and quotations offered as being factual; wire-service releases for rapid transmission of the asserted parameters of factuality; videos for television journalists, to ensure that they visualize the matter as the source sees it; audio clips for radio journalists, to ensure that they announce the matter as the source says it.

In many bureaucracies all of this is institutionalized through a public relations office and attendant formalization of who is authorized to say what. Most modern bureaucracies – especially those in the public realm, such as the police and government ministries – recognize that a dual strategy is required for policing knowledge: informal relations based on trust and formal relations based on censorship. In terms of the latter, the goal of public relations efforts is to appear to be disclosing more while actually enclosing on what is publicized. As a police administrator noted about the reorganization and expansion of their 'public affairs' operation, 'The more we disclose, the more we control.'

The public regions into which journalists are channelled to obtain their observational accounts are also designed to police knowledge and effect censorship. Most aspects of public organizations are not public. Regions that are public are still controlled in terms of what can be publicized. For example, what transpires in the courtroom cannot be publicized except through the filter of the law of contempt of court, the law relating to bans on publicity, the formal legal rationality of courtroom discourse, and the not-so-formal orchestrations of lawyers and judges who schedule cases and conduct hearings in a manner they hope will minimize publicity. Another example is provided by the legislature. The public face of the legislature is limited to a question period that is explicitly tailored to news requirements. Similar to the news conference, question period is a drama of political accountability and participation even while the actors' lines are limited to brief barbs about procedural strays.

Whether in the context of the courtroom, the legislature, or the official enquiry, knowledge is policed effectively. Political analysis and political philosophies give way to a discourse of administration and amusement. These official forums take on some of the character of news discourse, and news discourse in turn takes on some of the official, performative character of these forums. Faced with such cosmetic thinking, the citizen can do little more than spectate and speculate.

Partial knowledge is not just an accomplishment of official discourse. The news genre and media are also implicated in enclosure of knowledge. Secrecy and censorship are not creations of government and corporations exclusively, as the news media sometimes argue with protests over 'freedom of information.' They are also a product of the social and cultural organization of news outlets, which circumscribe the journalists' criteria of significance and ways of knowing. In most instances news organizations cannot compete with the knowledge resources of official or private corporate bureaucracies. Journalists typically lack specialist knowledge in the specific field being reported on. They are usually lacking also in detailed recipe knowledge about how any particular activity within the source organization was accomplished. Moreover journalists simply do not have the time to deal with the full official account – for example, to sit through an entire trial from beginning to end or to consult all the public documents pertaining to a court case – let alone to seek alternative, unofficial sources. Even though official knowledge has been filtered and censored by the officials themselves, there is more available than the reporter can manage to access. The court context typifies the general point that in most reporting tasks, parsimony takes precedence over testimony. The journalist limits herself to a few facts, quotable quotes, and related fictions to represent what she imagines to be the heart of the matter. News is circumscribed even further by the heavy reliance upon other news to decide what is newsworthy. The use of other reporters for knowledge, and the use of already published or broadcast news as the primary source of knowledge, compound journalistic procedures not to know.

From the perspective of sources seeking to police knowledge, these limitations of the news media can be a good thing. The perfection of the public-relations craft is to have journalists censor themselves in accordance with the image the organization wishes to present of itself. We witnessed this achievement, for example, in police relations with 'inner circle' reporters on their beat. However, reporters' self-enclosure was accomplished even more subtly and routinely at the courts.

Recalling the arrangements at the courts for policing knowledge allows us to capture the essence of the process. Reporters were closed out of locations where cases are decided, such as plea-bargaining sessions in the Crown attorney's office. The barrier was not physical, as much as social and cultural. That is, reporters did not have to be told to stay away from these plea-bargaining sessions. Moreover, just as they knew not to appear at these sessions, reporters also knew that what they were later told had occurred there was confidential except as it might become evident in the courtroom. In the courtroom, reporters were not allowed to make video or audio recordings of what happened; they were subject to legal restrictions; and they were asked to oblige particular requests for censorship. This channelling into the grooves of official discourse, combined with the resource constraints of their newsrooms, meant that court reporters adopted a particular focus: criminal cases; trials; the big case; outcomes rather than process; citing officials rather than the citizens involved; emphasizing not what is important in legal reasoning, but what is important for the ideological display of formal legal rationality. It is in the courtroom, and especially the trial, where the important ideological features of the law are displayed: its majesty, justice, and mercy. Kept out of the back regions and away from its forms of knowledge, reporters had little choice but to display legal form. The news media cannot penetrate legal form through coverage that is restricted to the courtroom, and therefore they cannot help but underpin the ideology of legal form. They end up communicating this ideology as common sense. Among the many and varied source organizations we examined, the courts came closest to perfecting the art of policing knowledge.

Controlling Organizational Life

Secrecy, confidence, censorship, and publicity are integral to the control of organizational life. News is used to control other units or levels within the same organization, as well as to control other organizations in the institutional environment. In the process of communicating intra- and inter-organizational control efforts, journalists involve their own news organizations in these exercises of control. Often news-relations specialists within source organizations see themselves in direct competition with journalists for news organizations: they each investigate a particular problem with an eye to taking the lead in publicity, and with the hope that this lead will ultimately bring them credit for having initiated control of the problem.

Publicity is an increasingly important component of achieving organizational compliance to laws and regulations. Most contemporary analyses indicate that the 'suasion' of publicity is the most important aspect of the compliance-enforcement process (e.g., Fisse and Braithwaite, 1983; Hawkins, 1984; Law Reform Commission, 1986). Moreover, with the increasingly complex and specialized division of labour in the knowledge society, there is a concomitant reliance upon compliance-modes of enforcement (Reiss, 1983, 1984, 1984a, 1987). Even agencies traditionally identified with a deterrence or command-penalty mode of enforcement, such as the police, increasingly deploy compliance strategies (ibid). As revealed in our analysis of the police beat, the police have expanded their publicity resources in an appreciation of its significance for policing.

Publicity has multiple functions in the achievement of compliance enforcement. Most fundamentally, it is a means to the end of general deterrence. In compliance enforcement, as in much of criminal punishment, the greatest deterrent is not the penalties provided for in law, but the stigmatizing effects of negative publicity. There is a great fear of the harmful effects of publicity, both at the organizational level and at the level of the individuals who might be held accountable and who wish to protect their personal reputations and positions (Dickens, 1974; Hawkins, 1984). As indicated in our source-interview data, when addressing the harmful effects of publicity respondents were most concerned about how it can damage reputations.

Similar to other components of compliance enforcement, the main controlling effect of publicity is in the *threat* it poses to those who fail to comply. It is in response to this constant threat that an organization polices knowledge about its compliance, so that its image remains positive, or not negative, or the least bad. When sustained negative publicity cannot be overcome, it is experienced as punitive. While most of the control effects of publicity are at the symbolic level, and more felt than seen, there are direct instrumental punishments available in publicity.

From the perspective of the enforcement agency, when formal action is taken it is usually with both the instrumental and the symbolic effects of publicity clearly in mind. Especially in the administrative-law context, to be seen publicly to be prosecuting an organization is often an end in itself. The ritual of 'crime and punishment' is assumed to have an educational and deterrent effect on others, while at the same time reproducing the legitimacy of the enforcement agency itself. 'Publicity makes possible the vindication of the agency as a credible enforcement authority. Public enforcement visibly displays regulatory rule-breaking as the law's business, dramatizing the success and effectiveness of the agency, and enhancing such deterrence as resides in the criminal process' (Hawkins, 1984: 194).

Beyond the specific rituals of deviance and control, publicity can be used to educate individuals and organizations about what is expected in their particular field of operations. Socialization about the norms of propriety in organizational life can be accomplished through news communications, which state expectations in the abstract rather than through particular instances of deviance and efforts at control. Often multiple organizations and institutions are involved. For example, the police sponsor an essay contest for school children about the role of the police officer, the winning entry is published in the local newspaper, and the winner receives prizes from private corporate sponsors whose names are identified with the goodness of police work and school work.

The use of publicity to achieve compliance among targeted organizations and individuals obviously varies according to what other options are available. As we saw in the case of public-service unions and police associations, news publicity is particularly important as a vehicle for mobilizing membership support, public sympathy, and concessions from supervisors, because they are denied the alternative of striking legally.

The news media are potentially open to any effort by one part of an organization to achieve compliance from another part of the organization, or from other organizations that have an interest in the matter. The only exception is when the effort at compliance and control is directed at a news organization itself. Efforts to criticize a news organization are met with denial of access, relegated to the personal-opinion format of letters to the editor, or framed in the context of exceptional mistakes in need of factual correction. Most of our respondents appreciated the futility of trying to use news communications to seek the compliance of the news organization that offends them.

In contrast, news organizations always have a dual agenda in publicizing the activities of enforcement agencies. They focus on the deviant targets the enforcement agencies are trying to control. In addition, news organizations scrutinize the procedural propriety of the enforcement agency itself as it goes about its control work. 'Police compliance often is at issue in police practice aimed at securing public compliance' (Reiss, 1984a: 107). The news media make a big issue out of compliance by law enforcers, institutionalizing as part of the discourse of policing a discourse about the propriety of the policing agency.

No organization is immune from news of procedural strays in its midst, including the news organization itself. And while the news organization gives itself relative immunity by deciding what it will publish, and by relegating published criticisms of its own activities to the status of personal opinion and/or exceptional factual error, it does thereby allow for a particular discourse about what it is doing wrong and should correct.

Publicity is not all bad. There is always the belief that good will come from pointing out what is wrong, erroneous, faulty, and in need of repair. There are many specific instrumental uses of publicity in mobilizing public opinion and using public pressure to achieve control of others. Sustained favourable publicity can be used to enhance an organization's resources, including news access itself as an important resource, as is evident in the case of legitimate and powerful organizations such as the police; however, publicity is also crucial for lesser organizations. The lawyer can use publicity of a prominent case she works on to create public recognition of her name, which generates business. Eventually the select few even have their cases covered by reporters simply because they are 'name' lawyers. For the marginal group of citizens with a particular interest, publicity is crucial to indicating that they are indeed organized and have knowledge relevant to an issue. Recognizing that organization and knowledge are key ingredients of power, they require news publicity to widen the range of other organizations and people who think they are worth listening to. The trick of the trade for the marginal group is to ensure that their imaginative efforts to achieve access – such as public demonstrations or news-conference theatricals – do not become publicized as extreme and have a delegitimating effect. Of course, the dilemma is the same for all news sources: they must work within prevailing criteria of rational acceptability, the culture and power of news as knowledge.

Beyond specific benefits for a career of an organization, and for the career of select individuals within the organization, news publicity can have particular operational uses. For policing agencies it serves as a public sentinel, warning of events or developments that might threaten public health and safety. It can help police, and others in the investigative trades, who are seeking the identity and location of suspects or witnesses. Even while offering material enhancement in these forms, the news is also serving as an ideological enhancement for the organization engaged in the good work.

Failure to control the news media can mean loss of control over organizational life and serious harms. Publicity can diminish organizational resources in a number of ways. The presence and pressure of journalists adds to the workload of the source organization's members. Members may have to change their routines – their timing, style, and location of work activity – to avoid publicity, or to minimize its potential damaging effects. Disclosure of confidential knowledge can have direct damaging effects, for example, blunting the competitive edge of a commercial operation or complicating the ability of the police to acquire adequate evidence for a prosecution. At the level of government policy and programs, distorted or unfavourable publicity can result in political and public pressure that has negative consequences materially and practically.

Often news discourse creates a political concern and pressure that are unrelated to the realities of the organizational environment. For example, it is well known that a moral panic over a particular problem of public safety can lead to unreasonable pressures on the police to solve the problem. When the problem remains unsolved because of organizational constraints within the police and in the wider community, police administrators may feel forced into scapegoating a particular investigative unit and police officers via a 'shake-up.' The police experience this as an injustice, because they see that public fear over health and safety is based more on news-media–generated fictions than on police knowledge of the facts. This is one reason why in recent years the police have devoted increasing resources to publicity aimed at convincing citizens that they need have little fear of victimization (Wilson and Kelling, 1982; Kelling, 1983; Reiss, 1984a). The police have come to appreciate as much as politicians that the news media are expressive in influence. The effects are in the heart as well as the head, and can only be overcome by further publicity that causes a change of heart. Failure to control public emotions can have the fundamental harmful effect of a loss of organizational legitimacy.

The stigma of unfavourable publicity is personal as well as organizational. While an individual source can enhance his organizational power and public influence by being designated an authorized knower in the news media, it is always at the cost of being accountable. He is responsible for the reality he represents, and if something goes badly wrong he risks becoming designated as the rotten apple who must be expended in order to save the mildly rotting barrel. Regardless of other organizational realities he knows about, he will fall from official grace if his account ability does not match news-mediated expectations about his accountability.

Just as the news media tend to personalize accountability, so does the news source. Thus, in the face of negative publicity experienced as biased, the source tends to blame the individual reporter who authored the item. Even experienced and sophisticated sources sometimes fail to see that the 'bad reporter' has usually been mandated by her newsroom to 'twist' things, in the hope that the news slant might set the source straight. When the source appreciates that the problem is organizational rather than personal, she can try to regain control of organizational life beyond the peculiarities of the particular journalist.

Beyond the particular journalist and her news organization there is the control of public discourse itself. Unless the source can speak in the terms of public discourse – fragmented conversations aimed at creating images with strobe-light effects – he is doomed to exclusion from the public conversation. Equally, unless the source can offset journalism's sporadic forays into his organization to ferret out procedural strays and to create order out of them, he is unable to capitalize on what the news really has to offer him. The source who falls short on either count is unable to share in the constitution of popular culture and the political myths on which it thrives. He thereby forfeits the ability to mobilize these myths as realities, realities that can make his news access routine and his organization's legitimacy incarnate.

Variation among Source Organizations

Sources vary substantially in their needs for secrecy, confidence, censorship, and publicity. Hence, they also vary substantially in their uses of regions and closures to police knowledge.

Many private corporations have little need for news publicity. They wish to limit public knowledge of their products to forms of advertising. If they can generate news stories that function as advertising, or that supplement the advertising that they pay for in the same news outlet, they are willing to oblige journalists. But when it comes to the bad-news formula of hard news, private corporations seek to minimize coverage and get out with the least-bad position. Faced with a strike by employees, or allegations that working conditions are unsafe, or the contention that they are polluting the environment, or imputations that their products are hazardous, the corporation wishes to discontinue the news coverage so that it can go about its business in private. For the private corporation, power over the news is power to stay out of the news.

This approach to the news by private corporations is evident in their public-relations operations. These operations typically combine advertising and news-publicity functions. Their news proactivity goes no further than reminding the news outlets that benefit from their advertising that the corporation would appreciate the odd 'free' news or feature item on the wonders of its products. When faced with bad news they often hire an outside public-relations consultant because he has knowledge about how to minimize the negative effects of publicity. This type of knowledge is often lacking in the advertising-oriented public-relations staff who work for the corporation full time. Moreover, the number of persons who can speak for the private corporation in news publicity is severely circumscribed. While many researchers have depicted the police as a kind of secrecy corporation, the police allow for a much greater range of spokespersons at all levels of their hierarchy than does the private corporation.

Organizations in the public sector know they are vulnerable to more systematic scrutiny by the news media, and they are therefore forced to organize to deal with journalists on a regular basis. While advertising is also available to public-sector organizations, and they are turning to it increasingly (Singer, 1986), its uses are more restricted than for the private corporation. Advertising is a format of self-interest, something public organizations cannot appear to be acting with. They always have to formulate knowledge of their activities within the public interest, and therefore news is the primary format of their legitimation work.

Each device established to accommodate journalists within public bureaucracies is also directed at controlling them. The physical, cultural, and social amenities extended to beat reporters give them special access to organizational activities and knowledge. This access creates the potential of negative influence, in the form of disrupting routines and publishing damaging material. However, extending the beat amenities gives advantages to the bureaucracy by assigning reporters to role expectations, including a sense of their appropriate time and place. In the eyes of officials we interviewed, the availability of beat reporters enhances the source's access to the news. It does so both in terms of formal role expectations, and through the cultivation of trusting relations, the key ingredient for both maintaining secrecy and sustaining favourable publicity.

Practices are not uniform among public bureaucracies. The courts have relatively little need for publicity, and thus can afford to effect tight control over regions and closures. Except for a few prominent lawyers, court officials are rarely proactive with the news media. The vast majority of our court respondents said they had never made a proactive contact with a journalist. They do not need to be proactive because their system of regions and closures, augmented by their own legal powers, ensures that news accounts reproduce the contours of legal form.

The police have also devised an elaborate system of regions and closures, hierarchized under the chief and channelled through a public-affairs office and official directive that influence who can talk and in what terms. Through public affairs the police have institutionalized their proactive newswork, issuing daily major-occurrence reports as well as releases about their good work. However, in spite of these measures, as a large bureaucracy the police are porous. They are therefore obliged to try to seal the leaks by solidifying trusting relations with journalists. This works routinely in relations with inner-circle reporters from popular news outlets, who are mandated to feed their newsrooms with a steady supply of copy to fill the available news space, and to embrace the police as the embodiment of consensus. With outer-circle reporters from quality news outlets it is a different story. They are mandated to uncover procedural strays among the police, as the police in turn pursue

stray members of the population. Nevertheless, in spite of the trouble they
cause for the police, it is arguable that outer-circle reporters join with their
inner-circle counterparts in the reproduction of police legitimacy. They are
all after using the police in the symbolic politics of order and consensus,
even if they use different routes for accomplishing this. Although not quite
as much conduit pipes as reporters on the court beat, police-beat reporters
work with their sources in policing the public interest, and reproducing their
version of consensual ideology.

While journalists join the courts and police in the manufacture of consensus, at the legislature consensus is problematic, equivocal, and always
at issue. The public culture of the legislature is defined in terms of competing interests. Hence, the beat is characterized by proactive pluralism and
fierce competition over accounts. Among the multiplicity of interests are the
news organizations themselves, who compete with one another as well as
with source organizations in rendering preferred versions of reality. Just as
source organizations have explicit political interests in particular issues, so do
news organizations. At the legislature, journalists' control of the environment
is substantial at all levels. In regular institutional contexts such as question
period, sources are sometimes turned into conduits for news outlets and the
agenda they have set. On the organizational level, journalists can make particular interests dependent on them, including not only political parties but also
citizens' interest groups with particular causes. On the level of individuals
there is substantial dependency on news outlets, especially among politicians.
Depending on the way they speak and shine in the media spotlight, political
personalities rise and fall. Politicians become news discourse incarnate.

In summary, the degree of control over publicity, censorship, confidence,
and secrecy varies substantially by source organizations, roles, and contexts.
It is hard to see a judge or police officer in the same light of media stardom
as a politician. The judge and police officer patrol their symbolic boundaries
in terms of a more distant institutional authority. The politician relies more
directly on personal symbolic images, in the hope of scaling new heights,
and eventually reaching the pinnacle of institutional authority. Squarely in the
hands of journalists, the politican is acutely aware that her task is the most
treacherous. The others are more protected by their institution's routinized
ways for appearing accountable, and have occasion to be grateful for that.

Variation among News Organizations

There is a substantial research literature on variation among news organizations in their coverage of particular topics. Studies based on news content
tend to emphasize convergence in coverage among popular and quality outlets in different media, but they also indicate some differences among them.

Studies based on observation in newsrooms give stronger emphasis to convergence among popular and quality outlets in all media. Previous research has given much less consideration to the perspective of news sources, whether they see differences between popular and quality news outlets in newspapers, television, and radio, and how this relates to their practices.

Our research indicates that sources perceive considerable variation among news organizations, and respond accordingly. Sources assess news organizations in a very pragmatic manner. Is the news outlet sympathetic to the source generally? Is the news outlet sympathetic to the particular issue before them? Does the news outlet meet a particular need at the moment, for example, to have widespread impact on the public, or to provide a more in-depth account of the source's position? Most important, what is the influence of the news outlet? on other news outlets that are likely to follow its lead? on other constituencies and organizations in the institutional environment that are likely to respond to what is being said? on mobilizing public opinion and generating public pressure? With these pragmatic questions in mind, sources are more concerned about news that is influential and helpful than about news that is impartial, accurate, and balanced. Objectivity is less an issue than political objectives.

At the court beat the main basis for news-media comparison is the medium of communication, rather than in terms of the popular/quality distinction. The court beat remains print-oriented. Here the term 'press room' is not anachronistic. With the exception of one television journalist and one free-lance, no regular reporters on the beat represented broadcast-news organizations. Reporters were prohibited from using the technological mechanisms of broadcast journalism – audio and video recording devices – in the primary news context of the courtroom. This is a more general reflection of the fact that court administrators, judges, and the legal profession persist in their preference for the more literate and formal logic of print. Printed documents and texts mediate transactions and decisions in the court, and the same is expected of news texts. The hope of court sources is that print journalism can provide depth; a permanent record; and subtle influence on other media, legal agents, and public opinion. This finding is consistent with court sources' hope for the impact of the law itself.

At the police beat the main basis for news-media comparison is the popular/quality distinction, rather than the medium of communication. All of the regular reporters with a desk at the police beat came from popular news outlets, regardless of whether they represented radio, television, or newspapers. The defining characteristic of this 'inner circle' was their empathy for the police lot, and concomitant portrayal of the police as the thin blue line between order and chaos. In contrast the 'outer circle' of reporters from quality news outlets were seen as a nemesis, always trying to pierce the veil of administrative decency to get at procedural strays who could be used in their own rituals of order.

The police did, however, show signs of gravitating towards broadcast news. There appears to be two basic reasons for this. First, there was an appreciation that television can be more powerful in efforts at legitimation. The opposite of the literate and formal logic of print, television traffics in image and rhetoric. As such it has *impact*. During our observations the police even embraced their fictional representation in entertainment programming to use in news contexts, holding a news conference with the star of a popular television detective serial to promote 'police week' and its 'cops are regular guys' theme. Second, there was an appreciation of the concomitant control qualities of broadcast news. Because its form works against its content, broadcast news can be used to gloss over detail and reproduce occupational ideology. Even at the level of preparing the story broadcast news can be easier to manipulate. The brevity of items, use of fewer sources, and use of verbatim clips make broadcast news less subject to decontextualization than newspapers are.

At the legislature beat, perceived variation in the influence of news organizations is not based as clearly on either the popular/quality distinction, or differences in the media of communication. There is a tendency of major bureaucracies and political parties to favour outlets with large circulation or audience figures. They also favour quality news outlets to a degree, because these outlets influence other media, other organizations, and the opinions of the élites. The effect of this favouritism is that bureaucracies rich in knowledge resources feed the more powerful news organizations. In the process both the rich source bureaucracies and rich news outlets become richer. The rest are left to take a lesser place in the knowledge structure of the beat, and to accept that their place means they have to follow news created by others instead of taking the lead.

Politicians clearly favour television. Politics in the age of show business means substituting images for initiatives, impact for analysis, as revealed in particular at election time, when politicians and their party organizers gravitate to television journalists, and spend their advertising dollars on television first, radio second, and newspapers last (Royal Commission on Newspapers [RCN], 1981; see also Diamond and Bates, 1984; Crewe and Harrop, 1986). It is also true in routine coverage at legislatures, where television journalists are usually leaders of the pack (RCN, 1981).

This does not mean that more in-depth coverage is not appreciated. It has its place for the ministry that wishes to promote its latest program, and the politician who wants his personality projected even more. In this respect, newspapers are important, especially the qualities. They are seen to provide depth, and a record that can be called back in the future. They also have influence: on other news outlets; on other organizations involved with the ministry or politician; and, through all of them, on the public at large.

Whether these perceptions of sources are evident in news content is a different matter. Questions related to variations in content (e.g., topics covered, sources used, and knowledge conveyed) among popular and quality news outlets in each of newspapers, radio, and television are central to our forthcoming volume (Ericson et al, forthcoming). However, regardless of what is revealed by aggregate patterns, it is the perceptions of sources that count in our present analysis. Sources perceive considerable variation among popular and quality news outlets and different media, and they take action in accordance with their perceptions. These perceptions are real. They are also real in their consequences because sources help to constitute the knowledge society as it is revealed in the news media.

Implications for the Knowledge Society

Knowledge-society theorists have focused on specialized knowledge, including scientific as well as professional and occupational knowledge (e.g., Böhme and Stehr, 1986). They have not thoroughly researched how specialists are called upon to translate their knowledge into common sense through news discourse (but see Nelson, 1984: chap. 4; Friedman et al, 1986; Goldstein, 1986). In this book we have addressed the translation process as it transpires among journalists and sources in their routine efforts to negotiate control over accounts of their activities. News sources provide a daily barometer of the knowledge structure of society: who is authorized by their own bureaucracies and by news organizations to speak in particular terms about key social issues and problems. This knowledge structure is reproduced at the level of transactions between sources and journalists, and revealed in the news content they produce. In this book we have shown how sources and journalists join together socially, culturally, and on beat locations as interdependent participants in knowledge production and use. In a subsequent volume (Ericson et al, forthcoming), we will examine the content of news, providing systematic readings of the knowledge structure of society that journalists and their sources make available in the news.

News is important because of the knowledge it provides about the knowledge structure of society. News provides knowledge about who are the authorized knowers, where they are in the knowledge hierarchy, and what claims they make to knowledge. In citing authoritative sources, news outlets not only underpin their sources' authority, they also reproduce their own authority. News organizations join with sources in representing the power/knowledge contours of organizational life, and thereby, the authoritative apparatus of society.

Sources are painfully aware that news does not mirror reality. They are equally aware that news does mirror images they help to construct. These images are crucial to the constitution of authority in the knowledge structure of society. Regardless of reality, the source who wishes to keep her place in the hierarchy of credibility must take the news seriously.

Journalists have considerable 'gate-keeping' influence over a source's position within the hierarchy of credibility. However, it is a mistake to assume that journalists are primary in determining the source's place in the knowledge structure. Journalists must deal with sources whose place has already been determined by their organizations and institutions. Source organizations have already decided who is best able to represent their own sense of hierarchy, and its place in the institutional environment. While journalists have influence, in the particular instance they typically operate within the prevailing knowledge structure.

Journalists must also operate within the prevailing institutionalized formats of the news-media. It is news media formats that contribute substantially to the structural framework of the knowledge society. It is through the established news communication formats that the knowledge structure is shaped, organized, presented, recognized, and acted upon by authorized knowers. Our analysis of the origins, changes, and consequences of reliance on one news format rather than another, as experienced by authorized knowers of different types, is therefore more than a study of the communication process, it is also a study of social change. News not only articulates the knowledge structure of society, it actively contributes to the constitution of that society and to the changes occurring within it.

Knowledge in the news about the knowledge structure of society provides for a sense of community participation and democracy. All news outlets, but especially those with a popular orientation, not only carry the voices of knowledge and authority but speak to the powerful on behalf of the people. The people are thereby given the feeling that they are brought into the public conversation. In this sense the news media provide for participatory democracy. Indeed, there are some senses in which democracy is enhanced: the news can provide some guidance as to where further knowledge might be discovered, and problems engaged, for the citizen who cares to look. In the main, however, the public conversation is experienced by the citizen as a prefabricated spectacle, making it seem that he is in the world but not of it.

All news outlets, but especially those with a quality orientation, speak *with* power. They carry the conversations that the authorized knowers are having with one another in their respective efforts at influence. However, even at these elevated levels of the knowledge structure, all are not equal. News as a form of cultural capital is differentially available. As we have documented, sources have differential access to the news media, and the news media have differential access to sources. This finding applies both to efforts at having something publicized and to efforts at keeping something out of the news. The news process reproduces the structured inequality of knowledge and its links to authority.

Thus, the news media are especially powerful. At the fulcrum of a variety of institutions attempting to capitalize on publicity and secrecy, the news media maintain a 'positional advantage' (Cook, 1977) over these other institutions. Certainly many sources we studied viewed the news media as the most powerful institution in society. Moreover, they were deeply concerned about this power because it contributed to the equivocality of their own institutional positions. With their authority mirrored in news images, they felt the social-control effects of news.

These features of news within the knowledge society are especially evident in our analysis of letters to the editor. These letters sustain the fiction that the newspaper provides a free market for ideas. However, a scrutiny of who gets published reveals that in this format as in other news formats, authorized knowers receive preference. The editor related his efforts at 'stroking' prominent writers. Among the most powerful predictors of whether a letter is accepted are if the source indicates her organizational affiliation and her organizational status and if she in turn cites other sources presumed to be in the know. As with news sources generally, the legitimacy of those who write letters to the editor underpins the legitimacy of the newspaper. It indicates that the particular newspaper is regarded by influential sources as the preferred outlet for public conversations. At the same time the newspaper bestows legitimacy on the letter writers it publishes, enclosing the hermeneutic circle on behalf of the knowledge-society élite.

Letters to the editor also allow the newspaper to sustain the legitimacy of its critical thrust and efforts at policing. By opening up the letter columns for criticism and policing of its own work, the newspaper gains licence for criticizing and policing other organizations. However this licence, too, has limits. A substantial proportion of letters are quibbles over facts, and they therefore help to sustain the web of facticity in news discourse. Indeed, the best predictor of acceptance of a letter is whether it deals with factual refinement, either correcting previously reported facts or adding further facts. Moreover, news organizations are like all other organizations in having regions and closures to patrol and control accounts of their activities. In the letters columns only certain kinds of complaints and imputations of deviance regarding certain spheres of operation are permissible. As a matter of policy letters of complaint about advertising are not accepted; thus complaints about more than 50 per cent of the newspaper's copy are excluded. Letters are excluded that take an offensive position, as so judged by the editor. Letters are excluded that address a longstanding issue, unless there is an *official* policy or legal change that signifies newsworthinesss in journalistic terms. Editors control letters as a form of filed copy according to the same criteria they use in judging any other filed copy. They are all the more powerful for that.

News typically fails to meet the expectations of those who use it, whether members of the public, regular sources, or news-media analysts. For their part, news-media analysts complain about the failure of news to provide adequate knowledge, that it is a means not to know. This is invariably true if one places the cultural template of news on a given social reality measured by some other criteria. However, it shows a lack of appreciation for the significant knowledge that is available in the news.

The news contributes to and articulates the knowledge structure of society. It incorporates important social dramas pertaining to community and democracy, order and change. These dramas are emotionally engaging. They help people to create their communities within the mythical configurations employed by authorized knowers. The myths become deeply embedded in consciousness, so that they do indeed direct our ways of knowing, as well as our knowledge of the world. News thereby solidifies the knowledge structure of society. News acknowledges order as it is preferred by members of the knowledge élites, and creates the class of political spectators. The systemic features of how this solidification occurs in everyday transaction between sources and journalists have been the subject of this book and our previous work (Ericson et al, 1987). The systematic features of how the solidity of the knowledge society is represented in news content is the subject of our next enquiry (Ericson et al, forthcoming).

References

Abel, R., ed. 1982. *The Politics of Informal Justice*. New York: Academic Press

Adams, B. 1984. 'The Frustrations of Government Service,' *Public Administration Review*, 44: 5–13

Adler, R., and R. Pittle. 1984. 'Cajolery or Command: Are Education Campaigns an Adequate Substitute for Regulation?' *Yale Journal on Regulation*, 1: 159–93

Alderson, J. 1982. 'The Mass Media and the Police,' in C. Sumner, ed., *Crime, Justice and the Mass Media*, pp. 7–24. Cambridge: Institute of Criminology, University of Cambridge

Altheide, D. 1976. *Creating Reality: How TV News Distorts Events*. Beverly Hills: Sage

– 1985. *Media Power*. Beverly Hills: Sage

Altheide, D., and R. Snow. 1979. *Media Logic*. Beverly Hills: Sage

Altheide, D., and J. Johnson. 1980. *Bureaucratic Propaganda*. Boston: Allyn and Bacon

Asworth, A., E. Genders, G. Mansfield, J. Peay, and E. Player. 1984. *Sentencing in the Crown Court*. Oxford: Centre for Criminological Research, University of Oxford

Atiyah, P. 1982. *Law and Modern Society*. New York: Oxford University Press

Atkinson, M., and P. Drew. 1979. *Order in Court: The Organization of Verbal Interaction in Judicial Settings*. Atlantic Highlands, NJ: Humanities Press

Balbus, I. 1973. *The Dialectics of Legal Repression*. New Brunswick, NJ: Transaction Books

Baldwin, R. 1984. *Regulating the Airlines: Administrative Justice and Agency Discretion*. Oxford: Oxford University Press

Ball, H., ed. 1984. *Federal Administrative Agencies: Essays on Power and Politics*. Englewood Cliffs, NJ: Prentice-Hall

Banton, M. 1964. *The Policeman in the Community*. London: Tavistock

Beckton, C. 1983. 'Freedom of Expression – Access to the Courts,' *Canadian Bar Review*, 61: 19–29

Berger, P. 1977. *Facing Up to Modernity*. New York: Basic Books

Bittner, E. 1970. *The Functions of the Police in Modern Society*. Rockville, Md: National Institute of Mental Health

Black, E. 1982. *Politics and the News: Political Functions of the Mass Media*. Toronto: Butterworth

Blumler, J., and M. Gurevitch. 1986. 'Journalists' Orientations to Political Institutions: The Case of Parliamentary Broadcasting,' in P. Golding, G. Murdock, and P. Schlesinger, eds., *Communicating Politics*, pp. 67–92. Leicester: Leicester University Press

Blyskal, J., and B. Blyskal. 1985. PR: *How the Public Relations Industry Writes the News*. New York: Macmillan

Böhme, G. 1984. 'The Knowledge-Structure of Society,' in E. Bergendal, ed., *Knowledge Policies and the Traditions of Higher Education*. Stockholm: Almqvist and Wiksell

Böhme, G., and N. Stehr, eds. 1986. *The Knowledge Society: The Growing Impact of Scientific Knowledge on Social Relations*. Dordrecht: Reidel

Bok, S. 1979. *Lying: Moral Choice in Public and Private Life*. New York: Vintage
– 1982. *Secrets: On the Ethics of Concealment and Revelation*. New York: Pantheon

Bolton, R. 1986. 'The Problems of Making Political Television: A Practitioner's Perspective,' in P. Golding, G. Murdock, and P. Schlesinger, eds., *Communicating Politics*, pp. 93–112. Leicester: Leicester University Press

Borrell, C., and B. Cashinella. 1975. *Crime in Britain Today*. London: Routledge and Kegan Paul

Boyce, G. 1978. 'The Fourth Estate: The Reappraisal of a Concept,' in G. Boyce, J. Curran, and P. Wingate, *Newspaper History*, pp. 18–40. London: Constable

Braithwaite, J. 1984. *Corporate Crime in the Pharmaceutical Industry*. London: Routledge and Kegan Paul

Braithwaite, J., and B. Fisse. 1987. 'Self-Regulation and the Control of Corporate Crime,' in C. Shearing and P. Stenning, eds., *Private Policing*, pp. 221–46. Beverly Hills: Sage

Brandt, R. 1969. 'A Utilitarian Theory of Excuses,' *Philosophical Review*, 78: 337–61

Brock, E. 1968. *The Little White God*. London: Allen and Unwin

Brodeur, J.-P. 1981. 'Legitimizing Police Deviance,' in C. Shearing, ed., *Organizational Police Deviance*, pp. 127–60. Toronto: Butterworth
– 1983. 'High Policing: Remarks about the Policing of Political Activities,' *Social Problems*, 30: 507–20
– 1984. 'Policing: Beyond 1984,' *Canadian Journal of Sociology*, 9: 195–207

Brogden, M. 1982. *The Police: Autonomy and Consent*. London: Academic Press

Burton, F., and P. Carlen. 1979. *Official Discourse*. London: Routledge and Kegan Paul

Cain, M. 1973. *Society and the Policeman's Role*. London: Routledge and Kegan Paul

Carlen, P. 1974. 'Remedial Routines for the Maintenance and Control of Magistrates' Courts,' *British Journal of Law and Society*, 1: 101–17

-    1976. *Magistrates' Justice*. London: Martin Robertson
Carriere, K. 1987. *Crime Stoppers: Reflections on the Public Portrait*. Edmonton:
     Discussion Paper 9, Centre for Criminological Research, Department of Sociol-
     ogy, University of Alberta
-    forthcoming. 'Crime Stoppers: A Case Study of Mass Media Organization
     and Criminal Control.' MA dissertation, Centre of Criminology, University of
     Toronto
Carson, W.G. 1970. 'White-collar Crime and the Enforcement of Factory Legisla-
     tion,' *British Journal of Criminology*, 10: 383–98
-    1982. *The Other Price of Britain's Oil: Safety and Control in the North Sea*.
     Oxford: Martin Robertson
Casey, W., J. Marthinsen, and L. Moss. 1983. *Entrepreneurship, Productivity and
     the Freedom of Information Act*. Lexington, Mass: D.C. Heath
Cassirer, E. 1956. *An Essay on Man*. New York: Doubleday
Cayley, D. 1982. 'Making Sense of the News,' *Sources* (spring): 126–8, 130–3,
     136–7
-    1982a. 'The Myth of the Free Press,' *Sources* (spring): 127, 138–42
Chibnall, S. 1977. *Law-and-Order News*. London: Tavistock
-    1979. 'The Metropolitan Police and the News Media,' in S. Holdaway ed., *The
     British Police*, pp. 135–49. London: Edward Arnold
Christiansen, J., J. Schmidt, and J. Henderson. 1982. 'The Selling of the Police:
     Media, Ideology and Crime Control,' *Contemporary Crises*, 6: 227–40
Christie, N. 1977. 'Conflicts as Property,' *British Journal of Criminology*, 17: 1–15
Clarke, M. 1981. *Fallen Idols*. London: Junction Books
-    1987. 'Prosecutorial and Administrative Strategies to Control Business Crimes:
     Private and Public Roles,' in C. Shearing and P. Stenning, eds., *Private Polic-
     ing*, pp. 266–92. Beverly Hills: Sage
Clement, W. 1975. *The Canadian Corporate Elite*. Toronto: McClelland and
     Stewart
-    1977. 'Overlap of the Media and Economic Elites,' *Canadian Journal of Soci-
     ology*, 2: 205–14
Clifford, J. 1983. 'Content Regulation in Private FM Radio and Television Broad-
     casting: A Background Study about CRTC Sanctions and Compliance Strategy.'
     Unpublished paper, Law Reform Commission of Canada
Cockrell, M., P. Hennessy, and D. Walker. 1985. *Sources Close to the Prime Minis-
     ter: Inside the Hidden World of the News Manipulators*. London: Macmillan
Cohen, S. 1985. *Visions of Social Control*. Cambridge: Polity
Cohen, S., and J. Young, eds. 1981. *The Manufacture of News: Deviance, Social
     Problems and the Mass Media*. London: Constable
Coleman, J. 1973. 'Loss of Power,' *American Sociological Review*, 38: 1–17
Cook, K. 1977. 'Exchange and Power in Networks of Interorganizational Relations,'
     The Sociological Quarterly, 18: 62–82
Cox, H., and D. Morgan. 1973. *City Politics and the Press: Journalists and the
     Governing of Merseyside*. Cambridge: Cambridge University Press
Cranston, R. 1979. *Regulating Business: Law and Consumer Agencies*. London:
     Macmillan

Craven, P. 1983. 'Law and Ideology: The Toronto Police Court 1850–80,' in D. Flaherty, ed., *Essays in the History of Canadian Law*, pp. 248–307. Toronto: The Osgoode Society

Crewe, I., and M. Harrop, eds. 1986. *Political Communications: The General Election Campaign of 1983*. Cambridge: Cambridge University Press

Dagenais, R. 1983. 'Aviation Safety in Canada: A Case Study on Compliance in the Canadian Air Transportation Administration.' Ottawa: Law Reform Commission of Canada, unpublished

Dennis, E. 1974–5. 'Another Look at Press Coverage of the Supreme Court,' *Villanova Law Review*, 20: 765–99

Diamond, E., and S. Bates. 1984. *The Spot: The Rise of Political Advertising on Television*. Cambridge, Mass: MIT Press

Dickens, B. 1974. 'Law Making and Enforcement – A Case Study,' *Modern Law Review*, 37: 297–307

Dominick, J. 1973. 'Crime and Law Enforcement on Prime-Time Television,' *Public Opinion Quarterly*, 37: 241–50

Doob, A. 1984. 'The Many Realities of Crime,' in A. Doob and E. Greenspan, eds., *Perspectives in Criminal Law*, pp. 61–80. Toronto: Canada Law Book

Doob, A., and J. Roberts. 1983. *An Analysis of the Public's View of Sentencing*. Ottawa: Department of Justice

Downing, J. 1984. *Radical Media: The Political Experience of Alternative Communication*. Boston: South End Press

– 1986. 'Government Secrecy and the Media in the United States and Britain,' in P. Golding, G. Murdock, and P. Schlesinger, eds., *Communicating Politics*, pp. 153–70. Leicester: Leicester University Press

Drechsel, R. 1983. *News Media in the Trial Courts*. New York: Longman

Dreir, P. 1982. 'The Position of the Press in the U.S. Power Structure,' *Social Problems*, 29: 298–310

Dunn, D. 1969. *Public Officials and the Press*. Reading, Mass: Addison-Wesley

Durkheim, E. 1947. *The Division of Labor in Society*. Glencoe: Free Press

Dussuyer, I. 1979. *Crime News: A Study of 40 Ontario Newspapers*. Toronto: Centre of Criminology, University of Toronto

Dyer, C., and O. Nayman. 1977. 'Under the Capital Dome: Relationships between Legislators and Reporters,' *Journalism Quarterly*, 54: 443–53

Edelman, M. 1971. *Politics as Symbolic Action*. New York: Academic Press

Elliot, B., F. Bechofer, D. McCrone, and S. Black. 1982. 'Bourgeois Social Movements in Britain: Repertoires and Responses,' *The Sociological Review*, 30: 71–96

Epstein, E. 1974. *News from Nowhere*. New York: Vintage

– 1975. *Between Fact and Fiction*. New York: Vintage

Ericson, R. 1981. *Making Crime: A Study of Detective Work*. Toronto: Butterworth

– 1981a. 'Rules for Police Deviance,' in C. Shearing, ed., *Organizational Police Deviance*, pp. 83–110. Toronto: Butterworth

– 1982. *Reproducing Order: A Study of Police Patrol Work*. Toronto: University of Toronto Press

– 1985. 'Legal Inequality,' in S. Spitzer and A. Scull, eds., *Research on Law, Deviance and Social Control*, 7: 31–78. Greenwich, Conn: JAI Press

– 1987. 'The State and Criminal Justice Reform,' in R. Ratner and J. McMullan, eds., *State Control: Criminal Justice Politics in Canada*, pp. 21–37. Vancouver: University of British Columbia Press

Ericson, R., and P. Baranek. 1982. *The Ordering of Justice*. Toronto: University of Toronto Press

Ericson, R., and C. Shearing. 1986. 'The Scientification of Police Work,' in G. Böhme and N. Stehr, eds., *The Knowledge Society: The Growing Impact of Scientific Knowledge on Social Relations*, pp. 129–59. Dordrecht: Reidel

Ericson, R., P. Baranek, and J. Chan. 1987. *Visualizing Deviance: A Study of News Organization*. Toronto: University of Toronto Press; Milton Keynes: Open University Press

– forthcoming. *Acknowledging Order: A Study of News Content*

Ericson, R., M. McMahon, and D. Evans. 1987. 'Punishing for Profit: Some Observations on the Revivial of Privatization in Corrections,' *Canadian Journal of Criminology*, 29: 355–88

Erman, M., and R. Lundman. 1982. *Corporate and Governmental Deviance*. New York: Oxford University Press

Feeley, M. 1979. *The Process Is the Punishment*. New York: Russell Sage Foundation

Fishman, M. 1980. *Manufacturing the News*. Austin: University of Texas Press

– 1981. 'Police News: Constructing an Image of Crime,' *Urban Life*, 9: 371–94

Fiske, J., and J. Hartley. 1978. *Reading Television*. London: Methuen

Fisse, B., and J. Braithwaite. 1983. *The Impact of Publicity on Corporate Offenders*. Albany: State University of New York Press

Fitzpatrick, P. 1984. 'Law and Societies,' *Osgoode Hall Law Journal*, 22: 115–38

Fleming, T. 1983. 'Criminalizing a Marginal Community: The Bawdy House Raids,' in T. Fleming and L. Visano, eds., *Deviant Designations*, pp. 37–60. Toronto: Butterworth

Foucault, M. 1977. *Discipline and Punish: The Birth of the Prison*. New York: Pantheon

Fraser, P. 1956. *The Intelligence of the Secretaries of State and Their Monopoly of Printed News 1660–1688*. Cambridge: Cambridge University Press

Friedman, S., S. Dunwoody, and C. Rogers, eds. 1986. *Scientists and Journalists: Reporting Science as News*. New York: Free Press

Fritz, N., and D. Altheide. forthcoming. 'The Mass Media and the Social Construction of the Missing Children Problem'

Gardner, M. 1987. 'Giving God a Hand,' *New York Review of Books*, 13 August, pp. 17–23

Garnham, N. 1986. 'The Media and the Public Sphere,' in P. Golding, G. Murdock, and P. Schlesinger, eds., *Communicating Politics*, pp. 37–53. Leicester: Leicester University Press

Garofalo, J. 1981. 'Crime and the Mass Media: A Selective Review of Research,' *Journal of Research in Crime and Delinquency*, 18: 319–50

Giddens, A. 1979. *Central Problems in Social Theory: Action, Structure, and Contradiction in Social Analysis.* London: Macmillan
- 1984. *The Constitution of Society.* Cambridge: Polity
Gieber, W., and W. Johnson. 1961. 'The City Hall Beat: A Study of Reporter and Source Roles,' *Journalism Quarterly*, 38: 289–97
Gilsdorf, W. 1981. 'Mediated Politics: Thoughts on the Relationship of Media to the Political Communication Process in Canada.' Paper presented to the Annual Meeting of the Canadian Communications Association, Halifax
Gitlin, T. 1980. *The Whole World Is Watching.* Berkeley: University of California Press
Glasgow University Media Group. 1976. *Bad News.* London: Routledge and Kegan Paul
- 1980. *More Bad News.* London: Routledge and Kegan Paul
- 1982. *Really Bad News.* London: Writers and Readers
- 1985. *War and Peace News.* Milton Keynes: Open University Press
Goffman, E. 1959. *The Presentation of Self in Everyday Life.* New York: Doubleday
- 1962. 'On Cooling the Mark Out,' in A. Rose, ed., *Human Behavior and Social Processes*, pp. 482–505. London: Routledge and Kegan Paul
Goldenberg, E. 1975. *Making the Papers: The Access of Resource-Poor Groups to the Metropolitan Press.* Lexington, Mass: D.C. Heath
Golding, P., G. Murdock, and P. Schlesinger. 1986. *Communicating Politics.* Leicester: University of Leicester Press
Goldstein, J., ed. 1986. *Reporting Science: The Case of Aggression.* London: Lawrence Erlbaum Associates
Gordon, M., and L. Heath. 1981. 'The News Business, Crime and Fear,' in D. Lewis, ed., *Reactions to Crime*, pp. 227–50. Beverly Hills: Sage
Gouldner, A. 1979. *The Future of Intellectuals and the Rise of the New Class.* New York: Macmillan
Graber, D. 1971. 'The Press as Opinion Resource during the 1968 Presidential Election,' *Public Opinion Quarterly*, 35
- 1980. *Crime News and the Public.* New York: Praeger
Greenberg, D.F. 1979. *Mathematical Criminology.* New Brunswick, NJ: Rutgers University Press
Greenberg, D.W. 1985. 'Staging Media Events to Achieve Legitimacy: A Case Study of Britain's Friends of the Earth,' *Political Communication and Persuasion*, 2
Greenstein, F. 1969. 'Popular Images of the President,' in A. Wildavsky, ed., *The Presidency*, pp. 287–96. Boston: Little, Brown
Gross, E. 1978. 'Organizations as Criminal Actors,' in P. Wilson and J. Braithwaite, eds., *Two Faces of Deviance; Crimes of the Powerless and Powerful*, pp. 199–231. Brisbane: University of Queensland Press
Gunter, B. 1980. 'Remembering Television News: Effects of Picture Content,' *Journal of General Psychology*, 102: 127–33
Gusfield, J. 1981. *The Culture of Public Problems.* Chicago: University of Chicago Press

Habermas, J. 1975. *Legitimation Crisis*. Boston: Beacon
- 1979. 'The Public Sphere,' in A. Matterlart and S. Siegelaub, eds., *Communication and Class Struggle Volume 1*. New York: International General
Hahn, D., and R. Gonchar. 1972. 'Political Myth: The Image and the Issue,' *Today's Speech*, 20 (3): 57–65
Hall, S. 1977. 'Culture, the Media, and the Ideological Effect,' in J. Curran, J. Woollacott, and M. Gurevitch, eds., *Mass Communication and Society*, pp. 315–48. Beverly Hills: Sage
Hall, S., C. Critcher, T. Jefferson, J. Clarke, and B. Roberts. 1978. *Policing the Crisis*. London: Macmillan
Harrell, D. 1985. *Oral Roberts: An American Life*. Bloomington: Indiana University Press
Hartley, J. 1982. *Understanding News*. London: Methuen
Hawkins, K. 1984. *Environment and Enforcement: Regulation and the Social Definition of Pollution*. Oxford: Oxford University Press
Hay, D. 1975. 'Property, Authority and the Criminal Law,' in D. Hay, P. Linebaugh, J. Rule, E. Thompson, and C. Winslow, eds., *Albion's Fatal Tree*, pp. 17–63. Harmondsworth: Penguin
Henderson, L. 1935. 'Physician and Patient as a Social System,' *New England Journal of Medicine*, 212: 819–23
Hepworth, M., and B. Turner. 1982. *Confession: Studies in Deviance and Religion*. London: Routledge and Kegan Paul
Herman, E. 1986. 'Gatekeeper versus Propaganda Models: A Critical American Perspective,' in P. Golding, G. Murdock, and P. Schlesinger, eds., *Communicating Politics*, pp. 171–95. Leicester: Leicester University Press
Hess, S. 1981. *The Washington Reporters*. Washington: The Brookings Institute
Heumann, M. 1978. *Plea Bargaining: The Experience of Prosecutors, Judges and Defence Attorneys*. Chicago: University of Chicago Press
Hickling-Johnston. 1981. *Metropolitan Police Management Study Report No. 2: Capability Requirements for the Future*. Toronto: Hickling-Johnston
- 1982. *Metropolitan Police Management Study Final Report: Managing Change within the Metropolitan Toronto Police*. Toronto: Hickling-Johnston
Hogarth, J. 1971. *Sentencing as a Human Process*. Toronto: University of Toronto Press
Hollaran, J., P. Elliott, and G. Murdock. 1970. *Demonstrations and Communication: A Case Study*. Harmondsworth: Penguin
Holy, L., and M. Stuchlik. 1983. *Actions, Norms and Representations: Foundations of Anthropological Inquiry*. Cambridge: Cambridge University Press
Hood, S. 1986. 'Broadcasting and the Public Interest: From Consensus to Crisis,' in P. Golding, G. Murdock, and P. Schlesinger, eds., *Communicating Politics*, pp. 55–66. Leicester: Leicester University Press
Hughes, H. 1940. *News and the Human Interest Story*. Chicago: University of Chicago Press
Hurd, G. 1979. 'The Television Presentation of the Police,' in S. Holdaway, ed., *The British Police*, pp. 118–34. London: Edward Arnold

Inbau, F., and J. Reid. 1967. *Criminal Interrogation and Confessions*. 2nd edition. Baltimore: Williams and Wilkins

Jacobs, J. 1977. *Stateville*. Chicago: University of Chicago Press

Jacoby, J., W. Hoyder, and D. Sheluga. 1980. *Miscomprehension of Televised Communications*. New York: Educational Foundation of the American Association of Advertising Agencies

Jefferson, T., and R. Grimshaw. 1984. *Controlling the Constable: Police Accountability in England and Wales*. London: Frederick Muller / The Cobden Trust

Johnson, C. 1980. *The Canadian Radio-television and Telecommunications Commission*. Study Paper, Law Reform Commission of Canada. Ottawa: Supply and Services

Jones, M. 1982. 'The Relationship between the Criminal Courts and the Mass Media,' in C. Sumner, ed., *Crime, Justice and the Mass Media*, pp. 55–69. Cambridge: Institute of Criminology, University of Cambridge

Katz, E., H. Adoni, and P. Parness. 1977. 'Remembering the News: What the Pictures Add to Recall,' *Journalism Quarterly*, 54: 233–42

Keen, C., and J. Greenall. 1987. *Public Relations Management in Colleges, Polytechnics and Universities*. London: Higher Education Information Services Trust

Keillor, M. 1982. 'Interview with Cameron Smith,' *Canadian Lawyer* (March): 14–16, 33–6

Kelling, G. 1983. 'On the Accomplishments of the Police,' in M. Punch, ed., *Control in the Police Organization*, pp. 152–68. Cambridge, Mass: MIT Press

Kingsburg, B. 1981. 'Complaints against the Media: A Comparative Study,' *Canterbury Law Review*, 1: 155

Kitsuse, J. 1964. 'Societal Reaction to Deviant Behavior: Problems of Theory and Method,' in H. Becker, ed., *The Other Side*, pp. 87–102. New York: Free Press

Knight, S. 1980. *Form and Ideology in Crime Fiction*. Bloomington: Indiana University Press

Konrád, G., and I. Szelényi. 1979. *The Intellectuals on the Road to Class Power*. New York: Harcourt Brace Jovanovich

Lane, J. 1923. *Muddiman: The Kings' Journalist 1659–1689*. London: Bodley Head

Law Reform Commission. 1986. *Policy Implementation, Compliance and Administrative Law*. Working Paper 51. Ottawa: Law Reform Commission of Canada

– 1987. *Public and Media Access to the Criminal Process*. Working Paper 56. Ottawa: Law Reform Commission of Canada

Leigh, D. 1982. 'Freedom of Information and the Criminal Justice System,' in C. Sumner, ed., *Crime, Justice and the Mass Media*, pp. 74–86. Cambridge: Institute of Criminology, University of Cambridge

Lundsgaarde, H. 1977. *Murder in Space City: A Cultural Analysis of Houston Homicide Patterns*. New York: Oxford University Press

McBarnet, D. 1981. *Conviction: Law, the State and the Construction of Justice*. London: Macmillan

McDonald Commission. 1981. *Commission of Inquiry Concerning Certain Activities of the Royal Canadian Mounted Police*. 3 volumes. Ottawa: Supply and Services Canada

McMahon, M. 1987. 'Police Accountability: The Situation of Complaints in Toronto.' Paper to the European Conference on Deviance and Control, Vienna

McMahon, M., and R. Ericson. 1987. 'Reforming the Police and Policing Reform,' in R. Ratner and J. McMullan, eds., *State Control: Criminal Justice Politics in Canada*, pp. 38–68. Vancouver: University of British Columbia Press

McWhinney, E. 1982. *Canada and the Constitution 1979–1982: Patriation and the Charter of Rights*. Toronto: University of Toronto Press

Macfarlane, D. 1982. 'The Practice of Law as a Business.' Unpublished paper, Centre of Criminology, University of Toronto

Mandel, M. 1982. 'The Discrediting of the McDonald Commission,' *The Canadian Forum* (March): 14–17

– 1983. *Law and Social Order*. Part I. Toronto: CBC Enterprises

Manning, P. 1977. *Police Work*. Cambridge, Mass: MIT Press

– 1980. *The Narcs' Game: Organizational and Informational Limits on Drug Law Enforcement*. Cambridge, Mass: MIT Press

– 1986. 'Signwork,' *Human Relations*, 39: 283–308

– 1987. 'Ironies of Compliance,' in C. Shearing and P. Stenning, eds., *Private Policing*, pp. 293–316. Beverly Hills: Sage

– forthcoming. *Secularised Dread: The Regulation of Nuclear Safety*

Mark, R. 1973. 'Minority Verdict,' *The Listener*, 8 November 1973

Marx, K., and F. Engels. 1972. *The German Ideology*. New York: International Publishers

Mattice, M. 1980. 'Media in the Middle: A Study of the Mass Media Complaint Managers,' in L. Nader, ed., *No Access to Law: Alternatives to the American Judicial System*, pp. 485–522. New York: Academic Press

May, A., and K. Rowan, eds. 1982. *Inside Information: British Government and the Media*. London: Constable

Mercer, D., G. Mungham, and K. Williams. 1987. *The Fog of War*. London: Heinemann

Merton, R. 1957. *Social Theory and Social Structure*. Glencoe: Free Press

Meyer, J., and B. Rowan. 1977. 'Institutionalized Organizations: Formal Structure as Myth and Ceremony,' *American Journal of Sociology*, 83: 340–63

Meyrowitz, J. 1985. *No Sense of Place: The Impact of Electronic Media on Social Behavior*. New York: Oxford University Press

Morand, Mr Justice. 1976. *Royal Commission into Metropolitan Toronto Police Practices*. Toronto: Queen's Printer

Morgan, D. 1978. *The Capital Press Corps: Newsmen and the Governing of New York State*. Westport, Conn: Greenwood

Morrison, D. 1969. 'On the Interpretation of Discriminant Analysis,' *Journal of Marketing Research*, 6: 156–63

Munton, D., and M. Clow. 1979. 'The Media, the Bureaucrats and Canadian Environmental Policy.' Paper presented to the Annual Meeting of the International Studies Association, Toronto

Murdock, G. 1982. 'Disorderly Images: Television's Presentation of Crime and Policing,' in C. Summer, ed., *Crime, Justice and the Mass Media*, pp. 104–21. Cambridge: Institute of Criminology, University of Cambridge

Murphy, C. 1985. 'The Social and Formal Organization of Small Town Policing: A Comparative Analysis of RCMP and Municipal Policing.' PH D thesis, Department of Sociology, University of Toronto

Nelson, B. 1984. *Making an Issue of Child Abuse*. Chicago: University of Chicago Press

Neuman, W. 1976. 'Patterns of Recall among Television News Viewers,' *Public Opinion Quarterly*, 40: 118–25

Nimmo, D. 1964. *Newsgathering in Washington*. New York: Atherton

O'Neill, J. 1981. 'McLuhan's Loss of Innis-Sense,' *Canadian Forum*, 61 (May): 13–15

Orwell, G. 1954. 'Politics and the English Language,' in *A Collection of Essays*. New York: Doubleday

Palen, F. 1979. 'Media Ombudsmen: A Critical Overview,' *Law and Society Review*, 13: 799–850

Paletz, D., and R. Entman. 1981. *Media, Power, Politics*. New York: Free Press

Perrow, C. 1984. *Normal Accidents*. New York: Basic Books

Pfohl, S. 1977. 'The "Discovery" of Child Abuse,' *Social Problems*, 24: 310–23

Pfuhl, E., and D. Altheide. 1987. 'TV Mediation of Disputes and Injustice.' Unpublished manuscript, School of Justice Studies, Arizona State University

Porter, J. 1965. *The Vertical Mosaic*. Toronto: University of Toronto Press

Postman, N. 1985. *Amusing Ourselves to Death: Public Discourse in the Age of Show Business*. New York: Viking

Punch, M., ed. 1983. *Control in the Police Organization*. Cambridge, Mass: MIT Press

– 1985. *Conduct Unbecoming: The Social Construction of Police Deviance and Control*. London: Tavistock

Reiner, R. 1983. 'The Politicization of the Police in Britain,' in M. Punch, ed., *Control in the Police Organization*, pp. 126–48. Cambridge, Mass: MIT Press

– 1985. *The Politics of the Police*. Brighton: Wheatsheaf Books

Reiss, A. 1983. 'The Policing of Organizational Life,' in M. Punch, ed., *Control in the Police Organization*, pp. 78–97. Cambridge, Mass: MIT Press

– 1984. 'Selecting Strategies of Control over Organizational Life,' in K. Hawkins and J. Thomas, eds., *Enforcing Regulation*, pp. 23–35. Boston: Kluwer-Nijhoff

– 1984a. 'Consequences of Compliance and Deterrence Models of Law Enforcement for the Exercise of Police Discretion,' *Law and Contemporary Problems*, 47: 83–122

– 1987. 'The Legitimacy of Intrusion into Private Space,' in C. Shearing and P. Stenning, eds., *Private Policing*, pp. 19–44. Beverly Hills: Sage

Reuss-Ianni, E., and F. Ianni. 1983. 'Street Cops and Management Cops: The Two

Cultures of Policing,' in M. Punch, ed., *Control in the Police Organization*, pp. 251–74. Cambridge, Mass: MIT Press

Richardson, G., A. Ogus, and P. Burrows. 1982. *Policing Pollution: A Study of Regulation and Enforcement*. Oxford: Oxford University Press

Robertson, G. 1983. *People against the Press*. London: Quartet

Robertson, S. 1981. *Courts and the Media*. Toronto: Butterworth

Rock, P. 1973. 'News as Eternal Recurrence,' in S. Cohen and J. Young, eds., *The Manufacture of News*, pp. 73–80. London: Constable

– 1986. *A View from the Shadows*. Oxford: Oxford University Press

– in press. 'On the Birth of Organizations,' *Canadian Journal of Sociology*, 13

Rodgers, D. 1987. *Contested Truths: Keywords in American Politics since Independence*. New York: Basic Books

Roscho, B. 1975. *Newsmaking*. Chicago: University of Chicago Press

Ross, H. 1970. *Settled out of Court*. Chicago: Aldine

Rothman, D. 1980. *Conscience and Convenience*. Boston: Little, Brown

Rousseau, J.-J. 1927. *Reveries of a Solitary*. London: Routledge and Sons

Royal Commission on Newspapers. 1981. *Final Report*. Ottawa: Supply and Services Canada

– 1981a. *Newspapers and Their Readers*. Ottawa: Research Studies on the Newspaper Industry, Supply and Services Canada

– 1981b. *The Newspaper and Public Affairs*. Ottawa: Research Studies on the Newspaper Industry, Supply and Services Canada

– 1981c. *The Journalists*. Ottawa: Research Studies on the Newspaper Industry, Supply and Services Canada

Rubinstein, J. 1973. *City Police*. New York: Farrar, Straus and Giroux

Runciman, W. 1983. *A Treatise on Social Theory. Volume I: The Methodology of Social Theory*. Cambridge: Cambridge University Press

Russell, P. 1983. 'The Political Purposes of the Canadian Charter of Rights and Freedoms,' *Canadian Bar Review*, 61: 30–54

Rutherford, P. 1982. *A Victorian Authority: The Daily Press in Late Nineteenth-Century Canada*. Toronto: University of Toronto Press

Salomon, G. 1979. *Interaction of Media, Cognition, and Learning*. San Francisco: Jossey-Bass

Samuelson, P. 1954. 'The Pure Theory of Public Expenditure,' *Review of Economics and Statistics*, 36: 387–90

Sandman, D., R. Brent, and D. Sachsman. 1982. *Media: An Introductory Analysis of American Mass Communications*. 3rd edition. Englewood Cliffs, NJ : Prentice-Hall

Schiller, D. 1986. 'Transformations of News in the U.S. Information Market,' in P. Golding, G. Murdock, and P. Schlesinger, eds., *Communicating Politics*, pp. 19–36. Leicester: Leicester University Press

Schlesinger, P. 1978. *Putting Reality Together: BBC News*. London: Constable

Schlesinger, P., G. Murdock, and P. Elliot. 1983. *Televising 'Terrorism': Political Violence in Popular Culture*. London: Comedia

Schmid, A., and J. de Graaf. 1982. *Violence as Communication: Insurgent Terrorism in the Western Media*. Beverly Hills: Sage

Schneider, R. 1977. 'Spelling's Salvation Armies,' *Cultural Correspondence*, 4: 27–36

Shapiro, S. 1984. *Wayward Capitalists*. New Haven: Yale University Press

Shapland, J., J. Willmore, and P. Duff. 1985. *Victims in the Criminal Justice System*. Aldershot: Gower

Shearing, C., and P. Stenning. 1981. 'Modern Private Security: Its Growth and Implications,' in M. Tonry and N. Morris, eds., *Crime and Justice: An Annual Review of Research, Volume 3*, pp. 193–245. Chicago: University of Chicago Press

– 1983. 'Private Security: Implications for Social Control,' *Social Problems*, 30: 493–506

– 1987. 'Reframing Policing,' in C. Shearing and P. Stenning, eds., *Private Policing*, pp. 9–18. Beverly Hills: Sage

Sherizen, S. 1978. 'Social Creation of Crime News: All the News Fitted to Print,' in C. Winick, ed., *Deviance and Mass Media*, pp. 203–24. Beverly Hills: Sage

Shibutani, T. 1966. *Improvised News*. Indianapolis: Bobbs-Merrill

Sigal, L. 1973. *Reporters and Officials*. Lexington, Mass: D.C. Heath

– 1986. 'Sources Who Make News,' in R. Manoff and M. Schudson, eds., *Reading the News*. New York: Pantheon

Singer, B. 1986. *Advertising and Society*. Don Mills: Addison-Wesley

Slayton, P. 1981. 'Competitive Applications before the Canadian Radio-television and Telecommunications Commission,' *Canadian Bar Review*, 59: 571–9

Smith, A. 1978. 'The Long Road to Objectivity and Back Again: The Kinds of Truth We Get in Journalism,' in G. Boyce, J. Curran, and P. Wingate, eds., *Newspaper History*, pp. 152–71. London: Constable

– 1980. *Goodbye Gutenberg: The Newspaper Revolution of the 1980s*. New York: Oxford University Press

Smith, C. 1982. 'Interview,' *Canadian Lawyer* (March): 14–16, 33–6

Soderlund, W., W. Romanow, E. Briggs, and R. Wagenberg. 1981. 'Newspaper Coverage of the 1979 Canadian Federal Election: The Impact of Region, Language, and Chain Ownership.' Paper presented to the Annual Meeting of the Canadian Communications Association, Halifax

Solicitor General of Canada. 1984. *Selected Trends in Criminal Justice*. Ottawa: Ministry of Supply and Services

Stanga, J. 1971. 'The Press and the Criminal Defendant: Newsmen and Criminal Justice in Three Wisconsin Cities,' PH D dissertation, University of Wisconsin

Stauffer, J., R. Frost, and W. Rybolt. 1981. 'Recall and Learning from Broadcast News – Is Print Better?' *Journal of Broadcasting* (Summer): 253–62

Steffens, L. 1931. *The Autobiography of Lincoln Steffens*. New York: Harcourt, Brace

Stern, A. 1973. 'A Study for the National Association of Broadcasting,' in M. Barret, ed., *The Politics of Broadcasting, 1971–1972*. New York: Cromwell

Stone, C. 1975. *Where the Law Ends: The Social Control of Corporate Behavior*. New York: Harper and Row

Straub, G. 1986. *Salvation for Sale: An Insider's View of Pat Robertson's Ministry.* Buffalo: Prometheus Books

Strauss, A. 1978. *Negotiations.* San Francisco: Jossey-Bass

Sudnow, D. 1965. 'Normal Crimes: Sociological Features of the Penal Code in a Public Defender's Office,' *Social Problems*, 12: 255–72

Sumner, C. 1982. ' "Political Hooliganism" and "Rampaging Mobs": The National Press Coverage of the Toxteth "Riots",' in C. Sumner, ed., *Crime, Justice and the Mass Media*, pp. 25–35. Cambridge: Institute of Criminology, University of Cambridge

Tatsuaka, M. 1971. *Multivariate Analysis: Techniques for Educational and Psychological Research.* New York: Wiley

Taylor, L. 1986. 'Martyrdom and Surveillance: Ideological and Social Problems of Police in Canada in the 1980s,' *Crime and Social Justice*, 26: 60–74

Tracey, M. 1984. 'Does Arthur Scargill Have a Leg to Stand On? – News,' *The Sunday Times*, 28 August, p. 43

Tuchman, G. 1977. 'The Exception Proves the Rule: The Study of Routine News Practices,' in P. Hirsch, P. Miller, and F. Kline, eds., *Strategies for Communication Research*, pp. 43–62. London: Sage

– 1978. *Making News.* New York: Free Press

Tumber, H. 1982. *Television and the Riots.* London: Broadcasting Research Unit, British Film Institute

Tunstall, J. 1971. *Journalists at Work.* London: Constable

Van Maanen, J. 1979. 'The Fact of Fiction in Organizational Ethnography,' *Administrative Science Quarterly*, 24: 539–50

– 1980. 'Beyond Account: The Personal Impact of Police Shootings,' *The Annals of the American Academy of Political and Social Sciences*, 425: 145–56

– 1983. 'The Boss: First-Line Supervision in an American Police Agency,' in M. Punch, ed., *Control in the Police Organization*, pp. 275–317. Cambridge, Mass: MIT Press

Van Outrive, L., and C. Fijnaut. 1983. 'Police and the Organization of Prevention,' in M. Punch, ed., *Control in the Police Organization*, pp. 47–59. Cambridge, Mass: MIT Press

Vining, J. 1986. *The Authoritative and the Authoritarian.* Chicago: University of Chicago Press

Voumvakis, S., and R. Ericson. 1984. *News Accounts of Attacks on Women: A Comparison of Three Toronto Newspapers.* Toronto: Centre of Criminology, University of Toronto

Wagner-Pacifici, R. 1986. *The Moro Morality Play: Terrorism as Social Drama.* Chicago: University of Chicago Press

Walden, K. 1982. *Visions of Order: The Canadian Mounties in Symbol and Myth.* Toronto: Butterworth

Walker, N. 1980. *Punishment, Danger and Stigma.* Oxford: Blackwell

Warnock, G. 1971. *The Object of Morality.* London: Methuen

Warshett, G. 1981. 'The Information Economy in Late Capitalism,' in L. Salter, ed., *Communication Studies in Canada*, pp. 178–95. Toronto: Butterworth

Weber, M. 1946. *From Max Weber*, H. Gerth and C.W. Mills, eds. New York: Oxford University Press

Weick, K. 1979. *The Social Psychology of Organizing*. 2nd edition. Reading, Mass: Addison-Wesley

Westell, D. 1984. 'Ottawa's Ad Outlay a Debatable Issue,' *Report on Business, Globe and Mail*, 5 May, p. B 1

Wheeler, G. 1986. 'Reporting Crime: The News Release as Textual Mediator of Police/Media Relations.' MA dissertation, Centre of Criminology, University of Toronto

Williams, R. 1976. *Communications*. 3rd edition. Harmondsworth: Penguin

– 1976a. *Keywords: A Vocabulary of Culture and Society*. London: Fontana

Wilson, C. 1974. 'The Effect of a Medium on Loss of Information,' *Journalism Quarterly*, 51: 111–15

Wilson, J. 1968. *Varieties of Police Behavior*. Cambridge, Mass: Harvard University Press

Wilson, J., and G. Kelling. 1982. 'Broken Windows: The Police and Neighborhood Safety,' *Atlantic Monthly* (March)

Wooley, G. 1985. 'Letters to the Editor,' in *The Times: Past, Present, Future*, p. 113. London: Times Publishing

Yanke, L. 1987. 'The Social Construction of the Missing Children Problem.' Unpublished manuscript, Centre of Criminology, University of Toronto

Index

418 Index

Stauffer, J., 250
Steffens, L., 91
Stehr, N., 3, 395
Stenning, P., 259, 302
Stern, A., 250
Stone, C., 273, 279
Straub, G., 279
Stuchlik, M., 27, 29
Sudnow, D., 87
Sumner, C., 166–7
Sun (Toronto), 35, 245, 317, 320, 370
Supreme Court of Ontario, 39, 46, 78
Szelenyi, I., 4

Tatsuaka, M., 355
Taylor, I., 152
television, 36, 39, 54, 65, 144, 147, 157, 179, 202, 203, 266, 301, 354; aid to police, 161–3, 394; complaint channels in, 328, 333–4, 335; control over meaning, 304–5, 378; and the cult of political personalities, 189–91, 211, 213–14, 241, 254–6, 292; dramatization of crime, 119–20; and evangelical organizations, 279–80; and political myth, 256–8; and police image, 149, 151, 154; and political coverage, 172–6, 180, 189–91, 214–15, 227–9, 231–2, 236, 239, 241, 246, 247–9, 254–6, 394; preference of private sector for, 292; regulations for access on police beat, 100; restrictions on court beat, 385, 393; and rise of political movements, 305; state regulation of, 264; use by marginal groups, 299–300; *see also* broadcast media
The Times (London), 340, 341, 343, 344, 348
Toxteth riots, 166
Tracey, M., 115
trial co-ordinators, 37, 52, 54, 58, 61, 69, 71
trials: and enclosure of knowledge, 65–70; and media focus on legal form, 46, 61, 68, 385; and police discretion in news releases, 99–100, 102, 127, 157–8; sense of theatre

in, 35, 44–6, 47, 70–1, 73–4, 84; as vehicles of publicity, 77–82, 84
Tuchman, G., 1, 4, 6, 15, 18, 240, 252, 331
Tumber, H., 140, 149
Tunstall, J., 34–5
Turner, B., 124, 290

unions, civil-service, 197–9, 206–7; need for spokespersons, 276
United Press International, 291

values, cultural, 23, 26, 27; and 'lawandorder' issues, 43, 169, 195, 204–8; and letters to editor, 351–2, 374; and news-media access, 213–14, 261–4, 279–80, 294–7, 304–5, 306–7; *see also* consensual ideology; public interest
values, reporting, 14–16, 49–51, 108, 110–11, 130–2; in letters to the editor, 359, 366–7, 370, 371–2, 375; and point/counterpoint methodology, 240, 248, 295–6, 366–7
Van Maanen, J., 21, 111, 129
Van Outrive, L., 92, 126
victims of crime, 151, 153, 157, 280
Vining, J., 57
Visualizing Deviance, 1, 2, 12, 308, 309
visuals, 100, 144, 147, 157, 203; aid to police, 161–3, 394; control over accounts, 304–5, 383; dramatization of news, 119–20, 213–14, 237; importance to politicians, 180, 189–92, 227–9, 243–4, 246, 394; and letters to the editor, 368, 373; and police image, 149, 151, 154; and the politics of image, 172–6, 247–9; restrictions on court beat, 385, 393; and rise of political movements, 305; superficiality of coverage, 214–15, 231–2, 236, 239; use of, by marginal groups for publicity, 299–300; *see also* broadcast media; television
'vocabulary of precedents,' 15, 51, 187, 281
Voumvakis, S., 116–17, 158
'vox pop' journalism, 15